Win 98 Rx

Solve Your Own Windows 98 Computing Problems Easily

*Kober, Buechel
& Baecker*

DATA BECKER

Abacus

Table Of Contents

Chapter 2:
Solving Frequent Windows Problems ----------- 43

Chapter 8:
The Active Desktop ----------------------------------- 359

Chapter 9:
World Wide Web Resources ------------------------- 373

Appendices

Chapter 1:
Preventive Measures

Chapter 1
Preventive Measures

I't's natural to blame yourself when your computer suddenly goes wacko or a peripheral no longer functions quite right. However, the problem is not always your fault. A computer or peripheral may breakdown even if you're very careful and treat it with care. Also, you shouldn't blame yourself for the small, inconspicuous programming errors that are hidden in many applications and programs. Don't feel bad if you cannot understand the various incompatibilities between hardware peripherals and software.

Errors in a computer system can come from several sources. Your computer system may have certain unknown shortcomings; no one can say what effects these shortcomings will have on work.

Fortunately, you can limit the potential damage from these problems. The best strategy is to anticipate and be prepared for problems. The measures and preparations described in this chapter will help you rule out some error sources in advance. It will demonstrate how you can make troubleshooting a great deal easier on yourself through the right preventive measures, so you don't have to stand by helplessly in an emergency.

Printing system information under Windows

Immediately after setting up your PC or after adding a new component, it's a good idea to look at the system contents. In other words, you should know the "state" of your PC. By printing the system information, you'll know everything about the hardware and software installed on your PC.

This information is invaluable if you need technical assistance or support. Technical support representatives will ask about your computer configuration and the entries in your operating system configuration files. You can have this information handy by printing the system information.

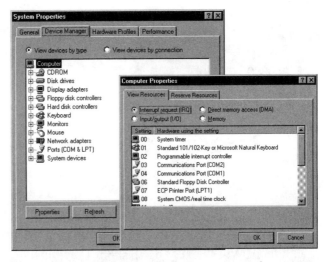

The Device Manager gives you the option of printing system information.

Printing this system information is simple. Date and store this information in a safe place after it is printed. Follow these steps to print the system information using the Windows Device Manager:

1. Double-click the My Computer icon on the Win98 desktop.

2. Double-click the Control Panel icon.

3. Double-click the System icon.

4. Click the "Device Manager" tab.

5. Then click the [Print...] button to view the system information printing options.

6. Select the "All devices and system summary" radio button and click [OK] to begin printing.

The following illustration shows how information about an installed sound card might appear:

1 *Preventive Measures*

Class: Sound, video and game controllers

Device: Creative Labs Sound Blaster

Resources:

  IRQ: 05

  E/A: 0240h-024Fh

  E/A: 0380h-038Fh

  DMA: 01

Device drivers:

  C:\WINDOWS\SYSTEM\mssblst.vxd

    File size: 17050 bytes

    Manufacturer: Microsoft Corporation

    File version: 4.00.330

    Copyright: Copyright c Microsoft Corp. 1994-1995

  C:\WINDOWS\SYSTEM\mssblst.drv

    File size: 38896 bytes

    Manufacturer: Microsoft Corporation

    File version: 4.00

    Copyright: Copyright c Microsoft Corp. 1991-1994

  C:\WINDOWS\SYSTEM\msopl.drv

    File size: 17856 bytes

    Manufacturer: Microsoft Corporation

    File version: 4.00

    Copyright: Copyright c Microsoft Corp. 1991-1994

Besides the allocated system resources, you will also see information on how peripherals and components are integrated in the system. This will probably be more information than you ever wanted to know about your computer system.

You'll probably agree the system information provides the most detailed information available about your computer system. This information cannot be obtained so accurately and quickly any other way. You'll know just how valuable this information can be when you have problems with a specific device and you need to call technical support. Date and store this information in a safe place.

Startup Disk for Emergencies

The most important precaution you can take for emergencies is to create a startup disk. Several occasions may arise when you'll need this disk (you may not be aware of some until it's too late). What would you do if some defect or error made access to the hard drive impossible? Maybe this startup disk would be your lifesaver. You will also need a startup disk if your computer becomes infected by a virus. Although the startup disk will not destroy the virus, you can boot "clean" and then load an anti-virus program to destroy the virus safely.

The right startup disk for Windows 98

You can create a startup disk when you install Windows 98. However, if you didn't create a startup disk at that time, we'll show you how to do it now. Follow these steps:

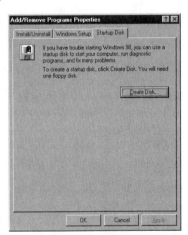

1. Double-click the My Computer icon.

2. Open the Control Panel.

3. Double-click the Add/Remove Programs icon.

4. Select the "Startup Disk" tab.

5. Click the [Create Disk...] button and Windows 98 will create a bootable startup disk.

It's easy to create a startup disk in Windows 98...simply follow the prompts.

This startup disk contains important programs that you will need in an emergency. However, if you require more than approximately 520K for DOS, you'll also need the memory managers. Copy the HIMEM.SYS and EMM386.EXE files from your Windows directory to the startup disk and add the following lines to your CONFIG.SYS (they should be the first lines in your CONFIG.SYS):

```
DEVICE=HIMEM.SYS
DEVICE=EMM386.EXE  NOEMS
DOS=HIGH,UMB
```

Then delete the line for the DISPLAY.SYS driver.

Insert an LH (Load High) before the entry for the KEYB program in your AUTOEXEC.BAT. This loads the keyboard driver into high memory and uses DOS memory more effectively. The following is how this line should appear:

```
LH KEYBOARD.SYS
```

You can remove the two lines starting with MODE.

Emergency startup diskette

What we have described so far is a basic startup disk. Although it can get your system up and running, it may not be enough in all situations. It still doesn't include any utilities that you will desperately need for certain emergencies.

What you should have on your emergency startup diskette

Since the startup disk may be all you have to get your computer running, make certain to include all the utilities that will help eliminate the problem. Windows 98 already provides some programs for this purpose. If you created a startup disk as we described, all you need to do is copy these programs to the diskette. Your startup disk for emergencies is then complete.

The following programs are handy in an emergency:

* SCANDISK.EXE   * FDISK.EXE   * SYS.COM

* DEBUG.EXE   * ATTRIB.EXE   * MEM.EXE

* FORMAT.COM   * MSD.EXE

All the files, except for MSD.EXE, are located in the COMMAND folder. You can either copy MSD.EXE to the startup disk from the Windows folder or from the Windows CD in the \OTHER\MDS directory.

If you installed a DriveSpace drive on your hard drive, then you will also need the DRVSPACE.BIN and DRVSPACE.SYS files from the COMMAND folder. Enter the following line in the CONFIG.SYS on the startup disk:

```
DEVICEHIGH=DRVSPACE.SYS  /MOVE
```

to make sure the driver doesn't use up any valuable DOS memory.

By adding these programs and utilities to the startup disk, you've got the best defense in case of an emergency.

Copy an anti-virus program to a "clean" diskette. Make certain to write-protect this diskette (the small write protect notch should be open). If your complete hard drive becomes infected with a virus, at least you'll know that the anti-virus program on the diskette is still "clean."

A special note to users of the CD-ROM version of Windows 98: If you need to use the startup disk to boot your PC and then reinstall Windows 98, you'll run into another problem when accessing the CD. Since you don't have the right drivers installed, you won't be able to access the CD.

In such a case, you'll also need the CD-ROM driver of your CD-ROM drive and the MSCDEX.EXE file on the startup disk. You'll also have to change your CONFIG.SYS and AUTOEXEC.BAT files.

We can simplify this process by copying the appropriate entries from your CONFIG.SYS and AUTOEXEC.BAT files on the hard drive. Then all you'll need to do is correct or delete the path names. This will give you access to your CD-ROM drive in emergencies and let you use the tools from the companion CD-ROM to get your system up and running again.

If you have other hardware that you absolutely must access in emergencies (e.g., an external SCSI device), then you'll also need those drivers on the startup disk. However, remember the startup disk is only 1.44 Meg and may quickly become full. If the disk becomes full and you can't copy any more drivers to it, you have two options:

1. Remove a program from the startup disk (we don't recommend this option).

2. Keep the drivers on your hard drive and specify their paths on the hard drive in the startup files. In this case, the drivers would be loaded from the hard drive when you boot from the startup disk. However, this only works if you are able to access the hard drive.

A final note if you installed one or more SCSI hard drives which have drivers installed in the CONFIG.SYS: Make certain to include these drivers on your emergency startup disk. You won't have access to the hard drive without these drivers in case of a problem. This means you won't be able to run software to eliminate the error or problem. If you don't have enough space on the emergency startup disk, remove another program so you have room for the drivers. Then copy the other program to a different diskette.

Security for BIOS with Setup and CMOS-RAM

The configuration data in the BIOS Setup contains the most important settings for your computer. If these settings are wrong, it's a safe bet your computer will respond with errors when you try to boot it the next time. You won't even get an error message in the worst case. The screen will remain dark and the computer won't even try to boot.

The different Setup entries vary between BIOS manufacturers. Therefore, we cannot describe their individual functions here. It's more important to know that the entire configuration of Setup is stored in the CMOS-RAM. This chip has a small memory area/address range for storing this information. A battery supplies the power for the CMOS RAM. This battery prevents the information stored in CMOS RAM from becoming lost when you switch off the computer.

When you change Setup, BIOS gives you the option of saving the current settings in CMOS RAM. This process occurs in software with the help of the BIOS program. In practice, you could write to CMOS RAM from any normal program, but any settings stored there would be lost forever. That would mean that incorrectly programmed software or virus programs could lockup your PC. Do you have all the settings memorized? For example, can you remember how the cache memory was configured?

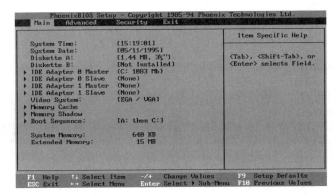

The CMOS RAM contains important information about the system configuration.

Most BIOS versions let you restore the most important settings using an option called **Auto-Configuration**. (This option may be called something similar in your version of BIOS.) Not all BIOS versions provide an option for reading out the parameters of the installed hard drive itself. If this is your situation, you'd better hope you've got this information written down somewhere. You'll have to enter it yourself. Also, you'll have to check the installed disk drives and video card setting. Make any necessary changes.

Fortunately, we know a way to make it easier: Back up all the settings of the BIOS Setup. Then you'll have them handy in emergencies. Then you can make all the necessary corrections in Setup and be confident they are correct. Your computer will reboot, but this time error-free.

Two methods are available for making a backup of your settings in Setup.

You could copy all the parameters from the screen, but that would be far too much trouble. Besides, you run the unnecessary risk of writing down an incorrect value from the screen. It's much simpler to print out all the information. You must be in the Setup program to do this, so restart the computer.

Pay close attention to the messages displayed by BIOS during the boot process. Use the appropriate key combination to interrupt booting. This takes you into Setup. Fortunately, most BIOS versions display the key or key combination necessary to interrupt booting while the computer is booting. A brief message appears, similar to the following:

1 *Preventive Measures*

Hit <DEL> if you want to run setup

The key combination you need depends on the manufacturer of your BIOS. Unfortunately, no standard exists for the key combination, so we've listed the most common keyboard commands for running Setup in the following table:

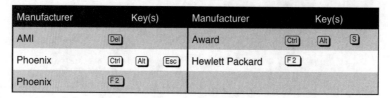

Manufacturer	Key(s)			Manufacturer	Key(s)		
AMI	Del			Award	Ctrl	Alt	S
Phoenix	Ctrl	Alt	Esc	Hewlett Packard	F2		
Phoenix	F2						

Once you're in BIOS Setup, simply press Print Screen to see a hardcopy of these settings. This instructs your printer to print a copy of the current screen. If your BIOS has several pages of settings, move to each page and press Print Screen. You'll soon have a hardcopy of all the settings. Make certain to store this hardcopy in a safe area in case of an emergency.

How to save the CMOS RAM

It's much easier if you use the PC_INFO program from the companion CD-ROM to save the contents of your CMOS RAM to a file. The program is located in the \BOOK\PC_INFO directory.

First, copy the entire PC_INFO directory to your hard drive. Then start the program in MS-DOS mode by entering:

```
PC_INFO
```

The **Save CMOS RAM/Restore** menu command lets you save the contents of the CMOS RAM to a file or copy the contents back to CMOS RAM.

When PC_INFO saves the contents of the CMOS RAM, it reads the bytes of the normal BIOS Setup from the CMOS RAM (except for the date and time). It saves the bytes to the current directory in a file called CMOS.RAM. Meanwhile, PC_INFO overwrites an existing file of the same name. If you want to restore the file contents, PC_INFO prompts you for confirmation. The CMOS.RAM file must be in the current directory or in a directory of the PATH line. Otherwise, PC_INFO displays an error message.

The **Save MBR/Restore** menu command lets you back up the partition sector and the first boot sector of C: to a file (PC_INFO.MBR). The file is saved in the current directory. If one of the two sectors is destroyed or infected with a virus, restore the sectors saved in PC_INFO.MBR. However, this only works when it is possible to address drive C:. Otherwise, you'll have to use more powerful methods such as the Norton Disk Doctor or DiskFix of PC Tools.

The PC_INFO.MBR file must be located in the current directory or in a directory of the PATH entry in the AUTOEXEC.BAT. Otherwise, the program outputs an error message.

If you change the BIOS Setup, remember to print a new hardcopy of the current settings. You could also make a new backup of the CMOS-RAM in a file. This method helps you avoid experimenting with old settings that may prevent your computer from running.

 The password is also backed up to the file if you enabled the password option in the BIOS. The password becomes active again if you need to restore the contents of the CMOS RAM from the file. So, remember the password if you want to back up the CMOS RAM to a file and you have a password enabled in BIOS Setup that you plan to change often. Then you can get into BIOS Setup again after restoring the CMOS RAM.

Backing Up

You've heard about it but how often do you do it? A regular routine of backing up data is the most important thing you can do for yourself, yet it's probably the most neglected preventive measure. Perhaps you've used one of the common reasons for not backing up data:

* Backing up involves work and takes too much time.

* I don't have the proper equipment for backing up.

* I don't want to back up hundreds of megabytes onto diskettes.

* Most users don't have programs for performing a backup.

Preventive Measures

1

However, what if your hard drive "bites the big one?" What if a virus destroys your entire database? What if DOS gets mixed up with the file allocation table again, leaving behind data chaos on your hard drive? Many other situations can develop where the data on the hard drive or the hard drive itself can become unusable. A hard drive rarely goes bad (especially suddenly). Yet no one can be completely protected. Only those users who perform backups regularly won't need to worry too much. Once these users have taken care of the problem, all these fortunate users need to do is restore their current backup and they can continue to use their computer.

Backing up vital files

Not only is it important to back up data on a regular basis, another part of the job is to back up important configuration and initialization files. Often such files contain entries which, if missing, make it impossible for the program to run. Besides the CONFIG.SYS and AUTOEXEC.BAT startup files, the WIN.INI and SYSTEM.INI Windows initialization files fall into this category. When something is wrong with these files, your computer becomes "programmed for disaster."

Windows includes the Emergency Recovery Utility (ERU.EXE) for this purpose. You'll find this utility on the Windows CD in the \Tools\ERU directory. Copy the files from this directory to your Windows directory. Then you can access them when necessary. If you own the diskette version of Windows 98, use the Explorer to search for ERU.EXE in your Windows directory. We'll explain how to use the Explorer to search for files a bit later.

ERU backs up the files to drive A: by default. You can specify a different drive, such as your hard drive, but we don't recommend doing this. If the hard drive develops an error, you wouldn't be able to get to the backup files.

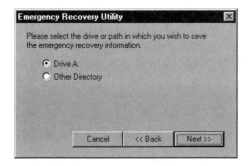

*You'll find the Emergency Recovery Utility (ERU.EXE) on
the Windows CD-ROM in the \Tools\ERU directory.*

Select the "Drive A:" radio button as your destination drive and click the Next >> button. Label a formatted diskette as "Emergency Recovery Disk." Insert this disk into the drive so you can save the files.

Make certain to use at least a 1.44 Meg diskette. In an emergency, you'll use the Windows startup disk that you'll learn more about later. After inserting the diskette, click OK to continue. An information window displays which files ERU is copying to your Emergency Recovery Disk.

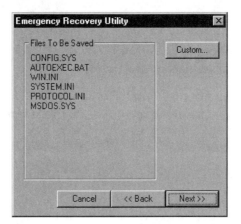

These are the files that ERU saves by default.

ERU copies the startup files, Windows initialization files, Windows system files and the registry databases to your diskette. You'll usually need the system files if you're intending to use a boot diskette for this backup. Since this isn't absolutely necessary, you can also deselect these files. To do this, click the (Custom...) button.

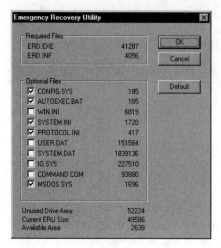

This is where you can choose the files for the backup.

If you don't want to use a bootable diskette, deselect the IO.SYS, MSDOS.SYS and COMMAND.COM files. The program then removes these files from the file list. Click the (OK) button to close the dialog box. Click (Next >>) to begin the backup. The program begins copying the specified files to the diskette.

Since diskettes are among the most unreliable storage media, make at least one extra copy of the diskette. To do this, simply repeat the procedure with another diskette. You then have a second copy of the Emergency Recovery Utility files in case the first copy is defective, erased or lost.

Backing up configuration and initialization files of other programs

Many programs have their own initialization or configuration files in which the various options and settings of the particular program are stored. Although these are usually only text files, they can be incredibly large, especially on larger programs such as Windows applications.

These files contain entries that are designed to provide error-free running of the application. In case of error, only few users can check these files manually with a text editor and correct the defective or missing entries. The programs themselves, if they'll start at all, don't give you the opportunity to check their configuration files and make any necessary corrections. All you can do is reinstall the program.

However, it's also better to back up these files to diskette. You then have got them available in emergencies. This saves you from the time-consuming task of reinstalling the application. All you need to do is determine which files to back up.

Locate all the files on your hard drive with the .INI and .CFG extensions. Use Windows Explorer to find these files. Select **Programs** in the **Start** menu of the Taskbar. Next, select **Windows Explorer**.

This opens the Explorer program window. Select the **Tools** menu and the **Find /Files or Folders....** command. This opens the Find All Files dialog box, where you can begin your search.

First, choose the drive where you want to execute the search in the "Look in:" list box. Then specify the file type you wish to look for in the "Named:" list box. Make certain to include the subfolders in your search so you don't miss any files.

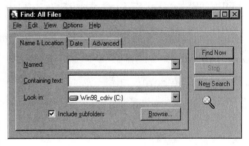

Check the "Include subfolders" check box (if it isn't already enabled). Then begin your search by clicking the [Find Now] button. Copy the files to your Windows directory so you can always access them.

You're now ready to search for the file.

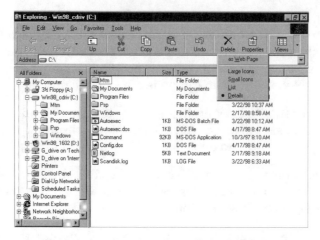

The Windows Explorer lists all the found files.

Windows Explorer displays the files it found in a list at the bottom of the window. Windows Explorer also specifies the directory in which the file is located. This lets you make inferences about the application program that is associated with the file. Long directory names are usually cut off by three dots. However, to assign the file to the application, you have to see the complete path.

To view the complete path, move the mouse pointer between the "In Folder" and "Size" fields. The mouse pointer should turn into a cross. Then double-click the left mouse button. The "In Folder" column widens far enough to display all the path specifications.

Now select those files from the list that you wish to back up (mouse click + Shift or mouse click + Ctrl). Select the **File** command and the **Send To | 3½ Floppy A** command.

> **TIP** Instead of simply copying the files to the diskette, create folders for the files, Name the folders after the application program whose files the folder contains. Check the Windows Help or documentation to find out how to create directories or folders.

16

This is similar to how you could set up the backup diskette.

Then select the files you wish to back up and copy them to the appropriate folders on the diskette. Repeat the procedure for configuration or initialization files with different file extensions.

After you finish backing up the files, make at least one copy of this diskette, too. You then have a second copy of these files in case the first copy is defective, erased or lost.

You have to determine which program configuration files to include in the backup. However, make sure that the files you back up are the current files. This also applies to the Windows files you backed up with ERU. If you aren't certain whether one of your programs changes its configuration files without first notifying you, back up the files regularly. This is the only way to be certain the backed up files are up-to-date. Otherwise, in case of an error or other problem, you might need to reinstall the complete program.

Backing up the contents of CMOS RAM

If you backed up the contents of your CMOS RAM to a file, remember to also back this file up to diskette. If you ever need this file and are unable to access the hard drive due to an error in the BIOS Setup, then your copy of the CMOS RAM on the hard drive will be of no use. Remember to copy the program that you used to create the copy of your CMOS RAM to the same diskette as well. How else can you restore the CMOS RAM to your hard drive?

17

1 *Preventive Measures*

Determining the type of backup copies

You're probably wondering whether all this is necessary. This is a legitimate concern. Some applications are so large that they require more than ten diskettes (if they're not already on CD-ROM). This is especially true for applications released before CD-ROMs became popular. If you own several of these older mammoth programs, making backup copies of all the diskettes not only requires time but can become expensive.

One thing you'll need to determine is whether to back up the application. In most cases, you won't need the program diskettes anymore once the program is successfully installed. When you upgrade your computer or buy a new one, some applications may require installing the appropriate drivers for the new hardware. If these drivers for the new hardware components aren't on a separate diskette, you'll have to go searching for the program diskettes that you've probably stored in a diskette box "somewhere."

A few other situations will force you to go hunting for your program diskettes. For example, if your hard drive stops working, you will need to reinstall your programs on the new hard drive. We all know that diskettes aren't exactly the safest storage medium. Files are repeatedly destroyed by defective sectors. In such cases, not even utility programs like ScanDisk can help. Fortunately, this isn't a big problem concerning original program diskettes. Most manufacturers will exchange the diskette or even an entire set of diskettes for new ones for a small fee.

The problem becomes larger when you cannot or do not want to wait for the manufacturer to exchange the diskettes. Therefore, if you work with a program that you simply cannot do without, not even for a couple of days, make a set of backup copies. This doesn't apply only for program copies. You should also back up driver diskettes that came with your hardware. These diskettes include the video card, CD-ROM drive or printer. Under certain circumstances, you won't even be able to use the hardware until you find a new driver diskette.

To make backup copies, double-click the My Computer icon in the desktop. Then move the mouse pointer to the 3½ Floppy (A) icon and press the right mouse button. Select the **Copy Disk...** command in the pop-up menu. Choose the source and destination drives in the Copy Disk dialog box.

TIP Make certain to write-protect the source diskette before copying (move the plastic button to expose the hole). Otherwise, you might mix up the source and destination diskettes and accidentally overwrite the original.

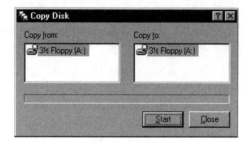

Windows includes a disk copying program you can use.

Click the [Start] button to begin copying. Windows reads the source diskette and then prompts you to insert the destination diskette.

Backing up preinstalled software

Many manufacturers sell their PCs today with Windows 98 and several programs and applications already installed on the hard drive. Besides the program directories, you will also find directories with the source files of the preinstalled programs. This saves you from performing the tiresome installation procedure.

Since these programs and applications are installed by the manufacturer, you do not have copies on diskettes. This may be a great drawback. If the hard drive becomes defective or a virus infects your hard drive, one of these preinstalled programs can be lost. It's not always easy to get the original diskettes for the program.

Since this is a problem recognized by many manufacturers, most preinstalled systems offer the option of creating "master diskettes." A program is usually available somewhere on the hard drive to perform this task. For more information, check the documentation of your computer.

We recommend using this option. It may be the only opportunity you will have to make backup copies of these preinstalled programs. Don't make any backups of the program directories, since the programs are never fully installed. Also, don't wait too long to make your master diskettes; even a new computer could have a defect.

Preventive Measures

Unfortunately, making master diskettes could be quite a hassle. This would depend on how the utility for creating master diskettes is programmed. If the programs won't run properly, visit your dealer. If the dealer can't provide you with a utility for creating master diskettes that really works, insist they give you original diskettes of your software as a replacement.

Determining which data files are most important

Determining which data files are most important is slightly different than it is with program diskettes. In emergencies, you've still have the original program or application diskette, but you might not have the originals of the documents, graphics or other data created with those programs. In case of a problem, all your work could be lost. Depending on the importance of your data, this could even result in considerable damage. Your only option might be to redo all the work.

Don't save your important data files only on the hard drive. Always make a backup of these files. If you don't have a tape streamer, save the files on diskettes. Even if tracking the files in various directories seems a tiresome chore, make the backups.

Optimum hard drive organization

A well organized hard drive is a prerequisite for effective data backup. It doesn't really help much if you start up your backup program and then have to go looking for the files you need to back up throughout various directories. You might overlook a file.

Furthermore, data files should not be located in program directories, or even in the root directory of your hard drive. Also, the directory tree should have a neat, well-organized structure.

A well-organized hard drive makes the job of backing up data much easier. The time required to backup a well-organized hard drive is much less than backing up a disorganized hard drive.

What's the best way to organize your hard drive?

Clear out the root directory

The best way to start is by clearing out your root directory. Create a temporary directory where you can move the superfluous or extra files. The following files should appear in your root directory:

* IO.SYS
* MSDOS.SYS
* COMMAND.COM
* DRVSPACE.BIN
* CONFIG.SYS
* AUTOEXEC.BAT
* CONFIG.DOS
* AUTOEXEC.DOS

You will also find some LOG files that Windows created during startup or operation.

Keep a start menu program in the root directory if you use such a program to launch your programs. You do not need any other files in this directory. If you aren't sure about a particular file, check the program documentation to find out whether the file has to be in the root directory. That takes care of the root directory.

A well organized directory structure

Now you need to create a new directory structure that is neat, well-organized and free of clutter. The following is an example of this type of directory structure.

Notice a folder is available for each program area. DOS programs are in the DOSPROGS folder. Each DOS program is in its own (sub)folder. We did the same with Windows applications. They don't belong in the Windows directory. The Windows applications should be in their own folders in the WINPROGS folder. We used the same model/system for game programs (DOS games and Windows games are also separated).

This is an example of a well-organized directory structure.

21

Finally, a folder called DRIVERS contains directories of driver files for installed hardware. You can place utilities in the UTILITY folder. If necessary, put programs that don't fit elsewhere in the MISC folder.

Naturally, you are free to choose different names for the folders. This example is only meant to give you an idea of which direction to follow.

If you organize your hard drive this way, remember to enter the changed directory names in your CONFIG.SYS and AUTOEXEC.BAT files as well. Otherwise you may be flooded with error messages the next time you boot. You may also need to change paths for applications in some configuration or initialization files. So, if you had to move programs to a different directory, be sure to check the CFG or INI files for path specifications.

Setting up a data directory

You should always have a folder named DATA on your hard drive. In fact, you should use a separate folder in DATA for each application installed on your system. Then you can store the data files that belong to the application in the corresponding folder. This is the only way to manage your data in truly well-organized fashion.

To use this structure, set the appropriate data directories in the options within the programs, so the applications automatically work in the right directory.

As an example, we'll assign a working directory to WordPad so its text files are automatically saved in C:\DATA\WORDPAD. First, we need to create a shortcut to the program. WORDPAD.EXE is usually located in C:\PROGRAM FILES\ACCESSORIES. Open the ACCESSORIES folder and drag the program icon to the desktop. Windows automatically creates a shortcut to the program.

Now right-click the shortcut and select **Properties** in the pop-up menu that appears. Now click the "Shortcut" tab.

A well organized directory structure such as this is important to control data and files.

Enter C:\DATA\WORDPAD as your working directory. Click OK to close the dialog box. From now on, start WordPad only from the icon of the shortcut. This way the working directory will be set right after you start the program.

Follow the same procedure with the other programs for which you created a data directory. Unfortunately, this procedure won't work with all Windows applications. Some programs, such as AmiPro, use their own setting options, and you need to set the working directory with these options. If necessary, consult the documentation of the program. Many DOS applications also have their own option. Again, check the program documentation.

If you organized your hard drive according to our recommendations, you now have a C:\DATA directory. This directory contains subdirectories in which all the data files for your programs are stored.

Specify the working directory in the Properties menu and the "shortcut" tab.

What advantage does this method have for you?

A well-organized, clutter-free hard drive makes data backup much easier. Because the installed program is unlikely to change, you usually do not need to backup program directories. When you need to back up your data files, you won't have to search through all types of different directories. All the data files are now located in subdirectories of the C:\DATA directory. All you have to do is back up the C:\DATA directory with its subdirectories. Then you've automatically backed up all the data files without overlooking any single file.

The best backup methods

Streamer tape drives are ideal as a backup medium because of their high storage capacity. If you don't have a tape drive installed on your system, then you'll have to use diskettes (a backup on diskettes is better than no backup at all). To reduce the chances of losing data, perform a backup regularly. If you're working with important data, you need to create at least two backups. What if you discovered that the backup medium is defective while attempting to restore the data? Moreover, most backup programs have a Compare option that compares backup data with the original. The program will alert you if it detects any errors. Always use this option, no matter which backup method and which backup medium you wish to use.

Preventive Measures

The first backup

Don't put all your faith in your backup software. You wouldn't be the first to pay for this mistake with serious data loss. Make certain your backup program runs smoothly and is fully compatible with the drive on which you want to create your backups. These programs usually prompt you to run a compatibility test the first time you run them. Don't rely exclusively on this test—run your own test backup.

Start the backup program and select some files from the hard drive as a test backup. We recommend using the following file types as a test backup:

* One system file

* One read-only file

* One hidden file

* One directory with files

* One empty directory

* One empty file, which is zero bytes (see below)

* One file with a long filename

* One file from a directory with a long name

If you do not have a file on your hard drive that is zero bytes large, start a DOS box and use the following DOS command to create a zero byte file

```
TYPE NUL > TEST
```

This gives you a file named TEST which is really zero bytes (remember, you cannot have a file or directory in your root directory with the same name). You could use IO.SYS and MSDOS.SYS from the root directory for your system, read-only and hidden files. To protect yourself from losing an important file, create a new directory with a long name and copy any file with a long filename to this directory. This is also an excellent way of testing the backup software's compatibility with Windows 98.

Now start the backup. If everything backs up satisfactorily, simply check whether restoring the data will also work. Make certain not to overwrite any files on the hard drive. Create a directory on the hard drive and restore the backup files to this directory. Specify this directory as the destination directory and start the Restore command. Now compare the restored files with original files. Use the DOS FC (File Compare) command if you don't have a utility such as PC-Tools or Norton Commander (Windows Explorer doesn't have a compare option):

```
FC /B [Drive:\][Path]Filename [Drive:\][Path]Original file
```

If all the files are comparable, you can be confident your backup software will work and is compatible with your hardware.

Building a backup system uses different strategies. Each strategy has its advantages and disadvantages. The strategies also differ in the backup medium used.

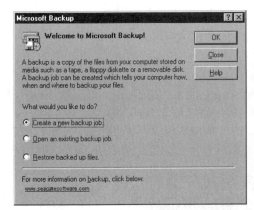

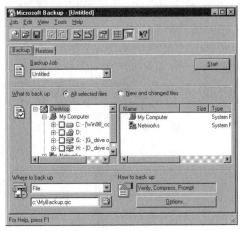

These three screens show examples of the options with MS-BACKUP of Windows.

Preventive Measures

Incremental backup

A good backup program gives you the option of backing up only files that have been changed since the last backup. An incremental backups typically start with a full backup that sets all file archive bits when done. Then each successive "incremental" backup saves only the changed files. The advantage is that it cuts down considerably on the time for a backup. The backup set requires less disk space on the backup medium.

Disadvantages of an incremental backup

If you notice while restoring a file that the backup medium has a defect, the file could be lost. This file won't necessarily be present on an older backup set.

Recommendation

Use this method if you wish to back up often. However, this method requires that you use at least two backup media. Alternate between media when you back up or create two identical backups each time. If a defect or error is found, you at least have the second backup to use.

Differential backup

In a differential backup, you specify which files you want backed up. For example, if you want to backup all text files, you'd specify *.TXT. However, the program does not reset the archive attribute for the files after the backup.

Advantages of a differential backup

When you specify file groups, all the files in the group are backed up, even if they haven't been modified. So, each file exists in each backup set. This becomes a big advantage in case something happens to the backup medium.

Disadvantages of a differential backup

Since common file groups are specified in this method, the backup sets are larger and require more disk space on the backup medium.

Recommendation

Use this method if you require a high amount of security for your data. Make certain to use at least two backup media.

Time backup

Finally, some backup programs let you specify a time frame. The program using this method backs up only those files whose date falls within this time span. DOS updates the modification date of a file with each write access.

Advantages of a time backup

No particular advantages.

Disadvantages of a time backup

You never know whether all the files you wish to include in the backup fall into the specified time range. You have to display the selected files to check. Moreover, you can't allow yourself to make a mistake when specifying the time range. You could easily overlook a file, which then would be excluded from the backup.

Recommendation

We don't recommend this method due to its disadvantages. Use this method only if other methods are unavailable.

Backup with streamer tape drives

To start a backup using streamer tape drives, first create a backup of your program directories. This saves you from having to reinstall the complete program in case of error. All you have to do is restore the directory to the hard drive and your application will run again. Then make two complete backups of your data directory (provided you already organized your hard drive as we described).

In the future, update your backups of the data directory regularly. Be your own judge of how often you need to back up. The safest method is, of course, to backup your data daily, but this could be too time consuming. After all, you don't spend all day every day working on each of your data files. Therefore, use one of the backup methods we described. This limits the amount of time you spend backing up.

You'll accumulate several backups over time, so you may have trouble locating the last backup of a particular file. The file in question doesn't always get backed up, but instead, only when the archive attribute is set. After three months, will you know when the last time you backed up this file was? Will you still remember which backup contains the file you're looking for? To prevent your backup sets from turning into mass confusion, create a complete backup of your data directory about once a month. Then you can delete or overwrite the "partial" backups made prior to this time.

Backup with diskettes

Backing up to diskettes usually requires more work than backing up to other media. Depending on the amount of data you have to back up, your collection of backup diskettes can grow into an unorganized pile. We don't recommend doing a backup of the program directories in this case. Any advantage compared to reinstalling the program with the original diskettes is negligible. Either way, you'd be changing diskettes all the time. It's a different story with the data files, however. If you value your data, follow the procedure we described earlier.

On the other hand, if you are fortunate enough to own a second hard drive, then you may be able to use a better method. If your data will fit on either hard drive, use the second hard drive as a backup medium. For example, if you have a data directory called C:\DATA on your C: drive, simply copy it to your second hard drive. This saves you the task of backing up to diskettes. We have never heard of two hard drives "biting the dust" at the same time. Even a virus only affects the current drive. Remember to copy the data directory to the second hard drive on a regular basis so your backup is up to date.

So, if you perform backups regularly as we described, then you don't need to worry about a defect in your computer or a virus. Your data is safely stored away on your tape or diskettes. Once you find the cause of the error and repair the computer, all you have to do is restore your backup without suffering a great loss of data.

Restore after replacing the hard drive

Of course your hardware can develop problems, too. Let's suppose that your computer no longer boots and your hard drive is defective. So you buy a new hard drive and install it in your computer. Since new hard drives are usually already bootable, you don't have to worry about reinstalling all your software including the operating system if you have a complete backup of the first hard drive.

However, it's important that the new hard drive boot with MS-DOS 7.00 and not with an older version of DOS. Check this by booting the computer with the new hard drive and then entering the following command at the DOS prompt:

```
VER
```

If the VER command shows that an older version of DOS is installed on the hard drive, you'll have to prepare the drive with the Windows startup diskette. To do this, boot the computer with the startup disk and enter the following:

```
SYS C:
```

This replaces the old DOS files with the new ones and adapts the boot sector.

To use your Windows backup program, you'll also have to reinstall Windows on the hard drive. As the owner of the CD version of Windows 98, you need to install the CD-ROM drivers first in order to be able to access your CD-ROM drive. Even if you have a Windows startup disk with the CD-ROM drivers installed on it, don't start the computer with this disk. This would considerably slow down the installation procedure of Windows, since the computer would constantly be accessing the diskette to call specific operating system routines.

Once Windows is installed, you can restore the remaining data of the backup. If you used a different program instead of MS-Backup, you'll have to install the program first, then perform the restore from your backup data.

Backup software updates

If you decide to install an update of your backup software, make certain to backup the old version first. It wouldn't be the first time that a new version turned out to be incompatible with the old version. If the old version is no longer available, all you can do is hope you never have to restore the old backup data.

Run a test backup followed by a restore as we described in this section. Also, check whether the new version also works with the old backup data. For this purpose, restore some of the files from the old backup to the hard drive. If this works cleanly or you are certain that you no longer need the old backup, then you can use the new version without worrying.

1 *Preventive Measures*

File System Maintenance

The best way to prevent errors in the file management system of the operating system is to occasionally organize your hard drive. This also makes troubleshooting for software errors easier and faster.

Keep in mind that because your computer is running smoothly right now doesn't mean everything is perfect on your hard drive. If you load your text file and discover that garbage characters have replaced part of your text, it's already too late. You could have avoided this error with some preventive maintenance. We'll show you how to keep your hard drive clean and avoid these and similar errors.

Removing unnecessary files

You may be unaware of the number of files on your hard drive that you never use or need. These files are simply wasting disk space on your hard drive. Many sources generate these files.

Backup copies of the startup files

A frequent source is when you install a new program or application. Some of these programs or applications change the CONFIG.SYS and AUTOEXEC.BAT files when they're installed. The CONFIG.SYS and AUTOEXEC.BAT files are the operating system startup files. The CONFIG.SYS can change, for example, when another driver is entered in the file. The AUTOEXEC.BAT may be changed by adding the name of the program directory to the list of search paths, *i.e.*, the PATH line. Other changes can be made to these files.

Before an application or program changes the CONFIG.SYS and AUTOEXEC.BAT files, it first creates backup copies. After all, it's possible that the computer won't boot properly after those changes have been made. If you cannot determine the error in the CONFIG.SYS and AUTOEXEC.BAT, you have the option of using the backup copies as the original files. That way you can boot your computer again.

However, such errors happen rarely. If you forget about the backup copies created by the program, they'll simply remain stored on your hard drive. The number of these backup copies can increase over time. Look in the root directory of your hard drive for these backup copies of the CONFIG.SYS and AUTOEXEC.BAT files. Usually the backups will have file extensions like .OLD or .BAK. A file called, for example,

30

CONFIG.OLD or CONFIG.BAK may be a backup copy, created in the manner we described above. If your computer boots properly, you can delete all the CONFIG files except for CONFIG.SYS and CONFIG.DOS. You'll need CONFIG.DOS if you kept your old version of DOS.

 Files called CONFIG.COM or CONFIG.EXE are not backup copies but are instead executable programs. However, such programs should not be in your root directory (move these files to your Windows directory). Don't delete any other CONFIG files. It's possible that you've also got a CONFIG.INI or CONFIG.CFG which the executable COM file requires.

The same also applies to backup copies of the AUTOEXEC.BAT. If you see several AUTOEXEC files displayed on the screen, you can delete everything but AUTOEXEC.BAT and AUTOEXEC.DOS. Don't worry about accidentally deleting an executable program. Nobody would write a program and name it AUTOEXEC.

Backup copies of data files

You probably have other backup copies on your hard drive that you no longer need. They can take up quite a bit of disk space on your hard drive. Some applications create backup copies whenever you save a file you have been editing.

For example, if you created a file in Word called EXAMPLE.DOC and you want to save it, Word will first rename EXAMPLE.DOC to EXAMPLE.BAK. Only then does Word save the file you are editing as EXAMPLE.DOC. The old file (the .BAK file) is now a backup copy.

Many applications use this method. Therefore, you can easily collect several hundred K or even a few megabytes of backup files on your hard drive. You won't normally need these backup copies (especially if you back up your data regularly). Therefore, it's usually safe to delete the backup copies. Most applications use .BAK for an extension. Read the documentation to find out which file extension the application uses for backup copies.

Searching for all these files manually is usually too time consuming. Instead, use Windows Explorer. Start Explorer from the Start menu. First, select **Programs** from the **Start** menu. Then click **Windows Explorer**. Select **Tools | Find | Files or Folders...** to display the Find All Files dialog box.

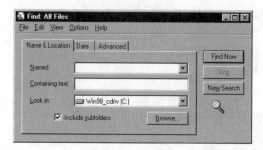

Track down unnecessary files the easy way with Windows Explorer.

Select the desired drive to begin the search. Enter the file type for which you are searching. Click the [Find Now] button to begin the search. Windows Explorer lists all the found files of the specified type. Select these files and drag them to the Recycle Bin. The recycle bin deletes these files from your hard drive.

Temporary files

Many programs create temporary files on the hard drive as you're using them. They do this by "misusing" the hard drive as RAM when the computer cannot provide sufficient free memory. These temporary files can sometimes be several hundred K in size. Most programs that work with temporary files save them in a directory specified by the DOS variable TEMP or TMP.

You can define these variables so all the programs will create their temporary files in the same directory. You can then delete these temporary files quickly because you know where they are all stored. The AUTOEXEC.BAT usually specifies these variables.

```
SET TEMP= C:\TEMP
SET TMP= C:\TEMP
```

Make certain to define both variables. Some applications use the directory specified for TEMP, and other applications use the directory specified for TMP.

Some applications delete their temporary files when you properly exit the application. Unfortunately, this is not always the case. Sometimes the computer may lock up or crash and you cannot exit the application properly. As a result, the application does not delete any temporary files. Also, some users thoughtlessly switch off their computer without first exiting the application. In this case, too, temporary files will remain on the hard drive.

Look at your TEMP directory occasionally. Files located in the TEMP directory will usually have the .TMP extension. It's normally safe to delete these files.

A few applications also work with temporary files, but do not recognize the directory for temporary files specified by the DOS variables. They simply store their temporary files in the program directory. You could probably tolerate this by using Windows to find all files with the .TMP file extension. You could then delete them. However, it's not quite that simple.

These programs use entirely different filenames and extensions. You'll find temporary files using extensions such as .$$$. Read the documentation for more detailed information about an application. With a little luck, you'll even find information about the program's temporary files.

Dead programs

The last type of unnecessary files includes all programs that you installed, but have not used in a long time. These are applications, programs, games or utilities that you probably won't need or use again. Don't keep these files; copy the files to diskettes if you feel you might need it someday. Then remove them from your hard drive. A better alternative is to back up those programs to a tape (if you have a tape drive).

While you're searching for old files, consider those old data files for which you no longer have any use. If necessary, copy them to diskette or tape and then remove them from your hard drive. Although you may need to keep a backup of the old data files, there is no need to keep them on your hard drive.

Getting Your Hard Drive into Shape

One of the most important components in a computer is the hard drive. It houses the operating system, the programs and data files. The hard drive "breathes life" into your computer. In the process, the hard drive is in constant motion (permanently rotating at 3,000 RPM). Also, the read/write heads are moving back and forth constantly. Data is constantly being read from or written to the hard drive. Therefore, the surface of the hard drive is reset each time.

1 *Preventive Measures*

Users must demand the highest reliability from the hard drive for data security. Today, a good hard drive normally has a longer life-span than its host computer. Even when you scrap your computer someday because of its hopelessly outdated technology, its hard drive will still keep your data safe.

So under normal circumstances, the hard drive won't wear out. If it's so reliable, why go through all the trouble of backing up? Actually, if it weren't for the operating system...

Now it's time to go into a bit more detail about hard drive organization and the FAT file system. You will find out that occasional "maintenance" of the hard drive is inevitable.

First, a new hard drive is partitioned using the FDISK program. In the process, the size and name of the partition is specified. Next, the partition needs to be formatted. The individual sectors on the hard drive are set up only after the partition is formatted. The FORMAT program automatically creates the FAT (File Allocation Table). The FAT records information about which clusters are free or allocated.

A cluster, or allocation unit, is a combination of several sectors. Depending on the size of the partition, a cluster can be 4, 8 or 16 sectors. This method is used to reduce the size of the FAT. For example, with a hard drive of 900 cylinders, 10 heads and 46 sectors (as in a 202 Meg hard drive), the FAT would require 414,000 bytes. If you combine 8 sectors into one cluster, and managed only the clusters in the FAT, and not the sectors, the FAT would only require 51,750 bytes. In the process, the operating system would create at least one additional copy of the FAT on the hard drive. After the partition is formatted, the root directory is also created and the hard drive is now ready for the complete operating system to be installed.

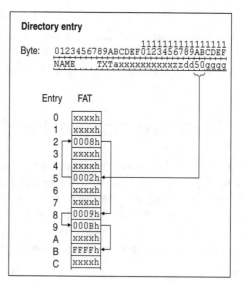

Files on the hard drive are managed using the directory and the FAT.

When a file is saved on the hard drive, the number of the first cluster at which the file begins is recorded in the directory entry for the file. This number is also the first number of the FAT entry. This FAT entry contains

34

another number representing the next FAT entry. This number also corresponds to a reference to the sectors allocated by the file. So, the FAT entries make up a chain that records which clusters are allocated by the file in question. Every single file on the hard drive is managed by DOS in this way. The FAT must be updated accordingly each time for all file operations, such as copying, deleting, moving or editing.

The following table explains the structure of a directory entry.

Byte	Meaning	Byte	Meaning
0...7	Filename, filled with spaces	18,19	Date of last modification
8...A	Filename extension, filled with spaces	1A	First cluster of the file, low byte
B	File attribute	1B	First cluster of the file, high byte
C...15	Reserved	1C...1	File size (in bytes)
16,17	Time of last modification		

The Windows 98 FAT system is called VFAT (Virtual FAT). It's based on the "old" DOS system we just described. VFAT is an enhanced version of the FAT, but maintains downward compatibility. The long filenames are achieved by using several sequential directory entries according to the "old" system. The number of entries used matches what the long filename requires. These entries are hidden with the help of the attribute byte. Therefore, FAT oriented programs cannot include these entries in the display.

We can only give you a glimpse into the file system of the operating system. It's only meant to show you the operating system has its hands full during file operations. Because of the complicated processes in file management, things can occasionally go wrong. This is why you sometimes have to "help" your operating system. It offers utilities that will help you to prevent many of these potential problems.

Reuniting file fragments with DEFRAG

When a file is saved on the hard drive, the operating system checks for free clusters in the FAT in which the data can be stored. A corresponding directory entry is created for this purpose. It contains the number of the first cluster that the new file requires.

Preventive Measures

Because files are usually longer than one cluster, the operating system must look for additional free clusters in the FAT. The operating system is unaware of whether the clusters it assigns are contiguous. For example, a file might allocate clusters 332, 333, 334, 874 and 516. Therefore, the file in question is split into three fragments. This is unimportant to you because you're unaware of the process. After all, your main concern is that the file is stored correctly on the hard drive. However, fragmenting also has some disadvantages that you won't notice until later.

The story doesn't end with just one file, however. Files are repeatedly written to the hard drive. This occurs when you install new programs or are editing your data files and saving them afterwards. Sometimes, starting with the first cluster assigned to the file during the save operation, not enough contiguous space is available on the hard drive. As a result, the file is split into fragments. An increasing number of fragmented files accumulate over time. This results in slower loading times for the files and programs in question.

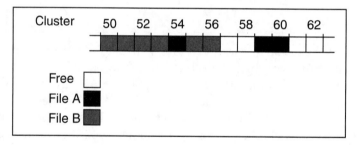

This is an illustration of fragmented files on the disk.

The clusters of a nonfragmented file that is loaded from the hard drive can be read in sequence. This prevents the read/write head from executing too many movements. With fragmented files, on the other hand, the heads have to move to each fragment. This slows the speed of the read/write head.

One fragmented file is fairly insignificant, but a large database could be split into countless fragments. These many fragments would slow the speed of the hard drive noticeably. Furthermore, errors can creep into the file system of a highly fragmented hard drive. These errors can lead to data loss.

Windows has a utility to combine the fragments of such files back into a single fragment. This utility is DEFRAG. To start DEFRAG, click the **Start** menu. Then click (in this order) **Programs | Accessories | System Tools**. Finally, click **Disk Defragmenter** to start the program.

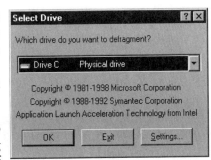

Choose the appropriate drive you want to defragment. Confirm your selection by clicking [OK]. The program displays the amount of fragmentation on the selected drive. If the percentage is low, you can decide for yourself whether to run the DEFRAG program.

Start defragementing by selecting the drive to be fragmented.

Run the program if the percentage of fragmentation is higher than 10%. The higher the percentage, the longer defragmenting will require.

Click the [Settings...] button to set more specific options of the DEFRAG program. (However, if you right click on a drive from the My Computer screen and then select the drive properties and tools, you won't get the Settings option before starting the defrag process.)

Choose options for DEFRAG in the Settings dialog box.

Click the [OK] button to begin defragmenting the drive.

Preventive Measures

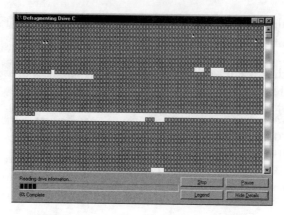

This is an example of DEFRAG at work.

Run DEFRAG on regularly (for example, once a month). This way, you'll keep your hard drive in tune and you'll prevent operating system errors. Perform a full defragmentation of your hard drive every few months. Since DEFRAG modifies the file system quite a bit, make certain to backup the hard drive before defragmenting. After all, DEFRAG could suffer a crash, through a programming error or due to programs or drivers tampering with memory. In the worst case scenario, this could result in data loss.

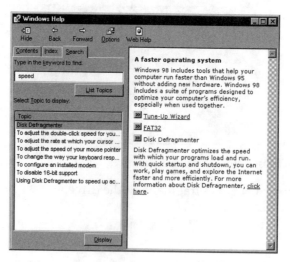

Be careful...another application could affect DEFRAG while
it's working if you followed this tip.

By following this tip, another application could hinder DEFRAG while it's working. Furthermore, some DOS programs or older 16-bit Windows applications could access memory areas that are normally inaccessible. Our recommendation: Don't trust Windows 98's crash-proof feature; the danger of data loss cannot be eliminated.

 If you have Windows 95, don't run any defragmenting programs that haven't been programmed for Windows 95. The control such programs have over the VFAT system is unreliable. This could result in your losing all your data.

If you have installed compressed drives with DriveSpace, don't use a hard drive defragmenter manufactured by any other company. Only DEFRAG, manufactured by the same company that produces DriveSpace, guarantees you the highest compatibility.

Checking the hard drive with ScanDisk

ScanDisk lets you search media for physical defects and, if necessary, repair them. ScanDisk is useful for checking physical defects on diskettes. You'll probably come across more errors with a diskette than your hard drive. Also, ScanDisk provides you with an ideal tool for checking DriveSpace drives. ScanDisk also finds defects in the logical file system. These defects include cross-linked files, lost file fragments, a destroyed directory structure or errors in the FAT. ScanDisk can repair many of these defects.

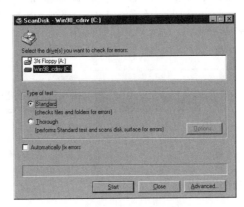

Starting ScanDisk in Windows 98.

To start ScanDisk, click the **Start** menu. Then click (in this order) **Programs | Accessories | System Tools**. Finally, click **ScanDisk** to start the program.

Click the (Advanced...) button to specify how ScanDisk works. Settings for cross-linked files and lost file fragments can be important. These settings let you convert defects in the file system to files. This ability can play an important part in data recovery. For more information, see Chapter 3. It discusses solving hard drive problems.

The advanced options of ScanDisk.

Cross-linked files

A serious error in the file system is present if ScanDisk detects cross-linked files. This error always affects at least two files. These two files, according to FAT, are both allocating at least one identical cluster. In this cluster, data of one file is overwriting data of the other file. That means at least one file is defective. ScanDisk and other utilities are unable to correct this mistake.

Although these errors rarely occur, they can be very disastrous. At best, ScanDisk can save one of the cross-linked files. How does the program know to which of the files the double-allocated cluster really belongs? With a little luck, ScanDisk will allocate the double-allocated cluster to the correct file. This is usually the file with the more recent date, because it was saved last. Otherwise, both files will be damaged. In this event, you'll need to use a backup copy of the files. Restore the backup file to the hard drive.

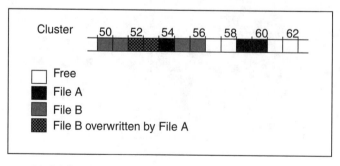

Multiple allocation of a cluster through cross-linking.

The number of cross-linked files will increase over time. You won't notice this until you attempt to load a cross-linked file. The consequences of doing this are unpredictable. Data files can be garbled and program files will be destroyed, since they can contain undefined/unspecified code. In the worst case, the computer will crash when you load such a file or program.

Lost file fragments

Lost file fragments are clusters that are labeled as allocated in the FAT, but no longer belong to a "valid" file. Sometimes the operating system just forgets to release deleted clusters in the FAT. We won't go into detail about how this happens. Such clusters take up valuable space on your hard drive. For example, a cluster on larger hard drives is 8,192 bytes long (8192 = 16 sectors of 512 bytes each). The following formula shows the amount of lost disk space for 127 lost clusters:

```
127 x 8192 = 1,040,384 bytes of lost disk space
```

Hundreds or even thousands of lost clusters are sometimes reported. The amount of lost clusters depends on how often the hard drive is accessed and the last time you used ScanDisk. ScanDisk gives you the option of freeing up this wasted disk space.

However, if you're afraid of losing valuable data, instruct ScanDisk to convert the fragments into files. The lost file fragments are then stored in the root directory in a file named **FILEnnnn** (*nnnn* represents a consecutive number). Most word processors, such as Write, can read this file. Unfortunately, WordPad in Windows 98 cannot read such files. You normally do not need to save fragments in a file. They usually belong to files destined to be deleted anyway. Otherwise, ScanDisk marks the affected FAT entries as free again and the disk space is again available.

To run ScanDisk, click the [Start] button. ScanDisk begins checking the file system and the hard drive. Checking the surface of the hard drive can take several minutes.

As with DEFRAG, run ScanDisk regularly to prevent errors in the file system. Also, use ScanDisk to check the hard drive surface occasionally. This will give you information

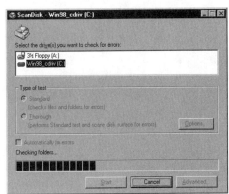

Example of ScanDisk at work.

about your hard drive before truly serious problems develop. If ScanDisk ever detects defective sectors, buy a new hard drive soon. These defective sectors will pile up and your hard drive will eventually become unusable or unstable.

> **TIP**
>
> If you installed any DriveSpace drives, don't use another manufacturer's programs for checking the hard drive. Only ScanDisk will guarantee the highest compatibility to DriveSpace drives. While ScanDisk is working, don't multitask any other programs. This tip also applies to DOS prompts despite Microsoft mentioning in the Online Help that this is possible.

> **WARNING**
>
> Don't use any competitor products not programmed for Windows 95. These products cannot communicate with the VFAT system, which could result in total loss of your data.

Don't forget to run a virus check

Naturally, regular use of a current virus scanner is also part of hard drive maintenance. Unfortunately, users don't do this often enough. Many users have unknowingly caught a virus only to discover it much later by accident. Unfortunately, by that time, quite a bit of data is already lost. To add to the problem, the virus was also saved each time the user did a back up. Refer to the chapter on viruses for more information.

This concludes our discussion of preventive measures. You'll be well prepared by following the suggestions and information provided in this chapter.

Chapter 2:
Solving Frequent
Windows Problems

Chapter 2
Solving Frequent
Windows Problems

Windows has become the most widely used operating system for home computers. Today's PCs are shipped either with Windows already installed or available for installation on a CD-ROM

Installing Windows 98 is usually quite simple. Windows is by definition user-friendly, quite clear and easy to understand, and beginners can easily get used to using it.

But, very few applications are ever 100% free of problems. One rule to remember is the larger the application, the more problems you're likely to have. Unfortunately, the same is true in Windows 98. Also, you must consider all the incompatibilities between other software or hardware.

Fortunately, this is somewhat less troublesome than it seems. Windows is really quite stable. It's only from time to time (but unfortunately time and again) that some problem or another makes itself noticeable in Windows. In an attempt to keep you from being frustrated, we explain the problems that occur most often in Windows.

The Safe Installation

Before installing Windows 98, you should understand the information in the following paragraphs.

Solving Frequent Windows Problems 2

README files

SETUP.TXT

Read the file called SETUP.TXT before installing Windows 98. The information in this file will help you avoid installation problems.

README.TXT

Windows 98 deletes some files from DOS and previous versions of Windows. Read the README.TXT file to see which files will be affected. Follow the steps outlined in the README.TXT file if you're uncertain whether you'll need these programs.

Problems with the DOS screen saver

Disable all screen savers installed with the original setup of your system before installing Windows 98. Otherwise, you may have problems with the Windows 98 Setup.

Do not use hard drive compression software

If you're trying to install Windows 98 on a hard drive that was compressed (using DoubleSpace, for example), Windows 98 will probably respond with an error message: The host drive has insufficient space to install Windows 98. You cannot install Windows 98 on a compressed hard drive.

At this point you have two options:

1. Use the compression software's setup program or the program itself to setup less compressed space and more uncompressed area.

2. Uninstall the compression software completely.

If you only have a small hard drive (under 200 Meg), you could reformat the drive exclusively for Windows 98. A better alternative is to buy a larger hard drive. It isn't only Windows that requires large amounts of space on your hard drive. Today's applications are becoming larger and require more hard drive space that ever before.

2 Solving Frequent Windows Problems

Automatic Hardware Detection (Plug and Play)

During installation, Windows will attempt to recognize your hardware and track its resources. This may result in a system failure. However, do not press Ctrl + Alt + Del if a system failure should occur. That would erase all necessary Windows information. Instead, press the reset button or switch off the computer. Then switch on the computer again and restart Setup.

Windows has already located and recognizes the hardware. It knows exactly which hardware has given the errors. With the new setup, a dialogue window will automatically appear. You will want to choose the Safe Recovery option. This instructs Windows to work around the problem hardware and avoid creating another system failure.

A new hardware failure could occur in a case where some exotic hardware exists. If so, you may need to repeat these steps several times. This hardware cannot be used directly after the full installation is complete. You must install them manually after Windows is installed. See Chapter 5 for more information.

Using a startup diskette

We stressed the importance of a startup diskette in Chapter 1. It's the most important precaution you can take for emergencies. This startup disk could be your lifesaver.

You can create a startup disk when you install Windows 98.

Follow the instructions in this dialog box to create a startup disk.

Creating a startup disk requires one floppy disk with at least 1.2 Meg capacity.

Use the startup disk to start your computer if you are having problems starting Windows. Insert the startup disk in your floppy disk drive before restarting. Then switch on your PC. Your PC starts from the startup disk instead of your hard drive.

Make a backup copy of the startup disk. Place both the original and copy in different safe locations.

Selecting the correct monitor

The Setup Wizard will show the computer settings which may be installed by Windows.

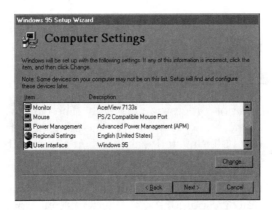

These are the settings which Windows selects.

You may not be familiar with the monitor name that Windows shows. If this is the case, you should enter your monitor type so Windows may list it among its choices. To use this option, click the (Change...) button.

2 *Solving Frequent Windows Problems*

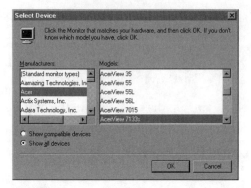

At this point you may choose your monitor type. Try a compatible monitor or "Standard monitor types)" if your monitor is not listed.

If your monitor is not among those listed, try a compatible monitor. Also, try selecting "(Standard monitor types)" for "Manufacturers:."

Failure during installation

Let's suppose the installation process ran perfectly. The Hardware Wizard indicates all hardware functions are working properly. The computer itself is found to be in order. However, the computer mysteriously crashed after you transferred files from the installation CD-ROM to the hard drive.

The origin of this error may be the BIOS boot protector or virus detector. If the boot protector is activated, a corresponding message will appear on the monitor. Reboot the computer and switch to the unit's BIOS Setup. Disable the virus and boot protectors and save the changes. Also, adjust any lines in the CONFIG.SYS and the AUTOEXEC.BAT that call the resident virus detector. This must be deactivated.

Also, disable any DOS screen savers and non-Microsoft file managers.

SETUP.EXE parameters

To remove the likelihood of additional installation problems, use SETUP.EXE with special parameters. The following table lists these parameters:

Parameter	Meaning
Batch	Specifies the name and location of the file that contains the Setup options.
/T:TMPDIR	Specifies the directory where Setup will copy its temporary files. If the directory doesn't exist, it will be created. Also any files existing in this directory will be deleted.
/IM	Skips the memory check.
/ID	Ignores the disk-space check.
/IS	Skips the routine system check.
/IQ	Skips the check for cross-linked files.
/IN	Runs Setup without the Network Setup module.
Note: The /N and /A options are no longer valid. Use NETSETUP.EXE instead.	

Problems with Startup and Using Windows 98

This section describes several problems which you may have starting or using Windows 98.

Startup problems due to incomplete installation

Before your computer is 100% operational, you must install Windows 98 completely and correctly. If installation is interrupted or incomplete and your PC locks up, follow these steps to run setup again. Restart your PC. Press [F4] when the opening message (**"Starting Windows 98..."**) appears on your monitor. If you're upgrading from an older operating system, the computer starts up with the original operating system and you will have to start the setup again.

2 *Solving Frequent Windows Problems*

First aid regarding start-up problems

You may be familiar with WIN.COM from earlier versions of Windows. However, Windows 98 is an independent operations system. It's no longer possible to simply operate Windows 98 with WIN.COM. Now Windows 98 starts without allowing any influence to be taken over its starting options. Microsoft fortunately added a built-in function that allows you to get around start-up problems.

Most of the difficulties concern the drivers for the memory managers or the graphic driver. In these cases, Windows will not run optimally, if at all. Reboot the computer. Press F8 when you see the "Starting Windows 98..." message. This interrupts the start procedure. The Microsoft Windows 98 Startup Menu will soon appear

Normal

Use this option to instruct Windows 98 to start up normally, as if the startup operation was never interrupted.

Logged (\BOOTLOG.TXT)

After you select this option, Windows will start and create a text file (BOOTLOG.TXT) of the configuration files and drivers loaded. This file helps you determine which device drivers might be giving you problems.

Safe mode

By starting in Safe mode, Windows ignores the two startup files, CONFIG.SYS and AUTOEXEC.BAT. Windows only uses the standard VGA driver. Windows does not load drivers for the network(s) (unless you select "Safe mode with network support").

Step-by-step confirmation

Here you're prompted to execute each line of the CONFIG.SYS and AUTOEXEC.BAT files. This gives you the opportunity to test the various drivers and to determine which is causing problems.

Command prompt only

This command starts the computer in DOS-Mode. The boot will end with a DOS-prompt. You may then start Windows by typing:

```
WIN
```

and pressing the (Enter) key at the DOS prompt. You may also enter various parameters by entering WIN/?.

Previous MS-DOS versions

If your system lists this option, it will start up on an older version of DOS. Make certain this point is in the startup menu if the "BOOTMULTI=1" entry exists in the MSDOS.SYS data. To edit this data you must change the following attributes:

* Hidden

* System

* Write protected

You must also select the file in Windows Explorer and use your mouse to choose the Properties option, where you can disable the file attributes. You may then use EDIT to load and make the changes to the file. After you edit the file, you must save the file and change the attributes back to their original state that were: Hidden, System and Write Protected.

We'll explain the steps later that you should take if a problem is detected with a driver out of the startup files. Systematically deactivate the driver files within the startup files CONFIG.SYS and AUTOEXEC.BAT to find the cause. See Chapter 3 for more information.

Dr. Watson integrated

Although at one time part of Windows 95, Dr. Watson is not included with Windows 98. However, Windows 98 has similar information available whenever you need it. Click the (Details >) button that appears inside the error window. As you can see in the following illustration, clicking this button displays detailed information about your problem.

Click the Details > *button to display detailed information concerning a system problem.*

As happened with Dr. Watson, most users are probably unable to interpret the information. If an error appears too often, call Microsoft Tech Support or the manufacturer of the software for a possible solution.

Using the help system

Windows 98 has a complete and well-organized help system. If you have problems with Windows, use the help system. Click the Start button and select Help.

Depending on the problem, Windows may have help available that could solve your problem.

Applying the registry

It's as important to save the registry on disk as it is to create a startup disk. It contains all the important information concerning the system's hardware and software configurations. The registry consists of the files SYSTEM.DAT and USER.DAT. You will find both of these in the Window's directory.

Thanks to the utility ERU, Windows 98 offers the possibility to save the registry and some configuration and system data.

Copy the ERU.EXE (Emergency Recovery Utility) to the hard drive when you are installing Windows 98. Find the ERU.EXE file on the CD-ROM and copy all files in its directory into the Windows directory. When you start the ERU program, you're prompted for a destination directory. Drive A: is the default.

The following illustration shows which files you can save.

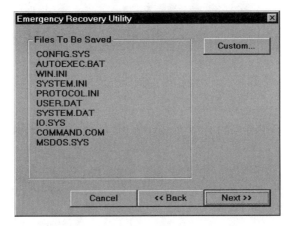

Select the files that you want to save.

Notice the [Custom...] button. Click this button if you want to remove or add files. We do not recommend using this option.

In the case of a registry error, restart Windows in the MS-DOS mode. Press [F8] when the "Starting Windows 98..." screen appears. In the following menu that appears, select "Safe mode." If you have saved on a server, choose "Safe mode, with network support."

Switch to the directory where the backup files exist. Start the program ERU.EXE. The saved files will be copied from there to the hard drive. Then your PC will work without the error messages.

The registry can also be saved by using Windows Explorer. Some data may be marked with the "Hidden" attribute. Click on **View | Option... | View**. You may select which data you would like to see in the file window. Click on **Show all Data**. Next insert a formatted blank disk. Copy the files to this disk.

If the files were damaged (or even erased) during the working process, an error message will soon appear.

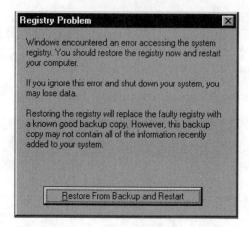

You'll see this window when the registry no longer exists.

Confirm the restoration process. In the Windows directory, you will normally find back up copies of the SYSTEM.DA0 and USER.DA0 files. This is the case if you haven't already erased it. These copies use Windows to restore the registry. The computer must be restarted to finish the process.

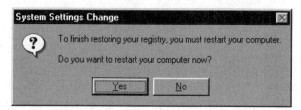

Click Yes *to restart Windows and put the changes into effect.*

Once you are certain that you have canceled the data, click No. Then open the Recycle Bin. Search for the USER.DAT and SYSTEM.DAT files. Once you have found them, select them. Click **File | Restore** to restore your files. If you do not find the corresponding items, go back to the registry. You can now start Windows Explorer and copy these files back to your Windows directory.

Be certain the SYSTEM.DAT and the USER.DAT have the "Hidden" and "System" attributes set. Otherwise Windows will display the same error.

If the registry fails during the initialization of the computer, the Microsoft Windows 98 Startup Menu will appear after the "Starting Windows 98..." message. In this case, start Windows 98 in Safe mode. Insert the backup disk and call up the program ERU.EXE.

You can also use the DOS copy command to restore the files. Use the ATTRIB command to remove the "hidden" attribute so you can copy the files. Enter the following lines at the DOS prompt:

```
ATTRIB -HA C:/*.DAT
```

Copy the registry files to the WINDOWS directory. Enter the following commands:

```
ATTRIB+H  C:\WINDOWS\USER.DAT
```

```
ATTRIB+H  C:\WINDOWS\SYSTEM.DAT
```

Windows 98 will run without problems after a new start.

Typical problems with DOS programs

Windows 98 normally runs DOS applications without problems. A problem can develop, however, when a DOS program demands too much of the system resources. This occurs most frequently with games.

The timelapse during the running of a program, such as those with graphic animation, could be noticeably effected. This is corrected by the DOS-mode that is to be installed into the program properties.

Click the right mouse button on a program's icon on the Windows 98 desktop. Select **Properties** from the menu and click Program. Then click the (Advanced...) button.

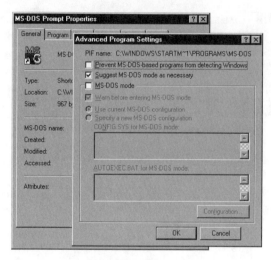

The DOS mode helps DOS programs run better.

Select the "MS-DOS mode" check box. Selecting this check box almost completely removes Windows from memory, giving the DOS program almost complete control over the system resources. The program runs problem-free again.

Also, you can apply individual CONFIG.SYS and AUTOEXEC.BAT files. This is very useful if the DOS program in question needs specific drivers to operate properly that the other programs might not need. This is a great alternative to earlier boot disk problems.

There is another problem that can occur with DOS applications that work in graphic mode and start in the full screen mode. If you don't disable the screen saver in the program properties, some unsightly distortions could appear in the graphics when the screen saver enables. Select the "Misc." tab. Then disable the "Allow screen saver" check box.

Disable the screen saver in the MS-DOS Prompt Properties.

Now, even graphic DOS applications should no longer pose a problem.

Driver problems

The Device Manager has primary control over driver problems. To get to the Device Manager, first open the Control Panel. Double-click the System icon. Select the "Device Manager" tab. Then you're set to install a new driver for the hardware in question. See Chapter 5 for more information on the Device Manager and the Add New Hardware Wizard.

Should you detect a DOS-driver that has been installed in CONFIG.SYS or AUTOEXEC.BAT, use the Microsoft Windows 98 Startup Menu to localize the driver. Restart the computer and press F8 when the "Starting Windows 98..." screen appears. Choose the command "Step-by-step confirmation." You'll be prompted to execute each line of the CONFIG.SYS and AUTOEXEC.BAT files. This lets you test the various drivers and determine which is causing problems.

When you've found the offending device driver, install an updated driver. It's also possible the driver file on the hard drive was defective. If you cannot remove the error, select a current driver for the concerned hardware. You can obtain this from your dealer or the hardware manufacturer. Also, check on-line services, the company's website or a local BBS for the file(s).

Problems with long filenames

Problems with long filenames have been discussed quite a bit in various books and magazine articles.

Longer filenames are not for everyone. Many Windows 3.11 applications can work with Windows 98, except for the long filenames. You also must be careful when using DOS applications.

If you're concerned, Windows lets you disable the long filenames option. First, click the [Start] button in the Taskbar. Click **Settings | Control Panel**. Double-click the System icon. This will open System Properties dialog box. Select the "Performance" tab. Click the [File System...] button. Then select the "Troubleshooting" tab. Check the "Disable long name preservation for old programs" box.

You should know that selecting this box can degrade the performance of Windows 98. Check these boxes only if you're troubleshooting.

Long filenames under DOS

DOS 7.0, included with Windows 98, abbreviates or truncates long filenames. You will see this when you use the DIR command in a DOS session. A file with the name:

```
LONGDATANAME.TXT
```

would be shortened to:

```
LONGDA~1.TXT
```

This doesn't seem to be much of a problem at first. However, another filename such as

```
LONGDAYFILE.TXT
```

would appear as

```
LONGDA~2.TXT
```

Adding several similar filenames in a directory could lead to confusion. This will become a real problem once you want to copy such files into another directory. For example, you find the above mentioned files in the directory C:\EXAMPLE. The DIR command would show:

```
LONGDA~1.TXT
LONGDA~2.TXT
```

Let's go one step further and say that a file exists in another directory with the name:

```
LONGDAYLIST.TXT
```

It would display in DOS with the name

```
LONGDA~1.TXT
```

Copy this file to C:\EXAMPLE list and type DIR command with

```
LONGDA~1.TXT
LONGDA~2.TXT
LONGDA~3.TXT
```

Now you don't know which file belongs to which long name. Fortunately, the longer name appears to the right of the shorter name. In DOS you can orient yourself with this.

Long filenames with old programs

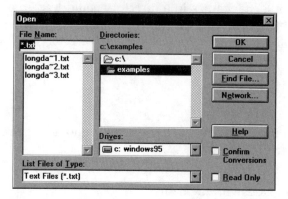

Trying to load a file with a long filename can be confusing.

The file requester in an older program will not display long filenames and it can be very confusing. This is especially true if you copied several files from one directory to another.

Consider whether you really want to use longer filenames if you are working with older programs.

Utilities and long filenames

Difficulties can arise when older utility programs encounter long file names. Using the latest version of software will avoid this problem.

If you cannot avoid installing an older utility, first use LFNBK.EXE to save, remove and later reinstall the longer filenames. LFNBK is an abbreviation for Long File Name BacKup. LFNBK.EXE is on the companion CD-ROM in the ADMIN\APPTOOLS\LFNBACK directory.

LFNBK.EXE is not, however, installed automatically. After you have closed all running Windows applications, run LFNBK.EXE from DOS.

```
LFNBK /V C:
```

Naturally you can also use other drives than C:. LFNBK transforms the long filenames in the old data name format and saves the long names in the LFNBK.DAT file. Now you can start your old utility program. It should run normally. After the application is finished you can again install the long filenames.

```
LFNBK /R C:
```

This command restores the original long filenames.

A warning concerning hard drive compression. Older disk compression programs that are not written for Windows 98 cannot handle longer filenames. Our recommendation is: If you want to use the compression program, then don't use the longer filenames. Deactivate the long filenames for older programs as we discussed before.

Limited data count in the root directory

If you have problems adding new directories or copying files into the root directory, your problem may lie in the limited number of entries in the root directory. The file count in the root directory is limited to 512 files. If you use long filenames, the count is even lower, because a long filename uses the space of more than one entry in the FAT.

Move all files that don't need to be in the root directory to another directory. Delete any files with .BAK or .TMP extensions in the root directory. Consider setting up a separate directory for your data files. See Chapter 1 for information on organizing a hard drive.

Trouble accessing the hard drive

If you have trouble accessing the hard drive, the new Windows 98 file system might be the source of the problem. This system allows complete 32-bit access, long filenames and new options for file sharing and file locking. Old 16-bit programs can be destroyed by this new file system. Try to determine which program is the source of the problem.

Disable some functions to determine which function of the new file system is responsible for the problems. If the program runs smoothly after you have disabled a function, you've found the error. Then you can decide whether to disable the file system function, remove the program or replace it with an updated version. Keep in mind, however, that disabling file system functions can degrade the performance of Windows 98.

To get to the properties of the file system, open the My Computer folder. Then open the Control Panel. Now click on the System icon, and then click the Performance tab. Click the File System button under Advanced settings to open the File System Properties dialog box. Then click the Troubleshooting tab to change the properties.

The Recycle Bin is a holding area for deleted files and directories that you want to remove from the hard drive. Deleted files and directories first go to the Recycle Bin. This means that the system will first file them in the directory named RECYCLED.

To empty the Recycle Bin, the files and directories must be deleted from the RECYCLED directory. Space is therefore reserved on the hard drive for the Recycle Bin. You can determine the size of this space. Click the right mouse button on the Recycle Bin Icon. Choose **Properties** to open the Recycle Bin Properties.

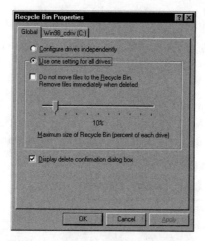

Change how the Recycle Bin is installed in the Recycle Bin Properties dialog box.

If you don't choose the Global tab, the hard drive space reserved for the Recycle Bin will be set automatically in proportion to the size of the hard drive. 10% of the drive's entire size is entirely adequate.

The Recycle Bin's reserved space can become full. If so, the oldest data is deleted automatically. If your hard drive has insufficient room to install a program, reduce the reserved space of the Recycle Bin.

Removing Windows 98

A re you unable to install or use Windows 98 for one of the following reasons?

* Insufficient workspace

* Processor is too slow

* Insufficient RAM

Unfortunately, in these extreme cases, you're likely to have only one alternative: uninstallation. How you uninstall Windows 98 depends on how you first installed it.

Uninstalling but choosing to keep old system files

The easiest method of uninstalling Windows 98 is if you installed it on a new hard drive. If you installed Windows 98 over an existing Windows and MS-DOS version, the method of uninstalling depends upon whether you saved the existing operating systems files. If so, a file called W98UNDO.DAT will be created.

It's no problem to uninstall Windows 98 using the UNINSTAL program. Restart your system with the Startup diskette in the drive and run UNINSTAL.EXE. Answer the prompts that appear on the screen. After 15-30 minutes your computer will return to its pre-Windows 98 condition.

Uninstalling Windows 98 if you've installed parallel with Win 3.x

If you have installed Windows 98 parallel to an existing Windows 3.x version, there is also no problem with the uninstallation.

Use a boot disk that has the SYS command from the Windows 3.x version. Transfer the system files by typing the following:

```
SYS C: Enter
```

This command transfers the system files to the hard drive. Make certain to rename the configuration files CONFIG.DOS and AUTOEXEC.DOS to CONFIG.SYS and AUTOEXEC.BAT. The next step is to restart your computer. It should boot with the Windows 3.x operating system.

Use a utility program such as PC Tools or Norton Commander to delete old directories or hidden files that may still exist in the root directory or Windows 98 directory. You can also use the Windows 3.x File Manager. Select **View | By File Type.** Make certain to select **Show Hidden / System files.**

The following files appear in the root directory. These files are part of Windows 98 and can be deleted:

✳ MSDDOS.—	✳ SYSTEM.1ST	✳ IO.DOS
✳ COMMAND.DOS	✳ SUHDLOG.DAT	✳ MSDOS.DOS
✳ BOOTLOG.DRV	✳ BOOTLOG.TXT	✳ DETLOG.TXT
✳ NETLOG.TXT	✳ SETUPLOG.TXT	✳ CONFIG.WIN

Verify filenames in case you used long filenames in Windows 98. Notice that these are in 8 - 3 format.

Using the DOS 6.0 Help System

MS-DOS 7.00 does not offer a Help system similar to DOS 6.x. However, if you're familiar with DOS 6.x, you don't have to abandon it. If you have not yet removed your old DOS, copy the following files to the \WINDOWS\COMMAND directory

HELP.COM   HELP.HLP   QBASIC.EXE

Moving the files to this directory makes sense because you'll probably delete the old DOS directory eventually. Then the DOS HELP would, of course, no longer be available.

You don't have to forget about the DOS-HELP in MS-DOS 7.00.

Don't become frustrated if you deleted the DOS 6 directory from your hard drive. Simply use the old DOS disk and copy the necessary files. The files QBASIC.EXE and HELP.COM are uncompressed on the MS-DOS 6.x disk. The data HELP.HLP is compressed, however. Use the command EXPAND.EXE, which is on the DOS disks. Next, copy this data into the hard drive.

Insert the disk with the HELP.HL_ file. Enter the following line at the DOS prompt:

```
EXPAND A:\HELP.HL_ C:\WINDOWS\COMMAND\HELP.HLP
```

This command expands, loads and stores the data in the command list. DOS help is available to you again. You can now delete the EXPAND.EXE data.

These files are also available on the companion CD-ROM in the \OTHER\OLDMSDOS directory.

The Windows 3.x File Manager

The Windows 3.x File Manager has a few advantages over Windows Explorer. Since you're probably more familiar with File Manager, it's faster for you than Windows Explorer. Plus, you can work with multiple windows in File Manager. This is not possible in Windows Explorer.

2 *Solving Frequent Windows Problems*

The following shows how you can install the Windows 3.x File Manager in Windows 98. The 3.11 File Manager is already part of Windows 98. Start Windows Explorer and search the Windows folder for the WINFILE.EXE file. Use the mouse to drag the file to the desktop. You then have an icon named WINFILE.EXE. Now simply double-click the icon to start the File Manager.

You can also continue using File Manager in Windows 98.

Using File Manager to delete files or directories

File Manager has one problem running in Windows 98, however. It doesn't recognize the Recycle Bin. In other words, any data you delete through File Manager won't be copied to the Recycle Bin. Therefore, the data can't be restored if you accidentally deleted important files.

The only way to avoid this problem is using a command like UNDELETE. UNDELETE is to the old DOS versions what the Recycle Bin is to Windows 98. The Recycle Bin, however, has replaced the UNDELETE command in both Windows 98 and MS-DOS 7.00.

Windows 98 3.x Write program

Windows 98 replaced the Write program with a new and improved version called "WordPad." Write was incapable of reading all data formats, but WordPad has this ability. You'll appreciate this ability when you're creating a text file. The program should be ready to read any text data, for example, files with .DOC, .RTF, .INI, .TXT and .WPS extensions.

If you have installed Windows 98 parallel to a Windows 3.x version, you can still use Write. Start Windows Explorer, locate WRITE.EXE and drag the file to the desktop. Now you have an icon for the WRITE.EXE program.

If you deleted the Windows 3.x version, insert the Windows 3.x disks in the disk drive. The Write program is compressed on the installation disk. This makes the installation a bit more detailed. You'll need the EXPAND command. You will find this either in the old DOS directory or on one of the Windows disks. Copy EXPAND.EXE onto the hard drive. To expand the program enter the following lines at the DOS prompt:

```
EXPAND A:\WRITE.EX_ C:\WINDOWS\WRITE.EXE
```

You may now drag the file over to the desktop. Now double-click the Write icon to start Write, and you may delete EXPAND.EXE from your hard drive.

Chapter 3:
Simple Tools And
Helpful Software

Chapter 3
Simple Tools And Helpful Software

The only "good" time for your computer to develop a problem is probably during the warranty period. A typical warranty period is from 90 days to one year, depending on the manufacturer.

Most manufacturers require that you return a defective computer to the dealer for repair during a warranty period. Besides the normal warranty period, many dealers also offer an extended warranty. For an additional charge, you can extend the manufacturer's warranty for another year or some other specified time.

The best type of manufacturer's warranty is an on-the-spot guarantee. If your computer is defective, simply call the service hotline number. Then schedule a time for a technician to come to your home and repair your computer. You can usually rely on fast, competent service from the manufacturer if there is a problem. It normally doesn't pay to make the repairs yourself.

It's another story if you need to return a defective computer to the dealer. However, if you need to return a defective computer, it's best if the dealer has a service center. Although you'll still be without the computer for a few days (or longer with serious repairs), at least you'll know the service is done "on site."

The time required for a repair can become longer if the dealer doesn't perform service work on site. In this case, the dealer must send repair work back to the manufacturer. It can then easily take several weeks before your computer is returned to you.

If you can isolate the defective component based on the error readouts, you won't necessarily have to return the entire computer to the dealer. Simply remove the defective component and exchange it with a new component. Make certain you have permission to remove the defective components yourself (ask your dealer or manufacturer); otherwise, you may be voiding the warranty. This shouldn't be a problem in most cases.

If you can simply exchange the defective component, this may save you from being without your computer for a long time. This could occur if the computer needs to be returned to the dealer or manufacturer for repair.

What you can repair yourself during the warranty period

It's usually safe to assume that you cannot do any repairs during the warranty period. Before opening the computer case, read the warranty information in the user's manual carefully. Repairs usually require exchanging hardware components, some of which you can do yourself. Your computer is composed of many individual elements. These include the different hardware components, such as the network cards, motherboard, memory, the drives and expansion cards. You can also include the external peripherals, such as keyboard, mouse, monitor and other devices.

With a few exceptions, you can conceivably do everything yourself during the warranty period, if you treat the various components as one unit. Simply speaking, you can, for example, exchange your defective graphic card for a new one yourself. Normally, you can even install a new motherboard or a new network adapter into the computer yourself.

Most manufacturers limit what you can repair during the warranty period. These limitations usually include only what can be plugged in or are otherwise easily exchangeable. These areas include, for example, the video memory, the CPU, the coprocessor, or other controller chips on the motherboard or on the expansion cards.

If you repair or exchange these areas, you must strictly follow the manufacturer's instructions. These instructions include using regulation tools and inserting original parts or alternative parts supplied by the manufacturer.

One example of what you cannot do is to exchange a quartz piece that controls the computer's time frequency for a quartz unit having a higher frequency. This is located (usually soldered) on the motherboard. Even if the computer operates perfectly and the time frequency is within toleration ranges specified in the CPU data sheet, the motherboard manufacturer can refuse the warranty claim if a controller chip failed due to the higher frequency (under the circumstances, this can be proven).

It's questionable whether the CPU manufacturer will replace the CPU without question if it failed as a result of such an action (despite maintaining the tolerances as stated on the data sheet).

3 Simple Tools And Helpful Software

Don't void the warranty

Unfortunately, the warranty agreement is sometimes very complicated and the accompanying documents are not always clear. Sometimes the warranty is so limited that you are not allowed to insert the memory yourself. If so, do not exchange the CPU yourself. If you're accused of handling a repair improperly, it can be very difficult to have the damaged part replaced. This is true even if you did not cause the damage.

> **TIP** Consult the dealer or the manufacturer if you're in doubt about performing warranty work yourself.

When repairing any part of your computer, use an antistatic wrist band and an antistatic mat. This will prevent static electricity from ruining the component on which you're working. Manufacturers can easily detect problems resulting from static electricity and will void your warranty.

Some manufacturers will seal or apply a warranty sticker to the computer case. The only way to open the computer is to break the seal. If the seal is broken during the warranty period, the manufacturer has the right to void the warranty. If you still, for example, want to add another expansion card yourself, first consult your dealer. Get any approval to continue in writing. This will prevent any future warranty problems if the computer has a defect.

What you should avoid doing

Avoid any soldering work on the motherboard or on other computer components (at least during the warranty period). Leave this work to an expert. For example, you may need to replace the CMOS-RAM battery. However, this part is soldered to the motherboard. Most, but not all, motherboards include a connector where an external battery can be connected. This lets you loosen the solder connection on the old battery and solder in a new one.

However, you can ruin the entire motherboard by using incorrect methods or the wrong soldering iron. Keep in mind that not every soldering iron is suitable for this work. The same is true for the solder connections that are located in the network card or in the keyboard port's entry circuit.

The basic rule: Don't do any soldering if you are inexperienced using a soldering iron. It's better to bring your computer or component to a repair shop. Then the repair shop is responsible if anything breaks.

Everything else is your call. Depending on how comfortable and capable you feel, you can try everything (within the limitations mentioned above). There is little (other than the soldering work) that you must hand over to a professional. You don't need to be afraid of the computer or of its inner workings.

If you're afraid to disturb or repair your computer, or if something seems too tricky, save the work for an expert.

Functional Tools

Some repairs require specialized tools. Fortunately, most computer jobs do not require specialized tools. You probably already own the most important tools. Most electronic stores sell these tools. You don't need to make a big investment to have the tools required for computer repairs.

The following tools can solve ninety percent of the problems:

* Small Phillips screwdriver

* Medium Phillips screwdriver

* Small slotted screwdriver

* Medium slotted screwdriver

* A set of torque screwdrivers

   Torque screwdrivers resemble Phillips screwdrivers, except their heads have a star-shaped indentation for the screwdriver instead of a cross shape. Unfortunately, most manufacturers (e.g., Hewlett Packard) use these screwdrivers to build their computers. Do not use a slotted screwdriver instead of a torque screwdriver. This screwdriver will easily wreck the star shaped indentation. This makes it difficult to loosen that particular screw. It is better to spend the money and buy the correct tool instead.

* Tweezers or small pliers

* Bootable emergency backup disk

3 Simple Tools And Helpful Software

We cannot describe in detail which tools you should use for a specific job. You'll learn more about that in the repairs section of this book.

The following tools are helpful:

* Small labels for labeling plugs and wires (and a pen)

* Small container for screws and other small parts

* Several jumpers in different sizes

* At least one preformatted blank diskette

* Multimeter (which measures voltage)

Refer to the repairs chapter to determine if you need these items. On certain jobs, for example, when working on the motherboard, we recommend the following tools:

* Antistatic mat (at least as large as the motherboard)

* Antistatic wristband

Most mats have a connection point for the armband.

An antistatic mat (at least as large as the motherboard)
and antistatic wristband prevent static charges.

The chances of static electricity damaging a component is very low (in five years, only one motherboard died on me as a result of static electricity). Nevertheless, the danger exists, so why take the chance. Electronic components are becoming more resistant to static charges, but you are responsible for assessing that risk.

The Best Software For Emergencies

Versions of DOS before 6.0 offered little or no support in case of an emergency. For this reason, you needed to use a utility program such as Norton Utilities, PC-Tools or CheckIt to diagnose errors. These programs have features that are missing in the operating system.

Norton Utilities, PC-Tools & Co.

MS-DOS version 6.20 included some good utility programs. Unfortunately, Windows 98 users have DOS version 7. Since you may not need to use Norton Utilities or PC-Tools, try the DOS utilities instead. You may need Norton DiskDoctor or DiskFix only in a few cases — for example, if you can't access a defective hard drive. Fortunately, these cases rarely occur. Therefore, carefully consider whether to buy a utility program if you already have MS-DOS version 6.20 installed.

It's different if you use Windows 3.1 or Windows for Workgroups 3.11. In this case, you only use DOS to boot up the system; DOS is not used again. The only utility offered by Microsoft is Undelete for Windows. As a result, third-party utility manufacturers released Windows versions of their programs (specifically Norton Utilities and PC-Tools).

Both programs are well suited for the standard functions. However, keep in mind that the Windows utilities are completely useless when there's a serious error. If the hard drive can't be booted, for example, you won't have a Window to use. DOS utility versions are available to solve the problem if a few functions cannot or may not be called up in Windows.

Windows 98 includes several utilities such as DEFRAG and ScanDisk in a Windows version. Most third-party utilities from Windows 3.1 and Windows for Workgroups 3.11 cannot be used in Windows 98. These utilities cannot master the new file system.

3 *Simple Tools And Helpful Software*

The diagnosis routines of the utilities included in Windows 98 are competitive with the well-known CheckIt program. These diagnosis routines let you test specific individual hardware components. You can test the mouse, keyboard, interfaces or the motherboard. The routines then weed out the defective parts. System information programs can determine the computer's configuration, which can also help you solve problems.

Finally, please note that we are specifically talking about emergency situations. We did not consider the other Norton Utilities and PC-Tools programs.

Utilities offered by Windows 98

The required utilities are included with MS-DOS version 6.20 and Windows 98. These utilities can "save your life" in an emergency. Many of these utilities have eliminated the need to buy third-party utilities. We'll only briefly mention the most important programs here. (For more information, refer to the chapter on preventive measures and error removal.) These programs are needed to care for data and to rescue data. Windows now offers the following utilities:

FDISK.EXE

FDISK creates a new partition sector, and boot viruses that infect the partition sector are eliminated.

SYS.COM

Creates a new boot sector and carries the system files to the indicated medium. An unbootable hard drive can often be put back into operation with this program.

SCANDISK.EXE

Checks and corrects the index and file structure on a disk and can also check for physical defects. You can easily use this program in the Windows 98 environment.

DEFRAG.EXE

Reassembles fragmented files. This prevents errors to the file system when used regularly. DEFRAG is only available in Windows 98 as a Windows version. Do not under any circumstances use an older DOS version of DEFRAG.

MEM.EXE

Checks the memory capacity.

DEBUG.EXE

DEBUG is a simple Assembler/Disassembler, with which, for example, port addresses for error diagnosis can be directly set out or read by interfaces. To this, DEBUG offers additional insertion areas which shouldn't be underestimated. Unfortunately, these advantages can only be used by users who have mastered Assembler language.

The most important programs have now been listed, and you are well prepared for an emergency.

Companion CD-ROM System Test Programs

The companion CD-ROM includes utilities for both DOS and Windows. We'll only summarize some of these utilities in this section so make certain to read the README file on the companion CD-ROM. This will help you avoid problems.

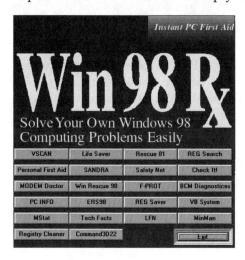

3 *Simple Tools And Helpful Software*

We have included the DOS applications (located in the DOSTOOLS directory on the CD-ROM) for you to use. There might be times or instances when you cannot use Windows. You may also find them very useful when troubleshooting and you have to use your trusty old DOS prompt.

Many of the programs featured on the CD-ROM are fully functioning *shareware evaluation versions* of the best programs available today. Shareware benefits both the user and the author. By avoiding distribution, packaging and advertising costs, prices of shareware remains low.

Keep in mind, however, that shareware programs are copyrighted programs. Usually the authors ask for payment if you use their program(s). You may try out the program for a limited time (typically 10 to 30 days). This should give you enough time to decide whether you want to keep the program. If you continue to use the program, you're requested to send the author a nominal fee.

Paying this fee makes you a licensed user of the program. Check the documentation or the program itself for the amount of the registration fee and the address where you send the registration form.

You'll find program instructions and notes on registering the shareware programs in text files. These text files are located in the program directory of each program. Refer to Chapter 8 for a complete description of the companion CD-ROM.

PC_INFO

The DOS utility program PC_INFO is basically a system information program. It has several service and test functions. The opening window in PC_INFO displays a general configuration summary. Use the icons to display detailed information on the listed components.

PC_INFO's overview displays general information on the computer's configuration.

PC_INFO can also assist you when you're buying a new computer or peripheral. PC_INFO can test whether the hardware that was installed is the same as the catalog or the retailer describes.

Besides the system information, such as computer type, bus system or BIOS, PC_INFO also provides detailed information about the processor's characteristics (if it's supporting the CPUID command).

If you have a question or need help using PC_INFO, press [F1]. Every information window displays a clearly written help text.

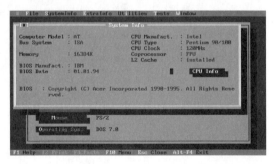

PC_INFO displays a explanatory text for the CPU information.

Additionally, PC_INFO provides information on the installed drives, available expansion cards and input devices. Furthermore, PC_INFO provides information on the different software interfaces, such as DPMI, MRCI or SCSI, that have been installed. The important thing here is the version number for the specification that is being supported. You determine which standard corresponds to the programming interface. This can be a deciding factor when buying new software or hardware.

3 Simple Tools And Helpful Software

Saving MBR area to a file.

PC_INFO also features service functions. In this menu you can save the boot hard drive's MBR area to a file and call it up again when needed. In doing so, the hard drive's partition section and first boot sector are saved. This is a valuable feature when fighting viruses. This is especially valuable if you have installed a boot manager or a disk driver such as the Ontrack-DiskManager so you can use a nonstop (universal) partition on hard drives larger than 504 Meg.

Furthermore, print functions are available through the service menu. Print the information through a printer or to a text file. You can select which information to print.

You don't always have to print everything.

Finally, use PC_INFO to test peripherals and components. It can test the mouse, joystick or an installed sound card.

Enter any hardware components that PC_INFO doesn't automatically recognize into an installation file (PC_INFO.INI). The hardware's resources are also registered in this file. These parameters are considered within the program.

The PC_INFO.INI file

PC_INFO attempts to automatically recognize your computer's hardware and your resources. Unfortunately, since not all hardware components have a defined programming interface or standard, not all hardware components can be identified by the program. This may result in the data on the engaged resources, such as the I/O ports, interrupts and DMA channels, being incomplete. Therefore, the PC_INFO initialization file can create its own data. PC_INFO reads the file at the start and evaluates the data found there.

The PC_INFO.INI file can be loaded using the file menu to an editor window. You need to be in the current index or in a PATH variable index.

The initialization file is divided into four sections (listed here in comment lines). Make certain the first character is a semicolon if you insert your own comment lines.

The OPTIONS section

Disable the automatic recognition of sound and graphics cards by entering the following (both lines may be necessary if PC_INFO crashes in the middle of checking the hardware):

```
SOUNDCARD=NO
```

or

```
GRAFICCARD=NO
```

 TIP When disabling graphics card recognition, data is still sent to the graphics card, but PC_INFO avoids directly programming the graphics card. Only a few graphics cards are no longer recognized. Alternatively, you can also disable automatic recognition when calling up PC_INFO with the parameters /S- (disables sound card recognition) or /G- (to overlook the graphics card).

The DOS section

The start files may have different names (for example, PTS-DOS) if you've installed an operating system other than MS-DOS. To load the start files using the file menu, enter these file names:

```
CFGFILE=CONFIG.PTS
```

```
AUTOFILE=AUTOEXEC.PTS
```

The WINDOWS section

You need to enter the Windows path here if it reads something other than
C:\WINDOWS. Your entry may look as follows:

```
PATH=C:\WIN31
```

This way, the Windows initialization files are accessible using the file menu.

The EXPANSIONS section

This is the most important section of PC_INFO. Insert the expansion cards that aren't
recognized by PC_INFO but which occupy the system's resources. The following is
the entry syntax:

```
name of device,I/O-Port,IRQ,DMA
```

The device name can be a maximum of ten characters. The port address is entered as
a hex number. PC_INFO requires that one of these lines must always have three
commas. Errors are not checked. If an expansion does not occupy a resource type, the
space in the line is ignored.

Let's assume that you have a network card installed in your computer. Network cards
are not recognized by the program. Therefore, the occupied port address and the
interrupt being used by the card are not displayed. The network card should use port
310h and interrupt 2, but not the DMA channel. Enter the following for the program
to recognize the card:

```
network,310,2,
```

Save the file. Then select **User entries read** from the **System Info** menu. PC_INFO
reads the data and enters it into its information. From this point, the network card will
be listed in the resource data.

If the network card occupies a 16-bit port, specifically 310h-31Fh, make an additional
entry so PC_INFO can recognize that I/O port 318h is also being used. (Refer to
documentation included with the network card for this information.)

```
network,318,,
```

You no longer need to indicate the interrupt. Different expansion cards use even more port addresses. Check the enclosed documentation. Enter the contacts according to the charts located in PC_INFO into PC_INFO.INI.

In this manner, PC_INFO can identify the occupied resources and you don't run the risk of doubly allocating resources when installing a new expansion card.

Modem Doctor

Use Modem Doctor when you have a problem using your modem. This program thoroughly tests your modem. After starting the program, you can immediately test the modem's equipment and the serial interface.

Interface and modem are checked.

You can also perform more specific tests besides the general tests. The serial interface is always an important factor in troubleshooting modem problems. Therefore, Modem Doctor features extensive tests for serial interfaces. A loopback connector is needed to connect different interface pins to one another. You'll find the corresponding technical manual in the program's loopback menu.

3 *Simple Tools And Helpful Software*

The serial interface is tested here.

Of course, even the modem can be tested in great detail. Modem Doctor features several testing options. Besides checking the modem's S register, you can also test the usual modem signals. Modem Doctor will immediately uncover any errors.

Modem Doctor is also useful for establishing modem paths. For this purpose, it maintains a simple terminal function. The test course is initiated at the modem on the other end and the pathway can be tested with the terminal.

InfoSpy

InfoSpy is an uncommon system information program. Hardware data isn't included in this program. Instead, InfoSpy is geared more toward the DOS/Windows operating system. The "tons" of information it uncovers is displayed in a window. Notice how deep InfoSpy digs into your computer system.

Simple Tools And Helpful Software 3

InfoSpy displays important information about the Windows system.

Besides the enormous quantity of information made available, InfoSpy has several monitors to guard the system resources. In addition, the program includes useful integrated tools and functions. This includes, for example, a File Manager and a Scheduler.

VBSys

This system monitor program displays the actual system load in a small information window. By using the integrated mini icon, you gain access to detailed information about the Windows system.

Information about how Windows works is displayed in the DOS and Windows Information dialog box. To view this, you need to click on the counter with red writing. It opens additional information windows.

85

3 *Simple Tools And Helpful Software*

VScan

McAfee's VScan is the first virus scanner for Windows 98. It distinguishes itself by its easily maneuverable menu system. After starting the program, the important options "Include subfolders" (also scans the submenu) and "Compressed files" (also scans compressed files) are activated.

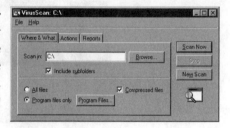

VScan normally scans files with the following file extensions:

* ✳ .386 ✳ .BIN ✳ .COM ✳ .VXD ✳ .EXE

* ✳ .DLL ✳ .DRV ✳ .FON ✳ .SYS ✳ .OVL

Click the [Program Files...] button to display the list and even enter additional file types. You cannot use wildcard characters in VScan.

Determine how the scanner should react to a virus by clicking the Actions tab.

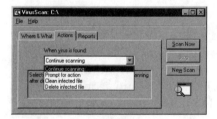

You select the scanner's actions here.

We recommend leaving "Continue scanning" enabled. A report file of the scan procedure is created in the Report tab.

Click the [Scan Now] button to start the actual scan procedure. Infected files are then arranged on a file list. It also lists which virus has affected the file.

Infected files are saved on a list.

From this point, fix the files either individually or at the same time. Double-click on an infected file to move to an information window where you can perform other functions. Clean the file ([Clean File]), delete the file ([Delete File]) or move it to another index ([Move File to]).

What will happen to the file?

If the file has been deleted, VScan examines it closely. A deleted infected file can't be restored from the Windows trash can.

Unfortunately, VScan doesn't have a virus data bank containing detailed information about the individual viruses, like F_PROT does.

Chapter 4:
Windows 98
Emergency First Aid

Chapter 4
Windows 98 Emergency First Aid

his chapter is probably the most important chapter of this book. This chapter deals with errors that occur frequently and provides you with solutions you can use. We organized the error symptoms by subject and divided them into sections.

Quick and Easy Fixes

his section talks about problems you may have booting your PC and starting programs.

Exiting and restarting a program

Be careful when programmers guarantee their software as "100% bug-free." No legitimate programmer should make this claim. The larger a software project is, the more errors can creep into the source code. Since some errors often are not noticed at first, they go undetected during the beta testing phase. When you purchase the software, you also get the errors.

Whether the error will show up on your system ultimately depends on your computer's hardware or software configuration. You don't have to be cynical to realize that eventually either your computer will crash without warning or the program won't do what you tell it to.

To exit a program when this happens (if the computer hasn't crashed yet), press Ctrl+Alt+Del. This calls the Windows 98 Task List.

You can exit crashed applications from the Task List.

Select the program and click [End Task] to exit the crashed program. Then restart it.

If you cannot start the Task List, simply press the Reset button or switch the computer off and back on. It's possible the error won't reoccur. Otherwise, call the manufacturer and ask for tech support. They may already have solutions to your problem.

Rebooting the computer

If the computer has completely crashed, perhaps the error will disappear after you reboot the computer. No one can say exactly which conditions cause such disturbances. There are too many variables. A bug (programmer error) is only one possibility. Another possibility is hardware incompatibilities.

While many programming interfaces for hardware have been standardized, there's always one maverick that interprets the definition of a standard differently. Also, many areas in hardware and software programming still lack a uniform standard. In such cases, problems and computer crashes are "part of the program."

Fortunately, disturbances that provoke computer crashes occur only seldomly. Just restart the computer, and maybe you'll never notice that error again. Otherwise, you'll have to read one of the sections of this chapter.

Windows 98 Emergency First Aid

README files

You'll repeatedly see one piece of advice in this chapter that urges you to read the README files. This advice also applies if you're upgrading or switching to Windows 98. Windows 98 also has problems with some hardware configurations. Known problems are recorded in text files so you can read them any time. Be sure to read these files before you purchase hardware. Windows 98 could have problems running with the particular hardware or peripheral that you're planning to buy.

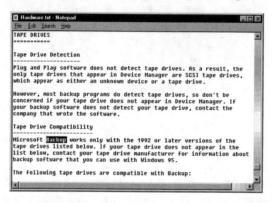

Don't ignore or overlook the information in README files.

If you're considering buying a new computer or system board, again, consult the README files. There are many situations where you could run into trouble.

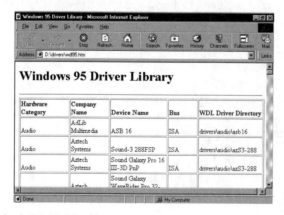

Always check README files..its information is too important to ignore.

You can avoid many problems by being well informed and prepared.

The Hardware Compatibility list

Windows also has other important information that you need to look at before adding hardware to your computer. Windows's Hardware Compatibility list contains many hardware components that have been tested and found to be compatible with Windows 98.

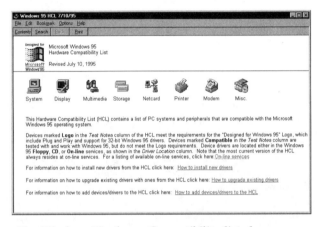

The Windows Hardware Compatibility list shows many hardware components compatible with Windows 98.

What that means for you, the user, is that when you install one of these components, you can expect the least amount of problems. You will find this list in the \DRIVERS folder of the Windows CD-ROM or, depending on the installation type, in the C:\WINDOWS\HELP directory. Double-click the HCL98 help file (HCL = Hardware Compatibility List).

For example, if you're considering buying a new video card, click the Display icon. Next, select Display Adapter from the list that follows. This list shows you all the video cards that are compatible with Windows 98.

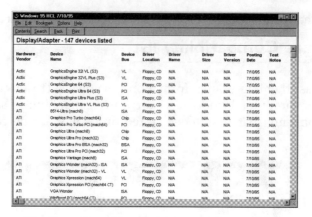

The lists of tested hardware components are huge.

If you find the hardware you selected in this list, look at the "Test Notes" column (the last column). If the column lists "Compatible", additional information is available. In our example, additional information is available about an Adaptec Controller.

You'll find more information available through the "Compatible" Test Note.

Double-click the word "Compatible". The Compatibility List displays additional information about hardware components that could be very important for use under Windows 98.

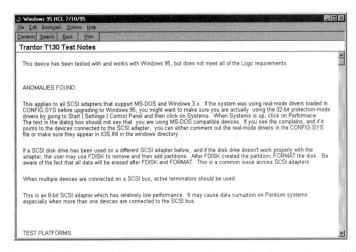

You'll also find help on installing components in the Hardware Compatibility list.

If the video card you're considering buying isn't in the list, it doesn't mean it won't run under Windows 98. It means instead the card hasn't been tested under Windows so there is no guarantee it will work. New hardware won't appear in this list because it didn't exist when the tests were run. Since Microsoft intends to continually update the compatibility lists, newer hardware components can also be quickly added to the list. Current lists will then be offered on the Microsoft network or other online services such as CompuServe. If possible, get a current Compatibility List before you buy expensive hardware.

Defective BIOS

A chip on the motherboard houses the program code of the BIOS (Basic Input/Output System). The BIOS program code is built-in and cannot be deleted. The BIOS is the first program code to be executed when you switch on the PC or after a reset. It is responsible for initializing the chips on the motherboard and the expansion boards and insures the various hardware will communicate.

Next, a system test called the "POST" (Power-On Self-Test) is run. The installed components of the computer are tested and counted. Among these components are drives, ports, the video card and the RAM. The configuration found in the test is then compared to the entries in CMOS Setup. If the POST routine detects discrepancies, it informs you by means of a beep code or an error message. On the other hand, if everything is found to be in order, the operating system is loaded. Usually, the computer searches the floppy drive first, then the hard drive. After that, BIOS acts as a programming interface between the hardware and software of other programs.

The CMOS RAM is usually located in a peripheral controller that is constantly supplied with power by a battery. Otherwise, there is a separate chip for this purpose. Some examples of this are the Dallas chip, and in older computers, the MC146818. The settings in the CMOS RAM would be lost when you turned off the computer if they weren't battery-backed. The CMOS RAM contains information on the configuration of the computer. Also, important settings for the chip set of the motherboard are stored in the CMOS RAM.

```
                    ROM ISA BIOS (204X2M11)
                    CHIPSET FEATURES SETUP
                    AWARD SOFTWARE, INC.

Auto Configuration      : Disabled    LOWA20# Emulation       : Disabled
Cache Read Burst        : 3-2-2-2     RC Reset Emulation      : Disabled
Cache Write Wait State  : 1 WS        System BIOS Cachable    : Disabled
DRAM Type               : Fast Page   Video BIOS Cacgable     : Disabled
DRAM Wait State         : 1 WS        Non-Cachable Block 1    : Disabled
Keyboard Clock          : 9.5 MHz       Block 1 Start Adress  :      0K
AT Clock                : CPUCLK/4      Block 1 Size          : 16KB
IO Recovery For ISA/PC8 : BCLK: 5/3
DMA/Master Cycle        : Hold 1-2T
Slow Refresh            : Disabled
Memory Remap            : Disabled


                                    ESC : Quit        ↑↓→← : Select Items
                                    F1  : Help        PU/PD/+/- : Modify
                                    F5  : Old Values   (Shift)F2 : Color
                                    F6  : Load BIOS Defaults
                                    F7  : Load Setup Defaults
```

The BIOS Setup contains data for the configuration of the chip set.

Check for incorrect Setup settings

Some BIOS types are designed so only the most necessary entries can be made. Others are built so you can adjust many varied settings. The AMI BIOS is one of these types. Incorrect settings in BIOS Setup can result in your computer no longer being able to boot. In the worst case, your computer hardware can even be damaged.

The setting for the bus clock in Advanced Chipset Setup is such a setting. It's only located on combination boards, which allow the computer to use different CPUs with variable clock frequencies. With the help of this menu item, you divide the clock frequency for the ISA bus. Usually, you can choose from CPUCLK/2 /3 /4 /5 and CPUCLK/6.

If you enter a divisor that is too low, the bus will work with a clock frequency that is too high, which not every expansion card can tolerate. On an ISA computer the bus clock is set at 8 MHz by default. However, there are also cards that work with 10 or 12 MHz.

There are advantages and disadvantages to this menu item. The disadvantage: Some older boards go along with tuning at a higher clock frequency at first. But after some time, the DMA controller can go out due to the high bus clock and the related increase in heat. This is the same as destroying the motherboard with today's SMD technology (Static Memory Devices).

The advantage to this menu item: If you have a board and cards that tolerate these high clock frequencies, the result is a considerable speed improvement. However, be very careful about increasing the bus clock.

System crashes are also frequently the result of a bus clock that is set too high. If you own a VLB or a PCI computer and have installed a corresponding video card and drive controller, then an increase of the bus clock won't improve the speed anymore. The VESA local bus already works with 33 or 40 MHz clock frequency in most computers. The PCI bus is specified with a clock frequency of 33 MHz.

If your CMOS RAM is so shot that nothing more runs, there are methods for restoring it. For more information, read the information "Activating BIOS default values" later in this section.

Restoring the backup CMOS RAM

If you don't know much about your BIOS Setup, then it will be easiest to restore your backup CMOS RAM with the PC_INFO program we've already described. Naturally, this is based on the assumption that you backed up your CMOS ROM.

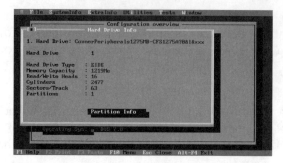

Use the Partition Info menu item to restore the backup CMOS RAM.

Then reboot the computer. Perhaps this will solve your problem.

Activating BIOS default values

There are BIOS types that automatically detect your hardware and, if necessary, enter it into the CMOS RAM during the autostart routine. This isn't possible with other BIOS types. In such cases, you can use either the **AUTO CONFIGURATION WITH BIOS DEFAULTS** or the **AUTO CONFIGURATION WITH POWER-ON DEFAULTS** command in the **Setup** menu to restore the default values.

The first program restores the default values for Setup. The second program is sometimes able to detect installed hardware and enter it in Setup. Both programs reconfigure Setup so the computer can boot up. Neither program enters any optimum settings. Nevertheless, you'll have to enter the majority of the values of standard CMOS Setup manually. Among others, this page has the settings for date, time and drives.

Looking for hard drive specifications for Setup

The values for BIOS setup is printed on many hard drives. What if your hard drive doesn't have them stamped on? The shareware market has several utilities that can read out the data from most hard drives. Naturally, you can also get the hard drive parameters from your dealer. However, that method is inconvenient and time-consuming. Your safest option is BIOS or the PC_INFO program from the companion CD-ROM. Read more about it in the next section.

Detecting hard drive specs with "Autodetect" or PC_INFO

Today, most BIOS manufacturers have implemented a tool that is able to read the hard drive parameters from the disk, and then enter them into CMOS RAM. If there is no hard drive registered in CMOS Setup, an error message similar to the following appears when you boot:

> No system or drive error
>
> Change and press any key

If the hard drive is configured with the correct parameters and has been set up and formatted with FDISK, then incorrect settings of the cylinders later won't result in an error of the booting procedure. Programs on the hard drive will be able to start up. No data would be lost during work on the hard drive with the wrong number of cylinders. You could run the programs. You couldn't determine whether errors or data loss would occur in long-term operation. Even so, to avoid errors you need to make sure the correct values are entered. If the data about the number of heads or sectors is incorrect, the computer will crash with one of the following error messages:

> C: drive error
>
> Press <F1> to Resume

> Operating system missing

> No system or drive error
> Change and press any key

If the wrong hard drive parameters are entered in the CMOS Setup, the hard drive would be formatted with the wrong parameters when you call the Format command. That means if you have a 340-Meg hard drive installed, but CMOS Setup only shows 100 Meg, your hard drive will be formatted as a 100-Meg drive.

To find the hard drive parameters of BIOS, boot the computer and go into CMOS Setup. Select the **Auto Detect Hard Disk** menu command. This menu item could have a different name with other versions of BIOS.

After selecting it, the program displays the parameters of the hard drive, which you must then confirm. If a second hard drive is installed, its data will also be displayed, and you will also have to confirm this information. After that, the hard drive parameters are entered into the CMOS Setup and you can reboot the computer.

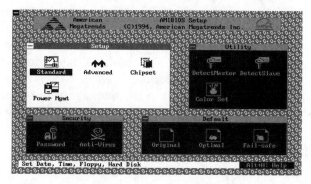

Determine the hard drive specs here through the Detect icon.

PC_INFO gives you another option. Start your computer with a bootable diskette that contains PC_INFO and call PC_INFO after booting up. PC_INFO can only read the hard drive specs from the controller if you start in DOS. Click the Drives button from the Drives menu item.

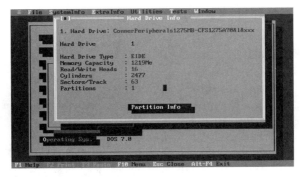

PC_INFO found the hard drive data for CMOS Setup.

Copy down these values and then enter them into CMOS Setup.

BIOS loses its settings

This suggests a weak battery. Batteries installed in PCs have different life expectancies. Depending on the type of battery, the life expectancy ranges from one to five years. Once a battery reaches its life expectancy, at first, the settings in Setup will disappear sometimes. Then the clock slows down, and sometimes the disk drive, or even all the drives, will disappear. Next, the intervals begin getting considerably shorter. Before anything worse happens and the setup data vanishes, change the battery.

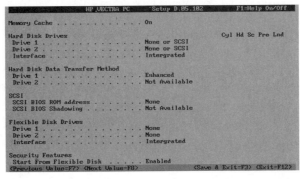

This computer appears not to have any drives installed.

Installing a new battery correctly

Some batteries are easy to replace because they plug into a socket. Others are soldered onto the motherboard. Don't remove the soldered batteries; they stay on the motherboard. Since they are long-life, later damage to the motherboard is impossible.

Plug the new battery into a slot provided for this purpose on the motherboard. Check the user's manual for your motherboard to see if you need to change a jumper. This depends on your type of motherboard.

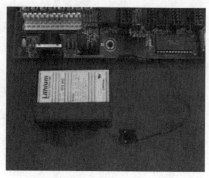

An example of a battery for the CMOS RAM.

To avoid losing all the settings in BIOS Setup when you change batteries, be sure the computer is switched on when you perform this task. Also, by having the computer on, you avoid the risk of destroying the motherboard through static charges.

If you would rather switch the computer off, remember that electrostatic charges can destroy the motherboard or the plug-in cards. Ground yourself beforehand. You can get the appropriate armbands with the right cable and clip at any computer store. Locate a good spot to attach the clip and properly ground yourself.

Back up the contents of the CMOS RAM to a file on a bootable diskette using the PC_INFO program from the companion CD. If you start the computer after changing batteries and the data from the CMOS RAM is gone, all you need to do is insert the system diskette. Boot from the system diskette. Ignore the other configuration errors in Setup. After booting, use PC_INFO to restore the CMOS RAM contents and your computer will boot perfectly from the hard drive again without giving you an error message.

Your computer doesn't work after you've experimented in Setup

Your computer will work at the maximum possible speed only if the right values are entered into CMOS Setup. Now and then you will find valuable tips for optimization in computer journals.

Let's suppose you change your settings and after rebooting, you notice that your computer comes to a standstill during the autostart routine. As long as you can still get into the Setup menu, this isn't so bad. Then you can undo the changes you just made. Seldom will you be unable to get back into Setup.

If your computer doesn't show any signs of booting up and you can't get into the Setup menu, there's no other choice but to delete/remove the CMOS RAM manually. Remove the computer case. Near the battery there is often a jumper that is used to set whether an internal or external battery is connected. If you disable this jumper, you've interrupted the power supply to the CMOS RAM (and the CMOS RAM data will be lost). The more modern boards even have a special jumper for this purpose. If you don't find a jumper or you're not certain whether it's the right one, consult the computer manual. In case of doubt, ask an expert.

Before you start experimenting in Setup, back up the contents of the CMOS RAM to a file on a diskette together with the PC_INFO program. This way you can easily restore the CMOS RAM in cases of emergency.

You forgot your password

This is more likely to be a user error rather than a BIOS error, but we'll give the solution to the problem. Besides other data, the BIOS password is stored in the CMOS RAM. If access to BIOS Setup is password-protected, forgetting the password can be very annoying. You won't be able to get into Setup any more the normal way.

Your only option is to delete Setup. Most motherboards have a jumper or a DIP switch for this purpose. Check the documentation for your motherboard. If you don't have this option, you'll have to disconnect the power supply from the CMOS RAM battery.

If your computer has an external battery plugged into an edge connector on the motherboard, all you have to do is unplug it and then plug it back in.

With a soldered battery, take a paper clip and short-circuit the battery for one second (naturally, you are shortening the life expectancy of the battery). Not only the password, but all the other data of the CMOS RAM, such as the hard drive information, will be lost. After rebooting, re-configure the CMOS and define your password again (and remember it this time!).

4 Windows 98 Emergency First Aid

The Computer Won't Boot Correctly

Now let's turn to problems with the computer itself. There are always situations in which the computer won't run at all. In this section we'll tell you the best methods for solving this problem. We'll also give you helpful information for those times when the computer crashes for no reason.

The computer shows no signs of life

If the computer shows no sign of life after you switch on the power, first make certain the power cord is plugged in properly. Check both ends of the plug. Sometimes the plugs can come loose but remain in the outlet.

If the power cord is plugged in properly and your computer still won't boot up, make certain the outlet is receiving power. We know an easy way to check this. Take an electrical appliance, such as a vacuum cleaner or radio, and plug it into the outlet. If the appliance doesn't run, check the fuse box to see whether all the circuit breakers are switched on.

A computer that still doesn't show any signs of life indicates a defective power supply or a defective switch. Some computers use a small lever as the switch to operate the power supply. Sometimes this lever becomes bent or broken; although you can press the button, the switch on the power supply won't get switched on.

Power supply defective?

Do not attempt to repair a defective power supply. Power supplies should only be repaired by an electronics specialist with the proper equipment. All you can do is measure the output voltage and check whether the microfuse inside of the power supply is still in order.

However, to check the microfuse inside the power supply, you have to open the power supply. If the guarantee for your computer hasn't yet expired, we advise you to refrain from this task, since the guarantee expires as soon as you open up the power supply.

WARNING

Make certain to disconnect the power cord before working on the power supply. The power supply when switched on, stores up to 1000 volts, and could even have more if something is wrong with it.

Unless you're 100% certain of what you're doing, do not repair a defective power supply. Either replace the defective power supply or leave any repair work to a qualified expert.

Microfuse switch defective?

Many switching power supplies have a small fuse. Some have a removable fuse, while others have a soldered microfuse. You cannot repair the power supply if the fuse in your power supply is defective and the new fuse blows after you replace the old one. You have to buy a new power supply instead.

We don't recommend repairing a switching power supply even if your computer store or electronics store offers to repair it. Very few service centers can repair such a complicated switching power supply, nor are they likely to even have the necessary measuring instruments. These service centers won't have the diagrams anyway. The cost of repair is too high compared to buying a new power supply.

How do you measure the voltage on the power supply?

Don't pull out the power supply for the motherboard to measure the output voltage. You won't get a correct measurement. Remove only the case of your PC. You can measure the voltage with a normal voltmeter or multimeter. The clips of the voltmeter must be long and thin so they can penetrate the plug from above and reach the noninsulated end.

The power supply furnishes voltages of +5V, -5V, +12V and -12V. The black conducting lines in the pins are the ground wires. The red conducting line conducts +5V, the white one -5V, the yellow one +12V and the blue line conducts -12V. We've included the pinout for the power supply of the motherboard in the Appendices.

What to look for when installing a new power supply

A power supply is only a little bit cheaper than a completely new case with a switching power supply. For this reason, maybe you'd prefer to purchase a new case instead. If you buy a bigger case, you won't have as many problems installing additional drives later. What is more, switching power supplies vary greatly in design, which means that you cannot install any power supply you wish into your old case.

Be very careful when working with your computer's power supply. It packs a lot of energy, and one miscue can be very hazardous. If you are at all uncertain about working with electricity, please allow a professional to do the job.

If you decide to keep your old case, there are a few things to keep in mind when replacing the power supply. First, find out what kind of power supply you have. When you buy a new power supply, make sure it delivers at least the same performance as your old one.

The new power supply should be able to provide approximately 200 watts. Your computer system will be well equipped with this much performance. If you install more hardware later, you won't need to buy a new power supply just because the old one doesn't deliver enough performance.

A standard power supply has two plugs with six conducting lines each that are plugged into the motherboard. Before removing the power supply, make sure the computer is turned off and the power supply is unplugged. Ground yourself before removing the power supply.

The plugs for the motherboard power supply aren't always coded, so it's possible to mix them up them. If the plugs are mixed up, it can destroy the motherboard and perhaps the expansion boards as well as the connected drives.

Before removing the power supply, mark the inside of the plugs with a waterproof marker.

Plugs for the power supply of the motherboard.

Use the color sequence of the conducting lines of the old plugs to see how to plug in the new ones.

Computer runs briefly, then everything goes off

The Power-Good signal is on a conductor that is usually orange (see the Appendix). This signal means the voltage provided by the power supply for the hardware components is at the proper level.

The Power-Good signal is very important when switching on a computer. About 100ms after the PC is switched on, this line provides a 5V current if all the other voltages are at the proper levels. If the peripheral controller of the motherboard doesn't receive this signal, it switches off all the data and address lines.

This happens to prevent undefined write operations from occurring in the CMOS RAM, which would prevent you from booting the computer. The power supply fan will even run when the motherboard isn't getting any voltage from the power supply. At least this tells you the computer is receiving its 220V of power.

A short circuit on a circuit board or the motherboard can also be the reason the computer is not starting. Make certain you don't have any screws lying around on the motherboard that could cause a short circuit. This could happen if you were doing some work inside your computer.

Also, the power supply, due to its built-in circuitry, is protected from overvoltage, excess current and excessive interior temperatures. If necessary, the electronic protective circuit will respond by disconnecting the voltage conductors. Then neither the motherboard nor the drives will be supplied with power. You can't switch on your computer again until the error has been eliminated.

Is the power supply overloaded?

The power supply will be disconnected due to overload whenever the computer detects the power supply is too weak. If your computer switches off after you have upgraded by adding new hardware, you'll also need to upgrade the power supply. A good power supply should output at least 180 watts. Power supplies in tower cases should have even higher output, because they're designed for adding many hardware components. Naturally, this also means more of a strain on the power supply. A server with four or more hard drives installed requires a power supply of at least 240 watts.

Hardware components today are usually designed to limit power consumption to a minimum. Although errors due to overload are rare, make certain to check the performance of the power supply when you buy a new PC or case. We don't recommend power supplies less than 150 watts.

Locating defective hardware

The power supply is not always the reason your computer won't boot. The error is more likely to be in another hardware component.

First, remove all unnecessary expansion boards and drives. Switch off the computer and remove all the cards from the motherboard except for the video card. You'll also need to unplug the disk drive and hard drive controller. The computer will display an error message if you boot it now, because the settings in CMOS Setup no longer correspond to the existing hardware. However, you at least know the computer functions correctly to this point.

However, if the screen stays blank, read the information called "When the screen stays blank" later in this section. If the computer beeps, continue reading the information in "Computer beeps several times after starting" later in this section.

You're in luck if the computer boots: The power supply, the motherboard and the monitor are not defective. Switch off the computer, plug in the drive controller and connect the hard drive. If the computer still boots, plug in the floppy drive next. If the computer boots again, you can plug in the remaining cards one by one and reboot after each card. Keep in mind, however, the computer must be switched off whenever you plug/unplug any of the components. This method will help you determine which card or drive is defective.

Detecting a defective motherboard

BIOS may be able to detect and locate an error on the motherboard during the POST. It will output a beep code if it detects an error. You can determine which chip of the motherboard is defective by referring to an error beep code list. Although error beep codes vary for different BIOS types, we've explained the beep codes in the Appendices. Your motherboard's manual should also explain these beep codes.

Most of the chips on a motherboard are soldered on, so it's unlikely you can replace defective parts. Do not under any circumstances use a soldering iron to try to remove a chip you believe to be defective. The SMD chips of a motherboard are quite sensitive to heat. The soldering iron could destroy chips next to the one you're removing.

The only parts on the motherboard which can be replaced are the CPU and, in some cases, the BIOS. Consult with a service center first and get an estimate of how much a repair would cost. Repairing a motherboard is possible and cost-effective in only a few cases. Instead, consider buying a new motherboard.

It's up to you to decide whether to upgrade your computer with a more modern motherboard. Basically, you can continue running all your other components on a new motherboard, such as expansion boards or drives, provided the new motherboard has the same bus system as the old one.

When the screen stays blank

Check the brightness control

Monitors attract a great deal of dust and other dirt particles. You should clean the monitor occasionally. Make certain to switch off the monitor first. An exceedingly high amount of voltage could escape through your body to the floor. Don't get the monitor too wet. A damp cloth is sufficient for cleaning the monitor.

Windows 98 Emergency First Aid

Don't panic if you switch your computer on and there's no picture on the monitor. Many monitors have the controls for contrast and brightness in an easy to access area on the monitor case. You probably adjusted these controls accidentally while cleaning. Set the contrast and brightness correctly and the picture should appear on the monitor again.

Many of today's monitors have their own Setup programs independent of the video card and the computer. Activate this Setup program from a control switch. Use this Setup program to set various properties to control the screen display. You can also adjust the contrast and the brightness. Check these settings and make any necessary corrections.

Check the power supply cable

Switching on the monitor places a strain on the power supply cable. If the cable is wedged in and you turn the monitor, the plug could slip out of its socket. The result is a blank screen. Most monitors have a light emitting diode or an illuminated display on the front to indicate it has power. The monitor is not receiving power if this LED doesn't light up. Check the plug to make sure it is correctly seated in the socket.

Your computer area may have cables that are wedged between tables or a table and the wall. Perhaps the cables on the floor are often carelessly run over by a chair or printer stand. This can eventually break some of the wires in the cable. Check your cable to make sure it doesn't have any broken conductors. If your monitor is still blank, replace the power supply cable with one that works.

VGA cable defective?

What we've said about the power supply cable also applies to the VGA cable running between the monitor and computer. Make certain this cable isn't damaged. If possible, replace the VGA cable with one that works. Unfortunately, this won't be possible with some older monitors, because the cable is physically attached to the monitor. If this is your situation, seek help from a qualified technician or replace the monitor.

Or, perhaps the video card isn't securely in the slot. Frequent plugging and unplugging of the VGA cable can loosen the card from its slot.

How to check your video card

Remove the case and check whether the video card is plugged tightly into the slot and screwed down. If the video card isn't screwed tight, it can get loose through frequent plugging and unplugging of the monitor cable. A proper connection between the video card and the slot of the computer then no longer exists. This could cause BIOS to output an error beep code when you switch on the computer. To find out more about the error beep codes, see "Computer beeps several times after starting" in the "The Computer Won't Boot Correctly" section in this chapter.

Is the computer running despite this?

It's easy to tell if your computer is booting, even if you don't have a picture on the monitor. Insert the Windows startup disk into drive A: and switch on the computer. The fan starts running immediately after the computer boots up and emits a more or less loud noise. You will hear a ticking on some computers while memory is being counted if this option hasn't been disabled in BIOS Setup. After the diagnostic routines of BIOS have been executed without error, the computer emits one short beep. Next, the computer addresses the disk drives and hard drives. You can tell this is happening by watching the LEDs of the drives. If you noticed the described sequence of events, after booting is complete, enter

```
DIR
```

If the disk drive starts up, there's nothing wrong with the computer. The source of the error is in the video system of the computer.

My onboard video card is defective, what now?

Many of today's motherboards have an integrated video card. If this onboard video card becomes defective, you don't have to run out and buy a new motherboard. The user's manual for the motherboard should include a section on disabling the video card. It's impossible without special hardware to operate more than one video card simultaneously, unless you add a monochrome video card to your VGA card. To replace the onboard card with a new color video card, you have to disable the onboard card. Disable the onboard video card using a jumper or a DIP switch. Then plug the new video card into a free slot. That's all you have to do.

If the new video card works, your onboard card is defective. Repairing the onboard card, if at all possible, is nearly as expensive as buying a new motherboard without a CPU.

Depending on the extent of the damage to the onboard video card, it's possible your new video card won't work perfectly even after disabling the old one. In such cases, you've no other choice but to buy a new motherboard. Fortunately, this doesn't happen very often.

Is the monitor defective?

If you were unable to find anything wrong with all the devices and cables you checked, then the source of the error can only be in the monitor itself. Contact a professional or buy a new monitor.

The computer beeps several times after starting

You switch on the computer, but instead of seeing the normal startup message on the screen, you hear strange beeps from the speaker or see a three or four digit number on the screen with an error message. The computer from this point doesn't communicate with you; resetting or switching it off and on again won't help.

There is a very simple explanation for the beeps and the error message. Every time you start the computer, BIOS runs the POST (Power-On Self-Test). The POST detected an error and displayed the error message.

The errors that occur here fall into three categories:

1. Video display

2. Errors connected with the motherboard

3. Errors originating from a complete breakdown of the system

Errors in the video system mean no more screen messages. Therefore, you'll hear beeps from the PC speaker instead. These beeps are called "beep codes," because certain sequences of beeps (short-short-long, for example) indicate specific errors.

Diagnostic error codes are output from the diagnostic routines of BIOS. The routines detect timer errors, DMA errors, keyboard errors, memory chip errors, port errors and similar errors.

For example, if you hear nine short beeps from the PC speaker after switching on the computer, it means there is something wrong with the checksum of BIOS (with an AMI BIOS). The bootup procedure is then aborted. The EPROM, in which BIOS is located, would then have to be replaced.

The different beep codes and diagnostic error codes are explained in the Appendices.

The computer doesn't boot correctly

Often, the computer may also stop in the middle of the bootup procedure. There can be several causes for this problem as well.

Computer stops after BIOS startup message

Using the wrong memory type?

Some motherboards require the parity type of SIMM chips. For example, if you upgrade the RAM in this type of computer and you use SIMM modules without parity chips, the computer will crash when checking the RAM. Perhaps you can find out whether this is the case using BIOS. If BIOS offers an option for the parity check, disable the option. If your computer runs after that, then you've actually got a SIMM module without a parity chip. You can either run the computer as is or exchange the memory chips at your dealer.

On the other hand, motherboards that don't support a parity check in BIOS can be equipped with SIMMs that have the parity chip.

Defective expansion card?

Naturally, with this system error you could also have a defective expansion card. We already discussed this in the information "Locating defective hardware" earlier in this section.

Computer hangs up while counting memory

As we mentioned, the computer performs a self test shortly after you switch it on. Among other tasks, the computer counts the available RAM and performs a simple test. If the computer hangs up while counting the memory, you can assume that one of the SIMM modules is defective. If you want to invest some of your time, you can locate the defective SIMM module and replace it with a new one. This requires that at least two banks be equipped, or you have a reserve SIMM module. We'll explain the procedure using a computer equipped with eight 1-Meg SIMM modules as an example.

Make certain to ground yourself to protect your computer from electrostatic charges.

Open the case and remove the SIMM module of bank 1 (the first bank is bank 0). Switch on the computer. The POST will determine that 4 Meg are missing and output an error message. Go to the Setup menu and change the entry for RAM if BIOS hasn't already done that. Exit BIOS by selecting the **Save & Exit** option (or whatever the option is called in your BIOS).

If you don't get an error message after rebooting, the defective module is from the SIMM modules in bank 1. Remove a module from bank 0 and don't put it with the other SIMMs. Take a SIMM module from bank 1 and plug it into the free spot on bank 0. Turn the computer back on. Does BIOS count the memory without finding an error? If the memory count is successful, plug in the next SIMM module. Repeat this procedure until you locate the defective module. It's very unlikely, although not impossible, that more than one SIMM module will be defective.

Computer displays a PARITY-ERROR message when you boot up

You can detect defective functions of the RAM using the parity check. There is an extra chip on the SIMM or PS/2 modules for this purpose. This additional chip is where the parity of the saved data is stored. The sum is either even or odd and is determined by hardware logic. If an odd sum is expected based on the data, but an even sum is written to the parity RAM due to the actual data, you have a parity error. The computer crashes and the error message "PARITY-ERROR" appears on your monitor. All you can do now is hit the Reset button.

Different viruses will also simulate a parity error (*e.g.*, the parity boot virus). Switch off your computer. Insert a bootable diskette containing a current virus scanner into the disk drive and switch on the computer again. After the computer finishes booting up, start the virus scanner and check your hard drive for viruses.

If you don't find a virus, you can assume that a memory chip of your RAM is defective. See the information called "Computer hangs up while counting memory" earlier in this section. It will tell you what action to take. However, if you happen to find a virus, see Chapter 7 for more information.

HIMEM.SYS reports unreliable XMS memory

If you don't disable the test function of the HIMEM.SYS memory manager through the parameter /TESTMEM:OFF, it runs a simple test on the availability of XMS memory prior to its installation. If everything is okay, the bootup process continues. If there is a serious memory error, the following error message appears:

> , ERROR: HIMEM.SYS has detected unreliable XMS memory at address XXXX:XXXX
>
> For more information, type HELP TESTMEM at the command prompt.
>
> To continue starting your computer, press ENTER.
>
> XMS Driver not installed.

You can be certain a defect is present in this case. You must find the defective memory chip. To do this, run the computer with the lowest possible amount of RAM. Equip only bank 0 with RAM and follow the procedure described in the information "Computer hangs up while counting memory" earlier in this section.

Not eliminating the error with this method, doesn't mean that all your memory modules are defective. This simply doesn't happen. Instead, the cause of the memory error will be in the cache memory. To check this, you'll have to take the computer apart to get to the cache memory. Make certain to use antistatic tools so you don't do more damage through static charges.

The owner's manual of the motherboard usually shows a diagram of the motherboard with the location of the cache chips marked. After removing the cache memory and putting as much of the computer back together as possible, you still need to disable the cache in BIOS. Then reboot the computer. Now the computer should run properly. Naturally, you'll notice the cache is missing when you work with the computer, but in a pinch, you can do without it.

Depending on the layout of the cache memory, you might even be able to find the defective chip. If possible, install only half the cache memory. Check the documentation for the motherboard to find out how to set the jumpers on the motherboard. Then you can find the defective chip by replacing the individual chips.

The BIOS outputs an error number or an error message

You'll always see error numbers or error messages on the screen when the diagnostic routines of BIOS detect a defect. (This is provided there is no serious damage to the video system, the CPU or the switching power supply). Then it is a diagnostic error code.

For example, the following error code may appear during bootup:

> 1782 Controller Failure

This number indicates the controller installed on the hard drive is defective and cannot be repaired. Try opening the computer and unplugging the power supply and the data cable, then plug them both back in. Now your computer may boot up again properly. In this case, the cause of the error was a poor contact to a pin/plug connection. However, if you get this error message again, you may have to replace the hard drive.

You'll find more information in "The computer beeps several times after starting" in the "The Computer Won't Boot Correctly" section in this chapter. The Appendix describes the beep and POST codes in detail.

"Configuration Error" appears

The computer runs a self test soon after you switch on. It then compares the hardware components it finds with the entries in the CMOS Setup. If any differences are found, one of the following error messages appears on the screen:

> Configuration Error

> Mismatch CMOS

These error messages, normally the result of the battery losing power or from a change in the CMOS Setup, are usually harmless. Press a key (usually F1) to run BIOS Setup so you can correct the entries. If you used the PC_INFO program to back up the CMOS Setup as we recommended, then choose Restore CMOS-RAM from the Utilities menu to restore the contents of the CMOS RAM.

"No ROM-BASIC, SYSTEM HALTED" appears

Early IBM computers had a BASIC interpreter integrated in BIOS. If it wasn't possible to boot from the hard drive, you could work with the BASIC interpreter. However, the functions of this BASIC interpreter are too limited to be useful now. Today, if the following message appears on the screen

```
No ROM-BASIC
SYSTEM HALTED
```

then there is no boot partition on the hard drive or the boot partition isn't active.

Boot with the Windows startup disk. Run the FDISK program. Then choose item 4 to display the status of the hard drive.

```
                        Microsoft Windows 95
                       Fixed Disk Setup Program
                  (C)Copyright Microsoft Corp. 1983 - 1995

                            FDISK Options

        Current fixed disk drive: 1

        Choose one of the following:

        1. Create DOS partition or Logical DOS Drive
        2. Set active partition
        3. Delete partition or Logical DOS Drive
        4. Display partition information
        5. Change current fixed disk drive


        Enter choice: [ ]




        Invalid entry, please enter 1-5.
        Press Esc to exit FDISK
```

How the screen should look after calling FDISK.

```
                          Set Active Partition

        Current fixed disk drive: 1

        Partition Status   Type    Volume Label  Mbytes  System   Usage
          C: 1         A   PRI DOS  C_DRIVE        1217   FAT16    100%






        The only startable partition on Drive 1 is already set active.

        Press Esc to continue
```

Status of the hard drive is displayed in this screen.

Is the boot disk or drive active? If it is, exit FDISK and use the SYS command to transfer the system files back to the hard drive. To do this, enter the following at the DOS prompt:

117

```
SYS C:
```

If for some reason the partition sector is destroyed, you'll have to use FDISK to create a new boot record. To do this, enter:

```
FDISK /MBR
```

Remove the diskette from the drive and reboot the computer. Now you should be able to boot from the hard drive again.

If your boot disk/drive is larger than 504 Meg (or 540 Meg, depending on your basis for calculation), you can have difficulties starting if any disk drivers were overwritten after using FDISK to restore the partition sector. For more help, see the information "After booting from diskette, the hard drive is not detected" in the "Hard Drive Crash" section in this chapter.

"Insert Bootdisk..." appears

After BIOS routines have been processed, the computer searches for a drive containing an operating system. If nothing else is set in the CMOS Setup, the computer searches drive A: first, then drive C:. If it doesn't find an operating system, it displays the following message on the screen:

> Insert Bootdisk
>
> Press Any Key

It's possible the operating system, consisting of IO.SYS and MSDOS.SYS, was accidentally deleted. However, the boot sector could also be defective. While IO.SYS and MSDOS.SYS are hidden and read-only, it's still possible you can display and delete these files.

In such a case, boot with the Windows startup disk. After bootup is completed and you are at the DOS Prompt, enter the following command:

```
SYS C:
```

You could also use the SYS command from the hard drive if it's not located on the diskette. To do this, enter the following line:

```
C:\WINDOWS\COMMAND\SYS C:
```

The SYS command recreates the boot sector and transfers the IO.SYS, MSDOS.SYS and COMMAND.COM files. Once these files are copied to the root directory of the hard drive, you will be able to boot the computer from your hard drive again.

Memory conflicts with ROM upgrades

Some expansion cards, such as the SCSI controller, network cards or a video card, have their own BIOS. This type of BIOS uses memory areas between 640K and 1024K. For example, the video card is always inserted at C000:0000 by default. If other cards are also using their own BIOS, areas can overlap, guaranteeing the computer will crash.

When installing cards that have their own BIOS, you can usually choose which area will be reserved for BIOS. You must, of course, know in advance which areas are used by the other cards to avoid later conflicts. To do this, use the PC_INFO program from the companion CD-ROM to tell you which ROM expansions are already present. For more information see the "Special cards with ROM expansions" information in Chapter 5.

"Controller Failure" or "Harddisk Failure" appears

This error message might appear, for example, after you have upgraded your computer with expansion cards. Cable connections or other cards could come loose when you plug in upgrade cards as a result of insufficient space inside the PC.

Reopen your computer. Make certain all the plugs and cards are properly seated. If necessary, unplug and then replug the controller card in the slot. Is the card screwed in tightly? A simple tightening of the screw could fix the error.

If everything is screwed tight, plugged in and connected properly and you get this error message, switch the computer off and back on again. If the error repeats, either the hard drive controller or the hard drive is defective. If you have a combination controller, which has the controller for the disk drives on the same card, it doesn't necessarily mean the controller for the disk drives is also defective. You could still boot from the floppy drive. Repairing the controller or hard drive is either impossible or not cost-effective. You'll have to buy a new controller card or hard drive. To find out which one is defective, replace a device for one that works.

You can get combination cards for the ISA bus starting at $20 at your favorite computer dealer.

4 Windows 98 Emergency First Aid

The LED for the disk drives won't go off

You can usually depend on your disk drive to operate for a long time. Usually, errors related to disk drives will have other sources. Often, the LED for the disk drives won't be lit anymore after you install expansion boards. Because the interior of the PC is so cramped, the floppy plug can come loose. Or, perhaps you had to unplug the floppy plug to add cards. You might have plugged it back in the wrong way. The result is an LED that doesn't light. Fortunately, improperly connected floppy plugs in this case won't damage the hardware.

First, make certain the plugs and controller card are properly seated. Disk drives and controller cards usually have a pin marked "1." The 32-pin floppy cable has a red conductor. This conductor must lead to pin 1 both on the drive controller and on the disk drive.

If you don't find any errors, the only other possible error sources are the controller card and the disk drive.

Do you have two disk drives in your computer with only one floppy drive LED that won't light? If so, ignore the error message during bootup and insert a diskette into the drive that is functioning. Use the DIR command to display the directory of the diskette. If that works smoothly, then the disk drive that has the LED permanently on is defective. Replace it with one that works. Make certain the Drive-Select on the new drive is set correctly. Check the old drive to see how it is configured. Use jumpers to set the Drive-Select. It specifies the priority of a drive. You can get to the jumpers from the outside.

They usually have the following labels:

DS0   DS1   DS2   DS3

If you only have one disk drive where the LED lights constantly, replace it with a new drive. Did the light go off? If not, you still have the option of replacing the controller card. Always switch off the computer first before replacing hardware components. If you don't have a spare drive or a spare controller, perhaps you can borrow one from a friend.

Bad or missing command processor

During the bootup process, the IO.SYS, MSDOS.SYS and COMMAND.COM files are loaded, one after the other. If the "Bad or missing command processor" error message appears on the screen, boot with the Windows startup disk and use the COPY command to copy the COMMAND.COM file to the hard drive. To do this, enter the following:

```
COPY COMMAND.COM C:\
```

Now your computer should boot without errors.

If you are using a different command processor, such as NDOS.COM or 4DOS.COM, don't copy COMMAND.COM to the hard drive. Instead, copy the command processor you have been using to the hard drive.

Computer stops after the "Starting Windows 98" message

If your computer makes it this far, then at least you can rule out a hardware error. It must be driver problems or memory conflicts that are affecting the rest of the bootup procedure.

Booting without startup files

To suppress these memory conflicts, you need to stop the operating system from processing the CONFIG.SYS and AUTOEXEC.BAT files. The error is likely in one of these files.

Press F8 when the Starting Windows 98 message appears on the screen. A Startup menu appears listing different troubleshooting options. Chapter 2 describes these options in detail. To start without running CONFIG.SYS and AUTOEXEC.BAT, choose the Safe Mode menu item. Windows starts up in Safe Mode. If Windows starts up free of errors, the source of the problem probably is a driver which is called by one of the startup files. We'll talk about this more shortly.

Memory conflict?

On a motherboard with an AMI BIOS, depending on BIOS version, it's possible to use memory area F000-F7FF as a UMB (Upper Memory Block). Do this by transferring parameters to the EMM386.EXE in the CONFIG.SYS.

This is possible because normally this memory area is used by the BIOS Setup program. After booting, the Setup program is no longer needed, so the memory could be overwritten or used by other programs or drivers. If you replace the motherboard, the computer may boot again after the "Starting Windows 98" message or the computer will simply crash.

The BIOS of the new motherboard probably doesn't have the option of making memory from BIOS area available as UMB. However, EMM386.EXE will keep trying to integrate the memory up to F7FF as UMB. The resulting memory conflict causes your computer to crash. Load the CONFIG.SYS with a text editor and remove the I=F000-F7FF parameter.

Before replacing a motherboard, reduce the CONFIG.SYS and AUTOEXEC.BAT startup files to only what is necessary. For example, delete Include statements of the EMM386.EXE (I=XXXX-YYYY). Do not delete the Exclude statements (X=XXXX-YYYY). REM out drivers for hardware.

After installing the new motherboard, enable all the drivers by deleting the REMs. If the new motherboard also has an AMI-BIOS, add the I=F000-F7FF entry to the call for the EMM386.EXE. If the computer runs with these settings, then you have an additional 32K available in the UMB. However, you won't be able to include this area on every board with AMI-BIOS.

Problems with the memory manager?

If you installed a different memory manager than the HIMEM.SYS and the EMM386.EXE of Windows 98, boot your computer first without the memory manager. To do this, REM out the appropriate lines in your CONFIG.SYS. If it works, the parameters passed to the driver are correct. Otherwise, refer to the program documentation or call tech support.

On the other hand, if you installed the Windows memory manager, then remove all Include parameters that are passed to EMM386.EXE. If the computer boots up, then add the parameters you removed, one at a time, and keep rebooting. This way you'll find the parameter that is causing the memory conflict.

Also, if at all possible, avoid using HIGHSCAN for the EMM386.EXE. This option gives EMM386.EXE additional control over the UMB. It checks whether high memory can be used as UMB or as a Windows EMS area. If necessary, it provides an area in the UMB to drivers or TSR programs. This area is not really free, and the result is a system crash.

Is another driver causing the problem?

If the suggestions above can't help you locate the source of the errors, then another driver must be causing the error. REM out all driver calls in the CONFIG.SYS and program calls in the AUTOEXEC.BAT. Now the computer should boot up properly. Begin deleting the REMs, one by one. Do the CONFIG.SYS first, then go to the AUTOEXEC.BAT. If the computer crashes again, then one of the entries you REMed out is the culprit. The driver or program at fault may be defective and needs to be reinstalled. Or you may need to buy a newer version of the driver or program.

The computer suddenly crashes

This is the most mysterious problem or error for your computer system. An occasional computer crash is often dismissed as "normal" if it rarely occurs. If you have bad luck, however, your computer will crash often. This can become an extremely annoying problem, and you'll have to start looking for the source of the problem.

However, just where do you start looking? The causes for occasional computer crashes are so many that you need incredible luck to find the error quickly. Many users frequently experiment with different solutions to solve the problem, and before you know it, the error isn't occurring anymore. However, the solution usually remains unknown because you (the user) simply didn't recognize it.

The following lists the most frequent reasons for such crashes. These explanations will help you solve problems if your hard drive often and suddenly crashes.

PARITY CHECK error message appears and the computer crashes

The parity check is responsible for checking data in RAM. A parity check error message is displayed if the logic in charge of the check detects discrepancies. This will cause your computer to crash. The only way to reboot the computer is to hit the Reset button. Frequent occurrences of this error under different programs can also have a different cause.

Defective memory chip?

RAM modules can be affected by temperature changes and old age. Electrostatic charges can also cause damage from constantly removing and reinserting the chips.

To find out how to locate defective SIMM modules, see the information "The computer hangs up while counting memory" in this section.

4 *Windows 98 Emergency First Aid*

Is a hard drive compression program the culprit?

Hard drive compression programs, like Stacker or DriveSpace, can sometimes cause problems on the computer, since the program code of such programs is deeply rooted in the operating system. Remove the hard drive compression program if your computer crashes unexpectedly.

If the errors no longer occur, then you have found the likely source of the crashes. Read the README files of both the compression program and Windows 98 carefully. You may find some helpful hints for solving your problem in these files. Otherwise, contact the manufacturer of the compression program. Perhaps an update is available which corrects the error.

How to check resource conflicts

Expansion boards such as sound cards, CD-ROM controllers or network adapters must include IRQs and/or DMA channels. These may be a frequent source of problems because some of the IRQs are already allocated by default. If an IRQ or a DMA channel is reserved for two or more resources, your computer can crash while attempting to access the card. So, it's important to determine which IRQs and DMA channels are still free before installing a new card. This avoids later conflicts. For more information on resource conflicts, see Chapters 5 and 6.

The computer always crashes with a specific program

It's possible that your computer will always crash with the same program. Naturally, this would make you suspect that something is wrong with the program. However, there can be other reasons for crashing.

Read the README files

Most software includes at least one README file. These files are also called READ.ME, INFO.DOC, README.DOC, etc. These files usually contain tips and tricks to solve problems that could occur using the software. For example, a README file might include a list of drivers or TSR programs with which the program has trouble. A README file also might list any hardware with which the program might be incompatible. A README file also usually describes solutions for the problems. If your program causes the computer to crash often, read the program's README files carefully.

Problems under Windows 98?

If you're running older programs under Windows 98, you definitely need to read through the Windows 98 README files. They may describe problems with the very software you are running. With a little luck, you'll also find some solutions.

Incompatible with the hardware?

Although software is rarely incompatible with hardware, you still need to consider it as a possible source of problems. This is especially true if the program is a hardware utility. It's impossible to test such programs with all the existing hardware. Are you using an exotic SCSI controller or an unusual network card? Again, check the README files for information.

Outdated program?

Don't underestimate the possibility that your program is simply too old to work with Windows 98. This is a real possibility if you've purchased new hardware and the program has been crashing frequently since the purchase. The program is either incompatible with the new hardware or has troubles with the new drivers of the hardware. You need to update the program to the most current version (preferably a Windows 98 version).

Bug in the application?

Lastly, if none of the causes we've listed applies to your situation, consider the possibility of a bug in the program. Contact the software manufacturer or author. You'll need to have certain information ready before you make the call (see Chapter 1). Tell them your computer configuration, the contents of your CONFIG.SYS and AUTOEXEC.BAT files and the possible circumstances for the computer crashes.

Other users may already have told the manufacturer or author about the error or problems. If the problem has been corrected, you'll probably be offered a bugfix (corrected version of the program) or an update of the program.

Since installing new hardware, the computer crashes sometimes

This is not as unusual as you might want to believe. The causes for such crashes can vary greatly, and it doesn't even have to be the fault of the hardware.

Read the README files

Depending on the type of hardware, a driver must also be installed before the hardware can be used. Besides the driver and the installation program, the diskette will also contain at least one README file. The README files will give you information about hardware and software that might create the new hardware problems. Perhaps you have some of the hardware or software mentioned in the README files. If so, follow the suggestions listed in the README files for solving the problem.

If a driver for Windows is also installed, take a look at the Windows README files as well. Maybe you'll find a solution for the problem there.

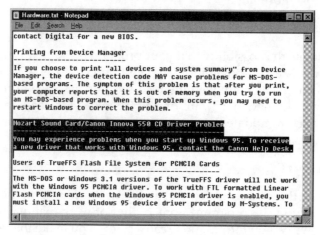

HARDWARE.TXT contains important information about hardware problems.

Problems with the driver?

If a driver or TSR program for the hardware in question is loaded in the CONFIG.SYS or AUTOEXEC.BAT, REM out the appropriate line. If a driver for Windows was also installed, you'll find the entry in SYSTEM.INI in the 386 Enhanced section (if necessary, check the hardware documentation). Place a semicolon ';' at the beginning of the line to disable this entry. This is especially necessary if the problems only occur under Windows. This of course means you can no longer use this hardware. If the computer stops crashing, there is probably a driver problem. Contact the manufacturer. They may already have solutions and can send you an updated driver. You should also see if the have a web site. If so, you may be able to download it.

Defective hardware?

If possible, test the hardware in question on another computer as well. If this computer also crashes, the hardware may be defective. Contact your dealer.

Am I using the right memory manager?

Memory managers (HIMEM.SYS and EMM386.EXE) are supplied with MS-DOS and Windows. To guarantee a smooth work routine, always use the latest version. The drivers are downwardly compatible, but often have new or improved functions for memory management. With the help of Windows Explorer, you can determine whether you are using the most current memory managers.

Select Windows Explorer and, in this order, select **Tools | Find | Files or Folders...** to find the HIMEM.SYS and EMM386.EXE files. Choose **View | Details** to display all the information and check the date. The most current driver will have the most recent date.

If you installed Windows 98, it will do your work for you. During installation, Windows automatically sees to it that you use the most current drivers.

It runs the first time, then crashes

Although this sounds like a serious error, it's likely to have a simple cause. It usually has to do with the system overheating or with the system components.

Wrong location?

You can shorten the life expectancy of your computer by placing it or using it in the wrong location. The worst possible locations for your computer are areas too close to radiators, heaters or refrigerators. Too much warm air rising from these devices can enter the computer. Not enough heat is dissipated when that warm air is combined with the amount of heat given off by the CPU and the video card. After a time, this can crash your computer. In the worst case, it could also destroy hardware components.

Also, don't expose your computer case to direct sunlight. This also contributes to excessive temperature increases inside of your computer. To make certain the vents provide the necessary air circulation inside the computer, don't place the computer too close to a wall or other obstruction.

4 *Windows 98 Emergency First Aid*

Components overheating?

Electronic components are subject to wear and tear caused by fluctuations in temperature. After a few years, the hardware components can become less resilient. As a result, your computer can crash after long operation. At least one chip simply gets too hot. When you reboot the computer, at first everything seems normal. However, then the intervals between crashes get shorter and shorter. You have to switch the computer off to give the electronic components time to cool off. Only then can you resume your work on the computer. At this point, you need to think about buying a new motherboard or expansion board.

Make certain the CPU is ventilated properly

This serious error can happen to computers with CPUs that have a high clock frequency. Such computers always have a CPU fan that provides sufficient cooling for the processor. Some manufacturers try to cut costs by installing inferior fans. These fans usually don't last too long. One indication that a fan is going bad is that it makes more noise than usual when it's running. The fan isn't achieving the required number of revolutions and can no longer cool off the processor sufficiently. A short time after you switch on your computer, the processor overheats and the system crashes.

Be sure to check the fan, replacing it if necessary. This helps you prevent premature destruction of the processor. If the fan is attached to the CPU, you're better off having an expert work on it. You can get a new fan at your favorite computer dealer or from one of the mailorder companies.

Heating problems caused by a dirty ventilation slot

You don't want your computer case to form an airtight seal around the interior hardware. Air must circulate through the computer to keep it cool. Most cases have extra air slots through which the air stream can flow. The fan in the switching power supply has the task of sucking in the air through these vents.

The stream of air sucked in through the slots whirls past the electronic components, picks up the warmth generated there and conducts it to the outside through the power supply. This guarantees the temperature inside the computer doesn't get too high and destroy computer components. SMD chips are especially sensitive to heat and must be protected from excessive temperatures.

Dust particles can also be sucked in along with the air. Over time, this takes its toll on the vent slots on the computer case, on the components themselves and on the power supply. As a result, the amount of air required for cooling off the insides of the PC is no longer able to pass through the slots. In turn, this means that less warmth is dissipated by the fan and the temperature inside the computer case increases. If the temperature becomes too great, the computer can crash. In extreme cases, hardware components can also be destroyed.

How to clean the inside of your computer

Once a year you need to give your computer a thorough cleaning. You will need a brush, a vacuum cleaner with a narrow head and a dust blaster or can of compressed air.

First, unplug the power plug. Then remove the cover of the computer case. Ground yourself. Now you're ready to go. Remove all the cards from the motherboard. Draw diagrams of where which cable goes to avoid future complications. Use the Dust Blaster to spray off the power supply and the disk drives. Do this outside, since things can get rather dusty.

After that, come back inside and begin vacuuming. Carefully pass the head of the vacuum cleaner over the motherboard and the case interior. If necessary, use the brush to help you remove dirt that won't come out. There may also be a lot of dirt accumulated under the motherboard. You might even have to remove the motherboard from the computer case.

Use the vacuum cleaner and the brush to clean all the circuit boards as well. After removing the dirt from all your computer components, you can plug all the cards back in and put your computer back together. Make certain the cables are all plugged in correctly.

Errors Accessing The Floppy Drive

Most users today have a modem, CD-ROM or both as part of their computer system. Otherwise, the only way for you to exchange data with the PC is through the floppy drive. Although CD-ROM drives are becoming more popular, the floppy drive remains a dominant method of storing data. Where do you boot from when the hard drive refuses to boot? Even floppy drives don't always work perfectly, and furthermore, the diskette is the least safe medium for data security. Still, there's a solution to almost every problem, which may help you out of one situation or another.

Cannot access the disk drive

A general problem accessing the drive doesn't necessarily indicate a hardware problem. One source for such a hardware problem could be a resident virus changing the disk interrupt. Cold boot the computer (hit Reset or switch the PC off, then on) with a "clean" boot diskette. If that works, scan the hard drive using a current virus scanner. If you don't find a virus and you cannot boot from the disk drive, then you probably do have a hardware error.

Drive Seek Error message appears

The BIOS detects this error during bootup. Fortunately, you may safely assume there's no problem with the drive. The source of this error is likely to be a mistake you made working on the disk drives. For example, maybe you changed, added or removed a drive. The drive seek error lies in the jumpering of the drives.

Each disk drive has jumpers which are used to set the Drive-Select. If the setting is incorrect, you will get the error message shown above when you boot the computer, and you'll have to check the jumper settings.

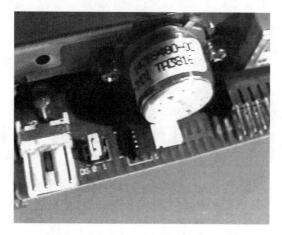

Set the Drive Select with this jumper.

We cannot offer specific information about the jumper setting, since it depends on various factors. The likely settings are DS0, DS1, DS2 and DS3 (DS = drive select), although some other drives have only DS1 and DS2. Normally, drive A: must be set with DS1 and drive B: must be set with DS2. However, two different models of bus cable are available to which the drives are connected. The first is the "straight" connection where each drive must have a unique drive select setting. The second model is the bus cable which has a twist on some of the wires between the two drive connectors, where the drives typically all use the same drive select setting. The jumper settings could be different for these bus cables.

If the default setting doesn't work, experiment with DS0, DS1 and DS2 until you find the right setting. Fortunately, only a few combinations are possible, so you should solve the problem quickly.

Read-write access errors

If you were working inside your computer, make certain the data cable of the disk drive is still plugged in tightly. Also, make certain the correct drive type is specified in BIOS Setup.

Is the diskette defective?

If the error only occurs with one diskette or with specific ones, then copy the readable data to another disk soon. These diskettes will not be usable for long. Defective sectors eventually will accumulate and your data will be lost.

If you cannot read some of the files during the copy, then attempting to repair them with a program like ScanDisk won't help either. ScanDisk does try to recopy the defective sector, but this generally won't work. At least ScanDisk marks the defective sectors in the FAT so you can also use a copy program for data backup. However, the diskette remains defective. Make certain to discard the defective diskette after backing up. This diskette should not be used for any purpose.

Defective drive?

If the error occurs with all the diskettes, the disk drive is probably defective. Repairing a disk drive can be expensive, so it may be to your advantage to buy a new drive instead.

Virus?

Scan your hard drive with an up-to-date virus scanner. Perhaps a resident virus is simulating this hardware error. Refer to the chapter on viruses to determine your best course of action if the scanner detects a virus.

Defective controller?

One last possibility is the drive controller. The hard drive is also connected to this controller. Try another controller (perhaps from a friend) if you've eliminated other possible sources of the error. You've found the source if the error no longer occurs.

Sector not found

This error happens when a file is being read. The error is in the FAT, and can no longer be repaired. Delete the defective file and copy a new, intact copy of the file to the diskette. Then use ScanDisk to check the diskette for possible errors. You can delete the lost allocation units; they probably come from the defective file. Perhaps you will also want to run DEFRAG to defragment the diskette. This creates a new FAT.

Positioning error message

Check whether the data cable of the drive somehow became loose. Also, make certain the data cable is plugged in tightly and correctly. The red wire plugs into Pin 1.

Another source for this error is an incorrectly adjusted read/write head. If you have problems reading your diskettes on other disk drives as well, you need to replace your disk drive.

Windows doesn't display any files

When you click the icon for the disk drive, Windows displays the number of existing objects but the file window remains empty. Windows may continue displaying the directory of the previous diskette after you have changed diskettes.

The source of this error is neither a defective diskette nor deleted files, but instead, is likely an error in Windows. Select **View | Refresh** (or press F5) and Windows will read the directory of the diskette again and display the correct files.

Dirty disk drive?

However, this problem can also have more serious causes. The hardware reports a change of diskettes through a switch or through the write-protect photoelectric beam. If the signaler is defective or dirty, the computer will no longer detect the change of diskettes.

The easiest way to remove the dirt is to blow the dirt away using a can of compressed air that you can buy at most electronics stores. To do this, remove the drive or at least open the computer case so you can get to the drive with the "straw" from the can of compressed air. You might also be able to a vacuum cleaner to remove the dirt from the drive if you don't have a can of compressed air. If this doesn't work, you may have to replace the floppy drive.

Defective data cable?

Although unlikely, another possible source for this error is a break in the data cable. The break would be in wire 34, which conducts the Disk Change signal (see the Appendix). Check the cable or the pin connection to see that it is properly seated and, if necessary, replace the cable.

Defective track 0

A defective track 0 is a serious error with diskettes. Windows 98 (or any operation system) cannot even format a diskette with a defective track 0. ScanDisk fails when track 0 is defective. Make certain to discard a diskette with a defective track 0 if there's no important data on the diskette. Otherwise, use a utility like DiskFix or DiskDoctor. These programs have an option for restoring a diskette's track 0.

Depending on the degree of destruction, the procedure for restoring a diskette can require several minutes. Disk Doctor has a high success rate, so there's a good chance it may restore the diskette. If the first attempt fails, try a second time. Perhaps the utility will succeed the second time around.

4 Windows 98 Emergency First Aid

Repairing diskettes with software

Unfortunately, access errors due to defective sectors occur more frequently with diskettes. At least one file is usually lost or otherwise unusable. DOS gives you an access error message. You can try to repair the defective diskette and perhaps save the file with a disk utility such as DiskFix, DiskDoctor or ScanDisk.

ScanDisk is located on the Windows 98 CD-ROM in the \WIN98 directory. Otherwise, if you've already installed Windows 98, select **Start | Programs | Accessories | System Tools**.

These utilities will, of course, also run into the access error. Unlike DOS, however, they won't abort the read attempt. Instead, they'll stubbornly keep trying to read the contents of the defective sector. Good programmers know that when an access error occurs on a diskette, it's necessary to start several read attempts immediately. DOS doesn't follow this rule, so it might report an access error when there is no error. If there is really nothing wrong with the sector, several attempts may be necessary to restore the data.

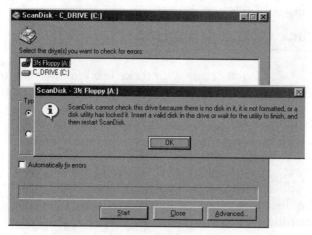

An example of ScanDisk repairing a defective diskette.

If the data seems to have been read at some time, then save the data to a different sector and correct the FAT of the diskette. If everything works, you can do a backup. Make certain to discard the defective diskette immediately.

Don't expect any miracles from these utilities. Attempting to recover data usually fails, and so the file remains lost. At least the defective sectors are marked in the FAT, so you can do a backup of the data still intact without any more access errors.

Recovering data when the disk jacket is defective

Yes, that can happen too. This is especially true with generic or other low-quality diskettes. Have you dropped a 3.5-inch diskette on the floor and watched as the metal sliding cover came off the diskette? Fortunately, this isn't a problem, because you can still insert the diskette into the drive and create a copy. Make certain to discard the defective diskette since it cannot be repaired.

You can also have trouble with 5.25" diskettes. On old diskettes, the magnetic coated disk will no longer turn. If you still need the data, then find a blank diskette. If you don't have a blank diskette, you'll have to store a disk's data on the hard drive temporarily. Now take out a pair of scissors and carefully cut open the top (the part that sticks out of the disk drive) of both diskettes.

Carefully cut open the top of the diskette jacket.

Remove both disks from their jackets and place the defective diskette in the jacket of the other diskette. Now insert it into the disk drive and you can copy the data from the diskette to the hard drive.

You can use the same trick if you spill soda pop or coffee on the diskette. If it's a sticky fluid, act quickly. Open the diskette and rinse off the magnetic disk under clear water. Air dry it and follow the procedure we described above.

This trick with the disk will also work with 3.5-inch diskettes. Since the case is glued together, you'll have to be careful not to destroy the case of the good diskette. Usually you can carefully pull apart the case on top. Since a little force is necessary, be careful not to injure your fingers. After getting the case apart, remove the disk and carefully insert the other disk. Nothing more stands in the way of recovering the data.

Do I need to clean my floppy drive?

Computer stores sell cleaning kits for both diskette formats. Usually, these cleaning kits consist of a diskette whose disk is made of rough white material and a liquid cleaning agent. Too many users reach for their cleaning kits when they get access errors on the disk drive. However, the cleaning kits are usually worthless for solving access errors. These errors very rarely are the result of dirty read/write heads.

We generally do not recommend using these cleaning diskettes. After all our years working with computers, we have yet to see one case where these diskettes helped eliminate access errors.

Hard Drive Crash

A defective hard drive is probably second only to a defective motherboard for providing users with awful nightmares. A defective hard drive causes nightmares because of the relatively high cost of replacement and because of the data and programs stored on the hard drive. To make matters worse, users seldom back up this data. That makes losing the data that much worse.

However, there are many ways to coax an unwilling hard drive back to running. Many times nothing is wrong with the hard drive. A properly maintained hard drive should outlast its "host" computer.

In this section you can read about the best course of action you can take with the various error symptoms. We've already dealt with some of the points in other sections, and you'll find references to those sections here.

The computer doesn't boot any more

This error doesn't necessarily indicate a defective hard drive. It can have many causes. Read the "The Computer Won't Boot Anymore" section earlier in this chapter for help locating the source of this error. The section also deals with the specific hard drive problems in connection with the bootup procedure and your options for troubleshooting.

Access to the hard drive is not possible

This problem can have several sources. You may also want to read the "The Computer Won't Boot Anymore" section earlier in this chapter.

Problems with removable frames

Computers with removable frames have experienced problems accessing the hard drive in the past that prevented you booting from the hard drive. Although it's possible to boot from a diskette, you still cannot access the hard drive. The source for this problem lies in contact difficulties in the removable frame. Pull the frame out and gently push it back into the bay. This should take care of the problem.

Make certain the frame is locked (if your removable frame is equipped with a lock). The computer cannot address the hard drive without this contact.

Motor won't start up

Another cause that we haven't mentioned yet lies within the hard drive. The motor on some early hard drives (e.g., Quantum 40AT and 80AT) may not start. To check, you need to unscrew the computer case. To give you the right feeling for the hard drive test, remove the hard drive from its mounting and hold on to it during the booting procedure. If the drive really doesn't start up, then shake the drive gently. The old Quantum drives will usually start up again. After warm booting the computer, you should be able to boot from the hard drive without any trouble.

It's time to back up once the hard drive is running again. A hard drive that is this defective won't last much longer.

Reviving the hard drive

However, if the hard drive runs and you still can't access it after booting with the emergency diskette (not even with FDISK or ScanDisk), try your luck at restoring the hard drive with Norton DiskDoctor or PC Tools DiskFix. If all other utilities and resources fail, these two programs might be able to bring your hard drive back to life. Depending on the seriousness of the defect, back up your data after repairing the damage (while you still can).

Low-level formatting

Perhaps the last option you have with a reluctant hard drive is low-level formatting. You can perform a low-level format using software available from the manufacturer, the dealer or from a bulletin board. If your BIOS has a menu command like **Hard Disk Utilities** in AMI-BIOS, then you've got another option for low-level formatting.

This type of formatting is not the ordinary DOS format. Low-level formatting prepares the structure on which the operating system will later set up sectors. Contrary to what you may have heard, this type of low-level formatting is completely harmless, even for AT bus hard drives. Many hard drives have been brought back to life with low-level formatting. If the formatting worked, then you can set up the hard drive with FDISK and FORMAT again. You won't have to buy a new hard drive, though naturally, the data is gone.

If you have a hard drive controller with its own BIOS, use its utilities rather than the computer BIOS utility. The following description of the SCSI controller shows you how to use this routine. The procedure is identical for other controllers with their own BIOS.

However, be careful with SCSI drives. Use only SCSI utilities (e.g., AFDISK from Adaptec) for formatting. If you don't have a program or if not even this program is able to access the hard drive, use the functions of the integrated BIOS of the SCSI controller, if you installed a controller with its own BIOS.

To call the BIOS program, boot with the emergency disk and start the DOS debugger by entering

DEBUG

A minus sign replaces the MS-DOS prompt. The controller's BIOS begins at a specific memory area which was set on the card through software or by jumpers. If necessary, consult the documentation or check the existing ROM extensions with PC_INFO.

We'll refer to the start address of this memory area as base address XXXX. For example, if you installed an Adaptec 1542B controller and reserved C800 for BIOS, then XXXX = C800. You'll need the address to start the BIOS utility with the debugger. This utility offers different services, including low-level formatting. You have to know the start address at which BIOS routine is located. It's usually in the controller documentation. If you cannot find it in the documentation, ask the manufacturer. The routine is located at XXXX:6 (or C800:6) with 1542B. In the debugger, enter the following (without the minus sign):

```
- G=C800:6
```

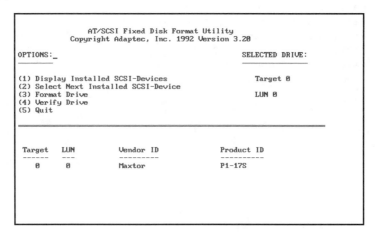

```
                    AT/SCSI Fixed Disk Format Utility
                  Copyright Adaptec, Inc. 1992 Version 3.20

OPTIONS:_                                        SELECTED DRIVE:


(1) Display Installed SCSI-Devices               Target 0
(2) Select Next Installed SCSI-Device
(3) Format Drive                                 LUN 0
(4) Verify Drive
(5) Quit



Target    LUN        Vendor ID           Product ID
------    ---        ---------           ----------
  0        0         Maxtor              P1-17S
```

The controller BIOS offers an option for formatting.

Then select the menu item for low-level formatting and follow the program's instructions. If the utility offers other options for diagnosing errors, try them out first.

Finally, exit the debugger with

```
- Q
```

If everything worked, you can reconfigure the hard drive.

4 *Windows 98 Emergency First Aid*

Controller diagnosis with DEBUG

The computer BIOS has a simple option for checking the hard drive controller. Functions 11h and 14h of Interrupt 13h are available for this purpose. Function 11h recalibrates the drive. Function 14h performs a simple diagnostic routine. If BIOS detects an error here, it returns a corresponding error number.

The following small listing gives the two functions and the error text for the error numbers. Enter the listing in an ASCII editor and save it, *e.g.*, as CHKIDE.DEB.

```
n chkide.com
a
jmp 01ef
db 'Controller Ok',0a,0d,'$'
db 'Controller error: h',0a,0a,0d
db '01h = Hard drive not present',0a,0d
db '05h = Error resetting the controller',0a,0d
db '07h = Error initializing the controller',0a,0d
db '20h = Defective controller',0a,0d
db '80h = Hard drive doesn't respond (Time Out)',0a,0d,'$'
mov ah,0
mov dl,80
int 13
jc 0203
mov ah,11
int 13
jc 0203
mov ah,14
int 13
jnc 021f
mov bx,0113
push ax
mov cl,4
shr ah,cl
or ah,30
mov b[bx+13],ah
pop ax
and ah,0F
or ah,30
mov b[bx+14],ah
mov dx,bx
jmp 0222
mov dx,0103
```

```
mov ah,9
int 21

mov ah,4c
int 21
rcx
12a
w
q
```

The blank line after the int 21 command is required. Then generate the executable COM file with the following command:

```
DEBUG < CHKIDE.DEB
```

You will also find the program as a ready-to-start COM file (CHKIDE.COM) on the companion CD-ROM in the BOOK\CHKIDE directory

This provides you with a simple program for diagnosing the controller. Naturally, our little routine is not meant to replace the more powerful utility programs, but it is useful in detecting many errors.

Defective controller?

Check your defective hard drive using another controller, perhaps from a friend's computer. It's possible that only the controller is defective, especially if your disk drive doesn't work anymore either.

Caution when using write-cache

Serious errors can occur when write-cache is enabled. The cache driver uses part of extended memory as a memory buffer for the hard drive. If an application requires data from the hard drive, then the cache driver checks whether the data is in the buffer. If this is the case, then the data isn't read from the hard drive but directly from memory. This increases the speed of the operation considerably. If data is to be stored on the hard drive, the cache driver intervenes again and stores the data in the buffer first. This lets you continue working without waiting for the memory procedure to be completed. The cache driver doesn't write the data from the buffer to the hard drive until it notices the processor is not so busy. This technique is called "write behind" (writing in the background or delayed writing) and can have dangerous consequences.

Data is lost if the cache driver hasn't yet written the data to the hard drive and the computer crashes for some reason. The same is true if you selected **File | Save** in the program and then switched off the computer without waiting for the write operation to finish. Any work you did is likely lost.

Programmers who start their programs from the compiler for testing purposes are in special jeopardy. You've just made extensive changes to the source code and start the program from the compiler interface to test it. The cache driver hasn't yet written the modified source code to the hard drive, especially since the processor is currently occupied with the execution of the program. If the computer crashes now due to a programming error, the source code changes are down the drain. When changes are made, the directory and the FAT will also be copied into the cached. If the programmer goofed and the program also messes up the cache driver through a programming error, the results can be disastrous.

So, if necessary, disable delayed writing to the disk. To do this, start Windows 98 and double-click the My Computer icon. Next, double-click the Control Panel and then the System icon. Select the "Performance" tab and then click the [File System...] button. Select the "Troubleshooting" tab from the File System Properties dialog box.

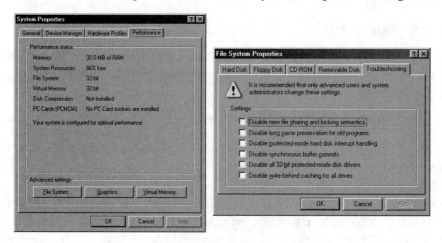

You may want to disable the write-cache.

You can disable write-behind caching in this dialog box by checking the "Disable write-behind caching for all drives" box.

Is the FAT or directory structure destroyed?

The organization of allocation units is managed in the FAT (File Allocation Table).

It specifies which allocation units belong to a specific file. The number of the first allocation unit of a file is stored in the appropriate directory entry. (See Chapter 1 for more information.) The two hard drive areas can be destroyed by defective software, a virus, a disturbance in the cache system (see above) or by improper use of hard drive optimizers such as DEFRAG.

Once the FAT has been destroyed, you have true chaos on the hard drive. The directories will contain huge files. We hope you don't find files with the most impossible of names. If so, then you've really had bad luck, because it means that your directory structure is also destroyed. You can only repair these hard drive areas with utilities such as ScanDisk, DiskFix or DiskDoctor. If you ever discover such chaos on your hard drive, switch off the computer and boot with the emergency disk.

How to save the data

You've really got a problem on your hands, because it's uncertain what will or could happen. You could even destroy the data currently not affected by this during the repair operation.

If you have a current backup, you may as well reconfigure the entire hard drive and restore the backup. Your most recent changes will, of course, be lost. If you don't have a backup, back up the important data that is still intact before starting the disk utility. If the backup program no longer works due to the defective file system, try copying the files to diskettes. Then you can begin performing the necessary repairs.

Usually, the operating system manages at least two FATs on one hard drive. If you're lucky, one copy of the FAT will still be intact. If so, ScanDisk can renew the defective FAT with the help of the copy. If the repair succeeds, then don't boot the computer from the hard drive right away. After all, there could be a virus that is responsible for the destruction of the FAT. See Chapter 7 for information on what measures to take.

However, if all the copies of the FAT have been destroyed, it's extremely unlikely you'll ever recover your data. Even disk utilities are powerless in this situation. All you can do is back up those files that you can still access. Then you'll have to completely reconfigure the hard drive.

Converting destroyed areas into files

During the repair, ScanDisk or whatever utility you are using will display error messages about many areas that can be converted to files. This usually is not worthwhile because you cannot restore lost files using these areas. Converting these areas to files only makes sense when you have important customer data on the hard drive, for which there are no copies. Then you have the option of sifting through the files created by ScanDisk to at least temporarily store the data in a text file.

To do this, start a text editor with which you can read the files created by ScanDisk.

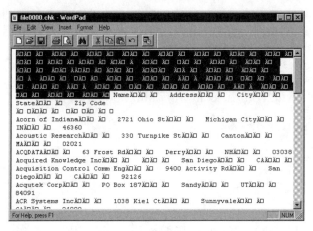

Use WordPad for data recovery if necessary.

Search for the data you need. Then highlight and delete the garbage characters. Although this method involves a great deal of effort, it's the best way to regain your lost data. For example, if you restored an address database, you'd have to prepare the addresses for adding to a database. Here's what to do:

* In the first line of the text document, assign the necessary field names (separated by commas).

* All the addresses are listed below. Each address has one line. Separate all "values" with commas.

* If an address is missing a value (e.g., the street, as shown in the following figure), add the comma anyway, so there would be two commas in a row.

Admittedly, that's a lot of work. However, if you must have the data and don't have a backup copy, you've no other choice. The following figure shows the results of the tedious work.

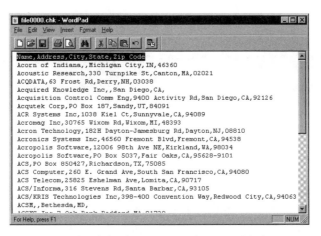

An example of the data converted to a usable format.

Now save the file as a text file (in other words, without formatting). You could name the file ADDRESS.ASC. Now the data is in ASCII format. You can read the data with many database applications and store it in a database.

Make certain to specify the comma as a separator when importing the ASCII file. Some database applications require using a semicolon instead of a comma as a separator. If this the case, use the **Find…** and **Replace…** commands in the text editor's **Edit** menu to replace the comma with the semicolon. For more information about importing data, consult the manual of the database program.

After booting from a diskette, the hard drive is not detected

This is not an actual hard drive error. Your computer probably doesn't have an EIDE capable BIOS. In addition, the hard drive controller also probably doesn't have its own EIDE BIOS either. To use the entire capacity in one partition with hard drives larger than 504 Meg (or 528 Meg, depending on the method of calculation), an extra driver is always installed. These drivers, such as the OnTrack Diskmanager or EZ-Drive, manipulate the partition sector in such a way they are loaded from the hard drive prior to the operating system. Not until then is it possible to access a partition larger than 504 Meg.

However, when you boot from the disk drive with the emergency disk, the driver is missing, since it is solidly anchored on the hard drive in the partition sector. As a result, access to the hard drive fails. This could be disastrous, for example if you were updating an operating system or installing a different one. The installation routine thinks it is dealing with an unformatted hard drive and naturally, wants to reformat it. The result would be a partition of 504 Meg. The remaining capacity would be unused, since the necessary driver wasn't installed.

However, drivers such as OnTrack or EZ-Drive offer an option for booting from diskette which allows access to the hard drive in its full size. When the computer boots and the OnTrack driver is installed, the following message appears on the screen

```
Press space bar to boot from diskette
```

Press *z* to continue booting from the disk drive. The hard drive is already installed and guarantees access to the hard drive. This way you can install a new operating system. Press *c* with the EZ-Drive driver instead of *z* to boot from diskette.

A Second Hard Drive Is No Problem

Do you have a second hard drive installed in your computer? Consider yourself lucky if you didn't have any problems installing a second hard drive. It doesn't always work the first time. However, if you're considering installing a second hard drive, make certain to read this section.

Installing a second hard drive

Master-Slave configuration

If you want to install a second hard drive on an ordinary IDE controller, make certain to configure the boot drive as the master and to configure the second drive as the slave. Do this by setting jumpers on the drives. This usually isn't a problem. However, problems can occur if there's no documentation about the jumpers. This is especially true when both drives are from different manufacturers.

After installing the hardware, it's not unusual if the second hard drive doesn't run or neither drive seems to be working. Another problem may be that one of the drives always wants to be the master, although you actually planned on booting with the other drive. It's also possible the two drives are not compatible with each other. You're then forced to replace one of the drives with a different make.

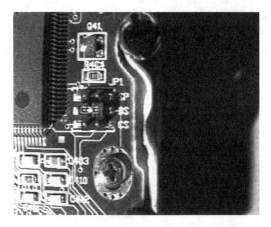

Use jumpers to set the Master/Slave option.

Problems with master-slave configuration can have several sources. Like other computer configurations, a uniform standard does not exist. Although the commands for programming the hard drive controller are largely standardized, some manufacturers will still deviate from the standard. These differences cause hard drives from different manufacturers to be incompatible with each other.

Use identical hard drive models so you're absolutely certain that both hard drives will run well together. At the very least, both drives should come from the same manufacturer. Other combinations are always risky business. Make certain you can exchange the second hard drive for a different brand if necessary.

The second hard drive won't run

At the very least you're using different models in this case. At the very worse, both drives are from different manufacturers.

Install the second hard drive in the computer by itself. This allows you to check whether the drive works.

If the drive won't run as the slave, experiment with the jumpers. Don't worry about damaging the hard drive. First, try it with no jumpers on the slave drive. Most slave drives have to be configured this way. If the master driver was running as a single drive before, then a jumper is usually already set on it.

Leave that jumper where it is and add another jumper. There's almost always an extra jumper set on the master drive to indicate that a slave drive is present. If the second drive still doesn't work, then test the other settings with the new jumper. With some luck, you'll find the right jumper position and the second hard drive will finally run.

If that doesn't work either, switch both drives on the bus cable. It's possible the second drive absolutely has to be the master. Experiment with the jumpers as described above. If that doesn't do the trick either, then you can assume the two drives are incompatible. You'll have to trade in one drive for a different brand. Ask your dealer for advice.

Tips on jumper settings

When you buy a new hard drive, sometimes you get documentation with the appropriate jumper settings for master-slave configuration. With other drives, you will find this information on the identification plate or sticker.

Otherwise, if you don't have this information, the following tables list the jumper configurations for the most common hard drives:

New Quantum Hard Drives			
Jumper	Single	Master	Slave
SP	* *	*_*	* *
DS	*_*	*_*	* *
CS	* *	* *	* *

Old Quantum Hard Drives			
Jumper	Single	Master	Slave
DS	*_*	*_*	* *
SS	* *	*_*	* *

New Conner Hard Drives			
Jumper	Single	Master	Slave
C/D	*_*	*_*	* *
E1	* *	* *	* *
CAM	* *	* *	* *

Old Conner Hard Drives			
Jumper	Single	Master	Slave
E1	* *	*_*	* *
E2	*_*	*_*	* *
E3	* *	* *	* *

New Seagate Hard Drives			
Jumper	Single	Master	Slave
1-2	* *	* *	* *
3-4	*_*	*_*	* *
5-6	* *	*_*	* *
7-8	* *	* *	* *
9-10	* *	* *	* *

Old Seagate Hard Drives			
Jumper	Single	Master	Slave
1-2	* *	* *	*_*
3-4	* *	* *	* *
5-6	*_*	*_*	* *
7-8	* *	* *	* *
9-10	* *	* *	* *
11-12	* *	* *	* *
13-14	* *	* *	* *

The Cable-Select option

For example, the newer Quantum hard drives offer a completely simple, sure fire method. They have an extra jumper position marked CS (Cable Select). This makes it possible for both drives to set themselves for master and slave operation. On both drives, one jumper is set to CS and the drives will immediately run smoothly together. Many CD-ROM drives also have such an option.

However, Cable-Select means that master slave selection is now made by the bus cable. For this to be possible, you must interrupt the bus cable at a specific place.

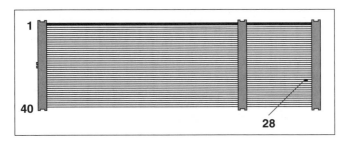

This interrupt is required for the Cable Select.

Use pin 28, which normally controls the spindle synchronization signal. However, IDE drives don't use this signal, so it's available for our purpose. The hard drive before the interrupt is always the master, and the other drive is the slave.

149

If your bus cable doesn't have this interrupt, you'll have to make it yourself. Unfortunately, this isn't so easy. Use a sharp knife or a razor blade to separate conductor 28 (conductor 1 is the marked conductor) from the neighboring conductors and then cut through it with a pair of scissors. Make certain not to cut the other conductors.

If you use hard drives that come with this option, you'll be able to totally circumvent the usual slave-master problems and can rest assured the two hard drives will run from the beginning.

It's possible that hard drives from other manufacturers also have such an option, but with a different name. In this case, the corresponding jumper will also be labeled differently. If necessary, ask your dealer or the manufacturer whether your hard drive has such an option.

Controller problems

It's not just hard drives that can give you trouble, the controller can also be the source of problems when configuring the master-slave. This problem often appears in the fact that both drives run perfectly as single drives, but only cause aggravation together. On some of the older controller cards, pins 34 and 39 of the IDE interface (see IDE layout/pinout in the appendix) are grounded, which completely prevents master-slave operation.

To check this, track the conducting paths of both connections. If the hard drive cable doesn't have a "cross over," or twist, then you can not set your hard drives as master and slave. If this is the case, it's probably better to spend a few dollars and buy a new controller. However, if you wish to continue using the old controller, you'll have to carefully interrupt the conducting paths on the controller card. Your could also pinch off the pins from the edge connector.

Several drives on an EIDE adapter

An EIDE adapter can manage up to four drives. The adapter has two ports on which two drives each can be connected. If you wish to run only two hard drives, you'll have an easier time with an EIDE adapter. Simply configure both drives as master or single. Run the slower drive on the secondary port, so it doesn't unnecessarily slow down the other drive.

The secondary port on many EIDE controllers supports only the IDE standard. Therefore, these ports cannot use the advantages of an EIDE hard drive. However, the EIDE standard still allows you to run drives such as CD-ROM or tape drives with the hard drives, provided they have an IDE or EIDE port.

EIDE doesn't entirely eliminate the master-slave problem, however. It always reappears when two drives are to be operated on one port. Both drives must be configured as master and slave as we described in the previous section. Configuration is accompanied by all the difficulties described in the section.

 "Non Hard Drive drives" such as CD-ROM or tape drives must always run as the slave when you run them from a port with a hard drive.

The following table shows the connection options on the EIDE adapter.

Primary, Master	Secondary, Master	Primary, Slave	Secondary, Slave
*Hard Drive	(none)	CD-ROM	(none)
Hard Drive			
Hard Drive		CD-ROM	
Hard Drive		Hard Drive	
Hard Drive	CD-ROM	Hard Drive	Either hard drive or CD-ROM drive
Hard Drive	Hard Drive		Either hard drive or CD-ROM drive
Hard Drive	Hard Drive	Hard Drive	
Hard Drive	Hard Drive	Hard Drive	CD-ROM
Hard Drive	Hard Drive	Hard Drive	Hard Drive
* This is actually the most desireable configuration in most instances			

The CD-ROM drive represents a "non hard drive drive." No other combinations are possible.

Since many EIDE adapters don't support the EIDE standard on the secondary port, make sure you're not running any IDE drives on the primary port. While you could do it, it would prevent you from using the EIDE features of an EIDE hard drive connected to the port.

Input Device Problems

Input devices are as important to a computer as the processor. Input devices form the interface to the user, controlling the computer, telling it what it is supposed to do. Without input, the computer would be as motionless as it would be if it didn't have any RAM or a CPU. The user must tell the computer what to do, be it through typing a DOS command, clicking on a button in an application or by moving the joystick to dodge the enemy in the spaceship. At any rate, the computer won't do anything on its own. The demands made on input devices are correspondingly high, since they have to withstand a great deal of stress.

However, problems can also occur with input devices. A defective input device seriously limits how you can use your computer. Have you tried running a Windows application using only the keyboard because your mouse didn't work? Try using your keyboard instead of a joystick in a fast paced computer game. Try entering a DOS command using your mouse when your keyboard suddenly goes bad.

This section describes some frequent problems. Perhaps you've already had a run-in with one error or another. If not, it's bound to happen sooner or later.

Keyboard problems

The keyboard is still the most important input device, and a computer without a keyboard would be inconceivable. The most frequent input is still made from the keyboard, and this won't change in the future either. When the keyboard goes on strike, it's the equivalent of a defective processor. The only difference is in the potential expenses.

The computer may give you a "Keyboard Error" when you boot. When the computer boots up, among other items, it checks whether a keyboard is present. If so, it checks whether the keyboard is in working order. You've probably noticed how the keyboard's LED lights up briefly as the computer is booting. The BIOS has already located the keyboard and is now testing the keyboard controller. By this time, the computer has determined the keyboard is in good working order. However, the computer could interrupt the booting procedure and use the "Keyboard Error" or "Keyboard Failure" error message to alert you that it found a problem. The computer beeps briefly and continues booting up.

Keyboard locked?

Check whether the keyboard is locked. Many computers still respond to a locked keyboard with this error message.

Check the setting on the switch

Some keyboards have a switch on the bottom that allows you to set the keyboard for "XT" or "AT." Make certain the switch is on the right setting. Beginning with 286 computers, the switch must be set to "AT."

Is the plug seated properly?

Check whether the keyboard plug is still seated properly. Pull out the plug, and then plug it back in. If that was the source of the problem, your computer will emit a short beep. This beep is to let you know the keyboard is functional again.

Defective keyboard?

If you believe your keyboard may be defective, connect a different keyboard to your computer. Then check to see whether your computer will work with this keyboard. If it does, then the problem is with your keyboard. You can buy a new keyboard for under $30. It's seldom recommended to have the keyboard repaired. Because either the keyboard controller is defective or there's a break in the keyboard cable, the cost of repair can be as much as a new keyboard. A new cable and plug costs almost the same as a new keyboard. You probably won't be able to buy a controller anyway.

If the second keyboard doesn't work with your computer, the source of the problem is likely to be in your motherboard. More about that later.

How to check the keyboard cable

You could save some money, if you have the ability, by opening the keyboard yourself. Make certain the keyboard is no longer under warranty. You'll need to determine whether there is a break in the cable. The keyboard cable requires five wires. The wires are soldered onto the keyboard circuit board. Use a multimeter to check each conductor.

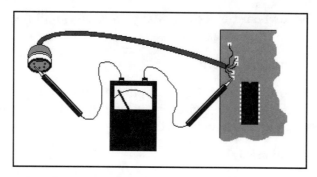

You have to test the wires of the cable individually.

The meter will react if the wire is OK as you scan the contacts. Follow the same procedure with all the other wires. If you find a break, you'll need a new cable. Write down the colors of the wires and note to which plug contact the colors belong. Then you won't get the wires mixed up. If everything was all right with the cable, it means the controller chip is defective. Since you cannot buy this chip and because it's soldered on, your only option is buying a new keyboard.

Defective keyboard fuse or filter chip?

Unfortunately, we're getting into more serious error causes here. If your motherboard is still under warranty, don't take the time to find the error(s). Depending on the motherboard, the signals from the keyboard are transmitted through filter chips that look like small coils with a ferrite core. These chips are always near the keyboard plug. If you cannot find these components, look for a soldered fuse resembling a small resistor. However, a few motherboards will have both components. The fuse is always one color (usually green).

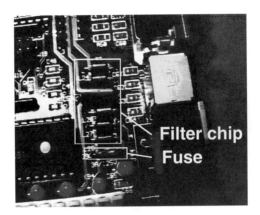

Make certain to check these components carefully.

Sometimes a filter chip or the fuse is broken. Make certain to ground yourself before continuing.

After uncovering the motherboard, use a multimeter to check the continuity through the chips. Their resistance is very low; the setting should be about 0 Ohms. If you find a defective filter chip, you may be able to buy a replacement at an electronics store, but it won't be very easy. If you can't find a filter chip, then bridge/shunt the solder connections of the defective chip with wire. If you do your work properly, you won't do any damage to the motherboard and the keyboard will function once more.

The same is true for a broken soldered fuse, but don't intentionally short circuit it with wire. Although this would work, these fuses are available at most electronics stores. Simply replace the defective fuse with a new one.

Defective keyboard BIOS?

If your motherboard doesn't contain filters or fuses, or the chips are not defective, then the keyboard BIOS is likely to be the source of the error. This is a 40-pin chip labeled 8x41 or 8x42. The "x" represents numbers such as 0, 1, 2 or 7. Fortunately, this chip is plugged into a socket on most motherboards, so you can replace it easily.

The 8x41 is several years old, and you'll only find it in old computers. You probably won't find a replacement for the 8x41 at any store. It doesn't really matter whether you use an 8142, 8242 or an 8742. The chips are identical in pinout and function. Unfortunately, you cannot always replace the 8x41 with an 8x42. Sometimes the keyboard will malfunction.

This is an example of a keyboard chip.

To determine whether the chip is the source of the error, buy a new one (about $5) or use a friend's motherboard. Once again, consider carefully whether you want to do the following work if the motherboard is still under warranty. Ground yourself before working on the motherboard.

If you don't have the right type of chip extractor, then use a small slotted screw driver or the tip of a knife to carefully pry the chip from its socket. The chip has a notch on one side. You have to insert the new chip the same way. Be careful not to slip and scratch any conductor paths on the motherboard. After freeing the chip from the socket, carefully insert the new chip. Make certain not to bend any of the pins. If the error causes described above didn't apply, then the keyboard will now work again.

The wrong keys

You pressed a "K" and your computer is displaying a "4" on the screen instead? This is a relatively rare, but confusing, error.

Error in the software?

First, see if the error also occurs with other applications. If you only have trouble with one specific program, call their tech support line (it should be listed in the user's manual). A programming error may have crept into the program.

Wrong or missing keyboard driver?

Check the Device Manager to make certain you have the correct driver installed for your keyboard. Begin in the Windows 98 desktop. Select the **Start** menu and the **Settings** command. Then click the Control Panel. Double-click the System icon and select the "Device Manager" tab. Finally, double-click the keyboard icon to display the entry for your keyboard.

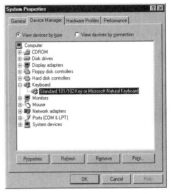

Display of the installed keyboard.

The default keyboard is usually installed. However, if the entry doesn't match your keyboard type, you must then install the correct driver. Select the correct keyboard type and click the [Properties] button. Select the "Driver" tab and click the [Change Driver...] button.

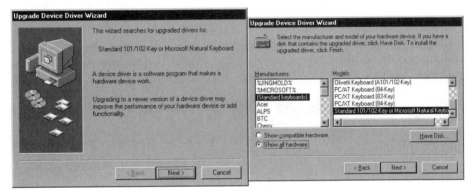

This is where you select the correct keyboard type.

Enable the "Show all devices" option so you can select the correct keyboard type. Confirm your selection by clicking [OK]. You'll have to restart Windows after you install a new keyboard driver.

Defective keyboard BIOS?

If the error persists, a defective keyboard BIOS is probably the source. For more information, refer to the information "Defective keyboard BIOS?" earlier in this section.

Virus in the system?

A resident virus could monitor the keyboard interrupt and simulate this hardware defect. Use a current virus scanner and scan your hard drive. If the scanner detects a virus, destroy the virus immediately. Then make certain to check your diskettes and CDs for the virus.

The keys are worn out or don't work

You probably use your keyboard more than all other input devices combined. Since the keyboard is subject to a great deal of mechanical stress, the keys can wear out. The main source of nonfunctioning keys is improper use. Too many users pound on the keyboard as if they were working on an old cast-iron typewriter. If you are in this category, don't be surprised if your keyboard "bites the dust" someday. If one or more keys no longer work, then you'll have to buy a new keyboard. As we mentioned, it's usually more expensive to repair a keyboard than it is too replace a keyboard.

It's a different story with sticky keys. This happens when you haven't cleaned your keyboard for a long time. We're also referring to cleaning the inside of the keys. You may be surprised by the amount of dust and debris that accumulates inside your keyboard over time.

The amount of dust and debris inside your keyboard may surprise you.

Fortunately, most keyboards today are designed so debris and liquid can't get to the contacts. This is important if you spill coffee or other liquid on your keyboard.

You'll find either springs or rubber stoppers underneath the keycaps. These generate the key strokes.

The rubber stoppers under the keycaps.

Any sticky debris will impede the key resistance over time. When this happens, the key either no longer comes back or comes back slowly after being pressed several times. Sometimes the rubber stopper is bent or snapped so it can no longer unfold. Use a flat object (a slotted screw driver will work) to pry the cap off the sticky key. Check the spring or rubber stopper to see that it is properly seated. Use rubbing alcohol to clean the rubber stopper, if necessary. After this, the key should work fine.

Cleaning your keyboard

Over time, a great deal of dirt falls between the keys of your keyboard. At some point you'll have to remove the dirt. If your warranty is expired, open the keyboard case. If you're lucky, this will only involve loosening a few screws. You'll see how much dirt has accumulated once the case is open.

If you have time and don't mind a little extra work, now is a good time to remove all the keycaps so you can clean the springs or rubber stoppers. Note the keyboard layout so you don't have to guess where each key belongs after you're finished. Blow all the lose dirt from the keyboard. You'll be surprised where dirt has fallen inside your keyboard. Use a very soft brush to remove dirt between the keys. If necessary, use this opportunity to clean the caps as well. Your keyboard will look like new again after this thorough cleaning.

After cleaning the keyboard, make certain the keys function correctly. To do this, use the test function in PC_INFO from the companion CD-ROM.

Mouse problems

If the keyboard is the most used input device, then the mouse is the runner-up. A mouse is indispensable if you're working with graphical user interfaces such as Windows 98. This operating system and its applications are designed to be used with a mouse. If your mouse suddenly develops a problem, operating these applications becomes virtually impossible.

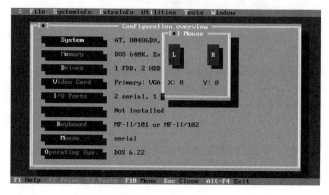

Use PC_INFO to test your mouse.

Basic problems

Is the mouse disconnected?

First, check whether the mouse is properly connected to your computer. It's possible the connector became unplugged.

Have you selected the correct port?

If you're using a serial mouse, make certain that it's connected to either COM1 or COM2. Some mouse-drivers only detect the mouse if it's connected to one of these two serial ports. In those cases you won't be able to use it with COM3 or COM4.

Is the correct driver installed?

Use the Device Manager to check whether the correct mouse driver is installed. From the Windows 98 desktop, click the **Start** menu (or press ⌐Alt⌐ + ⌐S⌐ to open the **Start** menu). Then press ⌐S⌐ for the **Settings** command. Click the Control Panel icon. When the Control Panel window appears, double-click the System icon. Select the "Device Manager" tab. Click the Mouse icon.

Windows 98 displays the mouse driver that is installed in your computer. If this mouse type does not correspond to the mouse you're using, you must install the correct driver. Click the [Properties...] button (or press ⌐Alt⌐ + ⌐R⌐). Select the "Driver" tab. Press [Tab] to move to the "Driver files" list box. This is where you can select the correct mouse driver. Use the ⌐↑⌐ or ⌐↓⌐ keys if you need to select a different installed mouse driver.

If you need to install a new mouse driver, click the [Upgrade Driver] button. Make certain to select "Show all devices." Use the ⌐↑⌐ or ⌐↓⌐ keys to scroll through the list of available manufacturers and models.

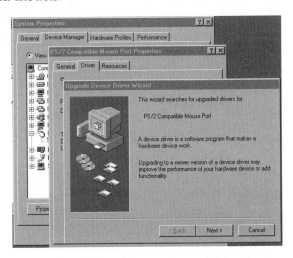

Reinstalling the correct mouse driver.

If you do not see either the manufacturer or model listed, try installing the driver from the installation diskette provided with your mouse. To do this, click the [Have Disk...] button. You'll be prompted to insert the diskette in the drive selected (usually A:).

Click [OK] to complete the installation. You'll have to restart Windows 98 for these changes to take effect.

The mouse refuses to work in MS-DOS mode

If the mouse isn't working under DOS, then the DOS mouse driver is probably not installed. This driver must be set up specifically for the MS-DOS mode. To do this, start the installation program provided with the mouse while operating in DOS mode. Then install the driver for DOS. The driver will have to be loaded at bootup in the CONFIG.SYS or the AUTOEXEC.BAT. You may need to reboot your PC for the installation to take effect.

Mouse pointer doesn't move smoothly

This is probably the most frequent problem you'll have with a mouse. The source of the problem is quite simple: the mouse's moving components are dirty. You normally move the mouse over a mouse pad or over the desktop. The rubberized ball transfers this movement to the roller sensors, which translate the motion into electronic signals. These signals pass through the mouse port and are transformed into mouse pointer movements by the mouse driver. Desk surfaces and mouse pads are seldom clean. Any dirt or dust that is picked up by the mouse ball collects on the roller sensors. This inhibits smooth movement.

Any dirt or dust that is picked up by the mouse ball can collect on the rollers.

The rollers eventually lose their ability to rotate freely and will reach a point where the only remedy is to clean the mouse.

162

Cleaning the mouse ball and rollers

The best way to clean the mouse ball and rollers is to open the mouse housing. Simply brush or blow off dirt that has accumulated on the surface of the ball. The rollers, on the other hand, must be wiped clean with a cotton swap dipped in rubbing alcohol. Also, make certain to clean the small retaining rings that hold the rollers. Be careful when cleaning these rings, because they're in direct contact with the electronic signal generators.

Once you've removed all the dirt, you may want to lightly lubricate the end of the rollers with some petroleum jelly (*e.g.*, Vaseline). Don't use too much, since this will cause dirt to build up at the bearings rings prematurely.

Is the spring-pressure too low?

Besides the roller sensors, the mouse also uses a pressure roller. With the help of a small spring, the pressure roller pushes the rubberized ball against the two roller sensors. If the spring is worn out, then the ball won't make positive contact with the two other rollers. This will also result in unsteady mouse pointer movement. Remove the spring and stretch it slightly. This may increase the pressure enough so the ball will fully contact the roller sensors.

Cleaning the signal generators is a little trickier

Another possible cause for unsteady mouse pointer movement is oxidation on the surface of the signal generators. This problem affects older Microsoft mice in particular. Disassemble the mouse so it's possible to use tweezers, wrapped with a cosmetic cleaning cloth, to rub the surface of the signal generator through a small opening in the surface. Make certain not to choose the opening through which you can see the delicate friction contact.

Insert the wrapped tweezers through the opening and exert just a little bit of pressure on the small disc. Then turn the roller so the entire surface of the disc is cleaned. You may want to consider whether this tedious job is worth the trouble for a $15 mouse—perhaps a newer mouse is a better alternative.

After cleaning and reassembling the mouse, you should have a mouse pointer that moves across your screen perfectly.

Is your audio CD-ROM player running?

You may also encounter the skipping mouse pointer if you're listening to an audio CD-ROM using the Windows Multimedia Player. Since this causes the mouse-events to be checked less frequently, the mouse pointer can move in small increments. The only remedy is to use another multimedia player that operates more effectively.

The mouse pointer won't move or only moves to one side

Is the mouse dirty?

If the mouse still doesn't work, remove the ball from the housing. Rotate the rollers with your fingertip. It's possible the rollers are so dirty they barely turn, if at all. In this case you'll need to clean your mouse as described above.

Defective port?

If your PC has a second serial port and you're using a serial mouse, check your mouse on the other serial port. Start the DOS mouse driver from the DOS prompt. If you don't have a DOS mouse driver, you'll need to restart Windows. If the mouse now works, you'll know the first port was not functioning properly.

It's possible the port is defective, although this is unlikely. It's also possible the port somehow became deactivated in the BIOS setup. Check your BIOS settings to determine if your BIOS supports this type of function. Also, make certain the port address doesn't conflict with any other address.

Conflicting interrupts?

If the previous test doesn't provide a solution, use another mouse to check whether your PC works with it. Make certain that you're using the correct driver. If this test also proves unsuccessful, an interrupt conflict may be the source of the problem.

By default, the mouse uses a hardware interrupt that is intercepted by the mouse driver to obtain the mouse signals. A serial mouse uses the default interrupt of the serial port. This is IRQ4 for COM1 and COM3 and IRQ3 for COM2 and COM4. Use the Device Manager to check whether the mouse interrupt is also being used by another expansion card. See Chapter 6 for information on this.

PS/2 mice use IRQ12, which must then also not be used by other expansion cards. If necessary, reconfigure the conflicting expansion card.

Is the mouse or the mouse cord defective?

If you got the second mouse to work, then the problem is likely in the mouse cord ("tail") or the mouse itself (specifically its electronics). Repairing a broken mouse is usually not cost-effective (you can buy a mouse for about $15).

If you want to save the few dollars, or if your mouse is a more expensive model, you may be able to repair it yourself. First, open the mouse. The cord is bent sharply on some types of mice just inside the housing. Conductors often break at spots like these.

Avoid this type of cable routing.

Refer to our section on keyboards to see how to check the cord's electrical continuity. If it is indeed discontinuous, you'll need to replace the cord. Check the cord's pin layout and write it down. If the cord has a sharp bend like the one we described, chances are the wire(s) is interrupted there. Cut the cable there. The newly cut end of the cord must now be insulated properly and soldered in the pattern that you wrote down. If the end of the cable was originally plugged in, the connector will not be reusable in most cases. Since such plugs can be difficult to obtain, you'll need to resort to the soldering iron in this case as well.

However, if the cord is in good condition, then the mouse's electronics are defective. Your best choice at this point is to replace the mouse.

A mouse button is not functioning

The likely source for this problem is a worn out mouse button. A quick solution is to switch the right mouse button for the defective left mouse button. (This is only a short-term solution and should be considered only if you don't often use your right mouse button.)

Your mouse driver may offer an option with which you can define your right mouse button as the primary one. However, this is also a temporary solution. You've probably developed a habit of using the left mouse button; suddenly switching to the right mouse button will be difficult.

If you're reluctant to replace the mouse with a new one, test your soldering skills. Either switch the wires for the two buttons, or the physically defective left button with the still working right button. You can always buy a new mouse later if necessary.

If you're using a three-button mouse and the primary button becomes defective, simply use the center button instead of the defective one. Very few applications support using the center mouse button.

Buy a new mouse if you can't work around a defective button, regardless of which mouse button is defective.

Problems with the mouse driver

Problems with the mouse driver often appear as jerky mouse pointer movement or simply a nonfunctioning mouse. These problems can arise when you start using a new mouse with your PC. Each mouse uses its own mouse driver. Since both mouse-electronics and mouse driver technology are constantly evolving, they are not necessarily downward compatible with older hardware or software. A new mouse driver, therefore, may not work with an old mouse, and a new mouse may not work with an old driver. This can be true even if both are from the same manufacturer.

If the mouse doesn't have a driver for Windows 98, at least try a compatible Win98 driver. Select the appropriate manufacturer and a compatible mouse type. If this allows your mouse to function properly, all you need to do is install the DOS driver. Otherwise, you'll need to install the accompanying Windows driver from the diskette. However, you should try to obtain the Win98 driver as soon as possible. In any case, make certain to install the DOS driver for your new mouse. Then you can also use it in MS-DOS mode as well.

After unplugging and plugging in the mouse, it won't work in Windows

In this case you've installed a PS/2 mouse. The interrupt handler of the mouse driver has detected the mouse was disconnected from the PS/2 port and therefore ceases to support the mouse on a software basis. You must exit and restart Windows 98. Depending on the BIOS version, you may even need to reboot your system to reinitialize the PS/2 port.

Testing your mouse

You have many ways to test whether your mouse is working well. Load the PC_INFO program and execute the mouse test. PC_INFO can recognize three-button mice, allowing you to check each of the buttons.

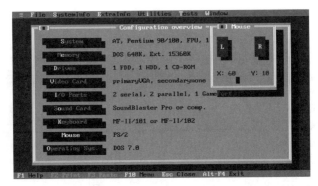

Use PC_INFO from the companion CD-ROM to test your mouse.

PC_INFO shows you which mouse button is being pressed. The screen coordinates are also converted into text mode and displayed

An alternative test is to simply open an application that supports the use of all mouse buttons. Then try using each of the mouse buttons within the program.

Joystick problems

Problems can also occur with joysticks. Many computer games use a joystick, since it's easier to control certain games this way. Using a joystick requires a game port to which the joystick is connected. You can usually locate the game port on the sound card. Combination controllers may also provide game ports. Also, a few expansion cards include a game port.

4 *Windows 98 Emergency First Aid*

The joystick is not being recognized

Games and testing programs fail to find the joystick

Say you've just installed the sound card or game port and the joystick doesn't work. First, check whether the game port is even activated. It's possible that it's deactivated as a factory preset of the expansion card and must first be turned on by switching a jumper. Check the expansion card's documentation and, if necessary, change the jumper settings.

Also, make certain the joystick is plugged into the game port. Finally, you may also want to check the Control Panel settings for the joystick. Make certain you're using the correct gameport software driver.

Joystick is not recognized, despite active game port

Instead of checking for a joystick that may or may not be plugged in, some applications check whether the configuration bit in the BIOS variable is set. If the BIOS failed to recognize the game port during bootup, which usually happens with AT machines, this bit in the variable will not be set. Most AT BIOS versions don't check the game port. So, if your software uses this bit to determine whether a game port is installed, it won't detect one. This is true even if a joystick is already plugged in. This problem can be noticed with many system information programs, since these usually check the configuration bit.

This problem occurs less frequently with games. Game programs usually check directly for the joystick and simply ignore the configuration bit.

Registering the game port using DEBUG

If your software is not recognizing the game port, even if it's installed and active, the following program may solve your problem. Open a DOS window and start an ASCII editor (for example, EDIT) and enter the following lines:

```
n gameport.com
a
push ds
mov ax,40
push ax
pop ds
```

```
mov al,[11]
or al,10
mov [11],al
pop ds
mov ah,4C
int 21

rcx
13
w
q
```

Notice the blank line following "int 21." This line is extremely crucial. Save the file under a name such as GAMEPORT.DEB. Exit the editor. Enter the following line at the DOS prompt:

```
DEBUG < GAMEPORT.DEB
```

The debugger reads the text file and compiles it to an executable COM file with the name GAMEPORT.COM.

The companion CD-ROM also includes this program in the \BOOK\GAMEPORT directory.

This program sets the game port bit in the BIOS variable and returns to DOS. From this point, the game port will be recognized by every program, making it possible to use the joystick.

> **TIP** If you have several programs that only recognize your game port with the help of this program, you may want to include it in your AUTOEXEC.BAT. If you've set up your hard drive as described in Chapter 1, add the following line to your AUTOEXEC.BAT:
>
> ```
> C:\UTILITY\GAMEPORT
> ```
>
> The GAMEPORT.COM program must be copied to the C:\UTILITY directory. You don't want to clutter up your root directory with small utilities. Your game port bit is now set each time you boot your PC.

4 *Windows 98 Emergency First Aid*

The joystick won't work, although several game ports are installed

First, check whether either of the game ports has even been activated. Check the expansion card's documentation for the correct jumper configuration. If necessary, activate one of the game ports.

Once you know that at least one of the game ports is active, make certain that it's the only active game port. None of the game ports will work if several are inadvertently activated. If your PC was factory equipped with a game port and your sound card also has one, deactivate one through either its jumpers or the Hardware Wizard.

The joystick doesn't work

This is a similar problem to the keyboard not working. Either the cord is defective or the joystick itself is at fault. Another possibility, although unlikely, is the game port is defective.

Defective game port?

Although we've yet to see a defective game port, anything is possible. Try a second game port, if one is available. First, uninstall the suspect game port and then activate the second one. You've discovered a rare problem if your joystick works after this.

Defective cord?

To check for a defective cord, open your joystick. Look for the solder points for the individual conductors in the cord. Use a multimeter to measure their continuity (see the information in the keyboard section). We usually don't recommend repairing a defective cord. You can buy a joystick for under $10 today.

Defective joystick?

The only remaining possibility is the joystick itself is defective. If PC_INFO was able to recognize your game port, use the joystick test functions. If this fails to detect any life in your joystick, the joystick is probably defective. Again, it's questionable whether any further effort is worth the trouble. Joysticks are usually constructed so that it's virtually impossible to repair these types of problems. You can buy a joystick for under $10 today.

A fire button isn't working

The source of this problem is likely wear and tear. The button itself is probably not salvageable, but you may be able to exchange a button from an older defective joystick. If the old button fits in the defective joystick, all you need is a little dexterity and a soldering iron to replace the button.

If you don't have an old joystick or if the fire button won't fit, it's still possible the defective joystick has additional buttons that you rarely use. Most joysticks include more than one fire button. If this is the case, simply switch the defective button with the one that's still working.

Calibrating your joystick

If you believe that your spaceship is no longer handling the way it should, run the game's joystick calibration routine. Most games should have such an option. Check the game's documentation on how to run its joystick calibration routine.

Once you've started the joystick calibration routine, you're prompted to move the joystick to the different corner positions and then press a fire button. Finally, you'll need to press a fire button with the joystick in its neutral position. Depending on how the procedure was programmed, it will run a little different than others. However, they're all basically the same. The program will store each of the values and will now use them in the game.

If your spaceship is still handling poorly, it's possible the joystick's potentiometers are dirty or oxidized. However, this is quite difficult to check due to the way these components are usually constructed. Again, the best thing is to replace the joystick with a new one.

Testing your joystick

Use PC_INFO to test your joystick. The test looks similar on the screen to that for the mouse.

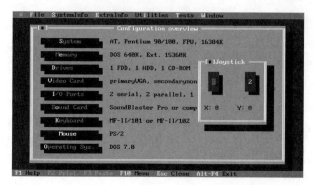

Windows 98 also provides a way to test your joystick. Click the Control Panel icon to display the Control Panel window. Double-click the Joystick icon. Then select the joystick you wish to test from the "Current Joystick:" list and the "Joystick selection:." Then click the [Test] button.

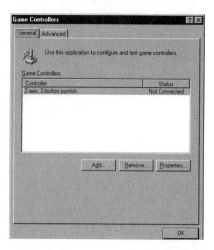

Windows 98 includes a method of testing your joystick.

You can also calibrate the joystick. However, the calibration in the Joystick Properties dialog box applies only to Windows 98 and not DOS games.

Video Card and Monitor Problems

The monitor and the video card are the most important output devices of your PC. Your PC responds graphically to input from the keyboard or the mouse through the monitor. This lets you perform tasks on your computer. If you're experiencing problems and suspect that your monitor is at fault, be extremely carefully if you decide to remove the monitor's housing.

 WARNING

EXTREME DANGER

The interior of the monitor contains voltages up to 25,000 volts. **NEVER open the monitor** if it's still connected to the AC power source. Even after you disconnect power to the monitor for several days, it can still store enough voltage to give you a serious electrical shock.

Also, if you're in the market for a monitor make certain the monitor has a low emissions rating (compliant with the MPR-II standard, or even better, the TCO-92 standard). The monitor should also be able to operate at a screen refresh rate of at least 70 Hz at the maximum resolution that you wish to use.

Screen interference

If you experience intermittent screen interference, regardless of what type of interference, and if this happens with different applications, consider the possibility of a computer virus. The Tremor virus, for example, causes the picture to occasionally vibrate. Scan your entire system for a virus by using a current antivirus program. Refer to the chapter on viruses for information on this procedure.

In graphics mode, the screen picture is too small or in the wrong spot

This error can occur if you're working with a higher resolution than the standard 640 x 480 pixels. The timing between the monitor and the video card must be recalibrated. Check the user's manual for the monitor to see whether it supports the resolution and refresh rate that you're using. Make certain not to select a refresh rate that exceeds the rate supported by your monitor. This could damage the cathode ray tube.

The drivers of most brandname video cards let you select and store the position and size of the picture. You must make the adjustments directly on the monitor, if this is allowed by your configuration. If your monitor does not support saved settings for different video modes, you may need to make these adjustments each time you switch between video modes (for example from MS-DOS mode to Windows).

The monitor image has a strong color tint

Sometimes the monitor picture can have a strong color tint. The picture may have a distinct yellow, red or blue tint. This means that one of the conductors in the VGA cable, which attaches the monitor to the PC, is severed.

Video cables often get pinched between the desk and the wall or between two desks, which can damage the cable in this way. Sometimes the PC or the monitor itself is placed up against a wall, which can also bend the cable too severely over time. Check to see if the pins on the connectors all still intact. If one of the pins is slightly bent, it will be bent over completely when you attempt to insert the connector into the socket. The result is a missing connection.

Check to see if the connectors are inserted firmly into their sockets. Make certain they're seated correctly and, if necessary, tighten the connector screws. Inspect the cable for physical damage.

If you were unable to find any of these problems, and the video image has not yet improved, replace the VGA cable. Before buying a new cable, borrow one that you know works. If this is not an option, use a continuity tester or an ohmmeter to check the cable. You can tell which connector is damaged by noting the color tint of your video image:

* A blue tint on the screen indicates that red is missing.

* A green tint on the screen indicates that blue is missing.

* A red tint on the screen indicates that green is missing.

Refer to the VGA connector pin diagram in the Appendix. This information tells you which wire is interrupted.

There are dark spots or bleeding colors

This is a frequent problem with large monitors (greater than 17 inches). The spots appear like dark clouds that may be distributed across the screen. They're often located in one or several corners of the screen (monitor 1), but they can also be distributed across the entire screen (monitor 2).

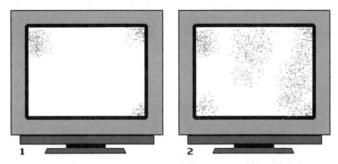

These types of spots can disfigure a monitor.

The best way to test the monitor is to use the Windows 98 version of Paint. Select the **Start** menu. Then select the following in order: **Programs | Accessories | Paint**. When Paint is loaded, select **View | View Bitmap**. The completely white screen makes it easier to examine your monitor's picture.

Dark spots or locally bleeding colors can be caused by external magnetic fields. Use the Degaussian function on your monitor (check the monitor's documentation to see if it is equipped with one). This demagnetizes the monitor's screen mask, reducing or eliminating the dark spots.

If this doesn't remove the spots, you should remove any electronic devices near the monitor which may produce a magnetic field (other monitors, printers, etc.). The user's manual for the monitor may contain a guideline for how far such devices should be kept from the monitor. Twelve inches should be enough. Activate the Degaus function again if necessary.

If the dark spots are still not eliminated, your monitor's mask is probably damaged. The dark spot is usually stretched across the full area of the screen. However, it can be damaged by rough handling or severe temperature fluctuations. If the monitor is still under warranty, contact your dealer or the manufacturer. Otherwise, you may have to buy a new monitor; this problem cannot be repaired at a reasonable cost.

The picture is not straight

This means the picture geometry has gone out of adjustment and is no longer perpendicular. The picture can be off on one or more sides. The following illustration shows this phenomenon (it's slightly exaggerated for a better demonstration).

The problem is usually caused by incorrectly or poorly adjusted deflection coils that are adhered to the picture tube. This causes the beam to not be deflected correctly at the edge of the screen, resulting in a tilted screen border. Errors in the horizontal edges (monitor 1) can generally not be corrected. Tilted vertical edges (monitors 2 and 3) can possibly be corrected using the monitor button field, if the monitor is equipped with a settings menu.

Examples of how a monitor picture can be out of square.

The settings in this menu let you correct bulge or trapezoidal distortions fairly easily. However, if the entire picture is crooked (monitor 4) the deflection coil may need to be readjusted. In that case you'll need to consult a qualified service shop.

Definitely contact your dealer or the manufacturer if any of these problems occur on a monitor that is still under warranty. They'll probably exchange the defective monitor for a new one. (Most newer monitors have adjustments to correct all these problems.)

The picture is flickering

Screen flickering is caused by a screen refresh rate that is too low. To provide an acceptable and stable image, the picture must be redrawn at least 70 times each second. In other words, the electron beam must trace the screen from the upper left corner to the lower right corner 70 times.

Select the refresh rate using the video driver included with your video card. Open the setup program for the video card in Windows and select the desired mode. The program may also provide an option that allows you to choose between the following two modes:

* Interlaced mode

* Noninterlaced mode

In the interlaced mode, your monitor works like a TV. During each pass the electron beam traces one half of the screen. The odd line numbers are traced first. Then, during the second pass, the even line numbers are traced. The beam must therefore trace the screen twice to construct the picture.

This method will always result in a certain amount of screen flicker. If you select an interlaced refresh rate of 70 MHz, the picture is drawn fully only 35 times each second. At a refresh rate of 70 MHz in noninterlaced mode, however, the picture is indeed drawn 70 times every second.

If this option is not available to you under Windows, a TSR program (Terminate and Stay Resident) may be provided with your video card that can be started in your AUTOEXEC.BAT. This type of program will also let you set the desired refresh rate. However, it's also possible that you'll need to reconfigure a jumper on your video card in order to select a higher screen refresh rate. Refer to the card's documentation for the necessary information.

The monitor image has too little contrast

Many newer monitors have a switch that allows you to change their input sensitivity from 0.75 to 1 volt. This is necessary when you're using an older or more exotic video card. The output voltage of such cards can deviate from the standard. By using this switch you can adjust your monitor to the card's output voltage.

The standard for normal video cards is 0.75 volts. However, if you're unhappy with the picture quality, try the other switch setting. Some high-quality monitors let you feed their VGA input signal through BNC connectors. If you're only driving one monitor with your video card, which is usually the case, you'll need to activate the 75 Ohm terminator through a switch. If more than one monitor is connected to a video card, the terminator only must be set at one of these monitors.

The settings menus of some monitors include an option that allows you to set the degree of color. It's possible to select two or more values. Don't hesitate to experiment with this option, since it can let you achieve better image contrast.

The screen has wavelike patterns

On smaller monitors at very high-resolution graphics modes, wavelike patterns can appear in areas of gray. This Moiré effect is caused by the monitor's shadow mask, which is unable to display this resolution. After all, it's impossible to display more pixels than are physically provided in the shadow mask. Select a lower resolution. This is also easier on your eyes with smaller monitors.

However, as always, a few exceptions exist (for example, under Windows). If you place a graphic into the background, small dot patterns can interfere with the dots of the shadow mask. This effect will disappear when you remove the graphic.

If your monitor has a settings menu with an option that controls the Moiré effect, you should take the following steps: Open the Windows 98 version of Paint. Select a color from the color palette that consists of differently colored pixels. Mixed hues of blue (the eleventh color in the top row of the default palette) are the best for this test. Use the Fill tool to fill the entire background with this color. Then select **View | View Bitmap**.

The wave pattern will be easily recognizable on this background. Now open your monitor's settings menu. Change the Moiré setting until the wave pattern disappears.

Setting the line and screen refresh rate in the BIOS

The computers of some manufacturers let you set the line and pixel frequency and the screen refresh rate using the CMOS setup. This can only occur if a video card is integrated into the system board and is activated.

Set the screen refresh rate in the CMOS setup under **Refresh Rate**. Specify the line and pixel frequency setting under **Monitor Type**. You'll find more information about these settings in your computer's documentation. You may damage your picture tube if you select a resolution or refresh rate that is higher than the maximum supported by your monitor. Before experimenting with the different modes, double-check your user's manual for the monitor. Verify the maximum resolution and refresh rate for the monitor.

Problems with SVGA modes and VESA modes

Most of the applications that run in graphics mode can display graphics at higher resolutions. These are the SVGA modes provide by Super VGA cards. This includes all resolutions above 640x480 at 16 colors. These applications usually have a setup option in which you can select the desired graphics mode.

See the graphics mode by accessing a video BIOS function, in which the number of the desired graphics mode is specified. This created several problems with the advent of SVGA cards, since manufacturers often used a different number for the same graphics mode. This doesn't support the idea of compatibility. If you had bad luck, and had a program that didn't know the number for a graphics mode of the video card installed in the system, you couldn't use that mode. Programmers then made it possible for the user to specify the graphics mode number manually in the program setup. Then a line such as

```
SVGA=65
```

or

```
SVgaMode=65
```

was stored in a configuration or initialization file. In this manner the appropriate number for a desired graphics mode (for the video card being used) was specified to the program. The correct number had to be taken from the documentation provided with the video card, and was different for most video cards.

179

The VESA standard was eventually developed. It defines which number corresponds to which SVGA mode. Since most applications today support the VESA standard, the problems described above are not met with VESA compatible video cards. The situation becomes difficult when you're using a video card that does not comply with the VESA standard and the application you're using is set up to work solely with VESA cards. In that case, you'll only be able to use standard VGA modes (at best 640x480 at 16 colors) in that application.

Use PC_INFO to check whether your card is VESA compatible and with which version of VESA it complies. This information is displayed in the window with the video card information.

Drivers have been developed for noncompatible cards that emulate VESA compatibility. They are available from BBSes, on-line systems or directly from the video card manufacturer. You may also want to check with your dealer; they may be able to get you the latest driver at no charge. The drivers must then be added to your CONFIG.SYS or AUTOEXEC.BAT.

Missing or defective video drivers

If you've purchased a video card that has just appeared on the market, it's possible the accompanying drivers are not bug-free or that drivers for certain programs aren't yet available. If so, you're at the mercy of your dealer. If they won't or can't get you the necessary drivers, contact the card's manufacturer or search various BBSes or on-line systems for the drivers. Also, don't hesitate to exchange the video card for another one that does come with the drivers you need.

Memory conflicts in the UMB

Each video card includes its BIOS that is superimposed onto the memory area starting at C000. However, the access to the BIOS through the bus and the video card is relatively slow. Therefore, the shadow RAM option is always activated in the CMOS Setup for the VGA BIOS. This copies the VGA BIOS into RAM at this address, increasing the access speed to the BIOS considerably.

Other cards, such as SCSI controllers or network adapters, also have their own BIOS. This BIOS uses memory areas above 640K of conventional memory. When installing these types of cards, make certain that none of these memory areas overlap. If this should happen nonetheless, your system will undoubtedly crash. Refer to Chapter 5 for more information on this topic.

Problems with S3 video cards

Video cards with S3 chipsets can cause problems on systems with four serial ports. Usually the S3 chipset uses the port address of COM4. There are almost always problems with devices connected to COM4. If possible, reconfigure the video card. If this isn't possible, you'll need to reconfigure COM4. Refer to Chapter 5 for information on how to do this.

Windows didn't recognize the video card

In this case Windows will install a default video driver during the installation. Unfortunately, this driver can't use the special functions supported by your card. You'll be able to install the video card's drivers from the video installation diskette using the Device Manager. Refer to Chapter 6.

Sound Card Problems

You probably won't realize the value of a sound until you no longer hear the wild explosions in an action game, Windows system sounds or even your music. In this section, you'll see that most sound problems can be solved with a small bit of know-how.

No sound

General problems

If you've just installed your sound card, first check whether the card is correctly seated in the expansion slot. Some expansion slots may require that you exert slightly more force to seat the board properly.

181

Check whether the speaker wires are connected properly to the output jacks on the sound card. Also, make certain the connector for the speakers are in the correct jack on the back of the sound card. The jacks for the input and output on the back of the board have the same diameters; it's easy to plug the connectors into the wrong jack.

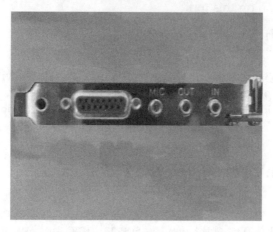

The connections on the back of the sound card.

Make certain the speakers are properly connected to their power supply (and are switched on). If you're using batteries instead of an AC adapter, make certain you're using fully charged batteries and they're inserted correctly (with the correct polarity). Replace old batteries.

Also, check the volume setting on your sound card; it's possible that it was turned too low. If you're using external speakers with a separate volume control, you'll also want to make certain that it's not turned down all the way. Some sound cards do not have a volume control, but use a software driver instead.

If the sound problems occur only with a certain application, check its options to see whether it actually supports sound or has its own sound level settings. Perhaps the sound board was never activated in the application settings.

Problems under Windows

If you still cannot hear any sound, despite all these checks, the sound card may not be installed correctly. This is not a rare problem. It's necessary for many sound cards to use jumpers to set the interrupts and DMA channels besides setting the port address.

If you find differences between the settings on the card and in Windows, the card will not be activated in the system when Windows is started. Select the **Start** menu and then **Settings | Control Panel**. Double-click the System icon and then double-click the "Sound, video, and game controllers" item in the device list. Scroll down to the desired sound card in the list. Click the (Properties...) button or double-click the icon corresponding to this driver.

The Properties dialog box shows the device status of the sound card.

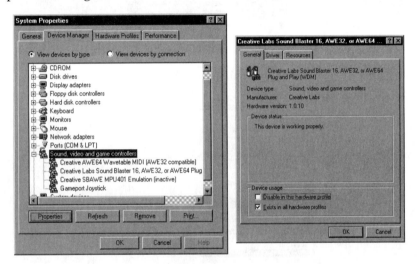

Device Manager with the sound card properties.

If the Device Manager shows the sound card is not active, take a closer look at the sound card settings under the "Resources" tab. You may need to make a new setting or change the existing one. Chapter 6 describes the operation of the Device Manager and setting resources.

Another possible cause for the problem is a resource conflict between the sound card and another system component. This would occur through overlapping port addresses, interrupts or DMA channels. In this case, one of the two conflicting components will not be activated when the system is started. Chapter 6 describes ways of resolving these types of conflicts using the Device Manager.

It's also possible the sound card driver isn't activated. Change this option by clicking the Multimedia icon in the Control Panel. Select the "Devices" tab.

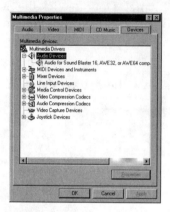

Check whether the sound card driver is activated by selecting the "Advanced" tab.

This shows the settings for the audio devices and where you can activate the audio driver.

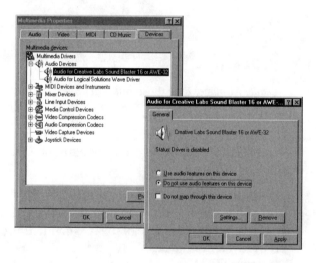

Here you can activate the audio driver in the Control Panel.

Problems in MS-DOS mode

First, check whether the program you're using even supports a sound card. If so, you should see whether the parameters selected in the program correspond to those of your sound card (same port address, interrupt and DMA). If you can't find your sound card in the list of supported types, you may be able to select another card type instead, with which your card is compatible. Most cards are compatible with either the SoundBlaster standard or the AdLib standard.

The port address, interrupt and DMA channel are set on most cards using jumpers. The parameters in the sound card driver must correspond with these jumper settings, otherwise the driver can't address the card. If you don't know the settings on your card, check the Windows Device Manager. Once you know the settings, you can configure the sound card driver correctly.

It's necessary with some sound cards (such as the ProAudio series by MediaVision) to activate the card in the system in MS-DOS mode using the device driver. The driver must be entered in the CONFIG.SYS using the DEVICE command. You'll find the necessary information in the user's manual for the sound card.

Please note that some sound cards are only SoundBlaster compatible through an additional driver (for example, the SB_ON.COM driver for the ProAudio Spectrum+). We recommend adding such drivers to your AUTOEXEC.BAT so the card is always SoundBlaster compatible.

If you're using a SoundBlaster or a SoundBlaster compatible card, use PC_INFO to check whether the SOUND variable is set. If you haven't installed PC_INFO on your system as an icon, you can start it from the desktop or Windows Explorer. Once PC_INFO has obtained the system configuration, you'll see the Configuration Overview. There you should select Operating System and click DOS-Variables in the next window. PC_INFO now shows all the variables defined for DOS, so you can see whether the SOUND variable has been set.

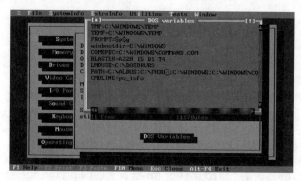

PC_INFO allows you to view the variables defined for DOS.

The SOUND variable allows applications to determine in which directory the sound card driver and the sound tools are located. It does this by simply checking the variable. If the variable is present, it's still possible that an incorrect directory has been specified. The Sound variable is set, or rather changed, in the AUTOEXEC.BAT. The following is the entry in the AUTOEXEC.BAT:

```
SET SOUND=C:\SBPRO
```

The "C:\SBPRO" in this line indicates the drive letter and path under which the sound card driver can be found. We've included it here only as an example, so you must enter the drive letter and path corresponding to your system. After adding the sound variable and then rebooting your computer, use PC_INFO to check whether the variable is being displayed correctly. If it's only displayed partially, or not at all, there is an error in the Environment. You'll find more on this topic in the information "Cruddy sound with some MS-DOS games" later in this section.

Another possibility is the BLASTER variable is missing. This variable is also needed for sound output with SoundBlaster or SoundBlaster compatible cards. However, since this problem really only occurs with games, refer to the information "Cruddy sound with some MS-DOS games" later in this section.

The PC crashes when sound is played

If you're using a SoundBlaster 16, you may experience problems with your 16-bit DMA transfers on certain system boards. If your computer and your sound card frequently refuse to work together, deactivate the 16-bit DMA channel and switch to a free 8-bit DMA channel.

186

The following explains what else you must take care of after this type of DMA channel switch. First, you'll need to change the DMA setting in the Device Manager. The BLASTER variable will also have to be set accordingly in your AUTOEXEC.BAT if it's needed in DOS mode.

You must restart Windows for these changes to take effect. Also, don't forget to reconfigure your MS-DOS games that require the DMA channel and which don't check the BLASTER variable.

Some sound boards, such as Turtle Beach Multisound, also require a memory window in the UMB. This means that all applications must remain out of this area. Like with the other resources of your sound card, reserve the memory area using the Device Manager. Refer to Chapter 6 for more information on this topic.

If, for some reason, you're still using Windows 3.1 drivers or can't reserve this memory area in the Device Manager, you can also do so in your SYSTEM.INI. To do this, you'll have to add the EMMEXCLUDE command to the [386Enh] segment, using the following command syntax:

```
EMMEXCLUDE=D000-D7FF
```

You'll also need to do the same for MS-DOS mode. This is also done in your CONFIG.SYS. Use an additional parameter with the entry for the EMM386.EXE memory manager:

```
X=D000-D7FF
```

The memory ranges specified here only apply for the default value of the Turtle Beach card. If your sound card has the same problem, check your card's documentation for the size and address of the required memory window.

Another frequent problem is an interrupt, DMA or port-address conflict with another system component. Refer to Chapters 5 and 6 if you suspect that you're experiencing one of these problems. These chapters describe information on detecting and fixing a resource conflict.

There is noise during printing

This problem is the result of an interrupt conflict that is caused by the interrupt setting on your sound card. Many sound cards are preset at the factory to interrupt 5 or 7. Unfortunately, the interrupts are usually used by the first (IRQ7) and second (IRQ5) parallel ports. To fix this problem, you'll need to change the interrupt used by your sound board. However, this can lead to sound problems with some older games, since these only accept interrupt 5 for the SoundBlaster card. If you change the sound card's interrupt, make certain to also change the setting in the Device Manager correspondingly. The same applies for any MS-DOS sound card drivers that may be needed, as well as DOS applications and games that support the sound card. If you're using the BLASTER variable, you'll also need to set it accordingly.

Chirping sounds when the screen is constructed or the hard drive is accessed

Other system components, such as the video card or the hard drive controller, are possible sources of interference. These system components, through the fast voltage fluctuations on their data, act like miniature transmitters. The sound card picks these up and makes them audible as chirping or similar sounds. The way to reduce this problem is to put as much distance between the culprit "transmitters" and your sound board. Another possible source of interference is power supply that is producing unclean voltages.

Cruddy sound with some MS-DOS games

Many reasons are possible for why you hear no sound or only partial sound with several games. The cause of the problem will vary depending on the type of sound card you're using.

Some games only support AdLib or SoundBlaster sound cards. Since some cards (such as the ProAudio Spectrum+ with the driver SB_ON.COM) only become SoundBlaster compatible with a driver, it's necessary to load the driver before the game is started. This is true even if the game is run under Windows. You should include the driver in your AUTOEXEC.BAT so it's always available.

The reason you don't hear any sound (and if you're using a SoundBlaster or a SoundBlaster compatible card) with older games (and some newer ones, like NHL Hockey 98) may be the BLASTER variable hasn't been set or is set incorrectly. This variable is needed to pass the sound card parameters to the program you're trying to run.

You can easily determine whether this variable is set by typing SET and pressing `Enter` at the DOS prompt. The operating system will display a list of all defined environment variables. You can also check the environment variables using PC_INFO. Refer to the "Problems in MS-DOS mode" information earlier in this section for information on how to do this. If the BLASTER variable is set, you should see the following item in the list:

```
BLASTER=A220 I7 D1 P300 T1
```

The "A220 I7 D1 P300 T1" in this line are the settings for the sound card. The application reads these settings. These parameters have the following meanings:

Parameter	Description	Value used in our example
A220	Port address used	Address 220h
I7	Interrupt used	IRQ 7
D1	DMA channel used	DMA 1
P300	Port address used for the MIDI port	Address 300h
T1	SoundBlaster version number (do not change!)	1

The numbers following the letters are only used as examples. Your values must correspond to the settings on your sound board. Please note the value "p," for the MIDI port, is optional; not all sound cards support this function.

SoundBlaster version code	Version number
T1	SoundBlaster 1.0 and 1.5
T2	SoundBlaster Pro
T3	SoundBlaster 2.0
T4	SoundBlaster 4
T5	SoundBlaster Pro MCV (Microchannel)
T6	SoundBlaster 16 ASP

If the BLASTER variable is not yet set in your system, you can set it now using this command:

```
SET BLASTER=Ax Ix Dx Tx
```

You'll need to replace each of the letters "x" with the appropriate parameters. However, the disadvantage of this method is that you'll need to enter the command each time you boot your system. Therefore, add the command to your AUTOEXEC.BAT so the variable is set automatically when you boot your system.

If your AUTOEXEC.BAT already contains this command, but the variable is still not set, it's probably because your environment area is too small, and the variable cannot be stored in the environment area. To test this, use PC_INFO. Select **Configuration Overview Operating System**. PC_INFO displays the total size of the current environment memory and the remaining amount of free environment memory.

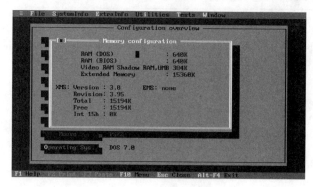

Use PC_INFO to check the amount of available environment memory.

If very little or no environment memory remains, increase the size of the environment range. Add a SHELL statement to your CONFIG.SYS (you can also do this using PC_INFO). The statement looks like this:

```
SHELL=C:\WINDOWS\COMMAND\COMMAND.COM C:\WINDOWS\COMMAND /P /E:512
```

The parameter "/E:" specifies the size of your environment area. The number to the right determines the area's size in bytes. The default environment size is 256 bytes, but can vary between 160 and 32,768 bytes. Optimal values are between 512 and 1,024 bytes. Make certain to include all the other parameters. Otherwise, DOS won't be able to function properly.

If your CONFIG.SYS already contains a SHELL statement, simply increase the specified value to increase the size of your environment area.

Don't delete any parameters we haven't mentioned that may be in your SHELL statement. Otherwise, you're more than likely to run into problems at your next bootup.

If your sound card is only playing normal audio signals and no digital effects, check your card's DMA settings. Older games tend to use only DMA channel 1. If your sound board is set to a different DMA channel, try changing it to DMA channel 1.

Use the Device Manager to make certain that this channel is not being used by another expansion card. This helps avoid DMA conflicts. Chapter 5 describes how to display the system resources (including the DMA channels). If the channel is already being used by another expansion card, try to reconfigure that card so that channel 1 becomes available for your sound card. In any event, you'll need to notify Windows of the change (see Chapter 6).

Many games have an insatiable hunger for conventional memory. If the operating system doesn't provide the game with enough conventional memory when the application is opened, the game may only partly support the sound card, if at all. Some games warn you at startup that your system doesn't have enough available conventional memory. You should be able to find more information on the amount of memory required by the game in its documentation or a README file in its directory.

The audio CDs won't play

This applies only if you've connected the audio-output of your CD-ROM drive to the sound board through a special audio cable. For other problems with the playback of audio CDs, see the "Smooth CD-ROM Operation" section in this chapter.

Check whether the driver for the sound card and the CD-ROM driver are configured correctly or have even been loaded. Use the Device Manager to check this by selecting the appropriate component by clicking it in the hardware tree. Then click [Properties...] to display the status of the device.

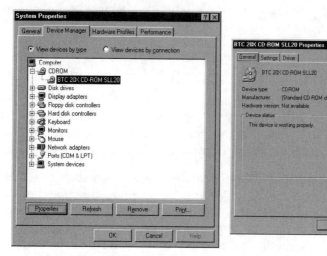

The device manager shows the current status of the CD-ROM controller.

If the Device Manager indicates a problem in the component's device status, see Chapter 6 for instructions on solving the problem.

Make certain the audio connector cable between the sound card and the CD-ROM driver is connected securely to both sockets. Also check whether you're using the correct audio cable. Unfortunately, because no standard exists for this cable, sound cards and CD-ROM drives use different sockets. So, it's possible the audio cable that was shipped with your CD-ROM driver won't fit into the appropriate socket on the sound card or that its pin-pattern doesn't match.

Example of a socket for the audio cable (circled in this illustration).

If you encounter this problem, find a cable that fits both connectors. If you have a wiring talent, locate a connector to replace the one that doesn't fit and solder it in its place. Select from two connector cable types (since no industry standard exists):

* Three-conductor cable
  uses a common ground for the two channels

* Four-conductor cable
  Uses two separate ground wires for the left and right channels.

The user's manual should list the connector layout for your sound card and your CD-ROM. Look under the layout for the LINE IN and LINE OUT connectors. If you can't find the necessary information, contact the sound card or CD-ROM drive manufacturer through their technical support lines. If this still doesn't help, try experimenting on your own.

Because of the lack of a standard, the fact that a cable fits physically doesn't mean that it will function correctly. Manufacturers use different layouts even for connectors that look the same (see the following table):

Pin number	CD-In SoundBlaster	Audio Out (MPC standard)	Audio Out Atapi	Audio Out Mitsumi FX001D
1	ground	left channel	right channel	right channel
2	left channel	ground	ground	ground
3	ground	ground	ground	left channel
4	right channel	right channel	left channel	ground

The following drives comply with the MPC standard:

* NEC-Multispin 4Xi
* Pioneer DR-U104X
* Plextor 4Plex PX-43 CD
* Chinon CDS 525S.

The following drives use an ATAPI audio:

* Sony CDU55E
* Toshiba XM 5302
* Mitsumi FX-300
* Mitsumi FX-400
* Mitsumi FX001DE.

Modify your audio cable according to the connector layout shown in the table. If your drive is not listed or if you aren't using a SoundBlaster card, refer to your user's manual. Also, call the technical support line of the sound card or CD-ROM drive manufacturer if your drive is not listed.

We'll use the Mitsumi FX001D and a SoundBlaster card as an example. The pin layout is reversed 180° between the two devices. However, since the connectors can only be plugged in one way, you can't simply turn the connector at one end around. Instead, pull the individual pins out of the connector and reinsert them in the correct pattern. Before you can pull the pins out of the housing, you have to carefully bend up a plastic retainer that holds a metal tab on the pin in place. Then you'll be able to pull the pin out of the housing.

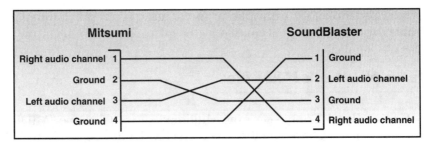

The pin layout of an audio cable.

Unable to record sound

It's possible that your software has some incorrect settings. First, check whether the recording levels are too low. If so, increase the settings.

Check the settings in the software that you're using to make certain the input selector is set to the device from which you wish to record.

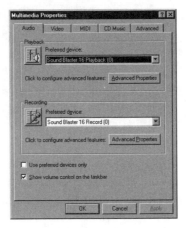

Setting the recording levels under Windows.

If you're trying to record through a microphone, make certain that it's connected correctly. The microphone might have an on/off switch. Check this switch setting. Not every microphone complies with the requirements of the sound card's microphone input. If the impedance of the microphone you're using is too small, the sound card won't be able to process the signal emitted by the microphone and thus won't be able to record anything usable.

Unable to play back MIDI files

Open the Control Panel. Double-click the Multimedia icon. Click the "MIDI devices and instruments" item. Check whether the correct MIDI device is selected. Besides supporting the internal playback through the built-in OPL synthesizer, most sound cards let you connect an external MIDI device.

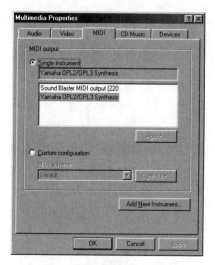

Selecting the desired MIDI device.

Windows also lets you turn off multimedia functions that you don't need. Double-click the Multimedia icon in the Control Panel to see whether the MIDI functions are active. Select the "Advanced" tab to look at the different settings.

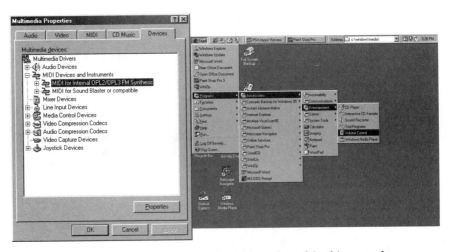

The MIDI playback on the sound card is activated in this example.

The Wavetable module isn't recognized

When Windows is installed, a Wavetable card (such as a WaveBlaster on the SoundBlaster 16) on the installed sound board won't automatically be selected as the default MIDI output device. Windows instead chooses the sound card's FM chip. Double-click the Multimedia icon in the Control Panel. Click the "MIDI" tab and select "Single instrument."

Then enable "MIDI for External MIDI Port." A Wavetable card on your sound board is treated the same way as an external MIDI instrument.

All WAV files are recorded with the incorrect sound quality

Windows provides several different recording qualities to match the particular application. Windows uses three different levels by default:

* CD-ROM Quality (44.1 kHz)

* Radio Quality (22.05 kHz)

* Telephone Quality (11 kHz)

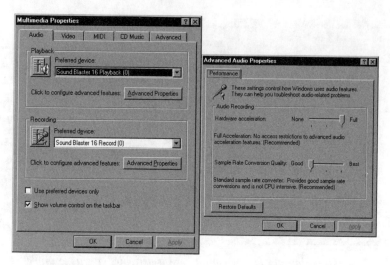

You can set the recording quality in the Control Panel.

Select the desired recording quality by double-clicking the Multimedia icon in the Control Panel. Select the "Audio" tab. The quality is set under "Preferred device:." Click the [Advanced] button to switch between mono and stereo for the selected data format.

Sound is inaudible or not loud enough

Like Windows 95, Windows 98 includes built-in volume control. Set the volume control by selecting **Start** | **Programs** | **Accessories** | **Multimedia** | **Volume Control**.

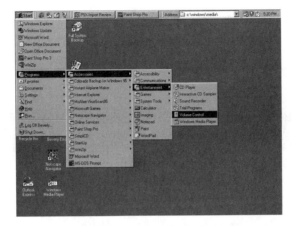

Accessing the volume control through the Start menu.

The Volume Control dialog box looks like a large mixing board. This "board" lets you set the volume for all your sound card's audio options.

Activating the volume control in your Taskbar.

A loudspeaker will appear next to the clock in your Taskbar. Click the loudspeaker to access the volume control. Double-click the loudspeaker to open the Volume Control dialog box (the mixing board).

Worthless digital sound effects

If your digital system sounds (audio schemes), for example, are nothing more than crackling sounds, or if other functions such as the playback of audio data isn't working right, you may be experiencing a DMA channel conflict. Read Chapter 5 on how to eliminate the resource conflict.

Sound problems with DOS applications

DOS games running under Windows usually don't need to access the DOS drivers they may otherwise need for the sound card (Windows 98 provides its own drivers).

However, if the application must be run in MS-DOS mode (in other words, if you need to exit Windows and the program is then started in MS-DOS mode), you'll need to make certain that any necessary drivers are included in your CONFIG.SYS or AUTOEXEC.BAT file. On the other hand, if the game uses its own MS-DOS configuration, it is executed through a PIF (program information file). If the PIF exists, simply click it with the right mouse button either on the Desktop or from Windows Explorer.

If the application doesn't have a PIF, select the program with your right mouse button. Select **Properties** from the pop-up menu. Select the "Program" tab in the Properties window. Click the (Advanced...) button. To create an MS-DOS configuration for the program, select "Specify a new MS-DOS configuration."

Edit the two startup files using the usual command syntax for CONFIG.SYS and AUTOEXEC.BAT. Once you've made all the necessary edits, click (OK) to close the window.

If the program did not yet have its own PIF, Windows will automatically give it the name of the program's startup file, using the .PIF file name extension.

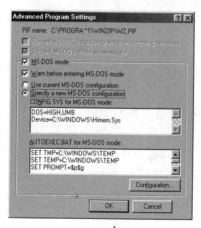

The necessary sound drivers for a Mediavision card were added in the Advanced settings.

Please be sure to also set the BLASTER variable, if it's used by your application. You'll find more on this topic in the information "Cruddy sound with some MS-DOS games" earlier in this section.

Windows doesn't provide the right sound card driver

The Hardware Wizard usually will recognize your sound card during the installation and automatically install the necessary drivers. However, if Windows doesn't recognize your card, you'll need to install the sound card driver manually.

If your sound card didn't come with a Windows 98 driver, or if you got the sound card before Windows 98 was released, you'll need to use an older driver. Refer to Chapter 6 for detailed information on how to install such a driver.

However, the preferred option is to obtain a Windows 98 driver for the card. Such a driver should be available by now. Check with your dealer or contact the manufacturer of your sound card. Perhaps you'll also be able to find the driver at a Web site.

Smooth CD-ROM Operation

Most new computers are now sold with a CD-ROM drive installed. Since many applications, and even operating systems, are shipped on CD-ROMs, error-free transfer of data from your CD-ROM drive to the PC is essential. This section provides tips and information to help you keep the CD-ROM drive working perfectly.

Types of CD-ROM interfaces

SCSI port

The SCSI port is a hardware-independent, 50-conductor port, so that SCSI devices can be connected to different computer platforms, such as a PC or a Macintosh. Unlike AT bus interfaces, the SCSI port is standardized across the industry. In addition to CD-ROM drives, you can attach other system devices such as scanners, tape drives or printers to the SCSI port. A special SCSI host adapter is needed to connect these devices to your computer. This adapter can accommodate up to seven SCSI devices. Keep in mind that although some sound boards include a SCSI port, few have the full SCSI command set so only the CD-ROM can be connected to this port.

ATAPI port or IDE

ATAPI (AT Attachment Packet Interface) drives are part of the newer generation of drives. These drives are connected to your hard drive controller through an IDE bus. Their name comes from an expansion of the IDE port within the command structure between the device and the driver.

Like the SCSI, ATAPI is an industry standard that is supported by all manufacturers. The connection consists of a 40-conductor cable, which makes it easy to mistake these for AT-bus drives. One of their advantages over AT-bus drives is they do not require an additional controller and therefore do not claim a port address and don't require any system resources in the form of interrupts or DMA channels.

An ATAPI drive is connected to the IDE bus similar to an IDE hard drive. It's configured in the same way as a master or slave drive. IDE controllers can only accommodate two devices, in this case a hard drive and a CD-ROM drive. Your system is already at capacity if it contains another hard drive and so cannot accommodate a CD-ROM drive. However, you can avoid this disadvantage by using an EIDE controller, a secondary IDE controller or a special controller card for the CD-ROM drive (which, however will cost you another ISA slot and an interrupt).

The drive is not recognized

To make things more clear, we've broken this problem down into several points. The first is Windows and MS-DOS mode problems. The second concerns problems specific to the interface used.

General problems

Check whether the cables are connected correctly to both your CD-ROM drive and the appropriate controller. Also check whether the cable is connected to the CD-ROM drive and the controller properly. Pin 1 of the data cable (its wire will be a specific color) must be connected to pin 1 of the appropriate sockets on both the CD-ROM drive and the controller board. It's possible that you won't find anything that identifies pin 1 on your controller or drive. Refer to the user's manual to determine which is pin 1.

This is also a good time to make certain the CD-ROM drive's power supply cable is connected to its socket securely. You may also need to check that the IDE interface is enabled in the BIOS.

If you're using a separate controller card to connect your CD-ROM drive, it's possible that this card isn't fully inserted in its expansion slot. Remove the card and carefully reinsert it until it is fully seated. If you're using an external CD-ROM drive, it's possible the drive is switched off and is therefore not being supplied with power. This would prevent the driver from recognizing the CD-ROM drive.

Windows problems

If you cannot access the CD-ROM drive under Windows, make certain the driver for the CD-ROM drive was installed correctly. Check this in the Device Manager. The Device Manager provides detailed information on the status of your CD-ROM drive. See Chapter 6 for more information on the Device Manager.

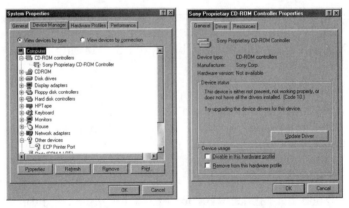

The Device Manager is alerting you to an incorrectly installed CD-ROM drive.

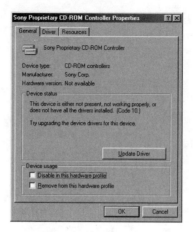

The Device Manager has detected an address conflict.

Another possibility is that you're experiencing a resource conflict with another system device. One of the affected devices will not be supported if such a conflict exists. Refer to Chapter 5 for information on how to detect and fix hardware conflicts using the Device Manager.

If you're using an old MS-DOS device driver for your CD-ROM drive because you can't use a corrected Windows driver, it's also possible the settings in your CONFIG.SYS and AUTOEXEC.BAT are incorrect. Check this by starting your PC directly in MS-DOS mode.

If you are then still unable to access the CD-ROM drive, it's safe to assume the problem is in the settings in these two startup files. Refer to the information in "Problems in MS-DOS mode" in the "Sound Card Problems" section for detailed information on this problem.

CD-ROM drive problems in MS-DOS mode

You've just installed the MS-DOS device driver for your CD-ROM drive and are unable to access the drive. If you now also automatically load a menu program in your AUTOEXEC.BAT, you may experience an installation error. If the installation program for your CD-ROM drive adds the driver MSCDEX.EXE at the end of your AUTOEXEC.BAT, *i.e.*, after the call for the menu program, MSCDEX.EXE will only be executed after the application that was started from the menu has been closed again. You can solve this problem quite easily by making sure the driver (MSCDEX.EXE) is loaded before the menu program.

Make certain the entry for the CD-ROM device driver is in your CONFIG.SYS. Verify that all its parameters are correct. You'll find the correct parameter syntax in the user's manual for your drive. If the drive works under Windows, use the Device Manager to look at the system resources reserved by the drive (see Chapter 6). This information lets you specify all necessary parameters correctly or add any missing parameters. You can also use the information from the Device Manager and perform an entirely new installation of your CD-ROM drive using the DOS installation program.

It's also possible that MSCDEX is not loaded when the MS-DOS mode is entered. When Windows 98 is installed, it will "REM out" the MSCDEX statement, if there is one, since Windows has its own driver and doesn't need this one. This modification may look like the following lines:

```
REM C:\BIN\MSCDEX /D:MSCD001 /M:10
REM - BY WINDOWS 98 NETWORK
```

For the CD-ROM drive to function under MS-DOS, you'll need to remove the letters REM in this statement. Use the correct path so the most up-to-date version of MSCDEX (included with Windows 98) is loaded. Using the above example, the corrected statement would look like this:

```
C:\WINDOWS\COMMAND\MSCDEX /D:MSCD001 /M:10
```

Also check the LASTDRIVE statement in your CONFIG.SYS. It's possible that you'll need to enter a higher drive letter. This statement specifies the last drive that DOS can use in your system. The default value is "E," in case you can't find the statement. When MSCDEX is loaded, DOS assigns the first available drive letter to the CD-ROM drive. Using the statement L:[drive letter], you can assign a specific driver letter to the CD-ROM drive. If the LASTDRIVE statement specifies a drive letter that is too low, you won't be able to access the CD-ROM drive. In that case, you'll get the following message when MSCDEX is loaded:

> Not enough drive letters available

However, we do not recommend that you simply enter an unnecessarily high drive letter, such as N or Z, since each unneeded drive letter uses memory.

When you load MSCDEX.EXE, the following error message appears:

> Device driver not found 'MSCD000' No valid CD-ROM device driver selected

The driver identifications that are specified with the "/D" parameter for the CD-ROM device driver (in the CONFIG.SYS) and for MSCDEX are different, as in the following example. Here is the device driver statement for the CONFIG.SYS:

```
DEVICE=DEV\MTMCDAE.SYS /D:MSCD001 /P:310 /M:20 /T:5 /I:11
```

and here is the MSCDEX statement in the AUTOEXEC.BAT:

```
LH C:\WINDOWS\COMMAND\MSCDEX /M:20 /D:MSCD000
```

Since you can use more than one CD-ROM drive with one PC, MSCDEX must use the correct name for the CD-ROM drive. Make certain that both names are the same and reboot your system. Another possible cause for this error message is the CD-ROM driver statement is missing from your CONFIG.SYS. This can easily happen under Windows 98 when you start the MS-DOS mode from Windows. Since Windows usually doesn't need the driver in the CONFIG.SYS, it's possible the statement was deleted. If so, add the statement to your CONFIG.SYS or reinstall the driver.

Although the CD-ROM device driver is being loaded properly, DOS crashes when MSCDEX.EXE is loaded and the following error message appears:

> Incorrect DOS Version

The driver diskette with some CD-ROM drives contains an older version of MSCDEX.EXE instead of the most recent version. If this older version is loaded, DOS recognizes that it's an older version of MSCDEX.EXE and displays the error message. Since the drivers are usually copied to their own directory when the CD-ROM drive is installed, simply change the path for MSCDE.EXE in your AUTOEXEC.BAT to C:\WINDOWS\COMMAND\MSCDEX.EXE. Do not change the succeeding parameters. Reboot your system; the error message should no longer appear.

AT-bus drives

Make certain the jumper settings on your controller card correspond to the parameters on the CD-ROM driver you're using. The port address must be the same on both. If you're using the drive in IRQ/DMA mode, you'll also need to check the settings for the DMA channel and the interrupt.

If you're using a sound card as the controller, you should also see whether the sound card even supports the CD-ROM drive you are using. Since these interfaces are manufacturer-specific, you won't be able to connect a Panasonic (Matsushita) drive to a Mitsumi interface, for example, even if both have 40-conductor sockets. If the sound card doesn't support your CD-ROM drive, you'll either need to obtain an appropriate controller or try to exchange the CD-ROM drive for one that is compatible with the controller on your sound board.

Although the AT-bus interface on your sound card allows you to set the DMA and the interrupt, you can't necessarily use the IRQ/DMA driver. Many sound cards (such as the Shuttle Sound System 48) only support the IRQ mode when used with the Mitsumi FX001D; in other words, you can't use them with the DMA mode. To block out the DMA mode, enter the parameter "/S" instead of the DMA channel with the installation of the MTMCDAE.SYS driver (in the case of the Mitsumi drive) in MS-DOS mode. This will put the CD-ROM drive into IRQ mode. If this also doesn't work, you'll have to resort to software polling.

Problems can arise with some sound boards with the internal CD-ROM interface when using a Mitsumi FX001D CD-ROM drive. These cards (such as the Orchid SoundWave 32 or the Terratec Sound System Maestro 32) only support software polling, since they don't offer any way of setting a DMA channel or an interrupt. If you don't have a special Windows 98 driver, you'll be forced to use the MS-DOS device driver MTMCDAS.SYS in your CONFIG.SYS.

If the sound card you're using supports CD-ROM drives by different manufacturers, for example Mitsumi or Matsushita, it will have a different socket for each of the different drive types. Perhaps you've connected the data cable to the wrong socket.

SCSI CD-ROM drives

Check whether you've specified the same ID number twice. If so, the host adapter usually recognizes neither device. Make certain the SCSI terminators are seated correctly. Only the first and last devices in a SCSI chain can have a terminator. Remove the terminators if any of the other SCSI devices have one. Make certain power is switched on for an external SCSI drive.

You'll read more information on problems with SCSI systems in the "SCSI Problems" section later in this chapter.

ATAPI IDE CD-ROM drives

The configuration jumper for the master/slave mode may be set incorrectly. Normally the CD-ROM drive is connected to the IDE bus next to a hard drive. The hard drive in such a situation must be configured as the master and the CD-ROM drive as the slave.

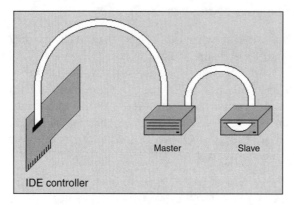

Connecting an ATAPI drive to an IDE-bus.

Unlike IDE controllers, to which you can only connect two IDE devices, an EIDE controller consists of a primary and a secondary adapter. Each of these can accommodate two (E)IDE devices. As with IDE controllers, these devices need to be configured as master or slave devices. The following table shows the device combinations possible with an EIDE controller:

Primary adapter		Secondary adapter	
Master	Slave	Master	Slave
HD	CD-ROM	-	-
HD	-	CD-ROM	-
HD	HD	CD-ROM	-
HD	HD	HD	CD-ROM

This example represents one possible option, with one ATAPI drive, to illustrate what kind of combinations are possible. You can also connect more than one ATAPI CD-ROM drive by using the available connections and configuring them as master or slave drives, as appropriate.

Follow these points to ensure perfect operation:

* ✳ Configure only one drive per adapter as the master; the other must be configured as the slave.

* ✳ All hard drives must precede the CD-ROM drive(s) in your system.

* ✳ Note that a secondary adapter or an EIDE controller uses interrupt 15 and the port address 170h. These settings cannot normally be changed.

* ✳ Additional controller cards, offered especially for ATAPI CD-ROM drives by the drive manufactures, also use interrupt 15. If this setting cannot be changed, you'll probably encounter an interrupt conflict. In that case you'll either need to reconfigure the other card, or if that's not possible either, refrain from using the additional controller card.

> **TIP** Because of the EIDE interface architecture, the adapter's data transfer rate is limited by that of the slowest device connected to the adapter. Therefore, a fast hard drive can be slowed by a slower ATAPI drive. To avoid this potential performance decrease, connect the CD-ROM drive to the secondary adapter. Keep the hard drive on the primary adapter.

The device driver of your CD-ROM drive recognizes the ATAPI drive on both adapters. Refer to the documentation of your CD-ROM drive for the correct driver configuration, or otherwise to an info file on the driver diskette.

If you have problems accessing your 32-bit hard drive under Windows after installing a CD-ROM drive together with an MS-DOS device driver, connect the CD-ROM drive to the secondary IDE adapter (if you have one). If this doesn't solve the problem or if you're not able to do this, try to get the current Windows 98 driver through the CD-ROM drive manufacturer or a Web site. If an appropriate Windows 98 driver is not available, look for an up-to-date MS-DOS driver. All current CD-ROM drivers should permit 32-bit hard drive access by now.

4 *Windows 98 Emergency First Aid*

Common CD-ROM problems

The Hardware Wizard doesn't recognize the CD-ROM drive automatically

Some CD-ROM drives are sold with special controller cards or have controller cards that can be purchased as an option. However, Windows 98's hardware recognition will only recognize the common, manufacturer-specific controllers of AT-bus drives (such as Mitsumi, Panasonic or Sony).

Windows won't necessarily recognize special adapters (also called "secondary IDE controllers") that are plugged into the ISA bus, for example, to permit the use of an ATAPI drive with the IDE hard drives already installed. Even SCSI devices are sometimes not recognized by Windows. Some manual work is necessary to use these devices under Windows 98. Chapter 6 tells how to register this hardware manually under Windows.

If more than one device is connected to a controller, note that all these devices must be supported by Windows 98 through a protected mode driver. If one of these devices is not supported by Windows 98, you will need to add MS-DOS drivers to your CONFIG.SYS for all the other devices as well. Contact your computer dealer or the device manufacturer for an up-to-date Windows 98 driver.

No usable Windows 98 driver

You own an exotic CD-ROM drive and cannot find an appropriate Windows 98 driver in either Windows or your driver collection. This is not a serious problem. All you need do is add the old MS-DOS device driver to your CONFIG.SYS. The same rules apply as in MS-DOS mode: Make certain the MSCDEX.EXE statement is also in your AUTOEXEC.BAT.

Use the most current version of MSCDEX that is included with Windows 98. Once you've added these statements to your two startup files and rebooted your PC, Windows 98 will automatically tie the CD-ROM drive into your system. Even if this allows you to use your CD-ROM drive under Windows, we recommend that you get a correct, Windows 98 driver soon. Contact your computer dealer or the device manufacturer. You may also be able to locate the driver on a BBS or on-line service if you have a modem.

The CD-ROM is not recognized

Did you insert the CD-ROM correctly? The printed side should face up. It's also possible the CD-ROM is not a Windows format, but another format, such as Macintosh. Look at the label on the CD-ROM to determine whether it's the Windows format. System information is sometimes listed on the CD-ROM.

Read any printed instructions that came with the CD-ROM. It's possible that it's not a computer CD-ROM, but is instead a CD-I, audio CD or even a Photo CD. Photo CD-ROMs, however, can usually be recognized by the symbol on the right.

Other types of CD-ROMs can usually be identified by their labels or descriptions.

If you just moved the CD-ROM drive from a cool location to a warmer one, it's possible that moisture has condensed on the lens. If so, the laser-beam may be unable to read the CD. Remove the CD-ROM from the drive and wait for the drive to warm up and the moisture to evaporate (may take up to an hour). You can leave the drive switched on during this time; the heat it produces will aid the drying process.

CD-ROM drive access is too slow

Check whether the CD-ROM is dirty or scratched. Fingerprints and dust can accumulate fast on a CD-ROM. Each sector on such a CD-ROM must be read several times, which slows the drive. Refer to the information "Dirty and scratched CD-ROMs" in the next section for information on cleaning and even restoring damaged CD-ROMs.

The lens of the CD-ROM drive can also collect dust and dirt. This results in read-errors and forces the drive to read sectors several times. If you're experiencing read-errors with several CD-ROMs, it may be time to clean the drive. Refer to the information "When the lens is dirty" in the next section to see how to clean the drives optics.

Windows uses several procedures to optimize the CD-ROM drive access. To specify the optimization for your drive type (such as single or double-speed drive) as well as the cache size, double-click the System icon in the Control Panel. Click the "Performance" tab. Click the File System... button. In the new dialog box, select the "CD-ROM" tab. Specify the desired settings in this dialog box.

Windows 98 Emergency First Aid

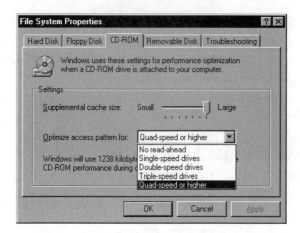

Tabbed page for optimizing your CD-ROM drive.

If you have problems while only in MS-DOS mode, follow these steps:

Check whether the size for the memory buffer for the CD-ROM driver is large enough or if it has been set up at all. You'll find this setting in your CONFIG.SYS under the parameters of the CD-ROM driver:

```
DEVICE=C:\DEV\MTMCDAE.SYS /D:MSCD001 /P:310 /M:20 /T:5 /I:11
```

This example uses the driver for the Mitsumi FX001D drive. The /M parameter specifies the size of the buffer. Depending on the manufacturer, this entry may use a different syntax (you'll find more information in the documentation with your CD-ROM drive). If the number is too low, simply change it to the appropriate value.

Use SmartDrive to increase the access speed of the CD-ROM in MS-DOS mode. Add SmartDrive to your AUTOEXEC.BAT using a command similar to the following:

```
C:\WINDOWS\SMARTDRV
```

For SmartDrive to support your CD-ROM drive, the MSCDEX driver must be loaded before the SmartDrive statement is executed. If you have problems with SmartDrive with your CD-ROM drive, refer to the information "SmartDrive won't support the CD-ROM drive in MS-DOS mode" later in this section.

It's possible the CD-ROM driver doesn't support the maximum drive speed or that you're only using a single-speed driver. This is sometimes true with CD-ROM drive packages at bargain prices. If you're not sure, look at the file creation date of the driver. It's possible that you're using a driver that is too old. Call the manufacturer's technical support line. Ask them for the version number of the most recent driver. The version number of the driver is usually displayed when the CD-ROM device driver is loaded during bootup. It's also found on the driver diskette. The manufacturer will be able to tell you how current your driver is and how to get the most recent version, if necessary.

The system crashes when the CD-ROM drive is used

If you use a PCI board with plugged-in PCI expansion , you may encounter interrupt problems with the ISA controller of your CD-ROM drive. The PCI slots are assigned interrupt number 10 by default. Some CD-ROM adapter cards (such as the Mitsumi FX001) also are set to interrupt 10. Avoid this problem by selecting a different interrupt in your PCI setup or on the CD-ROM adapter card. If the problems persist, switch the "DMA Line Buffer Mode" and "ISA Master Buffer Mode" settings in your PCI board chip setup from Enhanced to Standard.

You probably have an interrupt or DMA conflict with another system component. Since such a problem is quite complex, due to the large number of suspect components, refer to Chapters 5 and 6. These chapters provide information on how you can solve this problem.

Problems with audio CDs on SCSI drives

If you're experiencing problems with audio-playback, it's possible that your driver or the CD-ROM drive doesn't support the SCSI II standard. Some SCSI II CD-ROM drives let you activate or deactivate the SCSI II command set through a jumper setting. Some drivers let you activate the CD-ROM drive's proprietary command set through a parameter. The MS-DOS device driver ASPICD.SYS from Adaptec, for example, uses the parameter /Type:[drive manufacturer name] to make this setting. You'll find more information about this in the instructions to your CD-ROM drive or the ASPI driver.

Audio CDs won't play under Windows

You wish to play an audio CD under Windows, and even though you've inserted the CD correctly and started the playback, you can't hear anything. This may be due to the following problems:

If you've connected the loudspeakers or the headphones through the headphone jack on the front of the CD-ROM drive, it's possible the volume control is turned down too far. Perhaps the AC power source for your external speakers isn't connected or the power supply isn't receiving power.

Check whether the volume control of the audio CD output in the Multimedia properties in the Control Panel is set too low. Check this setting by selecting the "CD Music" tab.

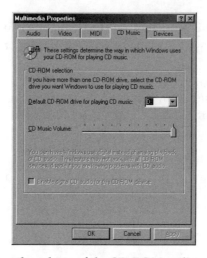

Setting the volume of the CD-ROM audio output

A message may appear in the CD Player window informing you a CD hasn't been inserted.

The CD-ROM Playback refuses to play audio CDs

The source of this error is that the driver for the CD audio device hasn't been activated in your Multimedia settings.

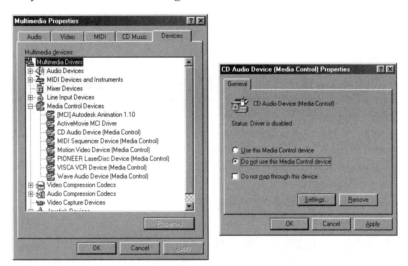

The CD-ROM audio device support hasn't been activated.

Open the Windows 98 Control Panel. Double-click the Multimedia icon. Select the "Advanced" tab. Then double-click the Media Control Devices. Then double-click "CD Audio Device (media control)" item. Click the Properties button. Make certain the driver is enabled and active.

If you still don't hear any sound from the sound card, see the information "The audio CDs won't play" in the "Sound Card Problems" section in this chapter.

The playback of audio CDs is noisy

If you've connected the audio output of your CD-ROM drive to the sound card or the CD-ROM controller using the audio cable included with the drive, the playback through these devices can have some interference. The interference radiation that is, unfortunately, always present in data cables is the source of these noises. Avoid this problem by moving the audio cable as far from the data cables as you can. If this doesn't eliminate the noise entirely, it will at least reduce it considerably.

Dirty and scratched CD-ROMs

Even if you're always very careful with your CD-ROMs, they somehow always manage to get at least a little dirty and scratched. By following our CD-ROM care program, you'll be able to clean your disks and remove any scratches, making them look almost new.

The best thing for cleaning your CD-ROMs is a soft and clean, lint-free cloth. Start from the center of the disc and wipe to the outer edge. Never clean a CD-ROM using a circular motion. Any particle that may be lodged under the cloth could create a circular scratch on the disc's protective layer. Since the individual sectors of the CD-ROM are imprinted on the disc in a spiral pattern, such circular patterns cannot only damage the data, but also the checksums of a sector. This leads to read-errors and unusable files. Although it's possible to scratch the disc when you wipe from its center outward, these scratches are perpendicular to the data path and therefore will cause virtually no damage.

Do not use cleaning agents or solvents. These agents or solvents can damage the disc's protective layer.

If you want to restore a scratched CD-ROM, buy a CD-ROM repair kit. Many computer or audio stores carry these repair kits. However, such kits are expensive and don't always work. Fortunately, we have a more economical alternative that uses something that you have in your house: toothpaste.

We've found that toothpaste can work in restoring a damaged CD-ROM. Use a clean, lint free, soft cloth and a small amount of toothpaste on the damaged CD-ROM. Carefully buff the scratches from the CD-ROM. Make certain to use only perpendicular motions to the data path — from the center of the CD-ROM to its edge. The toothpaste fills in the small scratches. Then carefully polish and clean the CD-ROM. The data should be readable again.

When the lens is dirty

Dusty or dirty CD-ROMs can literally blind the CD-ROM drive's laser. Fixing the problem requires a simple cleaning of the laser's lens. It's best to use a special cleaning CD-ROM (available from your computer or audio dealer).

If this does not solve the problem, or if you don't want to try something else, clean the lens very carefully by hand. Cleaning an older drive with an access lid that reaches the lens is quite easy. Otherwise, you must take the drive apart to reach the laser optics. Start by removing the housing, which exposes the drive's circuitry and mechanics.

Unfortunately, we cannot provide more specific information beyond this point. Drives are constructed entirely differently. Some drives will require you to remove circuit boards to reach the lens. These boards are connected to the drive mechanism through bundles of thin wires and sometimes thin, delicate ribbon conductors. Be extremely careful with these flat conductors, as they can be damaged very easily. They must not be bent sharply or creased.

Write down the correct connections when you unplug the wires from their sockets. Make certain to reconnect them in the proper orientation. Once the laser optics are finally exposed, use a lens brush to gently clean the lens (this avoids scratches on plastic lenses). Don't press too hard on the lens, since this could force the optics out of adjustment.

Once you've cleaned the lens, you're ready to start reassembling the drive. Before mounting the drive back in your PC's housing, test it to make certain it's working properly. You may otherwise have to remove it from the case again if you discover it's still not working right.

Unable to delete or edit files copied from CD-ROM

Since CD-ROMs are a read-only medium, all the data on CD-ROMs carry the read-only attribute. When you install programs from the CD-ROM to your system using their installation programs, the read-only attribute is usually deleted. However, if you're copying specific files manually, you'll probably need to delete this attribute.

To do this, select the file in its folder or use Windows Explorer. Press the right mouse button once to open the pop-up menu. Select **Properties** with your left mouse button. Disable the "Read-only" attribute in the Properties dialog box.

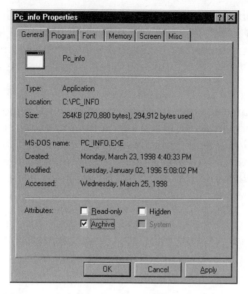

Removing the read-only attribute from a file.

This procedure also applies to any programs you've copied to your hard drive from our companion CD-ROM.

On the other hand, if you're working in MS-DOS mode, you'll need to use the ATTRIB command:

```
ATTRIB -R filename
```

Use the "/S" parameter to delete the read-only attribute for all the specified files in the specified directory, including all its subdirectories.

```
ATTRIB -R filename /S
```

Use the wildcards "*" and "?" to create a filename mask. This allows you to delete the read-only attribute from more than one file at a time.

CD-ROM video playback is not smooth

You need at least a 2x speed drive for acceptable video playback. The original single-speed drives are too slow to produce acceptable video playback today. In today's market, you have no excuse for going slower than 10x for a new CD-ROM drive.

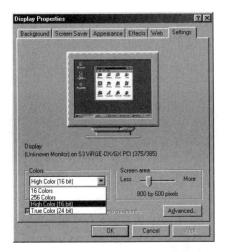

Reducing the color depth is one way to get smoother video playback.

If your CD-ROM driver supports more than one mode, such as the IRQ/DMA mode and software polling, set the driver to IRQ/DMA mode if it's not already in this mode. Do this under Windows by using the Device Manager (see the information "Switching a Mitsumi drive from polling to DMA mode" later in this section). If you're using the Mitsumi FX001D CD-ROM drive in MS-DOS mode, you'll need to use the driver MTMCDAE.SYS, which supports the IRQ/DMA mode, unlike MTMCDAS.SYS, which only supports software polling.

Also try reducing the color depth in the Control Panel. Double-click the Display icon. Select the "Settings" tab. Select a lower color depth under "Color palette."

Also, try decreasing the video window size. This may help provide a smoother picture motion. Do this under Windows by opening the Control Panel. Double-click the Multimedia icon. Select the "Video" tab. Change the picture size under the "Window" radio button in the "Show video in:" area.

Copy the necessary files to your hard drive from the CD-ROM. Run the application again to see whether the problem is with your CD-ROM drive or another hardware component. For example, you'll also need a sufficiently powerful video card for smooth video playback.

Decreasing the window's size is another way to produce smoother video movement.

For playback in MS-DOS mode, make certain the CD-ROM driver MSCDEX is loaded in your AUTOEXEC.BAT before the cache driver (SMARTDRV.EXE for MS-DOS). This assures the CD-ROM drive is also cached.

For playback in MS-DOS mode, increase the number of buffers in your MSCDEX driver using parameter "/M:." Try setting the maximum number of buffers with /M:64. Keep in mind that each buffer requires 2K of memory.

If you're running the video in MS-DOS mode, be certain to use the most current CD-ROM device driver version. Contact the technical support line of the drive's manufacturer. The representative should tell you the current version number. A more recent driver version may solve the problem.

Inserting the CD-ROM produces an error message

You try to load a CD-ROM in your CD-ROM drive and then directly read its directory or started an application. However, Windows responds with the message shown on the right.

MS-DOS mode displays the following (or similar) error message:

> CDR 101: Cannot read drive E: (F)ail, (R)etry, (I)gnore

This is actually only an "apparent" error. When you first load a CD-ROM into your CD-ROM drive, the drive requires a few seconds to initialize itself (the amount of time depends on your type of drive). You cannot access the drive during this initialization. You should also see the drive LED flash on.

The simple solution to this "problem" is to wait until the drive light is off again before accessing the drive. If you can't see your drive, wait about five seconds after inserting the disc before trying to access it.

The application can't access the CD-ROM

This problem occurs when an application requires data from a CD-ROM and doesn't find it at the specified path. Usually when the CD-ROM drive's driver software is installed, no specific drive letter is assigned, so that you can run into problems when you're using a removable hard disk, such as a Syquest or Jazz drive. When you boot your system, the driver of the high capacity drive checks whether a disc is loaded in the drive. If so, the first free drive letter is assigned to this drive, for example D:. The CD-ROM drive is then assigned the next available drive letter, in this case E:.

However, if the high-capacity drive does not contain a disc, the driver doesn't reserve a drive letter and the CD-ROM drive is assigned the drive letter D:. The path for your CD-ROM drive will either be set to D: or E: depending on how your software is configured. If this doesn't correspond to the drive letter assigned to the CD-ROM drive, you won't be able to access it and will get the error message.

Solve this problem by assigning a specific drive letter to the hard drive controller or the CD-ROM drive or both.

Under Windows it's particularly easy to reserve a drive letter for the CD-ROM drive. Open the Control Panel. Double-click the System icon. Select the "Device Manager" tab. Then single-click the small plus-sign next to the CD-ROM item in the hardware tree. This opens the entry for the CD-ROM drive.

Double-click the drive name to open another set of tabbed pages. Select the "Settings" tab. Now define a fixed drive letter for your CD-ROM drive.

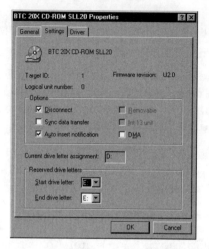

Reserving a drive letter for the CD-ROM drive.

It's also possible to reserve a drive letter in MS-DOS mode. Add the parameter "/L:[drive_letter]" to the MSCDEX statement in your AUTOEXEC.BAT. This parameter represents your CD-ROM drive.

```
C:\WINDOWS\COMMAND\MSCSEX.EXE  /D:MSCD001  /L:E
```

The CD-ROM drive is assigned letter "E:" in this example. Make certain all your programs access the CD-ROM drive using this path. If so, you'll no longer have this problem.

The disc tray is blocked or sticks

If you have this problem using a new CD-ROM drive, check the user's manual. It's possible there is a jumper that deactivates the drive door. Sony's CDU 55S CD-ROM drive, for example, has such a jumper. If this jumper is not set, you won't be able to open the disc tray through your software or the open/close button. Once the jumper is set, you'll be able to operate the door again.

You can set a parameter on the CD-ROM device driver with some drives that prevents the drive door from opening. Check whether the driver statement includes such a parameter in your CONFIG.SYS (for the Mitsumi FX-400, the parameter is "/U:1"). After removing the parameter from the statement in your CONFIG.SYS and rebooting your computer, the drive door should work fine.

The source of the problem may also be with the application you're running. It's possible that a program error is preventing the drive tray from opening. Close all your running applications and try opening the door again.

If the drive door seems to stick when you try to open or close it, the drive's mounting screws may be too long. They could be protruding too far into the drive's housing, thus blocking its tray mechanics. We recommend using the proprietary mounting hardware or the shortest screws possible.

An incorrectly inserted CD-ROM could be blocking the drive door. Try opening the drive by pressing the open/close button again. If this doesn't work, turn your system off immediately. You want to avoid overloading the tray motor. Refer to the CD-ROM drive's user's manual for the location of the manual door release.

Use a long thin rod (e.g., a straightened paper clip) to access the manual door release on some drives. The manual door release on other drives (such as the Mitsumi drives) requires that you turn a small screw. In any case, be careful to avoid damaging the CD-ROM or the drive. If you can't open the tray in this manner either, you'll have to remove the drive from your computer and take it apart to reach the CD. Refer to the "Dirty lens" section in this chapter for more information.

Problems with two CD-ROM drives

It's possible to use two CD-ROM drives in your system. Windows usually recognizes both CD-ROM drives automatically and adds them into the system. Under the section called "The application can't access the CD-ROM" we discuss how to assign a fixed drive letter to CD-ROM drives. The solutions that we discuss for single CD-ROM drives also apply to the other problems you may have with two CD-ROM drives in your system.

However, you must be aware of a few items in MS-DOS mode. All the necessary CD-ROM device drivers must be loaded in your CONFIG.SYS (each of the CD-ROM drives requires its own device driver statement). Use "/D:" to assign specific drive letters in each of the statements to the CD-ROM drive. The two drives, of course, must receive different drive letters.

The driver MSCDEX.EXE is located in the AUTOEXEC.BAT. You'll also need a "/D:" statement for each of the drives. These must correspond to the drive letters in the device drivers. The following example uses a Mitsumi FX-400 and a Mitsumi FX-001D. The statements in the CONFIG.SYS are as follows:

```
DEVICE=C:\DEV\MTMCDAI.SYS  /D:MSCD001
DEVICE=C:\DEV\MTMCDAE.SYS  /D:MSCD002
```

Our AUTOEXEC.BAT contains:

```
C:\WINDOWS\COMMAND\MSCDEX.EXE  /D:MSCD001  /D:MSCD002
```

This example is only intended to demonstrate using the "/D:" parameter. All other parameters, such as the port address, would also have to be included in a true situation.

Also, remember the LASTDRIVE setting in your CONFIG.SYS. Make certain that you have enough available drive letters.

No access to the CD-ROM drive from a network

To facilitate the access to a CD-ROM drive from a network in MS-DOS mode, the MSCDEX.EXE statement must contain another parameter. On the computer to which the CD-ROM drive is connected, load the AUTOEXEC.BAT in a text editor. Add the parameter "/S" to the MSCDEX statement and save the modified file. The change will take effect when the computer is rebooted and the CD-ROM drive will be accessible through the network.

SmartDrive doesn't support the CD-ROM drive in MS-DOS mode

If you're not sure whether SmartDrive is supporting your CD-ROM drive, enter "SMARTDRV /S" at the DOS prompt to see which drives SmartDrive supports. If this reveals that SmartDrive isn't caching the CD-ROM drive, then this might be due to the following problems:

You're using an old version of SmartDrive. CD-ROM drives are only supported by SmartDrive versions 5 and above. Version 5 was first shipped with MS-DOS 6.2x and Windows for Workgroups 3.11. It's best to use the current version for Windows 98, which you'll find in your C:\WINDOWS directory.

Suppose SmartDrive loads before MSCDEX.EXE, and therefore doesn't know that a CD-ROM drive is being used. Change your AUTOEXEC.BAT so MSCDEX.EXE is loaded before SmartDrive.

You've loaded SmartDrive with the "/U" parameter, which prevents the CD-ROM module of SmartDrive from being loaded. Because of this, SmartDrive is unable to support the CD-ROM drive. Remove this parameter from the SmartDrive statement in your AUTOEXEC.BAT.

Blankouts during the playback of audio CDs

You're using one of the Mitsumi drives (FX001 or FX001D) with the MS-DOS device driver. If the music-playback is plagued by blank-outs or skips, like a scratched LP, then your problem is not a faulty drive, but a defective CD-ROM device driver. Install a more recent driver version, version 1.16 or above, to solve this problem. Check with your computer dealer or the Mitsumi technical support line for a more up-to-date driver.

Another possible reason for blank-outs or skips during playback is dirt on the surface of the CD. Use a soft cloth to clean dust or finger prints from the CD-ROM, wiping from the center outward (see the "Dirty and Scratched CD-ROMs" section in this chapter).

Video CD-ROMs cannot be played back

If you want to play video CD-ROMs, you need a CD-ROM drive that complies with the White Book standard. Although the Mitsumi FX00D1 CD-ROM drive doesn't support this standard on a hardware basis, the manufacturer contends that CD-I CDs are supported with MS-DOS drivers versions 1.16 and above.

Another requirement for playing back video CD-ROMs is that your system must include a special MPEG decompression card. To fit more data on the CD-ROM, the video data is stored on the CD-ROM in a compressed format. Since a connector must tie the MPEG card to the VGA card, your VGA card must have a VESA compliant feature connector. It's also possible to get special VGA cards that have their own onboard MPEG decoder.

Problems with Photo CD-ROMs

If your CD-ROM is an older model, it's possible that it doesn't support the Orange-Book standard. Refer to your drive's user manual for information on its capabilities. If this doesn't get you anywhere, contact your computer dealer or the CD-ROM manufacturer's technical support line. Perhaps you're using a CD-ROM device driver that's too old and doesn't support Photo CD-ROMs.

If your CD-ROM drive can only read the pictures from the first session (the pictures that were saved to the CD-ROM the first time at the lab), then you probably have a single-session drive. These drive's don't support the XA standard and are therefore unable to read data that was written to the CD-ROM at a later time. If you do have a multisession drive, you're probably experiencing a driver problem. Perhaps your driver doesn't support multisession operation. Check with your computer dealer for an appropriate driver.

If you're using the SmartDrive cache program in MS-DOS mode and your system crashes just before it finishes loading an image from the photo CD-ROM, the problem is SmartDrive. Unlike hard drives and diskettes, Photo CD-ROMs aren't formatted all at once in their entirety before they are imprinted with data. Only the amount of space required for the pictures of the current session is formatted. A segment of 2,048 bytes remains unformatted between the individual sessions. Because of its built-in Read Ahead mode, SmartDrive attempts to read data ahead. If SmartDrive encounters such an unformatted section due to the predetermined block size of 8,192 bytes, you run into problems.

The following suggestions may help eliminate this problem:

Reduce the block size to 2,048 bytes using the "/E:" parameter:

```
C:\WINDOWS\SMARTDRV.EXE  /E:2048
```

Deactivate the CD-ROM drive caching. To do so, place a minus sign in front of the CD-ROM's drive letter. If your CD-ROM drive uses the driver letter "E:," the statement would look like this:

```
SMARTDRV -E
```

Once you've ended your Photo CD-ROM session, use the command

```
SMARTDRV +E
```

to reactivate the cache for your CD-ROM drive. This can become annoying if you work with Photo CD-ROMs frequently. You can use a simple batch file to automate these commands. The batch file could look like this:

```
@ECHO OFF
SMARTDRV -E
<program call>
SMARTDRV +E
```

You could then create a link on your Desktop for this batch file. Then start the application through this link in the future.

The other method of deactivating the caching consists of using the "/U" parameter. With this parameter, SmartDrive won't set up a cache for your CD-ROM drive.

```
SMARTDRV /U
```

The CD-ROM drive is extremely slow on the parallel port

The reason for this is the limited data transfer speed of the parallel port. Normally parallel ports top out at a transfer rate of 250K per second. However, even quad-speed or faster drives reach rates of 300K per second, not to mention the transmission rates of triple- or quad-speed drives. You can remove this bottleneck by swapping your parallel port for an EPP, an Enhanced Parallel Port. This port permits transmission rates of up to one Meg per second, which should be plenty for many of today's drives.

Switching a Mitsumi drive from polling to DMA mode

After Windows 98 was installed, it's possible that your CD-ROM drive was operating using software polling. However, now you wish to switch it to the faster DMA mode. It's easy to find out whether your drive is using software polling. Open the Device Manager in the Control Panel by double-clicking the System icon. Click the "Resources" tab in the CD-ROM controller's Properties. If you only find the E/A area under the Resource Settings, the drive is using software polling.

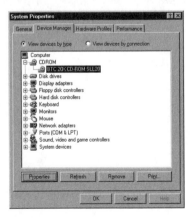

Windows 98 Emergency First Aid

When you try to change the resources, only the port address is displayed. First, remove the CD-ROM driver. Open the Windows 98 Control Panel. Double-click the System icon. Select the "Device Manager" tab. Click the desired driver ("BTC 20X CD-ROM SLL20" in the above example) and then click the (Remove) button.

Then the MTMCDAS.SYS driver (for software polling) in your CONFIG.SYS must be replaced by MTMCDAE.SYS (for the DMA mode), with all the necessary parameters (you'll find more information in the manual). Quit Windows and reboot your system. Once Windows 98 has booted, you'll need to re-register your CD-ROM drive.

Open the Hardware Wizard in the Control Panel by double-clicking the Add New Hardware icon. Let the Hardware Wizard locate the hardware.

It's the Hardware Wizard's job to look for the desired drive.

The CD-ROM drive is fully operational in DMA mode once the Hardware Wizard completes its task. To double-check, look at the settings that Windows selected in the Device Manager by selecting the "Resources" tab.

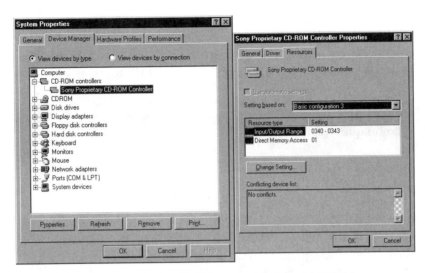

The driver for DMA/IRQ access has been installed.

Of course, you can also apply this procedure in reverse if a resource conflict forces you to resort to software polling.

Problems with NEC CD-ROM drives

NEC CD-ROM drives that use the NEC 3X firmware, version 2.2, may produce corrupt data. If so, Windows 98 will not support these drives. If you own such a drive, contact your computer dealer or NEC. It's possible they already have a solution to this problem.

Handling CD-ROMs

The widespread belief that CD-ROMs are indestructible and resistant to scratches or other damage is not true. Over time, a lack of care can result in an unreadable disc. Although a CD-ROM is approximately 1.2 mm (a little less than 1/16 in.) thick, it consists almost entirely of a polycarbonate carrier material. This carrier is coated with a very thin layer of aluminum (0.1 μm or about 4 millionths of an inch thick). This layer holds the actual data.

Only a protective coating that is 25 μm thick (approximately 10 millionths of an inch) protects the aluminum layer. Scratches usually don't damage the aluminum layer. However, scratches can divert the laser beam as it tries to read the data. The laser can also be thrown off by dust, dirt or fingerprints. All these problems will result in read-errors.

CD-ROM drives and audio CD players anticipate these read-errors, but the error-correction techniques vary considerably.

Any erroneous data on an audio CD player must be recovered or replaced quickly. This data must keep pace with a sample-frequency of 44.1 kHz. The player creates and uses a new value instead. The human ear cannot detect these errors.

It's a different story with CD-ROM data. An erroneous bit may crash an application. Because of the potential disaster these errors can cause, this necessitates an entirely different error-correction method. The primary goal is to obtain the correct data. Speed is only a secondary objective.

Manufacturers set aside 304 bytes on CD-ROMs strictly for check sums for each 2,352 byte sector. This is designed to facilitate the error-correction. Missing data can be regenerated using these check sums. However, if both the original data and the sector's check sums have become unreadable through damage to the CD-ROM, it's impossible to correct the read error, rendering the file unusable. If the aluminum data layer of a CD-ROM has been damaged, it is entirely beyond repair.

Following these tips ensures many years of trouble-free use from your CD-ROMs and CDs:

* Always store your CD-ROMs in their jewel cases. Buy extra jewel cases to store loose CD-ROMs like those found in many magazines.

* If you prefer using caddies, use the caddies for the CD-ROMs you use most frequently. Although these aren't exactly cheap (about $10 - $15 each), you'll save yourself the trouble of always swapping CD-ROMs in and out of the caddie. Another benefit of this approach is the CD-ROMs are protected from dust and physical damage.

* If you remove CD-ROMs from their protective jewel case and place them on your desk, make certain the label side faces down. Otherwise, the CD-ROM could unintentionally slide over the desk surface. This could result in scratches.

*   Handle the CD-ROMs only by their edges. Avoid touching the surface. Any oil or dirt from your fingers will remain on the surface of the CD-ROM. Also, this helps avoid scratching the disc, possibly resulting in read errors.

*   Never apply stickers to your CD-ROMs. The adhesive in the sticker could contain substances that might damage the CD-ROM's protective layer, possibly rendering it unusable.

*   Do not use an ink pen or pencil to write on your CD-ROMs. Sharp writing utensils (ball-point pens, pencils) can damage the transparent protective layer or even the aluminum layer that carries the data. Solvent-based pens may chemically damage the protective layer.

*   Instead, use pens specifically designed for labeling your CD-ROMs. Your dealer probably carries these special pens. Since they're free of solvents, they cannot damage the disc's surface.

*   Don't store CD-ROMs in direct sunlight or in excessively hot or humid places.

Important CD-ROM standards

The first standard was the Red Book or CD-DA standard (Compact Disk Digital Audio). This standard was created in 1982 by Sony and Philips, and was designed solely for the storage of audio data on compact CDs. Normal audio CDs use this standard.

The ISO-9660 standard was developed in 1988. It evolved from the High Sierra standard. Both standards describe the structure of the data format for CD-ROMs as CD-ROM data carriers. The maximum capacity of these formats was set at 650 Meg.

The Orange Book defines the recording process and data formats for writeable, optical storage media. These include, for example, the Kodak Photo CD-ROM and MO drives. Since these carriers receive their data in more than one write-session, CD-ROM drives that support this standard are "multisession capable."

The Green Book describes the CD-I standard, or Compact Disc Interactive. This standard is used to press videos to CD-ROMs that can then be played back on any drive that supports CD-I. Your system must include a special MPEG decoder card to view CD-I videos.

A mixed-mode CD-ROM has a data region and an audio region. The data region is at the start of the CD-ROM. It's followed by the audio region. The latter can also be played on a normal audio CD player.

The CD-ROM/XA standard (eXtended Architecture) by Sony, Philips and Microsoft was released in 1991. The XA standard is based on the Yellow Book and Green Book. It lets manufacturers store picture and sound data on a disc in alternating succession. This facilitates multimedia sessions, since the different data is automatically channeled to either the sound board or the MPEG board.

The White Book describes the MPEG-I process. This process allows manufacturers to store up to 74 minutes of video data and accompanying audio data on one CD-ROM. Your system must include a special MPEG decoder card to view these files.

The Photo CD-ROM is a development by Kodak based on the Orange Book. Photo CD-ROMs make it possible to transfer pictures taken on normal photographic film to CD-ROMs in a special laboratory. You can play Photo CD-ROMs on any multisession drive, although special software is required.

The Yellow Book makes it possible to access individual sectors on the CD-ROM. It also distinguishes between these two modes:

* Mode 1
  uses error correction and is intended for computer data.

* Mode 2
  dispenses with error correction and so is suitable for less critical information, such as video data.

Simple Printer Fixes

You've probably been here: sitting at your computer for hours, working over an important and urgent letter. At last you've made the final touches. It looks perfect in Print Preview. All that's left is a quick printout and a quick dash to the post office. You select the Print command and... nothing happens. Or perhaps your printer responds, but less than perfectly. Part of your work is mysteriously lost or the entire document is transformed into an unrecognizable jumble of hieroglyphics.

You should not let these setbacks reduce you to blathering hysteria. This section helps you resolve your printing crises with simple remedies and troubleshooting tips.

Printers can be divided into two main categories:

Impact printers

These printers work by mechanically striking the paper. By their nature, impact printers tend to be noisy. The dot matrix printer is probably the most widely used impact printer. Other types are used almost exclusively with large-scale computers.

Nonimpact printers

These printers include inkjet, laser and thermotransfer printers. As the name indicates, these printers have no impact mechanism. Therefore, these printers operate much quieter than the impact printers. One drawback, however, is their inability to use multicopy forms.

Another way to separate printer types is by the delivery sequence of the printed image.

Character printers

These printers output text one letter at a time. (Consequently, such printers may be somewhat confusingly called "serial printers," a term much more commonly used to mean those that connect to a serial interface.) Typical character printers are dot matrix and inkjet printers.

Line printers

These printers output an entire line of text at once. Line printers can print at rates to 1,500 lines/minute. These are found only in larger EDP installations.

Page printers

These printers print an entire page at once. Laser and thermotransfer printers are typical page printers.

Many problems can plague printing. Since many are restricted to certain types of printers, we have divided this section by printer type. This will make your troubleshooting efforts easier.

General printer problems

The following lists some problems that may occur on almost any printer, regardless of type.

The right paper

Although it sounds obvious, using the right paper is more important for quality output than you might suspect. The paper manufacturing process results in one side of the paper being smoother than the other. This is the side on which you should normally print. It's usually indicated by an arrow on the package.

Dot matrix printers are not so particular about what rolls across the platen. Laser and inkjet printers, however, demand higher paper quality. For laser printers, you can be safe using any paper that is appropriate for copy machines.

If you want to use other types of paper or transparencies, make certain they can withstand the high fixing temperatures of laser printers (over 300°F). Such temperatures make printing on adhesive labels especially risky. If the adhesive melts, a label may separate from the carrier sheet and lodge in the printer. This can damage a printer beyond repair.

Paper for inkjet printers should allow a slight running of the ink. Too much, however, makes the image look blurred. By experimenting a little, you can usually find a reasonably priced medium to solve your print quality problems. You should not have to resort to the more expensive specialty papers offered by some printer manufacturers.

However, an exception may be if you're using the full capabilities of a high-resolution color inkjet printer. Ordinary papers will not bring out the sharp image and brilliant color that these printers are capable of producing.

Simple but effective—switching the printer off and on again

This is the easiest way to solve many printer problems. Perhaps you have changed the settings on your printer's control panel. Now they conflict with the settings required by your word processor. By turning the printer off and then on again, you restore all settings to their initial defaults. The printer will also perform a self-test to check for hardware defects. Other possible causes of printing problems are bugs in the printer driver or using the wrong driver. After you correct the problem, your printer may still hesitate until you restart it.

The printer does not print

All control panel displays and indicator lights are off

First, make certain the printer is turned on. Note, however, that some models (for example, HP LaserJet 4L) actually have no on/off switch. Next, check the power cable to see that it is plugged in securely to the computer and to the power outlet. Are you using a power strip with a built-in switch? Then make certain the switch is on.

Test the outlet by plugging in another electrical device. If this also fails to operate, you may have blown a fuse or tripped a breaker. In this case, correct the problem and try your printer again.

Another possible cause is a defective power supply cable. Many printers have a removable power supply cable. If this is the case with your printer, exchange the defective cable with another cable. Then try to print again.

If you are setting up a new printer or one that was last used in another country, check for the proper voltage requirement. A plate is usually attached to the back of the printer providing this information. An unusually shaped power plug that requires an adapter to fit your outlet should be a warning to you.

Many printers have built-in fuses that are accessible from outside the housing, usually at the back of the printer. (Check your user's manual for fuse locations.) Remove and test any such fuses. With luck, a visual inspection may reveal the problem. If the fuse wire appears to be intact, test the fuse with a continuity tester. Buy replacement fuses at your local computer dealer or electronics store. Check the old fuse for an identifying number. This number is probably stamped on one of the contact surfaces.

If these suggestions don't solve your problem, the printer should be serviced by an authorized repair technician.

Control panel displays or indicators light up

When packaging electronic devices, manufacturers often insert safety clamps, shields or padding to protect sensitive components during shipment. Read the unpacking and assembly instructions carefully to locate any such materials or objects that require removal.

A good possibility is that your printer is simply offline. Depending on the type and model, this may be indicated by an unlit ON-LINE indicator or by a message on an LCD display. Switch the printer on-line, and printing should start. (Some printers have a PAUSE button rather than an ON-LINE button, in which case the status of the indicator light is reversed. When the PAUSE light is on, the printer is in offline mode.)

Another possibility is a defective or poorly seated connecting cable between the computer and the printer. If the cable seems to be fastened securely at both devices, try removing it and testing it on another computer system, or replacing it with a cable that you know is good.

Or, if your computer has an extra port of the same type, reconnect the cable, in case it is the port that is faulty. Remember to tell your software about the new port (direct the output to LPT2, for example, instead of LPT1). If your setup doesn't allow these options, try connecting the printer to a different computer.

An incorrect printer setting in your software may also be the source of the problem. Again, check for the appropriate port setting and printer driver.

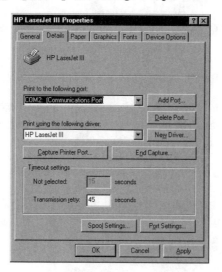

Changing the printer port.

Most printers have some type of door or cover. A microswitch or sensor prevents the printer from operating when this door or cover is not properly closed. A message such as COVER OPEN or an indicator light may alert you to the cause of the problem.

Failure to operate for inkjet printers may also be caused by a low ink supply. Some printers have a viewing window for monitoring the ink supply. Normally you are notified of a problem through a message or indicator light.

Many laser printers have an internal counter that electronically counts the number of times the image drum is exposed in printing. When this reaches the drum's life expectancy as determined by the manufacturer, the printer stops printing and displays a message. Some laser printers have a toner level sensor in the toner cartridge and may display a message when the toner is low before it stops printing. Remove the toner cartridge and shake it a few times and then replace it in the printer. You may be able to continue printing for a brief period. Otherwise, replace the toner cartridge.

Another problem that can occur in laser printers is improper installation of the toner cartridge. Remove the cartridge and reinsert it. Be sure it "snaps" into place correctly.

Be certain the Centronics cable you're using isn't too long. The signals degrade over long distances and may no longer be recognized by the printer. See the information "The printer stops working with a longer Centronics cable" later in this section.

Some printer models (e.g., Epson SQ2250, LQ2550) let you install an optional interface card. If present, this is automatically activated and all other interfaces deactivated. If you want to use one of the standard interfaces instead, you must remove the card from the printer.

Although we have listed some of the more likely causes for this symptom, a complete listing is beyond the scope of this book. Check your printer manual's troubleshooting section for additional suggestions specific to your printer.

Running the printer's self-test

A good way to check the capabilities of your printer is to run it in self-test mode. Begin this on character printers by pressing a certain key (LINE FEED or FORM FEED for Epson printers) while switching on the printer. The printer then produces a test printout of all the available characters in its character set. In addition, it normally prints the settings of any DIP switches.

To start the self-test on page printers you must use a menu item on the printer's control panel. Consult your user's manual for the appropriate keys or key combinations. (An exception is the HP-LaserJet 4L or 4ML, where you simply press the printer's single control button once.) Laser printers do not have DIP switches, but various option settings are printed with the test character set for available fonts.

The self-test prints only those fonts that are built into the printer or that reside on installed font cartridges. Software fonts, such as the Windows TrueType fonts, are not included.

A printer on the serial port prints incorrectly or not at all

While using a parallel interface involves only a simple cable connection, a serial interface has more complicated requirements. Both computer and printer must have the same transfer parameter settings. These consist of the data transfer (baud) rate, parity, number of data bits and stop bits, and the flow control (XON/XOFF or a hardware protocol).

If your serial port is sending garbage to your printer, first make certain the parity settings match. Another possible cause is a transfer rate that's too high. Reduce the speed until the output is correct. The self-test usually gives the data transfer parameters for the printer. Otherwise, consult the user manual for this information.

Select the printer under Windows by double-clicking the Printers icon in the Control Panel. Double-click the icon representing your serial printer. Select the **Properties** command in the **File** menu. Select the "Details" tab. Click the [Port Settings...] button. Then review the settings for the serial port and make any necessary changes.

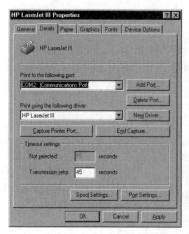 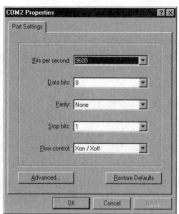

Serial printer interface settings under Windows.

Use the MODE command under MS-DOS to set the computer's data transfer settings.

```
MODE COMn [:] [Baud] [Parity] [Data] [Stop] [Retry]
```

The following explains the settings in the MODE command:

COMn
Gives the number of the serial port. The value must be from 1 to 4.

Baud
Gives the transfer rate of the serial port in bits per second. A shortened code is derived from the first two digits of the actual rate.

Code	Transfer rate	Code	Transfer rate
10	110 Baud	15	150 Baud
30	300 Baud	60	600 Baud
12	1200 Baud	24	2400 Baud
48	4800 Baud	96	9600 Baud
19	19200 Baud		

Parity
Determines the type of data checking used by the PC and printer.

N	None (no checking is performed)
E	Even parity
O	Odd parity

The default DOS setting for parity is "E."

Data
Gives the number of data bits used in the transfer. Valid values are from 5 to 8. The default is 8 data bits, which is the current standard for printers. A few older printers work with 7 data bits.

Stop
Gives the number of stop bits used. Valid values are 1 and 2. A data transfer rate of 110 baud normally uses 2 stop bits. Other baud rates use only 1 stop bit.

Retry

Gives the action to be taken when a timeout condition occurs during data transmission. If the Retry parameter is specified, part of MODE remains resident in memory.

P	Directs MS-DOS to try resending the data after a timeout condition. Without this setting, an error occurs when the maximum wait time is exceeded.
E	Directs MS-DOS to report timeout errors to the program issuing the print command.

The following shows how the command should look for a printer on COM1 operating at 9600 baud, with no parity, 8 data bits and 1 stop bit:

```
MODE COM1: 9600,N,8,1
```

The serial data cable is fine but the printer still does not print

Perhaps you have the printer connected to the wrong port. Unplug the cable and reconnect it to the proper port.

Check the printer settings for your software. A problem may exist with one of its parameters. Perhaps the wrong port may be specified.

If the printer can use a parallel port as well as a serial port, check the printer settings to make certain the serial port is active.

The DOS software supports only a parallel interface

Even if your software does not support a serial printer interface, you can redirect the output under DOS from the parallel to the serial port. Specify the parallel and serial ports involved as shown in the example below:

```
MODE LPT1: =COM1:
```

Any output sent to the parallel port LPT1 will now be redirected to the serial port COM1.

This arrangement redirects all the output sent to LPT1. If a parallel printer is connected there, it can no longer be used. In other words, make certain the port whose output you are redirecting is always available.

The printer inserts blank lines between lines of text

Printers have several commands to control vertical placement of the print head. The two most important commands are CR (carriage return) and LF (line feed). CR returns the print head to the left margin. LF advances the paper by one line. After printing a line of text from left to right, the printer must execute these two commands before printing the next line.

Print programs usually insert the CR/LF sequence at the end of each line of text to be printed. (The same effect can be produced if the sequence of the control commands is reversed to LF/CR.) Some programs, however, do not send these control sequences. They rely on the printer to advance on its own to the start of a new line when the current one is filled.

Consequently, newer PC printers include an optional automatic line feed function. You can disable this function when you are using software that generates the needed control sequences. Otherwise, the printer's internal commands will duplicate those of the software. The result will be double-spaced text where single-spaced is intended.

The printer prints garbage

This is another symptom of communication problems between your PC and your printer. The following lists some likely causes:

Wrong printer driver

Your program may be using the wrong printer driver. Check your settings and correct the driver designation if necessary.

Wrong printer emulation

You may be using the wrong printer emulation. This, of course, applies only to printers that have emulation capabilities and that do not recognize the proper emulation automatically (e.g., Brother HL-4 and HL-8). Most printers can use several emulations. In other words, they can simulate printers of other types.

The control commands that are transferred with the data sent to a printer are specific to the printer. The same control operation requires a different command for almost every brand of printer. If a wrong emulation is used, the printer misinterprets the commands and prints unexpected results. In this case, you must switch the printer over to the proper emulation.

Suppose, for example, that your DOS program is using a LaserJet emulation for the printer, but you try to print with a Postscript driver under Windows. The printer cannot interpret Postscript commands correctly and prints them as ordinary text. If you check the printout closely, you will see the actual text embedded within the command sequences.

Cable length or arrangement

Even if your printer cable is not too long, its arrangement may be causing problems. Excess cable gathered neatly into a coil to take up slack may look innocent enough, but actually this can cause interference in data transmission. Avoid looping the cable over itself or consider replacing the cable with a shorter one.

Defective cable

Another possible cause of garbled output is a hardware defect in the cable or one of its connectors. Try a replacement cable to test for such a problem.

Tracing errors with the hex-dump option

Most printers have this handy option. By pressing a special key or key combination while switching on the printer, you place it in hex-dump mode. All text printed will then be shown in hexadecimal numbers beside the regular ASCII output. Careful examination of a hex dump will reveal certain problems with data transmission through a parallel interface. (This method is not relevant for serial interfaces.) The following example illustrates a hex dump.

```
54 68 69 73 20 69 73 20 This is

61 20 74 65 73 74 20 70 a test p

72 69 6E 74 6F 75 74 20 rintout
```

The above dump was made with a good printer cable. Below you see the results of the same test using a cable with a broken conductor for the 1 data bit.

56 6A 6B 73 22 6B 73 22 Vjks"ks"

63 22 76 67 73 76 22 72 c"vgsv"r

74 6B 70 76 71 77 76 22 rknvowv"

See how only one small flaw in the cable can make the printed output appear completely worthless. You'll learn something if you look at the dump closely, however.

We used the MS-DOS Editor to type our sample text and send it to the printer. Each individual character is represented by 8 data bits (1 byte). A bit can have only one of two possible values, either 1 or 0. These values represent the two voltage conditions (high and low) that the computer's electronic circuitry can handle. As characters are stored internally as 8-bit binary numbers, they are transmitted as 8 data bits over as many separate conductors in the parallel cable. The printer translates the resulting binary value to its ASCII equivalent and prints the corresponding character.

	Computer	Centronics cable	Printer	Output
Databit 7	0	0	0	
Databit 6	1	1	1	
Databit 5	0	0	0	
Databit 4	0	0	0	D
Databit 3	0	0	0	
Databit 2	1	1	1	
Databit 1	0	0	0	
Databit 0	0	0	0	

Correct data transfer.

The character "T" is stored in the computer as the binary number 01010100, which is also the value that is sent to the printer. In hex-dump mode, our printer prints the number's hexadecimal value (54) as well as its ASCII code.

With the broken conductor for the 1 data bit, the cable can transmit only the other seven bits of data.

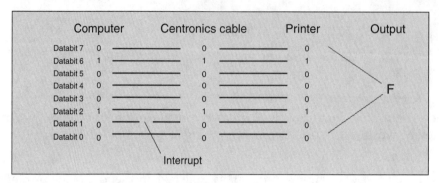

Data transfer with data bit 1 missing.

The perhaps surprising result of the missing bit is a value of 1 in that position for every character transmitted. This is a consequence of the design of the printer's circuitry, where an undefined input voltage, neither low (0) nor high (1), is brought high to give the input signal a valid status. Knowing this, you can analyze the binary values to detect the damaged conductor. For the characters that print improperly, the correct value for the affected bit position is 0, but it has been changed to 1. If 1 is the correct value for that position, the character prints properly.

Besides breaks in the conductor wires of the cable, defects in the interface adapters of the PC or printer can cause similar problems. You can learn more under the heading "The printer does not print."

Special characters are lost in MS-DOS mode

Getting your PC and printer to communicate in their "native" English is enough of a challenge at times. Trying to use foreign characters can introduce a whole new level of frustration. You can override the standard language setting with an International option when you install your PC's operating system. Teaching your printer a new language, however, is not quite that simple.

Windows has, to a large extent, solved such problems. However, if you work in MS-DOS mode with German text files, you've probably seen characters like ö, ä and ü get lost in the translation when you send them to your printer. Other special characters, such as the line-drawing symbols, can also be a problem. A box drawn neatly around your data changes to an unimpressive border of letters when you put the final output to paper.

The difficulty is the incompatibility between the character sets of your PC and your printer. IBM uses the upper 127 codes of the ASCII character set for special country-specific characters and the block graphic symbols. This extended character set is what constitutes code page 437, the normal (American) printer default.

Printer manufacturers, however, also equip their printers with specialized non-IBM-compatible character sets appropriate to the various countries in which the devices are marketed. Although these printers also have the IBM-compatible character set, it must be explicitly activated. Unfortunately, the manufacturers use different names to refer to this set, among them "IBM Standard" (NEC), "Graphic" (Epson), "PC-8" (Hewlett-Packard) and "Character Set 2" (IBM). Refer to your printer's manual. It should list the information you need. If the correct set is not apparent by name, there is another way to determine the one you need.

Use EDIT in MS-DOS mode to open a text file that contains the special characters and print it. Compare the screen with the printout. Where any differences occur, get the ASCII values for the screen characters. The values are available in PC_INFO under the command **Services | ASCII table**. Place the cursor on the character in question and the code will appear.

Refer to your printer manual and locate the set that attaches the desired character to that code. This should be the set you want. Check a few more characters to be sure. Follow the manual's instructions to activate this set using the printer's DIP switches or control panel. Now all the special characters should print properly under DOS, provided your application software is also using compatible settings. If your software is not compatible, you may have to change its settings or reconfigure your printer each time you use the application.

The printer sometimes feeds in more than one sheet at a time

When the paper is cut the edges can be left slightly rough. This sometimes causes sheets to stick together. To minimize this effect, first fan through it quickly to separate the sheets before placing it in the input tray of the printer.

The problem may also be the result of using a paper that does not meet the manufacturer's specifications for your printer. Check the printer manual for these specifications. The wrong weight paper or paper that is too rough, too smooth, embossed or damp may all result in paper feed problems.

4 *Windows 98 Emergency First Aid*

Perhaps you have simply loaded too many sheets in the input tray. Remove some if this looks like the problem. Many printers have the maximum stack height indicated by a symbol on the tray.

Some printers, such as the Epson SQ and LQ model series, have an envelope feed option controlled by a lever. Make certain you are not trying to perform normal page printing with the lever in the envelope feed position.

If your printer is an older pin or inkjet model, it may have only a semi-automatic page feed mechanism, designed to take just a single sheet at a time. If you load several sheets instead, they will not feed individually. Consult the user's manual for instructions on how to properly load paper in your printer.

The printer stops working with a longer Centronics cable

The technical specifications in some printer manuals call for a maximum cable length of ten feet. This recommendation is based on the fact that interference in data transmission increases with the length of the cable. Increased capacitance develops in the cable because the parallel conductors interact like small condensers. If this effect becomes too severe, the signal degradation will cause the printer to stop working, because it can no longer recognize the transmitted data.

The following lists some possible solutions.

Check the position of the cable. Avoid routing it alongside the power cord of the printer or computer. Keep them separate as much as possible.

Try replacing the cable with a shorter one. "The shorter, the better" is the rule. Consider moving the printer closer to the computer to minimize the length of cable required.

If you can't use a shorter cable, buy or use one that is specially shielded. Since these are rather expensive, however, there are a couple of other options to examine first:

Replace the interface adapter with one that works at higher voltage levels. If your parallel port is located on the system board rather than in an expansion slot, make certain that the new interface uses a different port address. Otherwise, address conflicts will occur. Set the port address using jumpers on the adapter card. For specific instructions, check the user's manual that came with the card and the system board.

Some computers (*e.g.*, HP Vectra VL2/xx) get the settings for an onboard port from the computer setup. If you're exchanging expansion cards, use the same interrupt. For an onboard port, use another interrupt, but avoid interrupt conflicts with other cards (sound cards, for example). If necessary, you can also disable the onboard port through jumpers on the system board or as a setup option.

The remaining possibility is to resort to a line extender for the Centronics interface. This is inserted between the PC and printer, as close to the PC as possible. This solution will work even if your port is on the system board and no expansion slots are available. If you're handy with a soldering iron, you can even make such a line extender. You'll find instructions in computer or electronics magazines. You can buy the necessary supplies from electronics mail order houses.

Letters "shift" in printing

This problem can occur only on character printers (dot matrix or inkjet printers) and then only when printing graphic characters or in graphics mode. TrueType fonts, for example, are printed as graphics and not individual letters (as ASCII codes). When the letter height exceeds that of a normal line of text, the letter is printed in multiple passes of the print head.

With bidirectional printing (the head goes from left to right on one pass, then right to left on the next), head placement is less precise than with unidirectional printing. The result is that successive passes may not line up exactly, and the letters may look wavy or jagged. If you're willing to sacrifice speed for improved print quality (bidirectional printing is faster because it minimizes head movement), turn off this option. Instructions can be found in the printer manual.

The printer continues printing when out of paper

A paper sensor is reporting the presence of paper in the printer. This problem may have one of the following sources:

A piece of paper from a previous jam may be blocking the sensor. Check for any scraps or particles and carefully remove them. Dust may eventually coat the sensor. You'll need to clean this area of the printer.

The paper sensor on some models (the Star NL10, for example) can be turned off. The printer is then incapable of recognizing the end of the paper supply and will continue printing. Consult the manual for directions to turn the sensor back on.

The final possibility is the most expensive. The sensor may be defective. In this case, you should have the printer repaired by an authorized dealer or technician.

The printer sounds like it's printing, but the page comes out blank

If this problem occurs on an inkjet printer, check the print head and ink cartridges for proper installation. You may have to prime the flow of ink in a model with a permanent print head. This is done by pressing a printer-specific key combination that flushes ink into the delivery system.

For dot matrix printers, check the condition of the ink ribbon. Replace old and worn ribbons. Make certain the ribbon assembly is properly seated and that the ribbon passes smoothly behind the print head.

An "Out of Paper" message appears when paper is loaded

Printers are made to accept print media within a specified range of dimensions. Paper or label stock that is too narrow will not engage the paper sensor. When the printer cannot "see" anything on which to print, it stops working and displays a diagnostic message. You can overcome this problem on some printer models by setting a DIP switch to turn off the sensor. This also means, however, that the printer will not sense the end of the paper and you run the risk of printing on the platen. It's always safer to use the recommended paper sizes and allow the sensor to perform its intended function.

This condition may also be caused by your software using the wrong paper source. Many printers are designed to feed paper from more than one input location. If the place where the program expects to find the paper supply is indeed empty, nothing will print. Change the paper source setting and issue the print command again.

The print head stops moving

The print head may become lodged in one position if it encounters a piece of jammed paper or other object in its path. This can damage the print head. Turn the printer off and remove the obstruction before attempting to resume printing.

The buildup of paper dust and gummy oil residues on the guide bar may also keep the print head from moving freely. Remove the buildup with a soft cloth and apply a drop of a resin-free oil, such as gun oil, to the guide. Then move the print head back and forth a few times to distribute the lubricant evenly.

Sheet feeding problems

Sheets will not feed into the printer

The paper may be improperly loaded. Make certain that the sheets are neatly stacked and lying flat in the input tray. Check the paper guide to see that it is adjusted for the correct width. The guide should not press too tightly against the edge of the paper.

For printers with add-on sheet feeders, the mechanism may not be fully engaged. Check to see that detachable parts are properly installed, levers flipped to the correct position, etc.

The paper intake rollers may need cleaning. Use a damp cloth to remove dirt and paper dust from the roller surfaces. If they have worn too smooth, you can restore their "grip" by abrading lightly with a fine emery paper. Certain Hewlett-Packard Deskjet models have developed problems with residue accumulation resulting from excessive wear of the rubber surface of the transport rollers.

Sheet intake is crooked

Check for excessive play in the adjustment of any paper guides.

Clean transport or guide rollers that are dirty or unevenly worn. Use fine emery paper if necessary to roughen the rollers.

Continuous-feed paper becomes torn or jammed

When using tractor-feed paper, make certain the guide holes are fitted properly over the sprockets of the tractor feed wheels. Also, check whether the wheels are set for the proper tension. The right wheel is movable for adjusting the tension. Be sure to lock it in place after making adjustments.

Position the paper supply near the printer. Check whether any obstacles, such as power cords or connecting cables, could interfere with paper uptake.

Do not allow the leading edge of the paper to be drawn back into the feed rollers after printing. Depending on your setup, you may have to experiment a bit to devise a guide configuration that conducts the printed paper away from the input mechanism for stacking.

4 *Windows 98 Emergency First Aid*

Problems printing adhesive labels

Be especially careful to avoid problems with uneven or obstructed feeding of label stock. Mechanical stress can result in nicking, tearing or bending of labels. This makes them more likely to delaminate during printing. Stock that has already passed through the printer once may have loose corners. If so, labels can catch and peel off inside the printer.

Never put adhesive labels through a laser printer twice. The excessive heat breaks down the glue, which can end up on the image drum, damaging its surface.

We cannot describe all label-printing problems here. Check with the user's manual for specific details concerning your printer. For laser printers, especially, follow the manufacturer's recommendations on exactly which labels can be used safely.

If you do lose a label inside your printer, use great care in trying to remove it. Tugging at it too forcefully will probably cause it to tear, since the glued side is most likely stuck to one of the printer's components. If you can't extract it with a gentle, even pull, take the printer apart. Wipe off any adhesive residue to avoid future paper jams. While you're at it, now is a good time for a general cleaning. Proper cleaning measures are described in the next section on printer maintenance.

Problems with thin lines in color printouts

If you print graphics with fine details, such as lines only one or two pixels thick, these details may deviate from the desired color. The appearance of bright yellow instead of green is especially noticeable. This effect is the result of a certain limitation in printer technology.

All the colors which you can print come from four base colors: cyan, yellow, magenta and black (collectively called "CYMK"). Color mixing is achieved by placing dots of different base colors close together. The eye cannot distinguish the individual dots and perceives the blended color instead. Very fine details may simply not have room for all the base colors needed. In the case of a green line, for example, yellow results because the cyan component is missing. The only solution is to avoid fonts and graphics that are too detailed for the resolution of your printer.

Proper printer maintenance

Clean your printer occasionally. Wipe the outside of the case with a soft cloth and some glass cleaner. Wipe the inside components with a dry, lint-free cloth. Use a natural-bristle brush for hard-to-reach places. Do not use a brush made from artificial fibers. These brushes generate static buildup that may damage the printer's electronics. Use a mini-vacuum cleaner or spray can of compressed air (available at electronics stores) to remove dust from inaccessible places. Wipe the platen on pin and inkjet printers carefully with rubbing alcohol. Use a cloth or paper towel to dab up any ink residue. Check for paper shavings or scraps that may cause a paper jam later.

Dot matrix printer

A white stripe appears in each print line

A stripe at the top or bottom of the print line may indicate a poorly positioned ink ribbon. Check and adjust the ribbon if necessary.

If the white stripe passes through the middle of the printed characters, determine whether the problem occurs only in Windows printing or in DOS mode as well. If limited to Windows, the problem may be caused by a bad printer driver. Reinstall the driver. If the problem persists, try to find another driver that is compatible with your printer. Contact the manufacturer's technical support line; you may be able to get the latest, hopefully bug-free version.

When the problem occurs in both DOS and Windows, one of the pins has a flaw. If you're lucky, it is simply gummed up and can be fixed with a good cleaning. We'll describe how to do this later in this chapter. The more serious possibility is that the pin has been broken off or pulled out. (This can happen when the print head is set back too far from the paper.) The damaged head could be replaced, but this repair is often so costly that it's better to buy a new printer.

The print is too light

The print head may be too far from the paper. Check the manual for instructions on adjusting this setting for different types of paper. Another possible cause is the ink ribbon. These eventually dry out and require replacement.

The print is too dark

The print head may be too close to the paper. Again, check the manual for instructions on adjusting this setting for different types of paper. Do not overcorrect this problem. Too great a gap between paper and print head may cause pins to be pulled out of the head during printing.

Sometimes a new ribbon or one that has just been re-inked will print too dark. If you can postpone your printing or use another ribbon in the mean time, set it aside and allow it to dry out a bit.

The printout has dark spots

Some of the pins are probably retracting too slowly. This problem is caused by a dirty print head. Follow the instructions later in this chapter on cleaning the print head. This prevents the pins from sticking and being pulled from the print head.

The printout varies between light and dark

If the variation is irregular, the ink ribbon may be starting to dry out. Replacing it with a new ribbon should correct the problem. If the output is uniformly dark on one side of the page and gradually lighter on the other, the platen may be crooked. This causes a gradual difference in the impact of the pins as the head moves along the platen. The necessary adjustment can be quite complicated and is probably not one you should undertake on your own.

If you have re-inked the ribbon, some parts may have absorbed more ink then others. Unless you can add more ink only to the drier portions, you will have to replace the ribbon to get uniform printing.

Colors are smeared in printing

Pigments from one color ribbon can adhere to the pins upon impact, then be deposited on another color ribbon in subsequent strokes. Regular cleaning of the print head will help the colors maintain their purity. However, this problem cannot be totally eliminated.

Caring for the print head

The print head of a dot matrix printer will eventually accumulate enough debris to affect print quality.

This print head is badly in need of cleaning.

Ribbon fibers catch on the pins and are ripped off by the high-speed movement of the mechanism. If allowed to build up on the pins, this debris may damage the print head and eventually cause pins to break.

Before starting to clean the print head, remove the paper from the printer and unplug the power cord. Next, remove the ribbon and carefully slide the print head to the center of the guide rail. Examine the way the print head is fastened. This varies between models. If you have doubts about how to properly detach it, it's probably better to let an experienced technician handle the cleaning.

If you decide to proceed, you may want to cover the printer with an old towel to protect it during the cleaning process. Remove the screws or loosen the stops that secure the head. Then gently pull it free from its mounting. Do not crimp or tear the thin foil that connects the head to the printer. This foil contains the conductors that carry electrical impulses to the pins to control their movement.

Begin cleaning the assembly, either with a special spray cleaner or a lint-free cloth dipped in rubbing alcohol. Do not use turpentine, thinners or solvent-based cleaners.

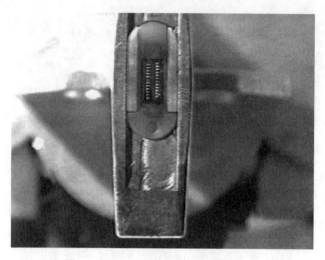

The print head can now be reinserted.

To reassemble the printer after cleaning, carefully place the print head back into its mounting. If your model has a ribbon guide (a thin metal plate between the head and platen), make certain the slot in the guide is positioned where the pins can pass through it to strike the paper.

Fasten the head securely by replacing the screws or tightening the stops, and the printer should again be operable. Before replacing the ribbon, however, you should load the printer with paper and run a self-test. This will clear the head of any remaining traces of debris and cleaning fluid.

When the printing comes out clean, you can safely replace the ribbon. Repeat the self-test and make certain everything prints correctly. If you encounter problems, shut off the printer, recheck everything, and repeat the assembly process if necessary.

Inkjet printers

How they work

Inkjet printers operate with two different processes. The older technology is the continuous-flow process, in which a constant supply of ink flows to the print head. We won't talk about this technology in detail, since it has largely been replaced by the drop-on-demand process.

In the drop-on-demand process, the flow of ink is controlled so ink reaches the print head only when it is needed. Drop-on-demand printing is accomplished through either the piezoelectric or the bubble-jet mechanism.

The word "piezo" is Greek for *to press*. A piezo element generates voltage when subjected to mechanical pressure. Printers put this phenomenon to use in reverse. Each ink jet in a piezoelectric printer contains a piezo element. When voltage is applied to the element inside a jet, the element changes shape and retracts. The resulting drop in pressure draws more ink into the jet from the reservoir.

When the voltage is removed, the element swings back, constricting the jet and forcing the ejection of ink droplets from the nozzle onto the paper. As the element returns to its resting position, the supply of ink is replaced with a new supply. This arrangement uses a permanent print head. The ink cartridge is housed separately and connected to the print head through tubes.

Bubble-jet printers have heating elements, rather than piezo elements, inside the jets. An element receives a short electrical impulse and immediately heats the ink within the jet to boiling. A gas bubble forms on the element's surface, which pushes the ink toward the nozzle opening, where it is ejected onto the paper. After a short time the bubble dissolves, and capillary action draws new ink into the jet. This process uses a print head that is integrated into the ink cartridge.

Printing is smeared or fuzzy

The distance between print head and paper is not set correctly. Adjust this distance for different weights of paper. Consult the manual for specific directions. Make certain you're using an acceptable paper for your printer. Also, check to see if you're printing on the proper (smoother) side of the paper.

Adhesive labels are smeared

Adhesive label stock is thicker than most paper because it consists of both label and carrier sheets. The extra thickness reduces the distance between the print head and the media surface, which can result in smeared printing. Check your manual for instructions on adjusting the print head setting.

The printed output contains thin white lines

The jets are probably plugged. Try flushing them out with the printer's cleaning function (see the manual for instructions on using this function). If this doesn't correct the problem after a few attempts, you will have to clean the print head manually. You can read how to do this in "Cleaning the print head," which is described below. If the printer uses a cartridge with an integrated print head, the control wire contacts may be dirty. Remove the head from its mounting. Use a cotton swab dipped in isopropyl (rubbing) alcohol and clean the contact surfaces.

If the problem only occurs under Windows, not under DOS, the fault is with the Windows printer driver. Try reinstalling the driver. If the problem persists, look for another driver that is compatible with your printer. An updated version may be available through the manufacturer's hotline.

Replenishing the ink supply

When the printer's ink supply is running low, you have two choices: buy a new cartridge or refill the old one. Refilling is much cheaper, and it's also easier on the environment. However, risks are involved in this practice.

First, if you plan to mix your own colors, expect a great deal of trial and error. You have to achieve not only the right color, but also the right consistency. If the ink is too thin, it will run on the paper. If the ink is too thick, it can start to dry out in the cartridge.

The most critical concern, however, is the effect that ink of the wrong consistency, or that contains impurities, can have on the jets. Once the jets become badly plugged with dried ink or foreign particles, you may have no choice but to replace the print head. If your printer has the type of head that is built into the ink cartridge, the only cost involved is some inconvenience and lost time. When you buy a new cartridge, the head is replaced anyway.

On the other hand, you can be looking at a serious repair bill with a permanent print head. Manufacturers explicitly warn against experimenting with ink refills because of their negative effect on the life of the unit. Some manufacturers will even void the warranty.

If you still want to follow the refill route, we know a better way. You can buy refill kits for many printer models. As long as you buy the right kit for your printer and use it according to directions, the ink should be suitable and safe. Some color ink cartridges are designed to be non-refillable. Third party manufacturers offer slightly modified multiple use replacement cartridges for these models.

The printer does not print with a new ink cartridge

The new cartridge may be installed incorrectly. Try removing and inserting it again. If the cartridge has an integrated print head, make certain to remove the protective foil that covers the jets.

Keeping the jets from plugging up

Inkjets can plug up when exposed to air. Therefore, you should keep the print head in its park position when the printer is not in use. A special cushion covers the jets when they're in the park position. This cushion keeps them from drying out. You should also protect your printer from excessive dust. You may want to consider using a dust cover, depending on your environment.

With printers that use removable ink cartridges (*e.g.*, some HP Deskjets), remember to put the cartridge you're not using back in its case immediately. This prevents them from drying out.

Cleaning the print head

The print head of an inkjet printer will eventually require cleaning. If your printer's head is built into the ink cartridge unit, you can simply remove it from the assembly.

Getting at a permanent print head is a little more work. Start by unplugging the power cord. Then remove the paper from the printer. Next, remove the ink cartridge. When the printer is turned off, the print head rests at the far left in a special cushion that protects the jets from drying out. The proper technique for removing the head from its rest position varies from model to model. Examine the assembly carefully before taking anything apart. If you have doubts about how to proceed, have an expert do the job.

The next step applies to some of the Epson models. To free the print head, carefully press back the plate on which the cushion is mounted. Slide the print head to the right. A thin foil between the print head and the printer contains conductors that carry electrical impulses to control the jets. Free this gently if necessary so the head can move. Be very careful not to crimp or tear the foil. If it is damaged, the print head won't operate correctly.

Undo the fasteners holding the head in place (depending on the model, these are either screws or stops of some type). Lift the head out of the printer. It will remain connected to the printer by the tubing that leads to the ink cartridge. It is not necessary to disconnect the tubing.

Start the cleaning process, which is the same for all models. Use a lint-free cloth that has been dipped in rubbing alcohol. Dab the jets carefully to dissolve the dried ink. Repeat this step a few times until all the jets are unplugged and free of ink buildup.

Then reassemble the printer and run a self-test. Don't be alarmed if nothing appears on the paper at first. It may take a while until the cleaning solvent is cleared from the jets and printing returns to normal. If problems persist, and if flushing the jets with the printer's built-in cleaning option doesn't help, switch off the printer and check everything. You may have to retrace your steps until you find a faulty connection or even repeat the cleaning process.

Laser printers

How they work

In laser printers, a laser beam paints a bit pattern on an image drum coated with a light-sensitive material. Before the drum is exposed to the laser, a corona wire places a negative charge on its surface. This charge is removed wherever the beam subsequently strikes the drum. Negatively charged toner then adheres only to the areas that have been discharged by the laser. It does not adhere to the remaining areas because like charges repel each other.

Next, as paper rolls past the drum, a positively charged corona wire underneath the paper pulls the negative toner particles from the drum onto the paper's surface. Finally, rollers draw the paper through a fixing unit, where the paper is heated to about 300°F. The extreme heat melts the resin in the toner and fuses the toner particles to the paper.

A very similar technology is used in LED and LCS printers. These types differ from laser printers only in the means used to expose the drum. The LED technology uses light-emitting diodes, while LCS uses a powerful halogen lamp whose light is directed through liquid crystal. Because everything else works the same, for practical purposes these are grouped in the same class as laser printers.

The printer processes data but does not print

Wishing to print out the CONFIG.SYS file, you type the following MS-DOS command:

```
C:\TYPE CONFIG.SYS > PRN
```

You watch the printer expectantly. The lights blink. The printer is receiving data. And finally,... nothing else happens.

As page printers, laser printers can print complete pages only. A page is not actually printed until the device has received more data than it can fit on the paper, or until the program sends it a FORM FEED command.

You can prompt the printer into action by issuing a manual form feed. Press the ON-LINE button to take the printer off line. Then press the FORM-FEED button. Finally, press ON-LINE again to restart the printer.

Another way around the problem is to send the escape sequence for the FORM-FEED (ASCII value 0D) from the computer to the printer. This is easily done using the ECHO command as follows:

```
ECHO ^L > PRN
```

Type the "^L" character by holding down Ctrl while pressing L. If you need to do this often, use the DOS editor to make a batch file containing the command line, and call it FF.BAT. Then you can generate a form feed by simply typing FF.

Now the printer will print your CONFIG.SYS file and eject the page.

A paper jam message appears

You should have a general indication of where the paper is jammed (depending on the model). Check your manual for specific instructions on accessing the problem area. Remove the paper carefully without disturbing any of the printer's operating components. The thin corona wires, which are very sensitive to damage, are visible in some models.

If the message persists after you have removed the paper, a small scrap may still be blocking the sensor. Another possible cause for this error is a sensor that has become smudged with toner.

Loose toner has collected inside the printer

When a paper jam occurs before print has been fixed by the fusing unit, loose toner can spill inside the printer. Some will also accumulate in the course of time with normal printing. Loose toner can be picked up and fused to the page in small flecks, blemishing subsequent output. To prevent this, use a lint free cloth to clean the inside of your printer. Be careful not to damage the corona wires that may be exposed in some printers (older models in particular).

The fine corona wires must be protected against damage.

You'll find more cleaning tips in the information "Proper printer maintenance," earlier in this section.

The print is gradually becoming lighter

The toner supply is running low. You can probably print a few more pages by removing the toner cartridge and gently shaking it. This helps distribute the remaining toner. However, you'll soon need to replace the cartridge.

The print is too light

An economy feature on some printers allows you to reduce the amount of toner used by about 50%. You can place the printer in this mode for development and testing, then switch to normal printing for the final output. The option is controlled by a setting on the control panel or through software. Some printers (for example, the Brother HL-8) have a regulator for setting toner saturation manually. Don't use too high a setting, as excess toner may end up loose inside the printer.

If your printer is already adjusted for darker printing, the toner supply is probably low. You can probably print a few more pages by removing the toner cartridge and gently shaking it. This helps distribute the remaining toner.

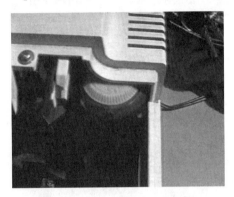

A control wheel allows adjustment of the toner output.

Another possible cause of this problem is paper that does not meet the manufacturer's specifications for the printer.

The toner does not adhere to the paper

You are probably using the wrong toner. If you have just installed a new cartridge, contact the dealer and try to exchange it.

A more serious possibility is a damaged fusing unit or corona wire. You'll need a trained technician to diagnose and correct these problems.

You have just replaced the toner cartridge, and printing still does not return to normal

You have probably forgotten to unseal the new cartridge. You must remove a plastic strip to open the cartridge before inserting it in the printer. Check the installation instructions that came with the cartridge.

A graphic prints across more than one page

This problem occurs when the graphic is too large for the printer's memory. Laser printers are page printers. They must load the contents of the page to be printed into their internal RAM. A very complex graphic may exceed the space available.

When the first part of the image fills the RAM, the printer prints a page with that portion of the image. Then the RAM is cleared, more data is sent to the printer, and another portion of the image is printed. Here are a few tips to make the most of your printer's memory.

You can reduce the printer driver's resolution setting, or shrink the image before printing it. Both options will degrade the print quality.

Some printers have special data compression capabilities. If this is the case with your printer, try setting your driver for a higher compression rate. This is also likely to affect output quality.

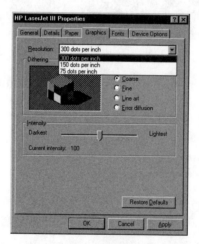

Lower the output resolution by changing your printer settings.

The ultimate solution is to add more memory. Refer to the user's manual for information on the type of memory expansion your printer uses and the steps required to install it.

The printout shows vertical white streaks

This is usually a sign that you are running out of toner. You can probably print a few more pages by removing the toner cartridge and gently shaking it. This helps distribute the remaining toner.

The optical components may also require cleaning. This part of the printer is specially shielded to prevent the scattering of light from the laser. The opening through which the beam is focused is covered with glass or plastic to keep out dust. Many printers (such as the HP 4P) have a special brush for cleaning this covering. Use this brush if it's included with your printer. Other devices can easily cause scratches. At this point, doing any more with this part of your printer can be dangerous and should be left to an expert.

A defect in the printer may also cause vertical white streaks to appear. If you suspect a problem, take it to your dealer or service technician.

The printout shows vertical black streaks

The light-sensitive layer on the surface of the image drum is probably scratched, in which case the drum will have to be replaced. Some printers have the image drum housed with the toner cartridge. If yours is such a model, replace the toner cartridge.

If the streaks are smeared, damage to the fusing unit is indicated. This is not a problem you can fix yourself. You'll have to take the printer in for repairs.

The printout contains black flecks

If the size and placement of the flecks changes from page to page, loose toner inside the printer may be the culprit. The toner can be removed by cleaning as described earlier. If this is not the problem, perhaps you're using the wrong type of paper or printing on the wrong side. A third cause may be damage to the toner cartridge. Installing a new cartridge will take care of the problem in that case.

If the flecks are always in the same place, the image drum is probably damaged. It may have been exposed too long to bright light when the printer was opened for cleaning or to clear a paper jam.

4 *Windows 98 Emergency First Aid*

GDI printers

How they work

GDI printers resemble laser printers mechanically. They have a bidirectional parallel interface and require the Windows graphic device interface (GDI) to run. Print data is sent directly to the printer as a raster graphic.

GDI printers cannot perform any data conversion because they lack certain components. These components include main memory and a RIP processor (raster image processor). This makes them correspondingly cheaper than normal laser printers with comparable features.

Because they receive the data ready for printing, GDI printers start printing faster than normal printers. A fast computer with at least eight Meg of memory is required, however, since the computer does the data conversion. A further disadvantage of these "dumb" printers is that they are designed for printing under Windows only. Printing from a DOS program can be done only by running the program in the Windows DOS prompt.

Printing takes forever

GDI printers do not prepare the data for printing. Instead, the Windows internal GDI module prepares the data. This requires processor time during which other applications must share system resources with the GDI module. The following are some suggestions to accelerate printing:

The quickest solution is to close unneeded applications. This will free up system resources. Otherwise, you may need to upgrade your system. While you should have at least eight Meg of RAM, the rule with GDI printers is "the more, the better." If you have a 386 or 486SX processor, consider upgrading to a Pentium if you're using a GDI printer.

Why is printing in the DOS box so slow?

Whenever you print on a GDI printer, even from the DOS box, the program's data must first be converted to a form the printer understands. This is more time-consuming than sending the data directly to a non-GDI printer.

The printer does not work in MS-DOS mode

This problem is inherent in the GDI printers and has no solution. You can learn more about this at the beginning of this section, under "How they work."

Thermotransfer printers

How they work

Thermotransfer printers are page printers. In this type of printer, a color ribbon passes over a heating bar that spans the entire page width. This heating bar consists of tiny heating elements. When an element is heated, the ink melts and is pressed from the ribbon onto the page.

The ribbon is divided into a series of four color sections. Each one of these sections is at least as large as the largest print format. A thermotransfer printer uses the same amount of ribbon regardless of how many pixels or characters it prints on the page. When the ribbon runs out, it must be replaced. Because they must print in four separate passes, these devices use very high-precision print mechanisms. Thermotransfer printers use ordinary, uncoated paper.

Pixels of color are incorrectly placed

The print mechanism is probably defective or out of adjustment. Because of their high-precision, these printers should be serviced only by a qualified technician.

The printout shows vertical streaks

A heating element is probably defective. This is not a repair you should attempt to make yourself. Take your printer to an authorized service person.

Printer problems under Windows

Nothing prints under Windows

Before you panic when none of your documents will print, make certain you haven't inadvertently selected the Work offline option for the printer. This is set under Printers in the Control Panel.

Printers

HP LaserJet 4000 Series PCL 5e

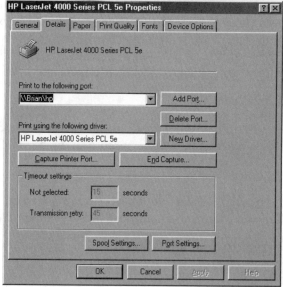

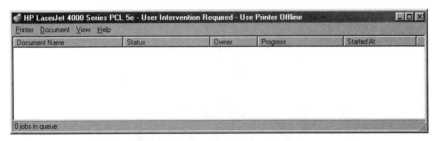

The Print Manager in offline mode.

If this isn't causing the problem, you might want to forgo any further troubleshooting and reinstall the printer. First, remove it by clicking **Start** | **Settings** | **Printers**, selecting the printer, then clicking **File** | **Delete**. Answer Yes to the prompt.

Removing the printer.

Then double-click the Add Printer icon. Answer the subsequent questions concerning your printer model. Once you reboot to implement the new installation, your problem will hopefully have cleared up on its own. This rather unconventional solution is in many cases the easiest way to address printer problems.

If the printer still refuses to work, try your luck with the Windows built-in printer help. Open the Control Panel. Double-click the Printers icon. Click the icon corresponding to your printer. Then select **File** | **Properties** and click the Print Test Page button.

The Print test page button is found under the General tab.

Clicking the Print Test Page button should initiate a test printout. If the printer fails to respond, click No in the dialog box. Then follow the instructions and suggestions offered by the Windows 98 on-line printer help.

No driver exists

With the number of printers available, it's possible that Windows 98 shipped without a driver for your specific model. One option is to install a different Windows 98 driver that is compatible with your printer. Many printers are compatible with printers from popular manufacturers ("LaserJet II-compatible," for example).

A compatible driver may still leave some of your printer's features unsupported, however. Another option is to install an earlier version of the driver for your printer through the Device Manager. Chapter 6 will explain how this is done. Remember, however, old drivers are not guaranteed to work with Windows 98. The best solution is to get the appropriate Windows 98 driver from your dealer, manufacturer or the internet.

Problems with Lexmark printers

If you experience bidirectional printing problems with a Lexmark Series 40x9 printer, check for a file called "LEX01.386" in the Windows\System directory. If it is present, add the following line to the [386 Enhanced] section of SYSTEM.INI.

```
device=*lex01.386
WPSLPT#=1
```

Replace the pound sign '#' with the number of the parallel port where the printer is connected (*i.e.*, WPSLPT1=1 for connection to parallel port 1).

Error 21 Printer overload, on an HP-LaserJet

If the above error message occurs on an HP-LaserJet, open the Control Panel. Double-click the Printers icon. Select (but don't double-click) the icon corresponding to your HP printer. Select the **File | Properties** command. Then select the "Device Options" tab. Make sure the "Page Protection" option in the "Device option" area is selected.

LaserJet 3 models require setting this option through the printer's control panel. If the page protect option is not available for the LaserJet 4, switch from raster to vector mode. Select the "Graphics" tab. An alternative is to reduce the complexity of the data you're trying to print.

Enabling the Page protect option for HP LaserJet drivers.

No TrueType fonts on inkjet printers

TrueType fonts are normally not available at low resolutions (75-150 dpi). Select a higher resolution in your printer settings to print TrueType fonts.

Modem Problems

A modem on your PC connects you with worldwide bulletin boards and online services. Communicate with friends and colleagues, even conduct financial business from the comfort of your home or office.

A modem offers many great advantages. However, they also offer frustration in getting the hardware and software installed and running. Connecting an external modem to the serial port, or even installing an internal one in a free slot, is the easy part. The real challenge is in configuring the setup. This challenge has frustrated even the most experienced computer user.

Learning a little about how hardware and software components work together can help make the job easier. Data is sent from the computer to the modem, which converts it to signals that can be carried over a phone line. The role of the serial interface is to package each data byte as eight successive bits. The modem then converts the bits to tones and sends them over the line. At the receiving end, a second modem converts the tones back to bits. The receiving computer's serial interface assembles the bits into bytes and passes them on to the computer. The data is then available for further processing.

The modem does not respond

If you start your terminal program and the modem does not respond, you have several possibilities to check. Some are specific to an internal modem that occupies a slot on the system board. Other possibilities are specific to an external modem that runs off one of the computer's serial ports.

An internal modem is configured like an additional serial interface. It's assigned a corresponding interrupt and port address. The computer's BIOS normally manages a maximum of four serial interfaces. These share interrupts in pairs. The following lists the standard arrangement:

```
COM1 and COM3 use Interrupt 4
COM2 and COM4 use Interrupt 3
```

Port addresses are specified in hex code. The following lists their assignments:

```
COM1 - 3F8h
COM2 - 2F8h
COM3 - 3E8h
COM4 - 2E8h
```

If your mouse is attached to COM1, do not put your modem on COM3. You will inevitably have interrupt conflicts that will interfere with the functioning of both devices. Configure the modem as COM2. If your computer is already using a second serial interface, it may have to be disabled. Combination controllers or interface cards have jumpers or DIP switches for enabling and disabling interfaces. Read your card's instructions to determine the proper settings.

The next consideration is whether hardware and software components agree on the interface parameters being used. The terminal program requires interrupt and port address settings to match those of the modem card. If the settings don't match, the software will not be able to communicate with the modem. Interrupts and port addresses often get doubly assigned, which can also produce this effect.

Make certain your system does not have two cards using the same interrupt and port address. PC_INFO lets you check these assignments for the hardware. Check for the same settings in your terminal program or the Datex-J/BTX decoder.

If you're using an external modem, interrupts and port addresses are not likely to be a problem. Troubles can often be traced to the connecting cable between the modem and the PC's serial port. You cannot use a null modem cable here. Both plugs must be connected at a 1:1 ratio. The Appendices shows how a connecting cable from serial port to modem should be wired.

Once you have ruled out any obvious hardware problems, have the Windows Hardware Wizard recheck your modem. Make certain the modem is turned on when this is done. If the Wizard fails to recognize your modem automatically, you will have to select one of the standard modem types manually to make the connection. In such a case, you will not be able to use the modem's special features, such as volume control.

4 *Windows 98 Emergency First Aid*

The modem does not dial

Most terminal programs use tone dialing as the default setting. Although this is available in some most of the U.S., some telephone networks still uses pulse dialing. If you use pulse dialing, you'll have to make some adjustments. The AT command must be changed accordingly. Instead of AT DT (for tone dialing), enter the setting AT DP (for pulse dialing) into your terminal program.

Open the Control Panel and double-click the Modems icon. Then click the *Dialing properties* button to access the settings for the dialing properties.

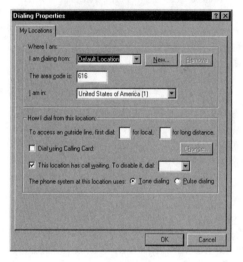

Selecting the dialing mode

Here you can choose between the two dialing modes.

The modem reports "No Dialtone"

The terminal program has a setting to control the amount of time the modem should wait for a dial tone after picking up the phone line. When this time has elapsed, the message "No Dialtone" appears on the screen.

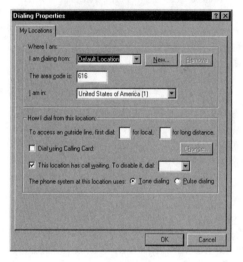

This message may result when the modem is not able to recognize the dial tone for a company's internal telephone network. The command AT X3 lets you turn off dialtone detection. To configure your modem for permanent use within the network, you can modify the initialization string accordingly.

The modem hangs up too soon

It takes time for two modems to establish communication with each other. The initial phase, in which they attempt to settle on common data transfer parameters, is sometimes called negotiation. If this process takes too long, as may happen with a bad connection, the terminal program hangs up. You can allow more time by increasing the value in the S7 register. To allow a connect time of 90 seconds, type S7=90 in your initialization string. Many terminal programs let you choose this setting with a separate menu option so you don't have to type the code yourself.

The modems negotiate but cannot establish a connection

If your speaker is turned on, you may hear the two modems 'talking' to each other during the negotiation phase, but after a short time the connection breaks off and the message "No Carrier" appears. There are two possible causes. The first is that one of the modems is not working properly. The very high-precision components of faster modems are especially sensitive to irregularities. If you can make contact with a different modem, yours is probably functioning correctly. If not, have the modem checked. It may be defective or require a ROM upgrade to improve its negotiating performance.

The second possible cause is that the modems cannot agree on the use of a common protocol. Both devices must adopt the same transfer speed and error detection method. If the receiving modem is set for V.32 with a data transfer rate of 14.4 bps, for example, while the calling modem is V.22 with a rate of 28.8 bps, they will not be able to connect. Make certain both modems are configured to adjust automatically to the required parameters. The modem's manual should describe how to code this option in the initialization string.

To access the initialization string under Windows, first double-click the Modems icon in the Control Panel. Then click the [Properties] button and select the "Connections" tab. Then click the [Advanced...] button. Here you can type the desired initialization string for the modem.

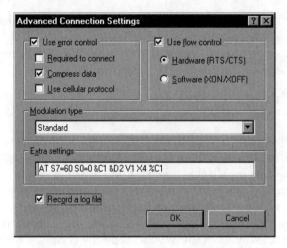

Special options can be set via the initialization string.

Devices with MNP 4 or V.42 (or V.90) error control can be configured with an AT command to refuse calls from modems without error control. To change this, you must modify the initialization string accordingly. Consult your modem manual for details.

Received data is displayed as 'garbage'

Once your modem has established a stable connection with the remote location, data transmission can begin. When your terminal program displays the incoming data on your monitor, it must use the correct settings to interpret the data properly. A garbled display indicates the wrong settings are being used.

The display of incoming data is garbled.

Check the protocol settings for your program. Most bulletin board systems require the following:

```
8 data bits, no parity, 1 stop bit (8,n,1)
```

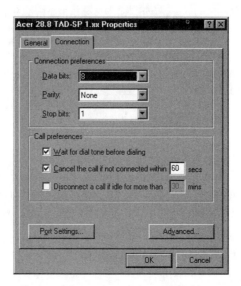

Protocol (transfer parameter) settings.

Also check for the proper terminal emulation. This determines the functions of control characters that are transmitted along with the data. The most widely used is ANSI. Others are TTY, VT-52, VT-100, VT-102, and AVATAR.

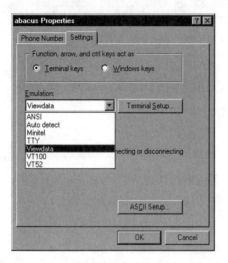

The proper terminal emulation is also required

The transfer speed between the computer and modem also plays a role. If the terminal program sends more data to the modem than it can transmit in a given time, the transmission will be faulty. The computer then uses the wrong transfer rate to interpret incoming data and undefined characters appear on the screen.

Typed characters are doubled

If every character you type appears twice on the screen, local echo is most likely enabled. First, the terminal program is displaying the character. Then it's being echoed from the modem and displayed again. You can correct the problem by turning the local echo option off.

In HyperTerminal, click the [Properties] button and select the "Settings" tab. Then click the [ASCII Setup] button to access the setting for local echo.

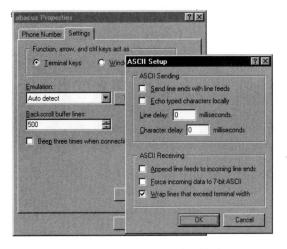

Local echo should be disabled.

Other terminal programs handle local echo differently, so it is possible that you will see nothing at all on the screen unless this option is enabled. Check the program documentation for selecting the required setting.

Transfer errors when uploading or downloading

If you have a high-speed modem, and your file transfers stop after the first few kilobytes, make certain your hardware parameters are set for hardware handshaking (RTS/CTS). The computer uses data compression to send data to the modem faster than the modem can transmit it. After a short time, the modem signals the computer that its buffer is full and transmission stops. The software handshake (Xon/Xoff) should never be used with a high-speed modem.

The modem suddenly disconnects

When data transfer proceeds normally for a time, but then is suddenly interrupted, the cause is usually a bad telephone connection. The fact that some transfer occurs indicates that the modem and port settings are correct. However, there may be noise in the line from electrical interference or the phone company's toll pulse. The connection is lost when the noise becomes too strong and obscures the carrier signal.

If you suspect this to be the problem, place a voice call over the line and listen for background noise. If you continually hear static or other disturbance, you may want the phone company to check your line. Special 16KHz band filters are also available from electronics stores to remove the toll pulse. Most external toll counters already have such a filter built-in. Make certain your modem is connected after the filter.

One more way to solve the toll pulse problem is setting your modem to tolerate a brief loss of the carrier signal. It will disconnect only after the specified tolerance interval has been exceeded. The interval is set in the S10 register in tenths of seconds. For example, the command:

```
AT S10=15
```

tells your modem not to disconnect unless the carrier signal is lost for more than one and a half seconds.

Problems with high transfer rates on serial interfaces

At very high speeds, incorrect or missing characters or the loss of a connection is more likely related to the computer than to the phone line. Transfer rates above 19200 bps can cause problems between the computer and the modem, especially for terminal programs running under Windows on slower computers.

If you need to work with higher transfer rates, your serial port can be equipped with a special UART chip. This is the 16550 or 16550AF UART chip. You can buy these chips for about $25 from computer dealers. Most standard interfaces use the cheaper 16450 UART instead. You can probably make the replacement yourself without a problem.

If you're uncertain which UART chip is in your serial port, use PC_INFO to tell you. Without the special chip, you should limit transfer rates to 19200 bps under DOS or 28.8 bps under Windows. The problem is not necessarily on your end, however. If you are sending data to a computer with a slower serial port, the data may transfer correctly to the receiving modem, but get bogged down between there and the receiving PC.

To access the settings for the UART 16550, double-click the Modems icon on the Control Panel, then click the [Properties] button. Select the "Connection" tab. When you then click the the [Port settings] button button, the dialog box for the FIFO components settings opens.

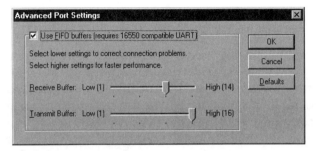

FIFO settings are made here.

Activate or deactivate the FIFO (16550), as required.

Throughput is slow despite a highspeed connection

You've upgraded your modem from 9600 bps to 28.8 bps but data throughput is slower than before. What's the explanation? Higher transfer rates are much more demanding of line quality. Minor interference that would hardly be noticeable at 9600 bps can wreak havoc on highspeed connections. This is one reason the latest and fastest modems have special error correction features.

With this error correction, each data block is checked for errors as it is received. If an error is detected, the modem requests that the block be retransmitted. Such precision can be a mixed blessing, however. With a very poor connection, almost every block transmitted may have an error, requiring repeated transmissions that can slow the overall throughput of data. If you have to contend with inferior line quality, use a slower transfer rate to minimize the necessity for repeat transmissions.

Hardware Run Amok

Can gremlins really control a computer? You try to access the CD-ROM drive in DMA mode and the system crashes. It works fine without DMA. Then the disk drive stops working. Suddenly even the sound card seems to be acting up.

We hope you'll never have to face such problems, but it can happen. If your system is plagued with hardware troubles of no apparent cause, check these troubleshooting tips.

I have resource conflicts

First, check the resources being used by the affected hardware components. It may not be safe to rely on PC_INFO. The type of hardware problem you're experiencing may cause the program to give false information. Instead, check the actual jumper settings of the devices in question. For cards configured from software, run the installation or diagnostic software provided by the manufacturer to check the settings. If you discover conflicts, resolve them and retest the hardware.

Is my systemboard defective?

Unfortunately, the trouble is more likely caused by a defective system board than a resource conflict. What the affected components have in common is their dependence on the DMA controller. Disk drives, CD-ROM drives and sound cards are among the devices that can use DMA (direct memory access) data transfer.

The DMA controller is one of the most sensitive components on the system board. High cycle frequencies and excessive heat can overwork the controller and eventually damage it. If the devices mentioned in the scenario above are giving you trouble, your DMA controller is definitely suspect. Since this is invariably located on the system board, and usually integrated into a peripheral controller as well, the board will probably have to be replaced. Before taking such a drastic step, however, you should test the peripheral devices on another computer.

SCSI Problems

Although it represents the most easily manipulated bus system for connecting peripherals to your computer, the SCSI (Small Computer System Interface) interface is not without its problems. You must follow certain rules when installing a SCSI bus system. If not, you're guaranteed to have trouble. This section gives you the basic information you need for error-free SCSI performance.

Termination on the SCSI bus

One of the most important principles of SCSI technology is terminating the bus. A mistake here is sure to be the source of problems.

Passive termination is usually provided by a set of resistors that plugs into a socket provided for this purpose.

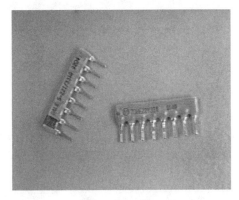

Terminator resistors

The internal construction of the resistor network requires proper orientation of the terminator plug. Pin 1 of the plug is usually marked with a small dot or a wide stripe. On the SCSI device, pin 1 is usually labeled on the socket. If you can't find such a label, look for the square hole (this is for pin 1) or check the documentation.

Some manufacturers are equipping the newer SCSI devices with active termination. An electronic switch replaces the resistors in active termination. You can turn active termination on/off through jumpers or software settings.

If your system consists, for example, of a SCSI host adapter and a single SCSI hard drive, both components should be terminated. If the system is later expanded by adding an internal CD-ROM drive, the new drive should be connected in the middle of the bus and should not be terminated. This means removing a passive terminator or disabling active termination, depending on the device.

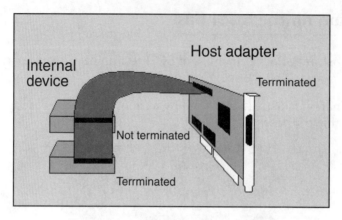

Termination with internal components.

If you add an external CD-ROM drive, on the other hand, this will require termination. The host adapter will now be in the middle. It should have its terminator deactivated or removed. If the system consists entirely of the host adapter and one external device, both should be terminated.

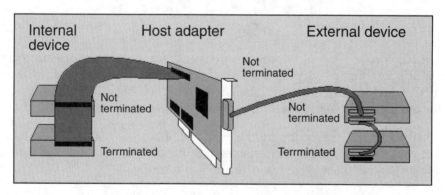

Termination with external and internal components.

Duplicating the power supply to the terminator can cause malfunctioning SCSI devices. The result can mimic the problem of duplicate SCSI IDs, where some components on the SCSI bus may fail to be recognized. The terminator power (TRMPWR) line is ordinarily provided through the host adapter, which also assumes the function of overload protection for the line. Many SCSI devices are factory preset to feed the TRMPWR line. To change this, you can disable the power supply to the terminating resistors via jumpers. Check the documentation for detailed instructions.

Some SCSI devices are not equipped with terminators. To use such a device as the last one on the chain, you must obtain a pass-through terminator and plug it between the device and the SCSI cable.

SCSI ID numbers

As many as seven devices can be attached to a single host adapter. These devices can include hard drives, CD-ROM drives, tape drives and scanners. Each device, including the host adapter, is assigned a unique SCSI ID number. This number is set using jumpers or switches.

The host adapter is usually factory preset for ID number 7. Do not change this number. The ID numbers 0 through 6 are available for the connected SCSI devices. If the computer boots from a SCSI hard drive, this drive must have ID number 0. The remaining IDs can be assigned in any order. However, no two components within a SCSI bus system can have the same ID.

Older host adapters are an exception to the above guidelines. Here, the IDs 0 and 1 are reserved exclusively for hard drives and should not be assigned to any other devices.

SCSI parity checking

A SCSI bus can perform parity checking to safeguard data integrity. This is invoked as an option by setting jumpers or DIP switches on the individual components (see the documentation for each device). You'll want to take advantage of parity checking and change the settings for any device that ships with the option disabled. You cannot mix modes on a SCSI bus system. It's an all or nothing scene—either all the components use parity checking or none do. To override parity checking, disable the option on the host adapter and on each individual connected device.

Most computers with an onboard SCSI host adapter have the NCR adapter, which is factory preset to enable parity checking. Although parity checking is part of the SCSI-2 standard, many of the older SCSI-1 adapters did not use this option. You should check whether it needs to be enabled when connecting any new components on your system.

4 *Windows 98 Emergency First Aid*

The troublesome SCSI cable

Some SCSI problems can be traced to the SCSI cable. Usually the ribbon cable used is relatively immune to electrical disturbances, since there is always a ground wire between two signal lines. If it is too close to a source of interference, however, such as the computer's power supply, problems can occur. Keep at least 3cm between such components and the cable.

A sharp kink in the cable can also result in interference. The SCSI-2 standard calls for a minimum clearance of one-half inch around the cable. If the ribbon is kinked, the effect is as if two cables were lying directly against each other.

Although they are rather expensive, you should use only high-quality SCSI cables for connecting external SCSI devices. This holds especially true if you are using fast SCSI components in your system.

Another problem can be excessive cable length. Normally, with a single-ended SCSI bus system, which uses the 50-pin ribbon cable, you can have up to 20 feet of cable. Problems may arise at even half this length, however, with time-outs being reported for SCSI devices.

BIOS or no BIOS?

Confusion seems to surround the issue of SCSI BIOS. Although a few SCSI host adapters come without their own BIOS, this is usually integrated into the adapter on an EPROM. A sound card, on the other hand, does not include the BIOS on its integrated SCSI interface. However, even this interface is essentially a full-fledged SCSI adapter.

A SCSI BIOS is usually not required. You can operate such devices as CD-ROM drives, scanners and even hard drives on a SCSI adapter with no BIOS. Such adapters have the advantage of being somewhat cheaper. You will need SCSI BIOS, however, if you want your computer to boot from a SCSI hard drive. In this case, make certain the BIOS on the host adapter is enabled. It will then be mapped into a reserved memory area in the computer's UMB (upper memory blocks).

When using the SCSI BIOS, do not enable the Shadow RAM option for the reserved memory area. The host adapter uses this area for data exchange and other functions. Shadow RAM would conflict with these purposes and invariably lead to trouble.

If the computer is to boot from a SCSI hard drive, you must, as we mentioned, activate the BIOS of the host adapter to which the disk is connected. In addition, the boot disk must be assigned SCSI ID number 0 for the boot process to work. There may also be a third requirement, that the host adapter be configured to a certain port address (for example, the Adaptec AHA 1542B adapter requires address 330h). If a specific address is required, the appropriate information will be explained in the documentation.

I have more than one host adapter in my computer

A system can have multiple SCSI host adapters installed. Each one represents its own independent SCSI bus system. This means that each one can have up to seven connected SCSI devices and, as a whole, is also subject to the other specifications we have discussed.

You may have a SCSI-1 bus system and a SCSI-2 bus system on the same computer. Make certain not to create any IRQ, DMA or port address conflicts with existing components when installing a new adapter. Also, be sure to enable the BIOS on only one of the adapters. This will be the adapter that controls the boot disk, if you are booting from a SCSI hard drive.

A SCSI adapter in addition to an (E)IDE adapter

Although this is possible, problems can occur, however, if both systems have an integrated floppy controller. This is likely to be the case. The computer then reports an "FDD Controller failure" when booting. Only the floppy interface of the primary controller should be active. The primary controller is the one connected to the boot drive. Disable the floppy interface of the other controller, following the instructions in the manufacturer's documentation.

The right SCSI driver

Normally, a SCSI system requires at least two drivers. These are called in the CONFIG.SYS file. The first driver is the actual SCSI manager. This driver is normally required, since it acts as the program interface to the host adapter. This adapter in turn relays all SCSI commands to the various device drivers.

The driver for Adaptec adapters, for example, is called ASPIxDOS.SYS. The equivalent for most NCR adapters is DOSCAM.SYS. Each device also needs its own driver to enable DOS to access it. Adaptec uses the driver ASPIDISK.SYS for hard drives. A device driver can usually support multiple SCSI devices of the same type.

A host adapter normally includes one or more diskettes. These diskettes contain the installation software and drivers for the SCSI devices. Many include additional utilities, such as diagnostic software and partitioning or formatting programs. Windows drivers may also be provided to let Windows access the SCSI devices.

Some SCSI setups do not require any driver at all. This is the case when a computer boots from a SCSI hard drive and the system contains no additional SCSI devices beyond a maximum of two SCSI hard drives. Here, the active SCSI BIOS assumes all driver functions. The first hard drive must have SCSI ID number 0, and the second, if present, must have ID number 1. If later another SCSI device is installed, at least two drivers will be needed: the SCSI manager and the appropriate device driver. Any hard drives on a second adapter also need their own drivers, since this adapter must have its BIOS disabled.

You save memory by eliminating the SCSI drivers on a system containing only one or two hard drives. However, a trade-off in terms of performance is the result. Access to the SCSI BIOS must occur through the adapter's EPROM, which is where the BIOS resides. This is the slowest type of access. Definitely install the drivers if you can spare the memory requirements. Then access to the SCSI BIOS will be handled exclusively by the drivers. They'll execute a great deal faster because they reside in memory.

You probably won't need to install any drivers under Windows 98, since 32-bit drivers for the most popular host adapters are already included. If you want to access SCSI devices under DOS, however, you will need to install their DOS drivers yourself.

When you do, leave the Windows drivers alone. Start by making a backup copy of the SYSTEM.INI file, which is usually found in the Windows directory. This will allow you to undo any changes that the driver installation software may make to the file. Some programs automatically update SYSTEM.INI entries for Windows drivers, without giving you a chance to override the changes.

When the installation is complete, restore SYSTEM.INI from the backup. In the unlikely event that you do have to install a Windows 98 driver for a particular device, use the Device Manager. Refer to the Chapter 6 for more information on this procedure.

Typical problems with SCSI devices

By now you have seen that installing a SCSI bus system involves certain pitfalls if you're not careful. Serious errors will result if you overlook critical details. The following explains the most common of these errors.

The SCSI utility program cannot find the adapter

This indicates a memory conflict in the UMB (Upper Memory Block). The UMB is the area of memory where the host adapter's BIOS is located. The memory manager EMM386.EXE usually recognizes the ROM-BIOS and excludes this area from the UMB. However, a conflict will occur if the Include parameter (I=xxxx-yyyy) has explicitly assigned it to the UMB. The host adapter's BIOS will not be functional, and the SCSI utility program will not detect the adapter. Correct the Include parameter, or assign another memory address to the ROM-BIOS. This is normally done using jumpers. Refer to the user's manual of the adapter for more information.

If the memory conflict is occurring without the Include parameter, try adding the Exclude parameter (X=xxxx-yyyy) to explicitly exclude the memory area for the ROM-BIOS from the UMB.

Another cause of this problem could be the SCSI utility itself. You may be using an outdated version, or one that is not designed for use with your host adapter. Buy an appropriate utility version from the adapter manufacturer or your computer dealer.

After an additional SCSI device is installed, both the new device and a previously existing one cannot be recognized

This indicates both devices have the same SCSI ID. Duplicate SCSI ID numbers are not allowed. Choose an available ID and reassign it to one of the devices.

A newly installed SCSI device is multiply recognized

Indicates the newly installed device has SCSI ID 7. This is reserved exclusively for the host adapter. Assign a different ID to the device from the numbers available.

A SCSI device will not work with the SCSI adapter

Indicates a problem probably related to parity checking. Perhaps an older SCSI device is not using parity checking, while the host adapter has this option enabled. Conversely, if you have a newer device on a SCSI-1 adapter, parity may be enabled on the device and not on the adapter.

The mixing of parity checking modes within a SCSI bus system is not permitted and will result in numerous errors. For enhanced data integrity, parity checking should be used whenever possible. Change the necessary settings to enable this option on all the system components (see the documentation for complete instructions).

After a new SCSI device is installed, none of the SCSI devices are recognized

This may be caused by duplicate power feed to the terminator resistors. Power is usually supplied through the host adapter. When you install a new device, make certain it's not set to supply power to the resistors as well. Many devices are shipped this way. You must change the setting before installing them on your system.

A particular SCSI device is sometimes not recognized

If the device is the last one on the SCSI bus, the SCSI cable could be the problem. Another possible cause is the terminator power supply. Refer to the earlier discussion on these subjects.

SCSI devices have fuses on the terminator power line to protect against short circuiting. A blown fuse could also cause this problem. Check the fuses with a multimeter or ohmmeter. They come in different styles. The normal style is easy to change. Simply pull it out and replace it with a new one of the same speed and amperage.

A fuse marked 2A M is a 2 Ampere, medium-delay fuse, for example. Another type of fuse looks like an ordinary resistor, but without colored rings. The amperage is printed on it. This type is more difficult to change because it's soldered in place. As you work, make certain you don't damage the device with static discharge. Another style is the SMD fuse. Changing this type of fuse should be left to a qualified technician.

Do not place your entire SCSI system at risk by bridging a blown or defective fuse with a wire. This could damage every device on the bus.

An external SCSI device is not always recognized

If you have ruled out the causes mentioned above, make certain that any external device with its own power supply is turned on before the PC. Otherwise, the driver will not detect the device. You'll have to reboot after turning the device on.

The new SCSI adapter produces permanent errors

You're probably using the SCSI BIOS, but have Shadow RAM activated for its area in the UMB. Go to BIOS Setup and deactivate Shadow RAM for the memory area in question. The exact location of the SCSI BIOS is determined by the configuration of the host adapter. Check the documentation for the adapter or run the PC_INFO program to find this location.

PC_INFO shows the reserved memory area assigned to the SCSI BIOS.

PC_INFO displaying more information.

Even in this case, when the ROM text string does not give any usable information on the SCSI BIOS, we know that the BIOS is for an Adaptec 1542B adapter. Other than the graphic card and the SCSI adapter, this computer had no expansion card with its own BIOS. Shadow RAM must be disabled for the indicated area.

Incorrect Processor is Indicated

This section talks about other areas where computer fraud has occurred. Besides non-functional caches, authorities have found some computers to contain relabeled processors. The upper surface of the housing is filed down to remove the manufacturer's logo and processor type. The component is relabeled as a more expensive one. For example, a Cyrix CPU is sold as an Intel CPU.

Unfortunately, such tampering is difficult to detect. The filing of the original label makes the edges of the housing somewhat sharper than normal. However, unless you're very familiar with the interior of a PC, you probably won't notice. Many processors have a cooling unit or heat sink mounted on top that hides the label.

The following are some other danger signs:

* A sticker covers the label on the top of the processor or on the metal plate below it. Reputable manufacturers would not place a sticker in this location. A sticker could interfere with the unit's cooling.

* PC_INFO or other software indicates a different processor type.

  Most test software provides a reliable diagnosis of the processor type. AMD and Intel CPUs are the most difficult to distinguish apart. A Cyrix or Texas Instruments processor are the easiest to distinguish. Ask your dealer to check your computer system completely.

* If the CPU supports the CPUID command, the CPU type given is completely reliable. Use PC_INFO on the companion CD-ROM to check this.

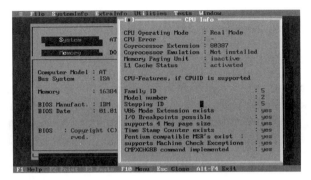

This CPU surrenders its manufacturer and type data via the CPUID command.

Precise type specifications include the family, model number and stepping ID. Report any discrepancy in this data to your dealer.

Unfortunately, the cycle frequency for which a processor was made cannot be determined using software. A 486/DX4 80MHz CPU, for example, can be installed to run at 100 MHz and sold as a 486/DX4 100MHz CPU.

Any test software would confirm this. Running faster than the intended frequency will shorten the processor's life unless adequate cooling is provided. Adding a cooling unit, of course, is a service for which a hardware pirate is not known.

Program Startup in MS-DOS Mode Problems

Simply calling a program at the DOS prompt can result in several error messages. The problem is also often simple and easily solved. The following are several likely errors and their solutions.

DOS prompt error messages

Bad command or file name not found

This is a common error message. Virtually every MS-DOS user has seen it at least once. The most likely cause is a simple typing mistake in the program name. Another possibility is that you have called a valid program, but DOS doesn't know where to find it.

DOS looks for the executable program file first in the current directory. If it cannot find the file by the given name in the current directory, it checks the directories that may have been listed in any PATH statement in the AUTOEXEC.BAT file. DOS then searches those directories. The error message is displayed if DOS still cannot find the file.

Solve the problem by switching to the directory where the program is located. Then reenter the command. If you intend to run the program often, save time by adding a PATH entry for its directory to AUTOEXEC.BAT. Then you can run the program without changing the current directory every time.

Open AUTOEXEC.BAT in a text editor. Make the appropriate changes to the PATH line. For example, if the program's directory is C:\DOSPROGS\DPAINT, extend the PATH line as follows:

```
...
PATH C:\;...;C:\DOSPROGS\DPAINT
...
```

Resave AUTOEXEC.BAT after making your changes. Reboot the computer. The DOS search paths now include the specified directory.

Not enough memory

This error message usually has one of two causes. The program requires a great deal of memory or your DOS startup file is not optimized to make the most efficient use of memory. In the latter case, install the memory manager EMM386.EXE in CONFIG.SYS. This lets drivers and resident programs be loaded into the UMB. More memory will then be available for your program.

Open CONFIG.SYS in a text editor. Add the following behind the line with the HIMEM.SYS entry:

```
DEVICE=C:\WINDOWS\EMM386.EXE  NOEMS
```

For the lines beginning with DEVICE=..., change this to DEVICEHIGH=.... Then the device drivers can be loaded high. Add the line

```
DOS=HIGH,UMB
```

to make the UMB area available.

For example, your CONFIG.SYS might look similar to the following:

```
DEVICE=C:\WINDOWS\HIMEM.SYS
DEVICE=C:\WINDOWS\EMM386.EXE  NOEMS  I=B000-B7FF
DEVICEHIGH=C:\DRIVERS\CDROM\MTMCDE.SYS  ...
DOS=HIGH,UMB
```

Since this system has a color graphics card, the Include parameter I=B000-B7FF allows the 32K video memory for monochrome graphics to be made available in the UMB.

AUTOEXEC.BAT should also be optimized for MS-DOS mode by specifying the LoadHigh command (LH) for resident programs. The following is an example AUTOEXEC.BAT:

```
@ECHO OFF
LH  C:\WINDOWS\COMMAND\DOSKEY.COM  /BUFSIZE=256
LH  C:\WINDOWS\COMMAND\MSCDEX.EXE  ...
LH  C:\DRIVERS\MOUSE\MOUSE.COM
PROMPT $P$G
...
```

Startup files optimized in this way give considerably more memory to executable programs in MS-DOS mode.

Wrong DOS version

This message appears when you try to run an older DOS version of a program under a newer version of DOS. The program itself checks the version number of the installed operating system. It reports an error if the number is higher than its DOS version number.

A likely candidate for this error is the CD-ROM driver MSCDEX.EXE found on the diskette included with your CD-ROM. The DOS version for which the driver was written may be older than the version installed on your computer. This error will appear when you install the CD-ROM drive and call MSCDEX.EXE from the AUTOEXEC.BAT file. Use MSCDEX included in the Windows 98 \COMMAND directory to correct this problem.

Many other drivers and programs assume a specific version of DOS. A well-written DOS driver or program will check the current operating system for this version number before running. If you cannot buy an update of the program, use a program called SETVER instead.

SETVER manages a list of program names that require certain DOS versions. When you run a program from the list, it will "misrepresent" the current operating system as the version required. You can simply add the program name and its DOS version number to this list.

If the program in question is called TEXTER.EXE, for example, and it only wants to run under DOS 5.00, type the following at the DOS prompt:

```
SETVER [Drive:Path\]TEXTER.EXE 5.00
```

TEXTER.EXE and its DOS version will then be placed in the SETVER list. Make certain to also add the following to CONFIG.SYS:

```
DEVICE=C:\WINDOWS\SETVER.EXE
```

or

```
DEVICEHIGH=C:\WINDOWS\SETVER.EXE
```

The "correct" version number will then be reported to the program. Make certain the program is compatible with the version of DOS you're using. Problems can occur if the program is incompatible.

Invalid drive specification in path

This error is not directly related to the program being called. It appears when AUTOEXEC.BAT contains a PATH entry with a nonexistent drive. This can happen in networks, for example, when the network software defines a path that later becomes unavailable.

Check the PATH entries and correct the invalid drive designation.

A strange error text appears when you start a DOS game

Sometimes games don't function at all. This may be related to the memory manager HIMEM.SYS or EMM386.EXE. It could also be related to the computer configuration itself. The games may work on other computers, even with the same operating system. You'll see a message that looks similar to the following when you try to start the game:

```
UNHANDLED EXCEPTION 0Dat 00EF:B602 Error code: FFFC
AX=000D      BX=FFFF     CX=0201      DX=0002
SI=FFFF      DI=005C     BP=0FA6      SP=0F98
CS=00EF      Limit=E4EF  segment #00 of RTM.EXE
DS=00EF      Limit=E4EF  segment #00 of RTM.EXE
ES=00EF      Limit=E4EF  segment #00 of RTM.EXE
SS=009F      Limit=FFFF  segment #00 of RTM.EXE
- 00EF:B5FA 8E D8 8E C0 56 FF 76 0A FF 5E 04 1F C7 06 70 39
```

You must subsequently do a warm boot or reset because most of your RAM is used. The message contains a brief and cryptic explanation of the error. This is followed by the contents of the processor registers at the time the error occurred and a partial dump of the affected memory area.

Such error messages seem increasingly likely to come from shareware games. This is probably due to the nonstandard programming of the XMS memory. This affects games that use the DPMI manager DPMI16BI.EXE and the run-time module RTM.EXE. According to convention, use HIMEM.SYS to make XMS memory available to Interrupt 15h. Older programs then can still use the XMS with this software interface. Problems occur in execution when HIMEM.SYS is used to invoke the Int15h option. Programmers of these games did not follow the convention.

The following entry in the CONFIG.SYS is how this would look:

```
DEVICE=C:\WINDOWS\HIMEM.SYS  /INT15=64
```

This would make 64K of XMS memory available using Interrupt 15h. Few programs still in use address the XMS memory in this way, however, so the unconventional programming in games is justified. Remove the parameter from CONFIG.SYS and the game should work.

What to Do with Processor Errors

You can find bugs in other locations than software. Hardware bugs can exist in the very heart of your computer: the CPU. A design error in the CPU, called a "masking error," can cause a system crash. This system crash seems as if it were caused by a program behaving badly.

Processor layouts have become so incredibly complex that incidental errors may never appear. This is true even during the most rigorous testing of the program. Yet, a very specific combination of conditions can be shown to result in a CPU error. Since the symptoms seem to indicate a software bug, months may pass before the real problem is discovered. Many defective CPUs may be sold during this time.

Once the error is known, programmers can stop using the affected processor commands. This will avoid using the conditions that produced the problem. The desired function can be simulated or replaced by other commands. The processor then works without an interruption.

We're including some of the most important CPU errors as examples. In reality, a complete listing of known CPU defects is much longer. Fortunately you won't need to worry about most CPU errors. Software developers take extreme precautions to avoid these errors.

Replacing the processor

Because the processor is the most critical (and the most expensive) component in your computer, don't attempt any repairs or replacement yourself unless you're familiar with such repairs.

Warning: If you do attempt the repair, make sure to protect the system board and CPU from static discharge by using an anti-static mat and bracelet.

Remove the computer case. Remove all the expansion cards to expose the motherboard. Raise the small lever beside the CPU, and gently lift the CPU from its socket. Then replace it with the new CPU. Fasten the new CPU in place by pressing back down on the lever. The computer should now be ready to reassemble.

In some computers, you can even access the CPU socket without removing any other components.

ZIF sockets greatly facilitate CPU replacement.

Place the old CPU in the package that contained the new one. This package is usually specially treated to eliminate static.

Chapter 5: Interrupts, DMA Channels, Port Addresses

Chapter 5
Interrupts, DMA Channels, Port Addresses

M any users are confused by interrupts, DMA channels and port addresses. For example, you must configure each expansion card so it can do its job in the system. Conventional expansion cards are configured by setting jumpers. But more advanced expansion cards are configured through software and Microsoft's Plug and Play convention, through which the card is automatically configured by the BIOS, is gaining in popularity.

After reading this chapter, you'll be able to install new expansion cards. You'll also learn to avoid and prevent resource conflicts. We'll use illustrations in this chapter to display the communication paths between expansion cards and the system.

Data transfer through the port address

Why do you need the interrupts, DMA channels and port addresses? Wouldn't everything be simpler without them? Yes and no. It would be simpler because users wouldn't have to mess with them. But, their expansion cards (sound cards, video cards, etc.) wouldn't be able to communicate with the system. Each card needs unique system resources to exchange data with the CPU and other cards. Without these, the CPU wouldn't know which devices were asking for what kind of information.

Each card is configured either through hardware (by jumpers) or through software. Once configured, the card will respond to requests at a certain address on the bus and accept the data present there. However, if a second expansion card is incorrectly configured so it uses this same port address, both cards will receive the data from the application. Depending upon the type of cards, nothing will happen.

However, the hardware may be confronted with data that it cannot interpret. The hardware will then refuse to cooperate with the computer. On the other hand, the computer will crash if an application wants to read from a port. Both cards will put their data on the data bus. This could corrupt the data. The application will then process the data incorrectly or the application will simply crash.

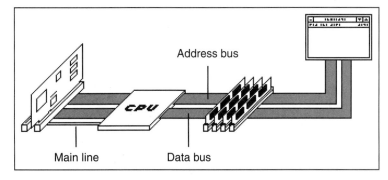

Everything runs through the CPU when transferring data through a port address.

Data transfer using a hardware interrupt

The card can use another option to handle data transfer. The method described above has one disadvantage. The application must first check whether data is ready to be read on the corresponding expansion card or whether the card is ready to accept data. That is an unnecessary waste of computer time.

Instead, a hardware interrupt is selected. If data is on the card ready to be read or the card is able to accept data, it will trigger the interrupt set on the card. The interrupt controller PIC (Programmable Interrupt Controller) will receive the signal and pass it along to the processor over the interrupt line. The processor will then interrupt the running program and process the associated interrupt routine.

By the time an interrupt handler has been triggered, it is able to react appropriately. Once the interrupt program is done, the processor will continue with the application. It now receives the message from the interrupt handler. It reads the data from the expansion card if the interrupt handler has not read the data itself.

5 *Interrupts, DMA Channels, Port Addresses*

However, if an interrupt is assigned to more than one card, the interrupt will be activated when the incorrectly configured card triggers an interrupt. This results in the application or the interrupt handler requesting to receive data from the proper expansion card. When the program receives completely unusable data, the computer may crash.

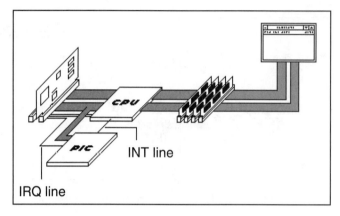

The PIC tells the CPU when a data transfer can occur.

Data transfer using a DMA channel

Some cards have to manage a large amount of data. This category includes drive controllers such as SCSI adapters or CD-ROM controllers. However, even sound cards have to process large amounts of data when reproducing sound. With data transfers of this type, the path through the CPU is undesirable, because it will block the processor for too long a time. This would be an unnecessary waste of computer time.

The path chosen in this case is through the DMA controller, so the data passed by the CPU arrives in working memory directly. This does not burden the processor as much. The application can read the data from memory, which goes much faster than through the port address of the card.

The willingness to accept a data transfer is not signaled by means of a hardware interrupt. Two cards that are configured so they use the same DMA channel can affect how the hardware components operate. If an incomplete DMA transfer is interrupted

302

by a new transfer, the result can be true chaos. This chaos is due to the incorrectly initialized DMA controller. The computer may not crash. However, the hardware components that try to use the DMA channel at the same time will usually not work.

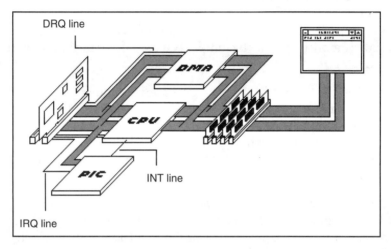

The CPU is not involved in DMA transfers.

ROM expansions

Finally, cards are available that have their own ROM expansions or their own BIOSes. These include, for example, SCSI adapters and network adapters. Graphic cards also may have their own BIOSes.

> **TIP** Remember this when you want to boot with the SCSI disk. When the separate BIOS in such cards must be used (i.e., SCSI adapters) , make certain no memory conflicts arise due to incorrect configuration. The computer will crash as a result. PC_INFO lets you view the ROM expansions already installed. PC_INFO also shows the memory block reserved by the ROM and its size. You can then set a correspondingly free memory block on your expansion card. This can be done with jumpers or with the help of the installation software.

Unfortunately, the topic of interrupts, DMA channels and port addresses is very complicated and could easily fill an entire book. However, it should be clear how the expansion cards operate within the total computer system.

What to Look for when Installing an Expansion Card

Whenever a new card is installed, the resources it will use must be set on this card. This is accomplished either by jumpers on the card or by the software that came with the card.

It's usually necessary to specify at least a port address and an interrupt. Depending upon the type of card, specifying a DMA channel and reserving the memory block for any BIOS present may also be required. For your card to be correspondingly configured, you must know which resources are still free. Avoid the accidental double assignment of resources. Only a few exceptions are possible in which double use is allowed.

Sixteen hardware interrupts and eight DMA channels are available in a standard AT computer. Certain computer components already use most of the interrupts; expansion cards cannot use these interrupts. Most of the eight DMA channels, however, are available for expansion cards. Refer to the Appendices to see the standard assignment of interrupts, DMA channels and port addresses in the AT computer.

The Windows 98 Device Manager is especially good for checking which resources are already used. It recognizes each piece of hardware installed and the resources reserved for it. The Device Manager displays this information in summary form.

Double allocation of already reserved resources can readily be avoided. Refer to Chapter 6 for more information on the Resource Manager. Chapter 6 also shows how you can display the resources used in the system. Use this information to avoid conflicts when installing a new component in your system.

We can provide only basic information in this section, so we'll ignore Windows 98's peculiarities with hardware. Again, refer to Chapter 6 for help with hardware installation using the Add New Hardware wizard and Device Manager.

ISA (Industry Standard Architecture) bus system

Managing an ISA bus is tough if you do not note the reserved resources. Unfortunately, not even the MSD utility in MS-DOS, or any other utility program, will help you. Such programs cannot determine the interrupts, DMA channels and port addresses used for all the ISA expansion cards. The data they return is unreliable and is valid only for standard cards. With these programs you can only check the standard assignments. You'll have to open your PC's case and check the settings of the cards configured with jumpers.

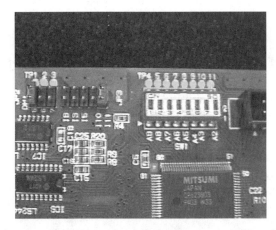

You have to check the settings of the jumpers or DIP switches.

Any cards configured with software must be checked with the associated installation software. Now is a good time to write down all the allocated resources for future reference, so you'll save the trouble of opening your computer again. Use the table in the Appendix.

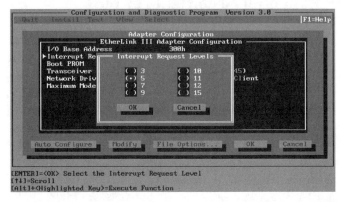

You determine the resource allocation with the installation software

5 Interrupts, DMA Channels, Port Addresses

EISA (Extended Industry Standard Architecture) bus controller

Computers with an EISA bus already offer a better way for checking the assigned resources. Such computers include a configuration program called CF.EXE. It's usually found in the EISA directory.

Expansion cards for the EISA bus include configuration files the CF program can access. All the setting options offered by the card are included in these configuration files. The configuration data of those cards already installed are stored in the expanded CMOS-RAM of the EISA computer.

It's then possible for the CF utility to detect any possible resource conflicts with the new card and propose alternative settings to the user. The new card is correspondingly configured and the new data stored in the CMOS-RAM. However, if a problem with resource allocation is present and the new card cannot be reconfigured, the CF utility will only suggest changing the settings of the second card.

Problems, like those on ISA computers, can arise on EISA computers only when ISA cards are also used. You're usually not provided with CFG files for an EISA system. The user must assume the responsibility for ensuring that no resource conflict will arise. Even if EISA cards are more expensive than their ISA equivalents, avoid using ISA cards.

MCA (Micro-Channel Architecture) bus

Configuring an MCA bus is as straightforward as working with an EISA system. Here, the expansion cards are configured with software, and the corresponding data is stored in the expanded CMOS-RAM. Resource conflicts are indicated immediately and can be avoided. The problems with ISA cards do not arise here because it's not possible to use them in such a system.

VESA (Video Equipment Standards Association) local bus

Expansion cards for the VESA local bus are configured similar to ISA cards. The VLB (VESA Local Bus) itself supports only the use of hardware interrupt 9. This can result in conflicts if you use several expansion cards for the VLB. However, such cards can be configured for the other interrupts as well.

The problems with the ISA bus are also inherited. Configuring VLB adapters is usually done with jumpers or with the help of installation software. You have the responsibility to avoid the resource conflicts.

Another problem results from the clock rate of the VLB. According to the specification, clock rates of 25 MHz or 66 MHz are possible. Two or three VLB slots are allowed on the system board (depending upon the VL bus version).

A higher clock frequency means fewer slots are present. One slot was available at 40 MHz for Version 1.0. This is still true for Version 2.0, with a frequency of 50 MHz. Most boards today operate at 66 MHz, and your next computer will probably use a 100 MHz frequency.

Difficulties begin with clock rates starting with 40 MHz. This is a result of capacitances between the traces on the system board. A system board not designed according to specification (having traces too close together, unfavorably routed or too many slots at high clock rates) leads to functional problems with the VLB cards.

Additional problems can arise from the expansion cards for the VLB bus themselves. The manufacturers do not always follow the VLB specification (this is true for expansion cards and system boards). Individual cards will not work at all on some system boards. Moreover, most cards are set up for only one specific clock frequency (usually 33 MHz), so their use in a VL bus running at a higher clock rate is impossible. If you want to swap your old VLB board for a newer VLB board, the existing expansion cards may no longer work on the new board.

When buying a new VLB card, make certain that it's also compatible with the VLB version implemented on your system board. The user's manual for the system board should include this information.

When buying a new VLB board, your old cards must be compatible with the VLB version on the new board. However, even then, there is no guarantee the VL bus will operate correctly. Overall, if you want to install a new system board, it's best to forget VLB.

PCI (Personal Component Interconnect) bus

The PCI bus has four additional interrupts added to the 16 conventional hardware interrupts of the AT computer. The connection of the PCI interrupts to the AT interrupt system causes more difficulties because nothing works by itself. PCI makes the interrupts INTA, INTB, INTC and INTD available for PCI adapters. As a rule, all PCI cards use INTA. The other three interrupts are intended for the rare PCI multifunction components. These are not used for standard adapters.

The PCI specification provides that all INTx lines of the PCI slot are crosslinked. Each INTx line is assigned a hardware interrupt. Several PCI adapters can then share a single hardware interrupt. Such interrupt sharing would theoretically save on resources. In practice, this method leads to problems on the software level, because the interrupt handlers of driver programs are only rarely set up for interrupt sharing. Therefore, each PCI slot has its own INTA line on the new system boards.

A hardware interrupt must again be assigned its INTA line. You still have the same resource problems you had with the standard ISA system. However, one advantage remains. Unused INTx lines of the PCI bus need not be assigned a hardware interrupt. This normally concerns INTB, INTC and INTD. If you use the options of the individual INTA assignments to the hardware interrupts, the resources for the remaining INTx lines will be lost.

Besides making certain the available resources are not allocated to more than one card, you must also make certain the PCI interrupts are rerouted to the hardware interrupts without conflict. This occurs by setting the jumpers on the system board, with the aid of the BIOS Setup or both.

How PCI adapters are best configured depends upon the type of card. The INTA line of a PCI-IDE adapter, for example, must be assigned to hardware interrupt 14 if the attached hard drive is to function. There is no exception to this rule. This requires, when possible, an individual assignment of the INTA line. Other modern PCI adapters can use interrupt sharing and assign a single hardware interrupt to all INTA lines. The associated drivers will then be able to work with this mode. Few system boards, however, offer the possibility of individually assigning the INTx lines.

However, that is still not everything in the PCI system. The PCI specification distinguishes between so-called "bus masters" and slave devices. Masters are those expansion cards that can trigger a data transfer automatically. Cards that merely react to write/read accesses are the slaves in the PCI system.

Not every PCI slot on a system board is capable of master operation. Certain expansion cards require a master slot to operate. These include network cards, IDE or EIDE adapters and SCSI host adapters. All PCI slots on newer boards have the capability for master operation, but not on older boards. If you add a bus-master card to such a system, a slave card may have to be moved to a different slot. The user's manual for the system board should have the necessary information concerning the PCI slots.

Now you're aware that you must work carefully in a PCI system to avoid problems.

Plug and Play

Plug and Play expansion cards give you fewer of these types of problems. To take advantage of Plug 'n' Play, you'll need a computer with a Plug and Play BIOS and an operating system like Windows 98 that has implemented true Plug and Play.

Plug and Play cards have no jumpers or DIP switches with which their required resources are set. You don't even need to use installation software to configure the card. The card is merely plugged into an unoccupied slot and independently configured by an available Plug and Play BIOS.

In a true Plug and Play system, where only Plug and Play components are used, the BIOS controls the PC resources. It knows exactly which resources are still available for assignment to a newly installed card. The card is then also automatically configured correctly and free of conflicts. The operating system supporting Plug and Play must recognize the resources used so its drivers for the hardware can be set correctly. The information necessary for that is in the Plug and Play BIOS.

Windows 98 supports Plug and Play even in computers that don't have a Plug and Play BIOS. Windows can recognize Plug and Play expansion cards in a conventional computer system. These cards are automatically configured according to the Plug and Play specification. Because Windows recognizes the resources reserved, it can allocate free resources to the new Plug and Play card. The configuration data is then saved in the registry.

When you're buying a Plug and Play card, make certain the Plug and Play specification of the card matches the version supported by the BIOS or operating system. Because Plug and Play is still relatively new, compatibility problems can arise.

Avoiding Resource Conflicts

Listing the resources allocated in your system is the best way to avoid conflicts with the interrupts, DMA channels, port addresses and BIOS expansions.

You can get this information in many ways. Use PC_INFO to display the reserved resources of standard hardware, such as the mouse, coprocessor, interfaces, etc. Then write down the allocations.

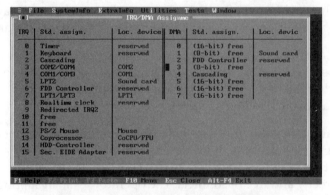

PC_INFO indicates the IRQ assignments.

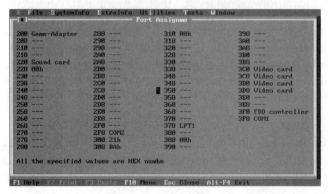

PC_INFO shows which port addresses have already been assigned.

Interrupts, DMA Channels, Port Addresses 5

If PC_INFO cannot recognize each piece of hardware installed, you'll have to take additional steps. If they are not displayed by PC_INFO, the settings of software-configurable cards are easily determined with the associated installation (or diagnostic) software. If you have installed expansion cards that are configured with jumpers, you may have to open the computer case to check them.

However, if a driver for the card in question is entered in the CONFIG.SYS or AUTOEXEC.BAT files, it may provide data on the card settings. Perhaps a DOS variable is defined in the AUTOEXEC.BAT file with the help of a SET variable that contains this data (for example, the BLASTER variable of sound cards). Look at the user's manual for the card. You may then save yourself the trouble of opening up the computer.

The Appendices include a table of allocated resources. Better still, copy the page and then save the copy with your computer's other documents. It may be necessary at some time to make changes in the table. You'll have an optimal summary of the resources. You can still allocate these for new expansion cards. You can also print the resource allocation with PC_INFO. For that purpose, mark the required information in the check-box window.

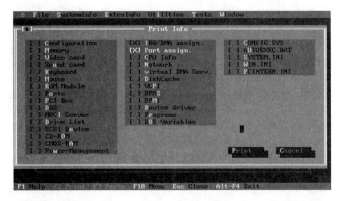

The data marked here is printed at the pressing of a button.

Click the [Print] button to print out the resource allocations. You can also redirect the output to the PC_INFO.REP file. Then load PC_INFO.REP into a text editor (for example, the DOS EDIT). Then you can make more changes if necessary.

311

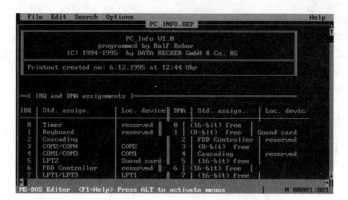

The PC_INFO.REP file can be edited in the Edit Window.

When the resources cannot be determined independently by the program, use the PC_INFO option of entering the already assigned resources in the PC_INFO.INI file. PC_INFO will show the following:

* Standard assignments

* Allocations by the identified computer components

* Expansion cards you entered with their associated configuration settings

You can then print the information.

When you install a new expansion card, remember to include the resources reserved by this card in the list. This reminder also applies when a card is removed or reconfigured. Always keep this list current so you won't need to deal with old problems at a later time.

Resource monitoring is simpler under Windows 98. You have a powerful feature available in the Resource Manager. It performs this task for you. To avoid resource conflicts before they start, install new hardware only through the Hardware Assistant. Also, take advantage of the capabilities of the Resource Manager. Chapter 6 describes the Resource Manager and Hardware Assistant.

Special cards with ROM expansions

If you are not using a SCSI adapter, then start the Shadow RAM for the memory range used in the BIOS Setup. The BIOS of the expansion card can be copied into RAM. This allows faster access to the BIOS.

Also consider blocking other applications from accessing the memory block. If you're working with EMM386.EXE, use the Exclude parameter. If the BIOS of your expansion card uses the memory range C800-D000, for example, add that as a parameter.

```
X=C800-D000
```

Although it's usually not necessary, you'll avoid memory conflicts in the UMB range immediately. This is the only way you can reliably prevent one of the drivers overwriting the BIOS of the expansion card.

That is also true for Windows. Windows installs its memory management immediately. This can lead to problems using ROM expansions. So, you should add the following entry to the [386Enh] section in the \WINDOWS\SYSTEM.INI:

```
EMMExclude=C800-D000
```

You cannot activate Shadow RAM for the BIOS of a SCSI adapter with memory mapped I/O. The BIOS of this SCSI adapter uses its own small address space in the UMB region for the hard drive data. Activating Shadow RAM for the SCSI BIOS renders this memory region inaccessible to the controller for writing. This can lead to unpredictable errors. Look at the user's manual for this card to determine if you can use the Shadow RAM option.

Avoiding memory fragmentation

> **TIP** Here's an important tip if you have installed additional cards with their own BIOS besides the graphics card (for example, SCSI adapters, network adapter cards). Configure the memory regions reserved for the BIOS so they follow one another in direct sequence. You'll avoid an unnecessary fragmentation or breakup of the memory.

When you load drivers or TSR programs high, fragmentation can be a problem. There may no longer be enough contiguous memory available in the UMB. In this case, you would have two smaller free memory blocks, instead of a larger contiguous block of memory. It may no longer be possible to load the program high. It would then occupy valuable main memory. Use the ROM expansion indicator of PC_INFO to configure the BIOS memory region correctly.

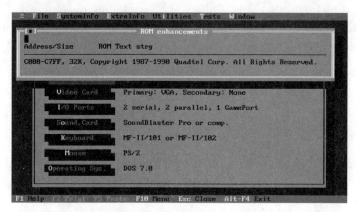

The BIOSes of the two cards reserve memory blocks which follow in sequence.

If the lower memory block of the UMB (starting at C800) on a card can't be configured, then use a memory block which lies directly beneath the system BIOS of the computer (this begins at F000). For example, if the SCSI controller above cannot be set for the C800-CBFF memory block, then choose the EC00-EFFF block.

What to Do when No More Resources are Available

Expansion cards usually do not have the ability to use all possible interrupts, DMA channels or port addresses. Only a few settings are normally possible. This can quickly lead to tight spots.

How reserved resources can be used

In these cases, it will be necessary to reconfigure at least one card. Also, don't forget to set the associated driver or corresponding application to the new parameters. The associated driver may have to be reinstalled.

You also must inform the Resource Manager, so the hardware in question will continue to run correctly. See Chapter 6 for more information on reconfiguring hardware.

If that is also unsuccessful, make certain a usable interrupt really isn't available. Standard interrupt assignments may not necessarily be in use. Most computers have two serial interfaces, but normally only one parallel interface available. Interrupt 5 would be immediately usable for expansion cards. Furthermore, if your computer does not have a coprocessor, interrupt 13 is then available.

Don't use interrupt 2 if possible. Cascading to the slave PIC (Interrupt 9) occurs over it. Use it only if there are no unreserved interrupts. Using interrupts 2 and 9 normally won't lead to problems, but problems can occur.

If you have installed a SVGA card, check in the user's manual whether it already uses interrupt 2. If that is not the case, then set the interrupt on your expansion card. Then check out your hardware thoroughly to make certain that it will operate correctly with this configuration.

Using software polling

Another option is the polling process. It allows an occupied interrupt to be released and made available to a different expansion card. This option is offered in part by CD-ROM drives, whose drivers have to be installed.

The ready signal for the data transfer with the polling process no longer occurs over the hardware interrupt. The driver in this case must determine whether a data transfer can occur. It must query the hardware continuously. This, of course, requires more computer time. Therefore, this method is not used, if possible.

If necessary, it could be implemented to release a hardware interrupt for a different card. If you're forced to use this option, check in the user's manual to see how polling is set up for the drivers in question.

Dangers with Resource Conflicts

Unfortunately, you'll probably accidentally find a way to become involved in resource conflicts. Therefore, they require closer consideration.

Serial interfaces

Problems can develop if more than two serial interfaces have been installed. This is true even if a device is connected to each interface. That will depend upon the hardware interrupts reserved for the serial interfaces. It's necessary to connect two interfaces to only one interrupt. IRQ3 is reserved for COM2 and COM4. IRQ4 is reserved for COM1 and COM3. You're probably using a serial mouse. This will also reserve the interrupt that belongs to the interface. If the mouse is connected to COM1, it will reserve interrupt 4 for itself.

This can lead to a conflict if there is another device connected to COM3 that also requires a hardware interrupt.

You have the option on the newer serial expansion cards of assigning COM2 and COM4 their own hardware interrupts using jumpers. However, you can use this feature only if it's also supported by your software.

Parallel interfaces

Conflicts with parallel interfaces are similar to those with serial interfaces. Interrupt 7 is reserved for LPT1 and LPT3. IRQ 5 is reserved for LPT2 and LPT4 (LPT4 is not, however, supported by the BIOS).

Most computers include only one parallel port. Conflict problems arise when more than two parallel interfaces have been installed. In this case, you must make certain that attached hardware will not collide with its interrupts.

If you have installed a sound card and want to add a second parallel interface, keep in mind that interrupt 5 is preset on most sound cards. It's frequently taken over when they are installed. Interrupt 5 is reserved for LPT2 and should no longer be used by the sound card. If possible, reconfigure the sound card.

Here, too, the more recent interface cards offer the option of assigning LPT2 and LPT4 their own interrupts using jumpers. However, make certain that your software can support this option.

VGA BIOS

You can use PC_INFO to display the ROM extensions in your PC. These will always include the VGA BIOS that lays claim to a specific block of memory. The standard memory allocation of the VGA BIOS is the C000-C7FF block. However, a few graphics cards (for example, the Paradise cards from Western Digital) have a BIOS that uses less, requiring only the C000-C5FF memory portion.

What is obvious here is to make the free region, C600-C7FF, available as UMB for drivers or resident programs. Although we don't recommend doing this, it can be done by adding the parameter I=C600-C7FF to the EMM386.EXE in your CONFIG.SYS file. Normally, the memory block for the VGA BIOS (C000-C7FF) is reserved in Setup as Shadow RAM. The free memory will consequently still be treated as Shadow RAM, even with the smaller VGA BIOS and not be available for use as UMB. If you attempt to make this memory region accessible through the memory manager, your computer will crash.

S3 graphics cards

Graphics cards with the S3 chip set use the 2EH8h-2EDh port-address block, among others, for programming. This memory block, per the AT standard, is reserved for the serial COM4 interface. Conflicts will occur if you have a COM4 available. It will then be necessary to reconfigure one of the two cards. Change the address of the interface only if the graphics card cannot be reconfigured. Remember, however, it may not be possible to set the software that works with COM4 to a different port address.

Chapter 6:
Device Manager &
Add New Hardware
Wizard

Chapter 6
Device Manager & Add
New Hardware Wizard

The two central locations for solving hardware or driver problems in Windows 98 are the Device Manager and the Add New Hardware Wizard.

They will help you regardless of whether you're installing Windows 98, installing new hardware and drivers or reconfiguring existing hardware.

This chapter illustrates working with the Device Manager and the Add New Hardware Wizard.

The Device Manager

The Device Manager contains all the hardware components reported by the Add New Hardware Wizard when you installed Windows 98. The system resources and the drivers for the individual devices are managed here. The Device Manager is, therefore, an important tool for solving hardware or driver problems.

Managing the system resources

The Device Manager summarizes which resources which have been allocated. Open the Control Panel, then double-click the System icon. Select the "Device Manager" tab. Then double-click the computer symbol. Windows 98 will display the resources in the system which it recognizes.

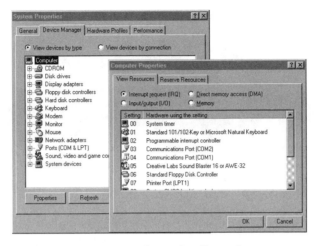

The Device Manager shows the allocated resources.

You can also print this information. If you want to install a new expansion card in the future, look first at the assigned system resources. Then you'll be able to configure your new card without risking a device conflict. Resources you do not see listed here can be used for new cards without worrying about potential problems.

What to do if a device conflicts

Even with the Hardware Wizard's help, hardware problems can still occur. Fortunately, Windows recognizes device conflicts early and reports them promptly.

Windows 98 discovers an error in the network adapter.

Don't immediately assume the hardware in question is really at fault. These or similar reports are usually the result of a device conflict. The Device Manager can give you more specific information about these problems. Open the Control Panel and double-click the System icon to start the Device Manager.

6 Device Manager & Add New Hardware Manager

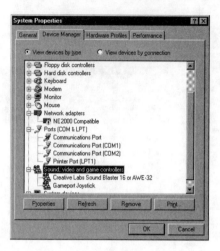

This exclamation point below "Network adapters" indicates a problem.

The Device Manager has already designated the network card with the exclamation mark. This exclamation point indicates a problem with this specific device or hardware component. Since a problem exists with this card, it cannot be used with Windows 98. To receive more detailed information, double-click on this entry. Alternatively, highlight the entry and click the (Properties) button. Then select the "Resources" tab.

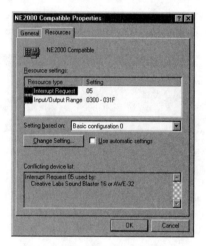

Windows has discovered a device conflict.

In the lower information window, Windows 98 shows that the network card conflicts with the installed sound card. Both expansion cards are using the same hardware interrupt. You must determine which card you want to reconfigure to resolve the conflict. We'll talk about how to do this below.

If you determine that a component suddenly no longer functions correctly (or perhaps not at all), look at the Device Manager first. You'll quickly solve most hardware problems from here.

Reconfiguring the available hardware

Here we assume that you have previously installed a sound card (for example, a Creative Labs Sound Blaster) and the new expansion card to be installed uses the same port address. The new card's port address, moreover, cannot be changed. Your only option then is to reconfigure the sound card to prevent a resource conflict. The card allows you to set one of the addresses (either 220h, 230h or 240h). If you do not know which of these addresses are still free in the system, check with the Device Manager as described above.

Open the Control Panel. Double-click the System icon. Select the "Device Manager" tab.

Use the Device Manager to access all system components.

6 Device Manager & Add New Hardware Manager

Select the Creative Labs Sound Blaster under " Sound, video and game controllers." Then click the [Properties] button. Select the "General" tab.

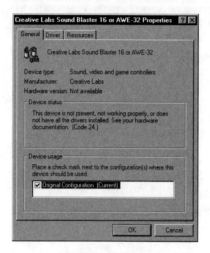

Set the resource settings by clicking the "General" tab.

You'll see general information on the hardware selected. Now you can select the window for the resource settings. Select the "Resource" tab.

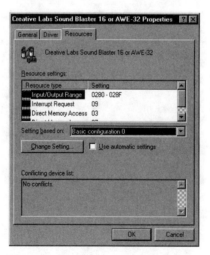

Adjust the resource settings by selecting the "Resource" tab.

Then select the resource to be adjusted. In this example, we want to adjust the first Input/Output Range. The second Input/Output Range setting concerns the AdLib ports here. Then we need to change the setting corresponding to the hardware configuration.

If the "Use automatic settings" box is checked in your case, first disable this setting. You must do this before changing the settings of the resources. Finally, click the OK button. You must exit Windows and restart your computer for these changes to take effect.

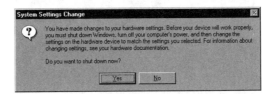

After reconfiguring, you have to restart Windows.

Now you can switch off the computer and reconfigure the sound card's jumpers, if necessary. When you restart, the sound card will be configured to work around the no-longer-conflicting device.

Add New Hardware Wizard

With the introduction of Windows 95, everything in the hardware field changed. Windows 98 continues this tradition. When you install Windows 98, it tries to automatically recognize the hardware components present in your system. It then arranges the resources used by these components. This is not a problem under true Plug and Play (providing only Plug and Play components are installed). Since Plug and Play installation is virtually problem-free, we won't discuss it further. However, problems can occur when there is no Plug and Play BIOS present or non-Plug and Play components are installed in a Plug and Play computer.

We'll first talk about hardware installation under Windows. We've attempted to make the following description very detailed. Then if you have to install hardware, you'll have detailed information available. In this section you'll learn what you need to do when Windows 98 is already installed and how you can then install hardware which may not have been recognized.

325

6 Device Manager & Add New Hardware Manager

No-hassle hardware installation

As an example, we'll install a sound card. If you install the hardware without help from Windows, resource conflicts can occur unless you know precisely which resources are already allocated to other components.

Before installing the hardware, start Windows 98. Then click the <![Start]!> button. Select **Settings** | **Control Panel**. Then double-click the Add New Hardware icon

The Add New Hardware Wizard helps with hardware installation.

The Add New Hardware Wizard is started. Click the [Next >] button here.

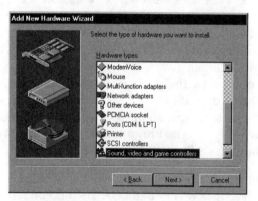

Select the type of hardware you want to install.

Indicate which device you want to install in this dialog box. Select "Sound, video and game controllers" as a device type. This obviously includes our sound card. When "Sound, video and game controllers" is highlighted, click the [Next >] button.

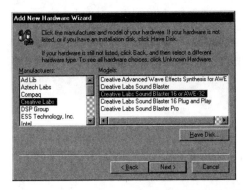

Windows already recognizes many devices and immediately offers suitable drivers.

Windows displays all the sound card manufacturers it recognizes in the "Manufacturers" box to the left. Our sound card is from Creative Labs, so we'll select that manufacturer. In the "Models" box on the right, select a model from the different sound cards listed. We're installing a Creative Labs SoundBlaster 16 / AWE32, so in our example we will select this.

If you also have an installation diskette for the sound card (which will probably be the case), you could then continue the installation by clicking the [Have Disk...] button to install the correct driver immediately. Use this option only if your hardware also has a current 32-bit driver for Windows 98.

However, if Windows offers a compatible driver, as in this case, Windows will then also have corresponding 32-bit drivers for this unit. In that case you shouldn't use the older 16-bit driver that is included on the diskette. If possible, use the drivers native to Windows. Click the [Next >] button to continue the installation.

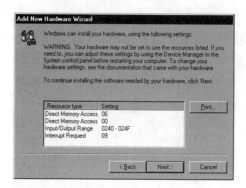

The Add New Hardware Wizard tells you which resources are free.

Windows displays a list of resources still unallocated in the system. Configure the sound card accordingly with jumpers, if necessary. If you then continue by clicking (Finish), Windows will finish installing the driver.

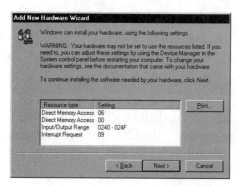

Windows is installing the driver.

Finally, Windows will prompt you to restart Windows. Then you can install the hardware, if necessary.

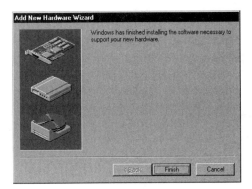

The driver installation is complete.

Exit Windows and switch off the computer. When you have inserted the sound card correctly, restart Windows. The sound card should now work satisfactorily.

If you installed the hardware before calling the Add New Hardware Wizard, you must let the Add New Hardware Wizard check the installed hardware again. This is necessary to allow the setup of the driver necessary for operation under Windows. The new hardware is also then entered in the Device Manager.

Chapter 7:
First Aid For A Virus
Attack

Chapter 7
First Aid For A Virus Attack

Computer viruses have been a problem for many years and continue to be a problem today. Even veteran PC users break out in a sweat when finding a virus. Regardless of how often or for what purpose we use our PCs, we've all experienced the following:

* An unexpected system crash

* A program that for some reason fails to start

* A file that has suddenly disappeared

* A small but noticeable slowdown in performance

However, these problems are usually either our fault or a harmless bug in the application we're using. Seldom is a virus blamed or even considered. A virus is something, after all, that happens to someone else. We can usually trace the problem to our error, a bug in the application software or some type of incompatibility. We then either fix the problem ourselves or get help from an outside source.

At some point, your application may come to a sudden halt. The screen goes blank. Then, with a few telltale words, such as "Darth Vader lives," your PC informs you that it has indeed fallen victim to a virus.

You might now say to yourself, "I'll just start my virus scanner—that should fix it." You reboot from a clean diskette (see Chapter 1), then you use a virus scanner to hunt down the virus.

As you run the virus scanner, you notice that many files show no evidence of a virus. You slowly begin to get that sinking feeling. Then your worst fears are confirmed when the virus scanner finishes: no virus was detected. The other virus scanner kept in your diskette box is also of no help to you. It too finds nothing. You either have a new virus or are using a virus scanner that is out-of-date.

Virus types

Viruses are classified into different types, depending on the mechanism and mode of transmission for the virus.

The following table lists the different types of viruses:

Virus type	Definition / Characteristic
File viruses	Attach themselves to the beginning or end of an infected program. This results in either lengthening or overwriting part of the program. File viruses are usually installed as resident in memory.
Boot viruses	Infect the boot sector of a diskette or the boot sector or partition sector of the hard drive. They install resident in memory.
Directory viruses	Install resident in memory and manipulate the File Allocation Table on the hard drive. No files need to be infected.
Resident viruses	Install undetected in memory and control DOS and/or BIOS functions.
Direct-action viruses:	Become active only when an infected program is called, thus are not installed in memory.
Hybrid viruses	Share the characteristics of both file and boot viruses.
Stealth viruses	Install resident in memory, are able to disguise their presence through highly sophisticated programming techniques.
Polymorphous viruses	Are basically resident file viruses with variable encryption routines, making their detection by virus scanners more difficult.
Companion viruses	Create matching COM files for EXE files. When the program is called the COM file starts before the EXE file at which point the virus becomes active.

All viruses, regardless of their type, have the goal of replicating themselves unnoticed until a certain time when they make their presence known. Viruses usually announce themselves with one of the following:

* Sound (beeps or melodies from the speaker)

* Graphics (text output or manipulation of the current display)

* Modification/destruction of data on storage media

How viruses avoid detection

The main task of a virus is to reproduce itself as many times as possible without being detected. A virus uses several methods to avoid detection (depending on the type).

Boot viruses

Boot viruses are transmitted through boot sectors of diskettes. A computer can be infected with a boot virus only if you boot the computer with an infected diskette. Before anything else, the computer loads the boot sector of the diskette so it can execute the boot routine located there. But the boot routine on an infected diskette has been replaced by the virus code. The virus checks the boot or partition sector of the hard drive, and if it has not yet been infected, it does so.

Finally, the virus installs itself in resident memory, then starts the original boot sector of the diskette. In the process of infection, the virus has copied the boot sector to a different sector. From this point, the virus controls several BIOS functions that are responsible for drive accesses. When the virus detects an access to a drive, it checks whether the corresponding boot sector has already been infected. If not, it copies the original boot sector to a different sector and overwrites the boot sector with its virus code.

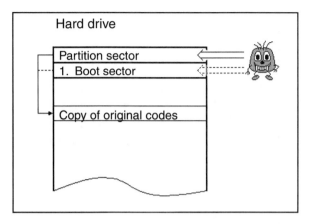

A boot virus infects the partition or boot sector and stores the original code elsewhere.

File viruses

File viruses replicate through executable programs, driver files or overlay files. The virus doesn't become active until the infected program is called.

A resident virus first checks whether the virus has already been installed in memory. If not, it quietly lodges itself there. It then controls execution of file accesses through DOS. When DOS accesses one of the above types of files, the virus checks if it has already infected this file. If not, it does so. It then allows the original DOS function to execute.

A nonresident virus usually looks for the file in the current directory and infects it if it isn't already infected. Depending on the virus, either the host program is simply overwritten or the virus attaches itself to the end of the program, thus altering its file header.

7 *First Aid For A Virus Attack*

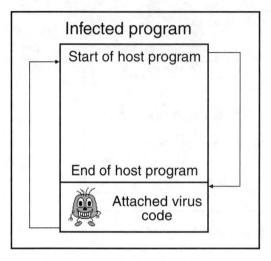

File viruses attack executable files.

Hybrid viruses

Hybrid viruses use transmission methods of both boot viruses and file viruses.

Antivirus organizations

Computer viruses steadily evolve over time. These viruses feature more diverse modes of infection and increasingly sophisticated methods of encryption and disguise. This is partly due to the vast body of literature available on existing operating systems, making their inner workings fully accessible to all. It's easy for the virus programmer to find the system's weaknesses and let the virus take advantage of them.

Viruses can also be programmed to sabotage the functioning of a particular virus scanner so the scanner won't be able to detect them. Virus scanner programmers must continuously update their programs to keep pace with the new developments.

Both sides no longer limit themselves to conventional file functions within the operating system. Viruses can now "bend" interrupt vectors, manipulate the Memory Control Block chain and control memory management. They do all this using convoluted techniques to outsmart the virus scanners.

Meanwhile, the virus scanners are not idle. In their effort to catch new, even unknown viruses, many identification methods have been developed with complex file analysis functions. It's a continuous battle as each side tries to outwit the other.

Virus scanning programmers work closely together, sharing new discoveries and incorporating them into their programs. One of the most active groups is the International Computer Security Association (ICSA). It's the leading membership organization. It provides educational materials, training, testing and consulting services to improve computer and information security, reliability and ethics.

ICSA supports over 1,600 members. These members represent commercial and governmental organizations. ICSA provides training through public and in-house seminars. The ICSA annual security conference provides a meeting ground for members and nonmembers to share experiences and learn about current technology and solutions.

Informational resources include books, research reports, training materials, conference proceedings and tools. These are featured in a 28 page information security resource catalog. ICSA manages a Web site (www.icsa.net) dedicated to computer security and ethics.

Unfortunately, virus programmers also cooperate with each other. Many virus programmers share ideas in developing new tricks to prevent virus scanners from finding new viruses in the system. They hold their meetings, too. Some even sponsor contests with awards for the best or most original viruses.

This leaves you, the hapless user, caught in the middle. All the above is aimed directly at you. One side makes your life miserable while the other wishes to protect you. One part is free, even if unwanted. The other costs money unless you're fortunate enough to have the latest shareware version of a virus scanner. The threat of viruses will always be with us, however, so it's up to you how much money and effort you invest in antivirus protection.

You should now have a basic understanding of what lies behind these dreaded parasites. We will now discuss how to prevent a virus attack on your computer and what to do if one occurs.

Your PC System Suddenly Begins Acting Strangely

We've all become used to the occasional system crash by now. Very little software is bugfree. This bug will eventually affect the program and, therefore, your work. If the systems locks up, you probably reach for the Reset button or press Ctrl + Alt + Del. If you're lucky, the bug may never affect your work again.

Other times, however, something really seems different. Something happens that you've never seen on your computer before. For an unknown reason, your printer no longer responds, yet you've just used it minutes before. No one with whom you talk has seen the problem before either. Then you notice an important file is suddenly missing. Then an entire directory has disappeared from your hard drive. It's only then you remember the many thousands of software viruses. You thought you were safe from a virus, until now.

> **TIP** However, before you panic, such strange phenomena can be the result of simple accidents. Many users have accidentally deleted one or more files in the Windows File Manager that shouldn't be deleted. The File Manager's confirmation to delete a file is easy to miss (it's even possible to disable this confirmation message). Many users don't even read the entire text in this dialog box anyway.

Also, printer settings are changed frequently inside applications. This is especially true when several users share the same printer. So, before assuming the worst, consider what occurred just before the problem.

BIOS issues a virus warning

Many BIOS manufacturers have included a simple virus protection feature in their BIOS. When the option is enabled, it prevents write accesses on the partition sector of the boot drive. This stops boot viruses from infecting your hard drive. It offers good protection, especially if you boot your computer from a diskette. No resident virus scanner can be active during the boot phase. Therefore, this simple BIOS option is your only protection against viruses that manipulate the partition sector. If a write access occurs, the BIOS interrupts the executing program and sends a message to the screen:

```
!!!Warning!!!
Disk Boot Sector is to be modified.
Type 'Y' to accept, any key to abort
Award Software, Inc.
```

The same message appears if you try to reformat the partition sector with FDISK / MBR or change the partitions with FDISK. The BIOS warning also occurs if you try to rewrite the stored MBR using PC_INFO or install a new operating system. If the access is legitimate, confirm by pressing Ⓨ. Otherwise, it's possible that a virus has just attempted to manipulate your partition sector. Just to be sure, run a current version of a virus scanner.

Locating a virus in your computer

In principle, simply use a current virus scanner to check your hard drive for a virus. You have your answer if the virus scanner detects a virus. However, you can't be certain your computer is virus-free even if the virus scanner doesn't detect a virus. We'll talk more about this later. Viruses frequently cause the following symptoms:

* The computer boots up when you call a program

* The computer seems slower than usual

* The computer no longer boots up completely

* The screen sometimes flickers

7 *First Aid For A Virus Attack*

* The printer sometimes prints garbage

* Key presses are interpreted incorrectly

* The PC speaker beeps periodically

* Identically named COM and EXE (executable) files exist in the same directory

* The system crashes with a PARITY CHECK or PARITY ERROR message

* Files, or entire directories, sometimes disappear

* CHKDSK reports conventional memory as less than 655,360K

If you notice any of these symptoms, immediately run a virus scanner to check your computer.

If the virus scanner doesn't detect a virus, too many users assume their system is virus free. These users simply put too much trust in their virus scanners. It's difficult today to pinpoint a particular virus because of the large number of possible symptoms. In the meantime, viruses have been programmed so well, they aren't detected until they intentionally announce themselves. At this point, it's already much too late. Symptoms that occur regularly should alert you to the possibility of a virus. These symptoms include the computer always crashing at 00:00 or files always being defective, although the hard drive is in order. You should then take appropriate measures as we describe below.

Simulated hardware or software errors

Unfortunately, not all viruses are designed to silently reproduce themselves. Most viruses are programmed to perform one or more specific actions at a particular time. These include viruses that delete your hard drive at a certain time or remove files or entire directories from the hard drive. These are, however, not even the most dreaded viruses.

More dreaded viruses are those that become active at irregular intervals and simulate hardware or software errors. Few users would consider a virus if their screens flickered at a particular graphics resolution. You would most likely look for an error in the graphic card, the monitor or the graphics driver of the application program.

340

Also, since the error appears infrequently and cannot be localized, you might consider replacing the graphics driver or even the hardware. The fact the problem is still with you becomes apparent only later, when the virus again becomes active. This might occur only after you spent quite a bit of money.

Also, few users would consider a virus responsible if the printer suddenly began printing nonsense. This is especially true if the printer starts working again after a warm start, at least for a while. After a few more times, perhaps you even buy a new printer cable.

The following is a short list of other examples where few users suspect a virus is causing serious problems:

* The mouse suddenly ceases to work.

* The computer crashes every so often

* One or more files are apparently defective or deleted

As you can see, you can never really be sure about viruses. The best insurance is using the current version of a virus scanner regularly.

When Your System Has A Virus

Once you discover that your system is infected with a virus, you can begin removing it. The best way to do this depends on the type of virus. Follow these instructions closely. If a virus isn't removed correctly from the system, it'll probably reappear very soon.

If you already know that your computer is infected, avoid using a Windows virus scanner — even if you have one available under Windows 98. A virus can trick the virus scanner even with a 32-bit operating system. We will discuss this in more detail later.

7 *First Aid For A Virus Attack*

Error-free use of virus scanners

Store the virus scanner that you'll be running on a write-protected diskette. If a virus has infected your hard drive, any virus scanner stored there might also be infected. If the virus has the additional capability of deceiving the virus scanner, it will infect all program files as the scan is occurring.

Besides the virus scanner diskette, you also need a write-protected bootable diskette (such as the emergency diskette from Chapter 1). You can boot your computer from the emergency diskette. You could, of course, also make the virus scanner diskette bootable with the SYS command (but only if your computer is "clean"). In this case, the diskette must also have a CONFIG.SYS file on it that installs a memory manager, such as DOS HIMEM.SYS. This way, if the virus scanner can't do it on its own, the memory manager will enable it to scan the HMA (High Memory Area) where a resident virus may be hiding.

First, switch off the computer. You want to restart it from the disk drive using the emergency diskette. If booting from the disk drive has been deactivated in your BIOS setup, you must now reactivate this option. Don't perform a warm start (don't press Ctrl + Alt + Del). Many viruses can bypass this and only pretend to warm start your computer.

A cold start with the Reset button may work, since this type of reset occurs through the hardware on the motherboard and cannot be intercepted by a virus. It restarts the BIOS and reinitializes all system components and variables. Any program or resident virus that is running inevitably stops.

However, depending on the BIOS version, pressing the Reset button for a cold start might not always completely clear the memory. When scanning the memory, the virus scanner would suspect an active resident virus and terminate with a corresponding message. So, the safest alternative is to turn the machine off entirely.

Insert the boot diskette in drive A: and restart the computer. BIOS loads the operating system from the diskette. This way the partition code and boot sector on the hard drive aren't executed. This prevents a possible boot virus or hybrid virus from starting. Start scanning the hard drive when the boot process has finished.

F_PROT virus scanner

We've included an example of a virus scanner (F_PROT) on the companion CD-ROM. Other virus scanners have similar options so we won't list them separately here. This a shareware program so make certain to read and understand the text files in the program directory for complete instructions on using F_PROT.

The program screen first appears when you start F_PROT. However, the virus scanner has already checked the memory (including the HMA) for resident viruses before this screen appears. Now select **Scan** from the menu.

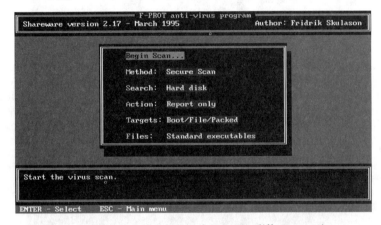

The F_PROT program screen has many different settings.

The program screen includes the setup options for the virus scanner. F_PROT checks for boot and file viruses in executable files on the hard drive by default. It generates a list as it scans the files.

Keep these settings. Then select **Begin Scan...** First, F_PROT checks the boot region of the hard drive. This includes the partition and boot sectors. It then begins to scan the files. F_PROT makes an entry into a report if it detects a potential problem. You can view this report on screen.

7 *First Aid For A Virus Attack*

```
Uirus scanning report  -  7. April 1995   21:48

F-PROT 2.17 created 10. March 1995
Uirus search strings created 9. March 1995

Method: Secure Scan
Search: Hard disk
Action: Report only
Targets: Boot/File/Packed
Files: Standard executables

Scanning MBR of hard disk 1
Scanning boot sector C:
Scanning volume MS-DOS_6
C:\DRIVERS\MOUSE.EXE  Infection: Tequila
Note: C:\DOSPROGS\SCANNER\TNT\TNTSCAN.EXE has been inoculated by Central
Point Anti-Uirus.

Results of virus scanning:

Files: 3132  (123.9 MB)
Scanned: 473  (34.2 MB)
PgDn - Page down    P - Print    S - Save    ESC - Cancel
```

The virus scanner has detected a virus

The Virus Info database in the virus scanner gives information on the type of virus encountered. This information can be critical to the next step of the process. The database first gives the virus's name, and, if known, its place of origin. It then gives the length in bytes and finally the virus type. Under Repair (remove) it tells you whether the virus scanner can remove the virus. Once the virus has been analyzed, additional information about the virus is also available. This information includes any possible harmful functions, etc.

```
========================= F-PROT anti-virus program =========================
                              Tequila
Name: Tequila
Origin: Switzerland
Size: 2468
Type: Resident  EXE-files  MBR
Repair: Yes

This virus was written by two brothers in Switzerland, 18 and 21 years
old.  The virus is related to the 'Flip' virus - possibly they wrote it as
well.  Tequila is difficult to detect as is uses a variable encryption
algorithm.  When an infected program is run, the virus will infect the MBR
of the hard disk, so the next time the computer is booted, the virus will
be active in memory, ready to infect .EXE files as they are run.  One
interesting effect of the virus is the display of a crude, character-based
Mandelbrot set image on the screen.

P - Print    ESC - Cancel
```

The Virus Info database contains detailed information about the virus

If the virus scanner has positively identified the virus by name and indicates that it's removable, go to the **Action** menu. Then select either **Disinfect/Query (remove with confirm)** or **Automatic Disinfection (remove automatically)**. Start the scan process

344

again and the virus scanner will remove the virus from your hard drive. If the virus is not removable, you must delete the infected files. Replace the deleted files with clean copies from a backup or the original diskettes.

When the virus scanner is unable to identify the virus, it will call it "Variant of..." In this case, don't let the virus scanner remove the virus completely. Keep one or two infected files and copy them to a diskette (if possible, use different types such as EXE and COM files). Then clean the hard drive with the virus scanner.

Use an editor to create a text file on the diskette. (The virus will not become active doing this.) Enter the name and version number of the virus as given by the virus scanner. Also, describe any symptoms this virus has caused on your computer.

Then write your name and address on the diskette label. Make certain to write "WARNING VIRUS" in big, bold letters on the disk label. Take this disk to a virus test center that a local user group or computer store might maintain. You can also contact ICSA at the address listed previously. Since this is a variant, it may have properties that are important to virus scanner programmers. When the virus is analyzed in a test center, the programmers receive a data sheet on the virus. This data sheet helps them compare the variant to the original and include it in their virus scanners.

Viruses and CD-ROMs

A virus on a CD-ROM is not unique, but it is pretty rare. A virus somehow manages to sneak its way past control mechanisms and establishes itself on a CD-ROM. You cannot remove a virus from a CD-ROM. Instead, avoid using the infected program. Stick a label on the CD-ROM (not just the jewel case) with an appropriate warning, so you won't forget that the CD-ROM contains a virus.

If you desperately need the program, copy the files to the hard drive and remove the virus with a virus scanner. You can then install the program and run it. We recommend contacting the technical support staff of the company that produces the CD-ROM that is infected. Let them know of the virus, and ask how you can replace the infected CD-ROM. Refer to your registration card for more details.

7 *First Aid For A Virus Attack*

Combating viruses with DOS

For computers that have fallen victim to a pure boot virus, the solution is quite simple. Although all virus scanners today can destroy boot viruses, we recommend using the operating system itself (for compatibility reasons). The Virus Info database in the virus scanner will tell you if you're dealing with a boot virus.

To remove a boot virus from your hard drive, you'll need a boot diskette made bootable by the same operating system that's installed on your hard drive. The diskette must also contain the DOS programs SYS.COM and FDISK.EXE. Use the emergency diskette that you created in Chapter 1. The "normal" Windows startup diskette can also be used.

Switch off the computer and insert the diskette in Drive A:. Switch on the computer again. When the boot process has finished, enter the following commands:

```
FDISK /MBR
SYS C:
```

The FDISK /MBR command reformats the partition sector of the hard drive. Any boot virus infecting this sector will be overwritten by a new partition routine.

SYS C: transfers the system files IO.SYS, MSDOS.SYS and COMMAND.COM to the hard drive. The SYS command also creates a new boot sector. If the boot virus has infected the boot sector on the hard drive, it will now be overwritten. The boot virus is destroyed, and your computer is again clean.

A somewhat more difficult problem is a hard drive with a boot manager that allows for multiple operating systems. The FDISK and SYS programs are incapable of recognizing such boot managers and modifying the sectors appropriately. Instead, they simply overwrite the boot manager. All you can do in this case is reinstall the boot manager.

However, PC_INFO lets you save the partition and boot sectors of the hard drive in a file called "PC_INFO.MBR." If you've used this option after installing your boot manager, you won't need to call FDISK or SYS. Simply use PC_INFO to rewrite the two sectors from the file. This overwrites the boot virus on the hard drive with the original sector contents. The boot manager remains fully functional.

Problems can also occur if you have an IDE or EIDE hard drive larger than 504 Meg and use a disk manager such as Ontrack or EZ-Drive to keep the entire hard drive within one partition. These disk managers change the partition sector so they're loaded before the operating system. FDISK /MBR would recreate the original partition sector so the disk manager couldn't be loaded.

You would have to reinstall the disk manager. This often requires you to reformat the drive. Save yourself this aggravation by using the same PC_INFO option and saving the MBR region in a file. When you rewrite the MBR with PC_INFO, you destroy the boot virus but the disk manager stays intact.

Determining the source of the virus

Although your hard drive is virus-free, your work is still not finished. You must now determine the source of the virus or you risk re-infecting your system. The following are a few suggestions:

* Consider which diskettes you've used most recently.

* Consider when you last downloaded a program. If you've received an infected program from a network, notify whoever is responsible so the virus cannot spread any further.

* Scan all questionable diskettes. It's better to scan one too many than one too few.

* Who else might have used the diskette that had the virus? Notify everyone who could've used the disk of the possibility of a virus.

* Scan original diskettes of programs you recently installed. Contact the dealer or manufacturer immediately if the virus scanner finds something. This also applies to pre-installed software.

The virus scanner may not find a virus for at least three reasons:

* Perhaps your computer isn't infected. The problems may come from other sources.

 ✱ The virus scanner is out-of-date and doesn't recognize the newer viruses. Always use a current version of the virus scanner. A better alternative is to use at least two virus scanners. Viruses not recognized by one virus scanner might be detected by another scanner.

 ✱ The worst case is when your virus scanner is current, but the virus is new and unknown. Fortunately, this occurs very rarely, but is not entirely impossible. When a virus doesn't identify itself (by sending a message to the screen, for example) you must know how to detect it. Then you must determine a course of action.

You have several ways to check whether an unknown virus has spread through your system. Many resident viruses lodge themselves in upper memory just below video memory. To prevent this region from being used by other programs, the virus decrements the BIOS variable that contains the amount of memory. This value is always 640K on a clean system. Use CheckDisk or PC_INFO to check this variable.

There's a 99% chance that you have a resident virus if one of the following is true:

1. If CheckDisk reports conventional memory as less than 655,360 bytes

2. PC_INFO displays memory according to BIOS as less than 640K.

The 1% uncertainty is because a small number of BIOS versions use 1K of memory for themselves. However if the reported value is under 654,336 bytes (639K), you can be sure that a resident virus is present.

Another option is comparing file sizes of frequently used programs with those of the original files. To do this, switch off the computer and reboot from a clean diskette. Use Windows Explorer to locate a program that you call frequently. One or more of these programs are likely to be infected if your system has a file virus. Infected files will be somewhat larger than the original files (you should have recent backups). Note their sizes and compare them with the originals. If a file on the hard drive has become larger, you know you have a virus. Send one or more of these files to a virus test center. Note any symptoms that you've observed.

Finally, use a virus feature that clearly signals an infection. Many viruses identify the programs they infect by manipulating the date or time. DOS saves this information in the directory with the filename. When you enter the DIR command at the DOS prompt, you will see the date and time on the screen. However, the seconds (time) and the century (date) remain hidden. Viruses exploit this "undocumented feature." They label infected programs with a seconds value greater than 59 or a century value greater than 19.

Enter the DIR command at the DOS prompt. A file whose seconds and year have been altered in this way appears similar to the following:

```
EXAMPLE EXE 13,992 03-28-98 21:12
```

The screen output does not distinguish between the years 1998 and 2098. The seconds are not displayed at all.

We're not aware of any virus scanner that checks these system values. This is odd, because any file alteration is an obvious sign of a virus (unless you've intentionally changed them yourself). Since this information is not so easily checked, a program called DT-SCAN (DateTimeScanner) was developed. It performs the task quickly and reliably. DT-SCAN is found on the companion CD-ROM in the directory \DT_SCAN. It checks the time and date entry for each file and reports any inconsistencies.

The following conditions will produce a warning:

Hours	> 23
Minutes	> 59
Seconds	> 59
Year	> 1999 (can be changed in INI file)
Month	> 12
Day	> 31

The data returned by the DIR command is also checked to catch even the most "flagrant" viruses.

Since stealth viruses can hide these manipulations, switch off your computer and reboot from a clean diskette. Insert a diskette with the DT-SCAN program. The syntax for calling the program is as follows:

```
DT-SCAN [Drive:] [/S]
```

If you omit the drive designation, the program scans the current directory. The /S parameter tells it to also check subdirectories.

DT-SCAN includes an initialization file called "DT-SCAN.INI." Make certain to store this file in the current directory. You'll find the entry YEAR= in this file. DT-SCAN issues a warning on any year above the value specified. This value has been set to 2000 initially, since MS-DOS cannot handle years greater than 1999. Higher numbers, therefore, indicate a virus.

Programmers must lift this restriction soon so years after 1999 will be possible. The DT-SCAN.INI entry must then be changed to avoid any error messages. The [FILES] section lists the filetypes that DT-SCAN should check. The maximum number of entries here is 16. The entries must follow one below another. The entries must always start with "*." followed by a three-character filename extension. The wildcard character "?" is a valid character.

You should boot the computer with a "clean" diskette before running DT-SCAN. Otherwise, a resident stealth virus can conceal itself from DT-SCAN and go undetected.

The memory size up to 640K is stored in a BIOS variable that always contains the value 640. If the number is smaller, there is a resident virus in your memory. Since no virus scanner tests this value, DT-SCAN includes an extra function for it. A message appears on the screen whenever DT-SCAN detects a change in the BIOS variable.

Other methods also exist for finding unknown viruses. However, these are very complex and generally reserved for "professional virus trackers."

Resident virus scanners

The shareware version of F_PROT also includes a resident virus scanner: VIRSTOP. VIRSTOP is started automatically from the CONFIG.SYS file. Refer to the program documentation for installation instructions. It monitors all file operations in the background that the operating system performs. VIRSTOP scans any executable program for viruses before it can be started or copied.

If VIRSTOP detects a virus in one of the files, the file operation is canceled and a message appears on the screen. It therefore detects a virus before that virus can spread in your system. VIRSTOP also looks for boot viruses by checking the boot sectors of hard drives and diskettes.

Another resident virus scanner for Windows 98 is VSHIELD from McAfee. VSHIELD uses the same method as VIRSTOP, but has the disadvantage of being called from the AUTOEXEC.BAT file. Since drivers called from CONFIG.SYS could be infected, it's possible a virus is already in memory when VSHIELD is installed. VSHIELD is then easily fooled by the virus.

Although resident virus scanners offer relatively good protection, don't rely on them exclusively. Instead, consider them enhancements that will make your virus scanner package complete. Resident virus scanners do monitor file operations. However, since they work in the background, they require processor time and are therefore unable to scan for all viruses. This job is left to the actual virus scanner, which now recognizes well over 5,000 viruses. If you had a resident virus scanner doing all this, Windows would require much longer to start.

Virus scanners and checksum modules

Most virus scanner packages offer additional protection against unknown viruses as checksum options. Several variations of checksums exist, but the basic principle is assigning a characteristic checksum to each executable file. The checksum is derived through various algorithms. It's usually appended to the files.

Other virus scanners create check lists in each directory containing the names, checksums and the first two bytes of each executable file in the directory. When the virus scanner is called, it validates the files' checksums besides the actual scanning. Resident virus scanners also validate checksums. If a difference is found, a warning appears on the screen. Something has modified the file. This could be the action of an unknown virus. Experienced virus programmers have already decoded the algorithms and developed viruses that are resistant to them. The checksum method is therefore vulnerable and offers only limited protection against unknown viruses.

Preventive Measures for Virus Protection

This section offers a few general rules you should follow to protect your computer from viruses.

General rule

Check any software you buy or receive for viruses. Do this regardless of how, where and on what medium you received the software.

Insert the diskette or CD-ROM into the drive. As an example, start the virus scanner VSCAN for Windows 98 in the directory \VSCAN on the companion CD-ROM. Enable the following options in the StartUp window: Include subfolders, All files and Compressed files.

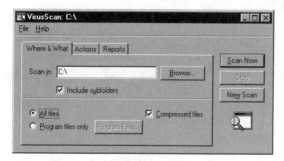

Starting the virus scanner.

Now select the drive to be scanned. On the Actions tab you can specify what should happen if the virus scanner finds a virus. For now, keep the default setting: Continue scanning. Start the scanning process by clicking [Scan Now].

The virus scanner now searches the data medium for viruses. VSCAN will make a list of all infected files.

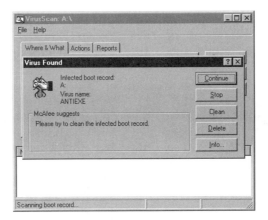

My test diskette contains a whole arsenal of viruses.

To remove a virus, double-click on the displayed file. VSCAN opens an information window where further actions are available.

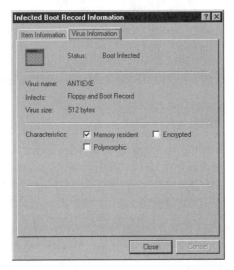

Next to the action switches, VSCAN gives only limited information on the detected virus.

Before destroying the virus, make a copy of the infected file so you can send it to a test center. For more information, see the details earlier in this chapter.

7 *First Aid For A Virus Attack*

If VSCAN is able to remove the virus from the file, you can continue with Clean File. The safest option (and the only option if VSCAN can't remove the virus) is Delete File, which deletes the infected file. You will then need to replace the file with a virus-free version.

Using this virus scanner will give you excellent protection against viruses. Keep in mind, however, that it is shareware. You may try out the program for a limited time (typically 10 to 30 days). This should give you enough time to decide whether you want to keep the program. If you continue to use the program, you're requested to send the author a nominal fee. Paying this fee makes you a licensed user of the program. Check the documentation or the program itself for the amount of the registration fee and the address where you send the registration form.

Fourteen rules to remember

Of course, there are quite a few other things you can do to protect your computer from viruses. The following rules will help you avoid unpleasant surprises.

1. Whenever possible, install only original software on your computer. Always write-protect the original diskettes so a virus cannot infect them. Viruses sold on original program diskettes are very rare. Most virus infections come from pirated copies that have been copied several times without being scanned.

2. Scan original diskettes, too, before installing the program. Although unlikely, even original diskettes can be infected.

3. If you bought a computer with pre-installed software, make certain to scan the hard drive first. There's no guarantee that such hard drives are virus-free. It's happened often enough—a virus is discovered shortly after you buy a computer and is traced back to the dealer.

4. Always scan diskettes that came from unknown sources. Even if the diskette contains only data files, it could still be infected with a boot virus.

5. Compressed archive files may harbor infected files. If your antivirus program is unable to scan archives, make a special directory on the hard drive and copy the archive into it. Then, if possible, immediately scan the archive file. If it's clean you can unpack the archive, after which you should also scan the unpacked files.

6. Before booting the computer, don't forget to take a look inside the diskette drives. A boot virus may be unknowingly transmitted in this way.

7. When buying new, preformatted diskettes, always scan at least one diskette in the package. Viruses on new diskettes are rare, but not new.

8. Scan new CD-ROMs for viruses. CD-ROMs are not immune to computer viruses.

9. Run the virus scanner before backing up your hard drive. This prevents you from unwittingly saving an existing virus.

10. Scan files that you are rewriting to the hard drive from unfamiliar streamer (or backup) tapes. It's easy for viruses to hide there.

11. Scan all files you receive from BBSes, e-mail or other internet services prior to use.

12. Scan your hard drive regularly for viruses. The more you work with "foreign" diskettes, the more frequently you should run the virus scanner.

13. Buy one or two up-to-date virus scanners. If you can't get them yourself, ask someone who has access to BBSes, e-mail or other on-line services. The latest shareware versions are available for most virus scanners from these sources. You can also check the ads in computer magazines that offer free test versions of virus scanners.

14. Don't assume the previous owner of your software has checked it for viruses. It's possible their virus scanner is outdated or incapable of finding certain viruses.

We won't list all the available virus scanners here with their options and extra utilities. The basic operation between virus scanners is the same. One might recognize fewer viruses while another has more options; essentially, virus scanners are the same. Also, the virus scanners are constantly being updated and improved, so any comparisons would soon be obsolete.

7 First Aid For A Virus Attack

Viruses and 32-bit Operating Systems

A 32-bit operating system, like Novell, UNIX, Windows NT, OS/2 and Windows 98, is not immune to viruses. These operating systems do, however, have effective built-in safety mechanisms, such as protection of memory from unauthorized use. Also, the file formats they use are different from the normal DOS file format. This makes it more difficult for viruses to spread.

However, since all this is implemented through software, software can also alter it. Therefore, what we've mentioned in this chapter also applies to 32-bit operating systems.

Boot viruses

There's also a special place here for boot viruses, which infect the partition sector of a hard drive. The partition sector is located at the same position on all hard drives, regardless of the operating system. During the boot process, before the operating system is even installed, the code in the partition sector is executed. This code then loads the boot sector, which in turn starts the installation of the operating system. By this time the boot virus has long since been active in the background. It simply waits for a diskette access and then continues to infect the diskette's boot sector.

Virus protection under Windows 98

Although Windows 98 is a 32-bit operating system, to maintain downward compatibility with DOS, its file system is not entirely new. The old system was merely expanded. All viruses that work with the DOS file format (DOS file system) also pose a threat under Windows 98. There is one advantage to this, however. Since the new file system is compatible with the old one, you don't need a new virus scanner (unlike with OS/2). The old virus scanner will work the same as before. Simply be sure to use a current version.

Warning, virus in the DOS prompt

You should be especially careful when scanning your computer with a DOS virus scanner. The 32-bit operating systems create "virtual machines" for open DOS prompts. Each DOS prompt is considered a separate computer with its own memory.

If you start an infected program in a DOS prompt, it infects the corresponding virtual machine. The virus becomes resident in the memory allocated to it. From there, of course, it can reach the hard drive and infect other files. If you now start the DOS version of a virus scanner in a different DOS prompt (which will happen if you generate an icon for the virus scanner on the Desktop), the virus scanner will get a new virtual machine with its own clean memory.

Before the virus scanner starts its job, it normally checks the memory first. However, since the 32-bit operating system has given the virus scanner a previously unused area of memory, it can't detect the resident portion of the virus in the other DOS prompt. Access to this part of memory is not available to the virus scanner. So instead of scanning all existing memory it scans only the memory in its own virtual machine. The following illustration demonstrates how this happens in Windows 98.

Special care must be taken with DOS virus scanners.

In the DOS prompt, we have installed the Vacsina virus by calling up an infected program. We then ran the virus scanner in the same DOS prompt. It scanned the memory of the virtual machine and immediately detected the resident virus code.

We again ran the virus scanner in another DOS window. Since this virtual machine also has its memory, the virus scanner was unable to detect any viruses.

Of course, you could free the hard drive of viruses. However, files would continue to be infected through the other DOS prompt. This still would not destroy the virus.

7 First Aid For A Virus Attack

If you must rely on a DOS virus scanner for your 32-bit operating system, start your computer with a clean boot diskette. Only if your operating system uses a DOS-compatible file system (e.g., Windows 98) can you be sure that a DOS virus scanner will remove the virus. Use a virus scanner designed for your specific 32-bit operating system. Even so, you should still close DOS prompts before scanning. The memory for a virtual machine can be protected from read accesses by outside programs.

Chapter 8:
The Active Desktop

Chapter 8
The Active Desktop

What is the Active Desktop?

The Active Desktop is the most visible addition to Windows 98. It can also be one of the most troublesome. This chapter will introduce some of the Active Desktop's important features, how to use them and, where appropriate, how to work around them.

The Active Desktop tightly binds the Windows operating system and the Windows World Wide Web browser (a.k.a. Internet Explorer). Your Windows 98 desktop has an icon layer (containing all your program and window icons, such as My Computer) on top of a background HTML layer. This HTML layer allows you to place any HTML document or element (a Web page, images, news and sports tickers—nearly anything that Internet Explorer can display) in your desktop's background. You can place elements in the background itself or position them on the background, in the icon layer. You can even add sounds to the background.

The Active Desktop is also closely linked to the new and improved taskbar, so we'll mention some of the ways this can make your work (or play) easier. And because of the tight integration of Microsoft's Web browser, you can even select a favorite Web page as the background, complete with live Internet links. True tech-heads can even create VBScript and Javascript routines into their backgrounds, building drop lists and animations, for example. We'll explain integrating "live" active elements from the Internet and how to work with automatic Web subscriptions.

> **TIP** The Active Desktop deservedly received bad press when it was first released with Internet Explorer 4.0. If you avoided it then, you may want to take another look at it now. The Active Desktop is much more stable and less intrusive in the Win 98 release than it was as an add-on.

The Active Desktop on your Computer

Desktop basics

The Active Desktop is a change from the Windows 95 desktop. Depending on whether you upgraded or purchased a new Win 98 computer, you may have the Active Desktop already activated. If this bothers you and you'd prefer to work with the now-familiar Windows 95 desktop, simply click the (Start) button, select **Settings | Active Desktop** and click **View as Web Page** to remove the checkmark and deactivate the Active Desktop.

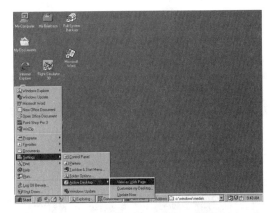

(Conversely, follow these same instructions to place the checkmark in order to experiment with the Active Desktop). Having many active elements on your Active Desktop can take a toll on your system resources. You may want to disable it if you will be running system-intensive applications.

You've probably already discovered that Win 98 offers several ways to view the contents of folders. These options are easily accessed in any window's **View** menu, but that setting only affects the current window. You can make this change once for all your folders by selecting the setting you want in the **View** menu, then click **View | Folder Options**, select the View tab, click "Remember each folder's view settings" to clear the checkbox and click the (Like Current Folder) button. Then click (OK). Now all your folders will appear just like this one.

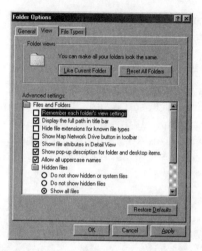

You can also create a custom toolbar on your desktop: First create a folder on your desktop by right-clicking and selecting **New | Folder**. Then copy everything you want to be in the toolbar into this folder: programs, hyperlinks, documents, etc.

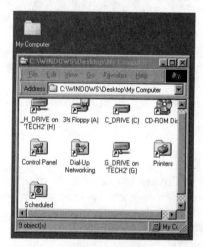

(Alternatively, if you already have a folder containing the items you want to appear in the toolbar, just copy this folder onto your desktop.) Now the most important step: drag this folder to the far edge of the desktop. Wow, each item in the folder is now a button on your new toolbar!

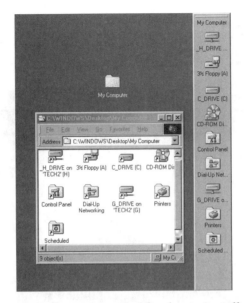

If you install many programs, then you probably also uninstall almost as many. These removed programs, and even some that you use frequently, install small programs that launch automatically everytime you start the computer. Sometimes these are useful, sometimes benign, and sometimes they actually impede your computer's performance, especially when one has outlived its usefulness. These may be hiding in the startup menu, an *.INI file or somewhere else. Windows 98 provides the System Configuration Utility to manage these programs, so you don't have to poke into all the obscure corners of your hard drive. To run the System Configuration Utility, click the Start button, then **Programs | Accessories | System Tools | System Information**.

8 *The Active Desktop*

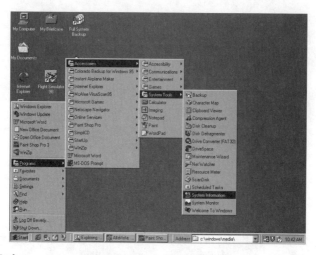

In the System Information program, click **Tools | System Configuration Utility**. Once here, it is not a bad idea to make a backup of the current configuration by clicking the [Create Backup] button on the General tab. (If your edits create problems, you can return to this saved configuration by clicking the [Restore Backup] button.)

Now move to the Startup tab. The list here contains all the drivers and programs loaded by WIN.INI, SYSTEM.INI and the Startup group. To prevent an item from loading at startup, simply clear the checkbox in front of it, then click [OK] or [Apply].

One of the Active Desktop's most hyped features is the HTML wallpaper, which allows you to place almost anything you can see on the Web as your desktop's background (including Java, ActiveX, Dynamic HTML and more). If you are inexperienced at creating Web pages, the easiest way to use a Web page as a background is borrow one from the Web. Go to your favorite Web site (maybe one with news or appealing graphics) and save it (**File | Save as...**) to your Windows\Web\Wallpaper folder. If the page contains any graphics, right-click on each, select **Save Picture As** and save it to the same folder (you may need to open the document in an HTML editor and adjust the pointers to these graphics). With the Active Desktop enabled, right-click on the desktop and select **Properties**. On the Background tab, select the Web page in the wallpaper list.

On the Web tab, check the box labeled "View My Active Desktop as a Web Page".

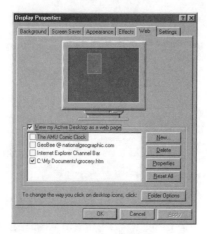

Individual images from the Web can also be used as your desktop background. Just right-click on the image and select **Set as Wallpaper**. You may tile or center the image on the Background tab of the Display Properties.

If you have just a little experience creating a Web page, or would like to gain some, the next easiest method is to click Start, **Programs | Internet Explorer | FrontPage Express**. This diluted version of Microsoft's FrontPage Web builder helps you quickly create and place HTML elements without requiring manual coding. When you are finished, save the Web page to Windows\Web\Wallpaper and proceed as above.

If you feel your Web background is more important than your desktop icons, you may hide these icons by right-clicking the desktop, selecting the Effects tab and checking the box labeled "Hide Icons When the Desktop is Viewed as a Web Page."

Don't worry if your Web page doesn't behave exactly as it should in the Active Desktop. Advanced features, such as FrontPage's Timestamp WebBot or 'script programming, don't always work properly in the background.

Toolbar

Microsoft has also made the taskbar much more user friendly. It now does much more than simply tell you which programs are open. Now it contains QuickLaunch shortcuts, desktop icons, an address bar, even custom toolbars. But if you enable even half of the taskbar options that are available to you, the taskbar becomes very cluttered. You can clean this up by right-clicking on an empty area of the taskbar to open a context menu. Select **View** to choose large or small taskbar icons.

This context menu also allows you to toggle the text of icons, the title of toolbars and even the presence of the individual toolbars. You may resize these taskbar toolbars by positioning the cursor between two toolbars until it becomes an arrow pointing left and right. Then click and drag to resize the toolbars.

To add a frequently used program, document or other icon to the QuickLaunch bar, simply drag that icon onto it. To remove one, right-click on it and click **Delete**.

To create a custom toolbar, right-click on the taskbar and click **Toolbar | New Toolbar**. Then locate the folder you'd like to become a toolbar. Each item in the folder becomes a button on the toolbar.

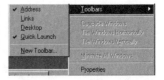

Windows Update

One of the most useful features of Windows 98 is the Windows Update, located in the [Start] menu. Selecting this option will connect you to Microsoft's Web site.

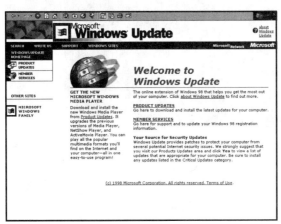

8 The Active Desktop

Just a few clicks later, Microsoft will analyze your software (drivers included) and recommend any downloads that will bring your system up to date. Then follow the instructions to download and install security patches, driver updates and bonuses, such as entertaining desktop themes. This is the first step in creating a "smart" machine that can fix itself. If you run into errors indicating an obsolete driver or requiring a new version of a file, the Windows Update can be a great resource.

The Active Desktop and the Internet

The feature of Active Desktop that Microsoft touts most is the tight bond between the OS and the Internet. This allows you to place "live" content on your desktop and to "subscribe" to Web sites, creating automatic updates that you can view offline.

Active Items

Active content on your desktop can be almost anything that you can see at a Web site, including DHTML, Java or ActiveX. Some of Microsoft's partners are creating content specifically for the Active Desktop. To see what is available, click Start, **Settings | Active Desktop | Customize My Desktop**.

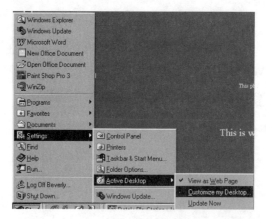

Be sure the "View my Active Desktop as a Web page" option is enabled and click New.

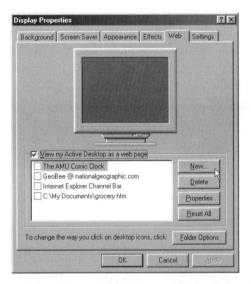

When the dialog box asking if you'd like to browse the Active Desktop gallery appears, click [Yes].

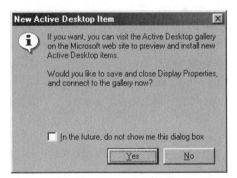

This launches your browser and takes you to Microsoft's Active Desktop gallery, where you can preview and download Active Items. Currently, 42 sites have prepared desktop elements, including CNN, National Geographic, MTV, ESPN, Fortune and The New York Times. Here you'll find stock tickers, sports scores, trivia quizzes, animations and much more. Simply click on the items that interest you and follow the instructions.

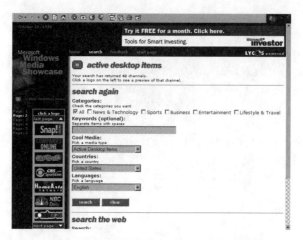

But Windows doesn't always place these items in the appropriate place. You can move Active Items just as any other window: Place your mouse cursor over the window until the window's frame appears. Then you may drag the window by clicking and holding the mouse button down on the top edge of the window, or resize it by moving the cursor over an edge of the window until it becomes a double-ended arrow.

Web subscriptions

Windows 98 also supports Web subscriptions. These allow you to download favorite (and often slow-loading) Web sites while you work on something else or even leave your computer. When you're ready, you can view the Web site off-line without waiting for each page to load. You can also arrange for updated content to arrive automatically on your desktop, such as a news or stock ticker.

By default, you'll also find Microsoft's Channel Bar on the Win 98 desktop. This provides single-click access to Internet content provided by some of Microsoft's commercial partners, many of which also provide active desktop content. But overall, the Channel Bar is a useless feature that occupies a lot of desktop space. To rid your desktop of the Channel Bar, right-click on the desktop and select **Properties**. On the Web tab, select the Internet Explorer Channel Bar in the list of Active Desktop items and click Delete. If you'd prefer to remove the Channel Bar without deleting it, click the box before it in the list to clear the checkmark. Click here again to replace the checkmark to restore the Channel Bar.

If you use a few features of the Channel Bar, but don't need the entire thing taking up desktop space, you can easily edit it to your preference. Simply right-click on an unwanted icon and select **Delete**. You may streamline the Channel Bar by dragging icons for subscribed channels out of their subject categories and onto the main bar—then delete the unnecessary category icon.

Besides Microsoft's Channel Bar partners, you can subscribe to any site on the Web to receive automatic updates for off-line viewing. This allows you to schedule updates so your computer will automatically download your selected Web site(s). When you return to your computer, the Web sites will be waiting for you to view them off-line, so you won't have to wait for data-heavy pages to download. You can arrange subscriptions in several ways. One of the easiest is to open your browser and visit the site to which you wish to subscribe. Drag its icon from the address bar to the desktop. Right-click on this new desktop icon and select **Subscribe**.

Click the [Customize] button and follow the prompts to declare how many pages deep you want downloaded and when the page will be updated. You may choose to download several layers of linked pages, but all the pages must be on the same server, and .CGI scripts won't download properly either (which means you get many pages without advertising—no great loss).

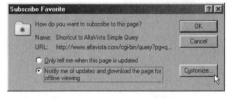

8 *The Active Desktop*

The tight bond between the OS and the Web browser isn't always a good thing. For instance, if your browser hangs or crashes, you can say Goodnight to your OS as well. A browser crash can easily lock up your entire system, forcing you to reboot. This can be avoided with sufficient system resources (a minimum of 32 MB RAM for Win 95/98). To loosen the browser's hold on the OS, launch Internet Explorer and click **View | Internet Options**, select the Advanced tab and check the box labeled "Browse in a New Process".

Click OK and restart the computer to make the change effective. This will create a new IE window for each new browser task. If one of these fails, you can close that window without affecting the entire desktop.

Automatic subscriptions can also launch your Internet connection software when you'd rather it didn't. To stop Windows from launching your dialing program, run Internet Explorer and click **View | Internet Options**. Select the Advanced tab and clear the checkmark from the box labeled "Enable Scheduled Subscription Updates".

This disables all automatic subscriptions, so you will need to update these manually (by clicking **Favorites | Update All Subscriptions** in Internet Explorer).

Chapter 9:
World Wide Web
Resources

Chapter 9
World Wide Web
Resources

This book addresses the most common problems that people encounter when using Windows 98. But we don't have the time or space to write about absolutely everything that can go wrong with a Windows system. Plus, the variety of hardware with which Windows must work creates very individual problems, and it simply isn't practical to address every possible component conflict.

But that doesn't mean we won't do everything we can to help you solve your problem. Many troubleshooting resources are at your disposal on the World Wide Web. We've identified a few of these for you here. Simply open your Internet connection, launch your favorite browser and type the Web address (also known as an "URL") into your browser's Location or Address text field.

Netscape Navigator/Communicator users can visit these sites even easier by importing the bookmark.htm file into their browsers. To do this, launch Netscape's browser and place the companion CD-ROM in your computer's CD-ROM drive. In version 4.05, click **Window | Bookmarks | Edit Bookmarks...** to open the Bookmarks window. In the Bookmarks window, click **File | Import...** Use the Import dialog box to select the sites.htm file on the companion CD-ROM. Click Open and the bookmarks for these sites will be added to your Navigator's bookmark list. (This procedure may be slightly different for other versions of Navigator, but is essentially the same.)

Windows 98 Homepage

www.microsoft.com/windows98/

No place is better to learn about Windows 98 than Microsoft's Windows 98 homepage. Here you may tour the main attractions of Windows 98, learn which programs best take advantage of Win 98's new features, download demos and updates and even get assistance if you need it.

World Wide Web Resources 9

Microsoft Personal Computing Windows 98 Guide

www.microsoft.com/magazine/guides/windows98/

The best answers to software questions usually come from the creator(s) of the software. And so we point you to Microsoft's official Windows 98 guide, where you can "Find out how Windows 98 can help you work and play better," "Order Windows 98 online," "And more!" Do you really need to upgrade? This site will explain why Microsoft thinks you do. Frequently asked question files, installation tips and features round out the information.

Tom's Hardware Guide

www.tomshardware.com

This German doctor's hobby is sharing his broad and deep knowledge of hardware resources. Tom enthusiastically explains motherboards, chipsets, CPUs, RAM, hard drives, video adapters, BIOS, overclocking and still more. His hands-on previews, reviews and tutorials are clear and well-written, as are his trade show wrap-ups and industry forecasts. This is a very good site for any hardware questions you may have.

Web Novice—Internet "How-to" in Plain English

www.uscities.net/webnovice/

This award-winning site is a great resource for computer beginners and anyone who has an unanswered Internet question. Web Novice will teach anyone to use Internet services and resources. The Cyberbabble Decoder (a glossary) clearly explains Internet and computer terms in everyday English. The tips, tutorials, articles and other informative materials will easily take you from Web novice to Web pro. If you still need more, this site will point you to books, top Web sites and other resources that will answer your remaining questions.

Your Source for the Best Windows 98 Information

www.windows98.org

This Web site's interesting design simulates a Windows desktop in your browser window. The page itself looks like the desktop, and the hyperlinks are designed like desktop icons. The Information icon will take you to news about Windows, tips for

375

World Wide Web Resources

using Windows and reviews of the program. The Resources icon will connect you to many tools you may use to learn more about Windows, including Web sites, books, newsgroups and software.

System Optimization Information

www.sysopt.com

The SysOpt site has won many awards, and for good reasons. You can discover the problems and solutions encountered by other users in the PC hardware chat and message boards. If you're considering buying or building a new computer, you should explore the component information (covering BIOS, motherboards, memory, CPUs, chipsets, etc.) and product evaluations and surveys. If you're interested in tweaking your present machine, read the tips, tutorials, technical information and FAQs. Or maybe you just want to sign up for a free computer magazine? You can do all this and more at SysOpt.

The Windows 95/98/NT Troubleshooting site

www.fixwindows.com

This site offers a unique and very easy to use flow chart for diagnosing and correcting many common Windows problems. Besides the news, feature articles, and tips and tricks, you can also browse technical support numbers and download more than 200 utilities.

The Computer Network

www.cnet.com

This excellent site is your portal to many sites focusing on people and the computers they use. This is the parent site of News.com (bringing you breaking technology news), Computers.com (a consumer's guide to computers and peripherals), Builder.com (focusing on Web authoring and scripting), Gamecenter.com, Download.com, Shareware.com, Browsers.com, Search.com and Shopper.com. Cnet.com brings you technology news, daily download recommendations, features, articles, tutorials and more. Visit this site a few times to see how useful it is.

Windows 98 Megasite

www.cmpnet.com/Win98/

Associated with the online version of *Windows Magazine*, this site offers many tips and resources for Win98 users. Read the Technology Guide to learn what's under the hood of Microsoft's latest operating shell upgrade. You can also find hot technology news, 100s of tips, guided tours and utilities here. The resources page will connect you to books, Web sites and other helpful links.

Windows Magazine Online

www.winmag.com

The online edition of *Windows Magazine* offers many valuable resources for you: the Windows tips, computer news, a buying guide, an upgrading guide, discussions, previews and Internet resources offer much useful information. If you need software, the software library and top 100 freeware and shareware lists should have what you need.

Ziff-Davis Net

www.zdnet.com

Ziff-Davis is one of the most prolific publishers in the computing industry; this is their homepage. In addition to links to many magazines in the ZD stable (*PC Magazine, PC Week, PC Computing, Interactive Week* and more), here you also have access to chats, downloads, games, free e-mail and more. Specifically, you can uncover Windows secrets (such as taming the active desktop or turbo charging your browser), read breaking news and reviews, follow tutorials and much more.

The Ultimate Guide to Windows 98

www.zdnet.com/products/windows/98.html

Hosted by Ziff-Davis, the Ultimate Guide offers you the inside story on Windows 98's pluses and problems. This site's feature articles, lab tests and Q. & A.s explore the new features, utilities, power management and improved hardware support brought to you in Windows 98.

377

World Wide Web Resources

Make Windows 98 Fly

www.zdnet.com/zdhelp/howto_help/win98tips/win98tips_3.html

Another aspect of the Ziff-Davis Web site, this page encourages you to tune your PC with Win 98's included utilities. Disk Cleanup will seek and destroy orphaned and unnecessary files, for example. Others will protect your PC from viruses, extend your laptop's battery life, schedule automatic updates and much more.

Windows 98 Spotlight Software Library

www.hotfiles.com/spotlight/windows98/index.html

This self-described "Download deluge" offers more files than you can download in a day. Here you'll find the Win98 upgrade toolkit, daily hot files, registry utilities and much more. All your bases are covered here, whether you want to customize your workspace, clean out your cookies or increase your computer's security. Plus, you may also peruse Ziff-Davis's articles and product reviews.

Downloads for your PC

www.zdnet.com/zdhelp/dl_help/dl_inside_help.html

Here you can retrieve free benchmark programs, storage solutions, memory managers, diagnostic tools, system monitors, file trackers, print utilities, etc. The information on or linked to this page will help you cure hardware conflicts, recover data, and perform do-it-yourself technical support.

ZDNet's Download Help

www.zdnet.com/zdhelp/dl_help/dl_help.html

These are some of the best freely available files, regardless of your operating system, but especially for Win 98 users. You may search for a particular program or browse the most popular categories: security (encryption, protect your e-mail and avoid cookies), Internet (whether you're a webmaster or a simple browser), tests and utilities (performance benchmarks, graphic tests and troubleshooting tools) and applications. There's even a special area focusing on MS Office (teaching you how to protect Word from nasty macro viruses, for instance).

The Editors' Picks of ZDNet's Software Library

www.hotfiles.com/epicks.html

The Ziff-Davis editors see more programs in a day than many people see in a year, and these are their picks of the litter. Current favorites include a Win 98 upgrade toolkit, shareware office suites and weekend webmaster tools. You may also browse the shareware awards and the monthly picks for the best of the best.

Quarterdeck's Tuneup.com

www.tuneup.com

This is your one-stop, online PC service station. Tuneup.com offers a unique online maintenance program. Anyone can visit for tips and articles to avoid PC problems. Members get much more, including updated virus protection, online data backups, a directory of technical support contacts and a searchable library. The subscription is fairly inexpensive, and the first 30 days are a free trial period.

Symantec Corporation

www.symantec.com

Symantec's products are some of the best tools you can use to protect and maintain your computer. The highly acclaimed Norton Utilities is a suite of diagnostic, preventative and repair utilities that will monitor your system, protect it from crashes, and troubleshoot difficulties. Norton Anti-Virus offers some of the best protection from digital nasties, and the Web site offers detailed virus information in the Symantec Antivirus Research Center (SARC). Visit this site to find and fix problems in your PC and improve its performance.

PC Tune-up

www.pctusa.com

PC Tune-up offers computer sales and services through this Web site. It also answers your computer and repair questions, explains error codes and teaches about viruses. While here, you may want to browse the glossary of computer terms or glean tips on tweaking the Windows registry. You can even learn to test your PC for the millennium (Y2K) bug.

9 World Wide Web Resources

Win 95/98/NT Links from My Virtual Reference Desk

www.refdesk.com/win95.html

My Virtual Reference Desk (www.refdesk.com) is one of the best link pages on the Internet. This page has MVRD's Windows links, which connect you to all sorts of Web pages devoted to the many aspects of Microsoft's flagship programs. From here you may link directly to Microsoft's homepage or support center, find the hidden utilities in Win 98 and teach it to behave as you wish it to. You can also preview the best downloads for your operating system or check the clock of Bill Gates's personal wealth to find out what he's worth at this minute.

Excite's Computer and Internet Channel

www.excite.com/computers_and_internet/

Excite is one of the best search engines on the Net. The computers_and_internet page is Excite's collection of the best Web resources for information about the Web. Each heading, such as Hardware, Software, Internet and Networking, links you to technology magazines, hot topics, feature articles, news, even chats and message boards for discussing your computer and its ills with other users.

Yahoo's Windows Information

www.yahoo.com/Computers_and_Internet/Software/Operating_Systems

/Microsoft_Windows/

Yahoo, possibly the most popular search engine on the Internet, lets you search for specific topics or browse subject categories. The page cited here is Yahoo's collection of pages regarding Microsoft Windows. From here you can explore books, user groups, frequently asked questions and Web sites. The Web sites referenced on this page lead to many valuable resources, including a trouble-shooting flow chart, drivers, tips, tricks and secrets.

Appendix

Standard Assignment Of System Resources

Appendix A lists the default assignments of system resources in PC/XT and AT computers. These include the assignments for port addresses (I/O ports), the hardware interrupts and the DMA channels. Refer to Chapter 4 for more information on the special features of resource assignments for different computer and bus systems.

Standard Assignment for Port Addresses		
Component	PC/XT	AT
1. DMA Controller (8237A)	000-00F	000-01F
1. Interrupt Controller (8259A)	020-021	020-03F
Timer	040-043	040-05F
Peripheral Controller (8255A)	060-063	-
Keyboard Controller (8x42)	-	060-06F
Realtime Clock/CMOS-RAM (MC146818)	-	070-07F
DMA Page Register	080-083	080-09F
2. Interrupt Controller (8259A)	-	0A0-0BF
2. DMA Controller (8237A)	-	0C0-0DF
Coprocessor	-	0F0-0F1
Coprocessor	-	0F8-0FF
EIDE Adapter, Secondary Port	-	170-17F

Standard Assignment Of System Resources

Standard Assignment for Port Addresses (continued)		
Component	PC/XT	AT
Hard Drive Controller/EIDE Adapter, Primary Port	320-32F	1F0-1F8
Game Port	200-20F	200-207
Expansion Unit	210-217	-
LPT2	-	278-27F
COM4	2E8-2EF	2E8-2EF
COM2	2F8-2FF	2F8-2FF
Prototype Card	300-31F	300-31F
Network Card	-	360-36F
LPT1	378-37F	378-37F
Monochrome Video Card (MDA)	3B0-3BB	3B0-3BB
Parallel Interface to monochrome video card	3BC-3BF	3BC-3BF
Color Video Card (EGA)	3C0-3CF	3C0-3CF
Color Video Card (VGA)	3D0-3DF	3D0-3DF
COM3	3E8-3EF	3E8-3EF
Diskette Controller	3F0-3F7	3F0-3F7
COM1	3F8-3FF	3F8-3FF

Standard Assignment Of System Resources

Standard Assignment Of Hardware Interrupts		
IRQ	PC/XT	AT
0	Timer	Timer
1	Keyboard	Keyboard
2	-	2. Interrupt Controller
3	COM2/COM4	COM2/COM4
4	COM1/COM3	COM1/COM3
5	Hard Drive	LPT2
6	Disk Drive	Disk Drive
7	LPT1/LPT3	LPT1/LPT3
8	-	Realtime Clock
9	-	Redirection to IRQ2 / VESA Local Bus
10	-	free
11	-	free
12	-	PS/2 Mouse
13	-	Coprocessor
14	-	Hard Drive
15	-	EIDE Adapter, secondary port

Table for user entries

The table on the following page is designed so you can enter the assigned resources of the expansion cards installed in your computer. Then you'll always have them available for future reference.

Standard Assignment Of System Resources

Appendix A

Component	Reserved Port Addresses	Reserved IRQs	Reserved DMA channel

Appendix

Beep Codes & POST Codes & Diagnostic Error Codes

BIOS outputs beep codes when serious errors occur. The number of beeps is often helpful to users since such errors usually mean that not even the video system can operate to display an error message on the screen.

AMI-BIOS		
Beeps	Error	Description
1	Refresh Failure	The Memory Refresh chip is defective
2	Parity Error	Parity error in the first 64K of memory
3	Base 64kB Memory Failure	Memory error in the first 64K
4	Timer not Operational	Memory error in the first 64K or Timer 1 of the motherboard doesn't work
5	Processor Error	CPU on the motherboard is defective
6	8042-Gate 20 Error	The Keyboard Controller (8042) is defective, the BIOS cannot switch to 'Protected Mode'
7	Processor Exception Interrupt Error	CPU generates an exception interrupt
8	Display Memory Read/Write Error	Video Adapter not present or video RAM is defective. Not a serious error
9	ROM Checksum Error	The ROM checksum is incorrect
10	CMOS Shutdown Register Read/Write Error	The Shutdown Register of the CMOS RAM is defective
11	Cache Error/External Cache bad	The external cache is defective

Beep Codes & POST Codes & Diagnostic Error Codes

Appendix B

AWARD-BIOS	
Beeps	Error/ Description
1x short	Not an error, system is booting
1x long, 2x short	Error in video card
2x short, followed by PRESS F1 TO CONTINUE	Some type of error
1x long, 3x short	Error in keyboard controller

IBM BIOS	
Beeps	Error/ Description
None	Power supply or motherboard completely damaged
Continuous	Motherboard severely damaged
Short	Normal POST run, system is in order
2x short	POST error, text of the error message displayed on the screen
Short... (repeats continuously)	Power supply or motherboard damaged
Long, short	Motherboard
Long, 2x short	Video Adapter (MDA,CGA)
Long, 3x short	Video Adapter (EGA)
3x long	3270 Keyboard Adapter

Phoenix-BIOS	
Beeps	Error/ Description
1 1 3	Read/Write of the CMOS RAM
1 1 4	ROM-BIOS checksum
1 2 1	Programmable Timer chip (8253)
1 2 2	Address and/or counter register of the DMA controller Channel 0
1 2 3	Read/Write of the DMA 'Page-Register'
1 3 1	RAM refresh
1 3 3	Chip or data line of the first 64K of RAM

Phoenix BIOS (continued)	
Beeps	**Error/Description**
1 3 4	Error in lower 64K of RAM: odd/even logic doesn't work
1 4 1	Error in the lower 64K of RAM: Address bus
1 4 2	Parity error occurred in the first 64K of RAM
1 4 3	Security Timer (only with EISA BIOS)
1 4 4	Software of the NMI interface (only with EISA-BIOS)
2 1 1	Bit 0 in the first 64K of RAM defective
2 1 2	Bit 1 in the first 64K of RAM defective
2 1 3	Bit 2 in the first 64K of RAM defective
2 1 4	Bit 3 in the first 64K of RAM defective
2 2 1	Bit 4 in the first 64K of RAM defective
2 2 2	Bit 5 in the first 64K of RAM defective
2 2 3	Bit 6 in the first 64K of RAM defective
2 2 4	Bit 7 in the first 64K of RAM defective
2 3 1	Bit 8 in the first 64K of RAM defective
2 3 2	Bit 9 in the first 64K of RAM defective
2 3 3	Bit 10 in the first 64K of RAM defective
2 3 4	Bit 11 in the first 64K of RAM defective
2 4 1	Bit 12 in the first 64K of RAM defective
2 4 2	Bit 13 in the first 64K of RAM defective
2 4 3	Bit 14 in the first 64K of RAM defective
2 4 4	Bit 15 in the first 64K of RAM defective
3 1 1	Register Test DMA Controller (Slave)
3 1 2	Register Test DMA Controller (Master)
3 1 3	Register Test Interrupt Controller (Master)
3 1 4	Register Test Interrupt Controller (Slave)
3 2 4	Test Keyboard Controller

387

Phoenix BIOS (continued)	
Beeps	Error/Description
3 3 4	Video RAM
3 4 1	Initialization of video RAM
3 4 2	Screen retrace test
4 2 1	Timer chip (87253) (tick test)
4 2 2	Shutdown/Restart
4 2 3	Gate A20 failure, Address line 20
4 2 4	unexpected Interrupt in 'Protected Mode'
4 3 1	RAM test from 64K
4 3 2	Programmable timer channel 2
4 3 4	Realtime clock
4 4 1	Serial port
4 4 2	Parallel port
4 4 3	Math coprocessor defective or missing
L1 1 2	(first beep lower) Chip-Select on motherboard defective
L 1 3	(first beep lower) Error in extended CMOS RAM

Diagnostic Error Codes

The error codes listed here are output on the screen by BIOS when errors occur.

Hewlett Packard	
Code	Meaning
000F	Microprocessor Error
001X	BIOS ROM Error
008X	Video ROM Error
009X	Option ROM Error while testing address range C800-DFFFh
00AX	Option ROM Error while testing address range C800-DFFFh
00BX	Option ROM Error while testing address range C800-DFFFh
00CX	Option ROM Error while testing address range E000-EFFFh
00DX	Option ROM Error while testing address range E000-EFFFh
011X	RTC Error while testing CMOS register
0120	RTC Error
0130	RTC/System Configuration Error
0240	CMOS Memory/System Configuration Error
0250	Invalid Configuration
0241	CMOS Memory Error
0280	CMOS Memory Error
02C0	EEPROM Error
02C1	EEPROM Error
02D0	Serial # not present*****
030X	Keyboard/Mouse Controller Error
0311	Keyboard/Mouse Controller Error
0312	Keyboard/Mouse Controller Error
032X	Keyboard/Mouse Controller Error
033X	Keyboard/Mouse Controller Error
03E0	Keyboard/Mouse Controller Error

Hewlett Packard (continued)	
Code	Meaning
03E1	Keyboard/Mouse Controller Error
03E2	Keyboard/Mouse Controller Error
03E3	Keyboard/Mouse Controller Error
03E4	Keyboard/Mouse Controller Error
03EC	Keyboard/Mouse Controller Error
034X	Keyboard Test Failure
035X	Keyboard Test Failure
03E5	Mouse Test Failure
03E6	Mouse Test Failure
03E7	Mouse Test Failure
03E8	Mouse Test Failure
03E9	Mouse Test Failure
03EA	Mouse Test Failure
03EB	Mouse Test Failure
0401	Protected Mode Failure
050X	Serial Port Error
0510	Serial Port Error
0520	Serial Port Error
0543	Parallel Port Error
0545	Parallel Port Error
0506	Datacomm Conflict
0546	Datacomm Conflict
06XX	Keyboard Key Stuck
07XX	Processor Speed Error
0800	Boot ROM Conflict

Hewlett Packard (continued)	
Code	Meaning
0801	Boot ROM Not Found
081X	Integrated Ethernet Interface Errors
0900	Fan Error
110X	Timer Error
1200	Timer Error
1201	Timer Error
20XA	Memory Mismatch
21XX	DMA Error
22XX	DMA Error
30XX	HP-HIL Error
4XXX	RAM Error
5XXX	RAM Error
61XX	Memory Address Line Error
62XX	RAM Parity Error/Memory Controller Error
630X	RAM Error Test
6400	RAM Error Test
6500	BIOS RAM Shadow Error
6510	Video BIOS Shadowing Error/System ROM Error
6520	Option ROM Shadowing Error
65A0	Shadow Error probably caused by system board memory
65B0	Shadow Error probably caused by system board memory
65C0	Shadow Error probably caused by system board memory
65D0	Shadow Error probably caused by system board memory
65E0	Shadow Error probably caused by system board memory
65F0	Shadow Error probably caused by system board memory

Hewlett Packard (continued)	
Code	Meaning
66XX	Shadow Error probably caused by memory on accessory board
7XXX	Interrupt Error
8003	Bad Drive Configuration
8004	CMOS Drive/System Configuration Error
8005	Bad Drive Configuration
8006	Bad Drive Configuration
8007	CMOS Drive/System Configuration Error
8X0D	Controller Busy/Controller Error
8X10	Controller Busy/Controller Error
8X12	Controller Busy/Controller Error
8X20	Controller Busy/Controller Error
8X21	Controller Busy/Controller Error
8X38	Controller Busy/Controller Error
8X3C	Controller Busy/Controller Error
8X40	Controller Busy/Controller Error
8X45	Controller Busy/Controller Error
8X0E	Hard Disk Error
8X0F	Hard Disk Drive Mismatch
8X11	Hard Disk Drive Control Error
8X13	Hard Disk Drive Control Error
8X30	Hard Disk Drive Control Error
8X39	Hard Disk Drive Control Error
8X3A	Hard Disk Drive Control Error
8X3B	Hard Disk Drive Control Error
8X41	Hard Disk Drive Control Error

Hewlett Packard (continued)	
Code	Meaning
8X42	Hard Disk Drive Control Error
8X43	Hard Disk Drive Control Error
8X44	Hard Disk Drive Control Error
8X49	Hard Disk Drive Control Error
8X4B	Hard Disk Drive Control Error
8X28	Hard Disk Drive Splitting Error
8048	Hard Disk Drive Identity Error
804A	Hard Disk Drive Identity Error
8050	Hard Disk Drive Controller Conflict
84XX	Bad Boot Sector
9XXX	Flexible Disk Drive Error
9X0A	Flexible Disk Drive Conflict
9X10	Flexible Disk Drive Conflict
A00X	Numeric Coprocessor Error
B300	Cache Controller Error
B320	Memory Cache Module Error
CXXX	Extended RAM Error
EXXX	Bus Memory Error

IBM BIOS	
Code	**Meaning**
01x	Not classified
02x	Problems with the power supply
1xx	**All the following error messages concern the motherboard (Error code 1)**
101	Interrupt Error
102	Timer Error
103	Error at interrupt of timer
104	Problems with Protected Mode
105	The last 8042 command was not accepted
106	Conversion logic (8/16 Bit) of slots defective
107	Hanging NMI
108	Bus test of timer failure
109	Error in memory addressing
11x	**The following error messages concern motherboards of PS/2 systems**
110	Parity Error
111	Error in memory upgrade
112	Arbitration error in the Micro Channel
113	Arbitration error in the Micro Channel
121	Hardware interrupt with unknown source
131	Only for PCs: Failure checking the cassette port (with inserted plug)
161	CMOS RAM battery empty
162	Checksum error in the CMOS RAM
163	Realtime clock doesn't work
164	Memory size in CMOS RAM not set correctly
165	PS/2: System not configured
166	PS/2: Adapter Timeout

Appendix B

IBM BIOS (continued)	
Code	Meaning
199	PS/2: Specified INSTALLED DEVICES list incorrect
2xx	The following error messages refer to the memory test
201	Defective RAM cell, address output in hexadecimal
202	Addressing Error Lines A0 to A15
203	Addressing Error Lines A16 to AZ3
215	PS/2: Defective RRM on the motherboard
216	PS/2: Defective R451 on the motherboard
3xx	Keyboard
301	Keyboard doesn't respond to software reset or reports sticky key - in this case the appropriate scan code is output in hexadecimal.
302	Keyboard locking is active
303	Error in keyboard or control system
304	Error in keyboard or control system, cycle line hangs at '1'
305	PS/2: Keyboard power supply fuse on the motherboard is defective
4xx	Monochrome Display Adapter (MDA) error
4xx	PS/2: Parallel port error
401	Error checking video RAM, horizontal synchronization frequency or video chip
401	PS/2: Parallel port defective
408	Diagnostic routines: User specified error: Character attributes
416	Diagnostic routines: User specified error: Character set
424	Diagnostic routines: User specified error: Mode 80x25
432	Error at parallel interface on the MDA card
5xx	Color Graphics Adapter error (CGA)
501	Error checking video RAM, horizontal synchronization frequency or the video chip
508	Diagnostic routines: User specified error: Character attributes

IBM BIOS (continued)	
Code	Meaning
516	Diagnostic routines: User specified error: Character set
524	Diagnostic routines: User specified error: Mode 80x25
532	Diagnostic routines: User specified error: Mode 40x25
540	Diagnostic routines: User specified error: Graphics mode 320x200
548	Diagnostic routines: User specified error: Graphics mode 640x200
6xx	Error on floppy drive/controller
601	Error during floppy drive/controller self test
602	Boot record of diskette destroyed
606	Sensor for diskette change doesn't work
607	Diskette write-protected
608	Drive reports invalid command
610	Error formatting: Track 0 unusable
611	Timeout (drive doesn't respond)
612	Controller chip defective
613	General DMA error
614	DMA error: 64K limit exceeded
615	Index timing defective
616	Rotation speed of drive incorrect
621	Track switching error
622	Checksum error of read data
623	Sector head information not found
624	Sector head information invalid
625	Track switching error due to defective controller chip
626	Error comparing data after write operation
7xx	Error in math coprocessors 8087, 80287 and 80387

IBM BIOS (continued)	
Code	Meaning
9xx	Error at parallel port
901	Error at parallel port during test
10xx	Error at second parallel port
1001	Error at second parallel port during test
11xx	Error at serial port
1101	Error at serial port during test
1102	PS/2: Error of serial port or serial interface
1106	PS/2: Error of serial port or serial interface
1107	PS/2: Error of serial port or serial cable
1108	PS/2: Error of serial port or serial interface
1109	PS/2: Error of serial port or serial interface
1112	PS/2: Error of serial port on the motherboard
1118	PS/2: Serial port error on the motherboard
1119	PS/2: Serial port error on the motherboard
12xx	Error of second serial port
12Xx	PS/2: Error of double serial adapter
1201	Error of second serial port during test
1202	PS/2: Error of double adapter or serial port
1206	PS/2: Error of double adapter or serial port
1207	PS/2: Error of double adapter or serial cable
1208	PS/2: Error of double adapter or serial port
1209	PS/2: Error of double adapter or serial port
1212	PS/2: Error of double adapter on the motherboard
1218	PS/2: Error of double adapter on the motherboard
1219	PS/2: Error of double adapter on the motherboard

IBM BIOS (continued)	
Code	Meaning
1227	PS/2: Error of double adapter on the motherboard
1233	PS/2: Error of double adapter on the motherboard
1234	PS/2: Error of double adapter on the motherboard
13xx	Game control error
1301	Game control error in test
1302	Joystick error
14xx	Dot matrix printer error
51x0	Error in synchronous serial ports (SDLC adapter)
1510	Port B of 8255 defective
1511	Port A of 8255 defective
1512	Port C of 8255 defective
1513	Timer 1 of 8253 cannot be decremented
1514	Timer 1 of 8253 permanently active
1515	Timer 0 of 8253 cannot be decremented
1516	Timer 0 of 8253 permanently active
1517	Timer 2 of 8253 cannot be decremented
1518	Timer 2 of 8253 permanently active
1519	Error on Port B of 8273
1520	Error on Port A of 8273
1521	Timeout with 8073 command or read action
1522	Error on interrupt-level 4
1523	Ring Indicate permanently active
1524	Receive Clock permanently active
1525	Transmit Clock permanently active
1526	Test Indicate permanently active

IBM BIOS (continued)	
Code	Meaning
1527	Ring Indicate permanently inactive
1528	Receive Clock permanently inactive
1529	Transmit Clock permanently inactive
1530	Test Indicate permanently inactive
1531	Data Set Ready permanently inactive
1532	Carrier Detect permanently inactive
1533	Clear to send permanently inactive
1534	Data Set Ready permanently active
1535	Clear to send permanently active
1537	Error on interrupt-level 3
1538	Results of a data receive interrupt defective
1539	Error comparing mirrored data
1540	Error in DMA channel 1
1541	Error in DMA channel 1
1542	Error during error checking or status query of 8273
1547	Interrupt on level 4 with unknown source
1548	Interrupt on level 3 with unknown source
1549	Timeout during interrupt arbitration
16xx	Error codes during emulation of screen control systems (327x, 5520 and 525x)
17xx	Hard drive error
1701	Hard drive error during self test
1702	Controller error
1703	Drive error
1704	Controller or hard drive error that cannot be localized
1780	Error at drive 0

IBM BIOS (continued)	
Code	Meaning
1781	Error at drive 1
1782	Controller error
1790	Error at drive 0
1791	Error at drive 1
18xx	Error in slot expansion case
1801	Error during self test
1810	Error during Enable/Disable
1811	I/O expansion card inactive
1812	Higher order address lines inactive
1813	Wait state generator inactive
1814	Enable/Disable mechanism not addressable
1815	Wait state generator permanently active
1816	I/O expansion card permanently active
1817	Higher order address lines permanently active
1818	Disable mechanism not addressable
1819	Defective configuration of wait state generator
1820	Error during self test of receive adapter of I/O expansion
1821	Higher order address lines of receive adapter defective
19xx	Error codes of add-on cards of PC 3270
20xx	Binary synchronous port (BSC-Adapter) error
2010	Port A of 8255 defective
2011	Port B of 8255 defective
2012	Port C of 8255 defective
2013	Timer 1 of 8253 cannot be decremented
2014	Timer 1 of 8253 permanently active

Appendix B

IBM BIOS (continued)	
Code	Meaning
2015	Timer 2 of 8253 cannot be decremented or is permanently active
2017	Data set ready of 8251 permanently inactive
2018	Clear to send of 8251 missing
2019	Data set ready of 8251 permanently active
2020	Clear to send of 8251 permanently active
2021	8251 doesn't respond to hardware reset
2022	8251 doesn't respond to software reset
2023	Error flag of 8251 cannot be cleared
2024	Transmit Ready of 8251 missing
2025	Receive Ready of 8251 missing
2026	Overrun flag of 8251 cannot be set
2027	Timer interrupt missing
2028	Interrupt error sending
2029	Interrupt error sending
2030	Interrupt error receiving
2031	Interrupt error receiving
2033	Ring Indicate permanently active
2034	Receive Clock permanently active
2035	Transmit Clock permanently active
2036	Test Indicate permanently active
2037	Ring Indicate permanently inactive
2038	Receive Clock permanently inactive
2039	Transmit Clock permanently inactive
2040	Test Indicate permanently inactive
2041	Data Set ready permanently inactive

Beep Codes & POST Codes & Diagnostic Error Codes

Appendix B

IBM BIOS (continued)	
Code	Meaning
2042	Carrier detect permanently inactive
2043	Clear to send permanently inactive
2044	Data Set ready permanently active
2045	Carrier detect permanently active
2046	Clear to send permanently active
2047	Send interrupt with unknown source
2048	Receive interrupt with unknown source
2049	Error comparing send and receive data
2050	8251 reports overrun
2051	Data Set Ready lost during data mirroring
2052	Receiver timeout during data mirroring
21xx	Error codes of second binary synchronous port (BSC-Adapter)
2110	Port A of 8255 defective
2111	Port B of 8255 defective
2112	Port C of 8255 defective
2113	Timer 1 of 8253 cannot be decremented
2114	Timer 1 of 8253 permanently active
2115	Timer 2 of 8253 cannot be decremented or is permanently active
2117	Data set ready of 8251 permanently inactive
2118	Clear to send of 8251 missing
2119	Data set ready of 8251 permanently active
2120	Clear to send of 8251 permanently active
2121	8251 doesn't respond to hardware reset
2122	8251 doesn't respond to software reset
2123	Error flag of 8251 cannot be cleared

402

IBM BIOS (continued)	
Code	Meaning
2124	Transmit Ready of 8251 missing
2125	Receive Ready of 8251 missing
2126	Overrun flag of 8251 cannot be set
2127	Timer interrupt missing
2128	Interrupt error sending
2129	Interrupt error sending
2130	Interrupt error receiving
2131	Interrupt error receiving
2133	Ring Indicate permanently active
2134	Receive Clock permanently active
2135	Transmit Clock permanently active
2136	Test Indicate permanently active
2137	Ring Indicate permanently inactive
2138	Receive Clock permanently inactive
2139	Transmit Clock permanently inactive
2140	Test Indicate permanently inactive
2141	Data Set ready permanently inactive
2142	Carrier detect permanently inactive
2143	Clear to send permanently inactive
2144	Data Set ready permanently active
2145	Carrier detect permanently active
2146	Clear to send permanently active
2147	Send interrupt with unknown source
2148	Receive interrupt with unknown source
2149	Error comparing send and receive data

IBM BIOS (continued)	
Code	Meaning
2150	8251 reports overrun
2151	Data Set Ready lost during data mirroring
2152	Receiver timeout during data mirroring
22xx	Error codes of cluster adapter (in LANs)
24xx	Error codes for the EGA card
24xx	PS/2: Error codes for VGA on the motherboard
26xx	Error codes of XT/370
27xx	Error codes of AT/370
28xx	Error codes of emulations adapter 3278/79
29xx	Error codes of Color/Graphics Printer
30xx	Error codes of Primary PC network adapter
3001	Error checking processor
3002	Invalid ROM checksum
3003	Error checking device ID-PROM
3004	Error during RAM test
3005	Error while checking the controller for the interface to the file server of the network
3006	Plus/Minus 12-Volt power supply defective
3007	Error during data mirroring
3008	File server reports defective interface controller
3009	Synchronization error, no GO signal
3010	File server interface OK, no GO signal
3011	GO signal set, command 41 missing
3012	Interface card not installed
3013	Interface card: Error in digital section
3015	Interface card: Error in analog section

Appendix B

IBM BIOS (continued)	
Code	Meaning
3041	Carrier signal detected, not for this card
3042	Carrier signal detected for this card
31xx	Error codes of second primary PC network adapter
3101	Error checking the processor
3102	Invalid ROM checksum
3103	Error checking device ID-PROM
3104	Error during RAM test
3105	Error checking controller for the interface to the file server of the network
3106	Plus/Minus 12-Volt power supply defective
3107	Error during data mirroring
3108	File server reports defective interface controller
3109	Synchronization error, no GO signal
3110	File server interface OK, no GO signal
3111	GO signal set, command 41 missing
3112	Interface card not installed
3113	Interface card: Error in digital section
3115	Interface card: Error in analog section
3141	Carrier signal detected, not for this card
3142	Carrier signal detected for this card
33xx	Error codes of compact printer
36xx	Error on GPIB (General Purpose Interface Bus)
38xx	Error codes of data acquisition adapter
39xx	Error codes of professional graphics Adapter
71xx	Error codes of voice communication adapter
73xx	Error codes of external 3½ inch floppy drive

IBM BIOS (continued)	
Code	Meaning
7306	Sensor for diskette change doesn't work
7307	Diskette write-protected
7308	Drive reports invalid command
7310	Error formatting: Track 0 unusable
7311	Timeout (drive doesn't respond)
7312	Controller chip defective
7313	General DMA error
7314	DMA error: 64K limit exceeded
7315	Index timing defective
7316	Rotation speed of drive incorrect
7321	Track switching error
7322	Checksum error for read data
7323	Sector head information not found
7324	Sector head information invalid
7325	Track switching error due to defective controller chip
7326	Error comparing data after write operation
74xx	PS/2: Error code of VGA card
85xx	Error code of XMA (Expanded Memory Adapter)
86xx	PS/2: Error codes for graphical input devices
8601	PS/2: Error code for graphical input devices
8602	PS/2: Error code for graphical input devices
8603	PS/2: Error codes for graphical input devices or defective motherboard
89xx	Error code of Music Feature Card
100xx	PS/2: Error codes of multiprotocol adapter
10002	PS/2: Multiprotocol adapter or serial port defective

IBM BIOS (continued)	
Code	Meaning
10006	PS/2: Multiprotocol adapter or serial port defective
10007	PS/2: Multiprotocol adapter or serial connection cable defective
10008	PS/2: Multiprotocol adapter or serial port defective
10009	PS/2: Multiprotocol adapter or serial port defective
10012	PS/2: Multiprotocol adapter or motherboard defective
10018	PS/2: Multiprotocol adapter or motherboard defective
10019	PS/2: Multiprotocol adapter or motherboard defective
10042	PS/2: Multiprotocol adapter or motherboard defective
10056	PS/2: Multiprotocol adapter or motherboard defective
104xx	PS/2: Error codes for ESDI hard drives
10401	Hard drive error during self test
10402	Controller error
10403	Drive error
10404	Non-localizable error on controller or hard drive
10480	Error at drive 0
10481	Error at drive 1
10482	Controller error
10490	Error at drive 0
10491	Error at drive 1

Phoenix BIOS	
Error code	Meaning
101	System interrupt
102	System timer
103	System timer interrupt
104	'Protected Mode' problems
105	Keyboard communication
106	Logic test
107	NMI test
108	System timer test
109	Problems with lower 64K RAM
161	Battery/Accu empty or defective
162	Checksum CMOS RAM not correct
163	Time and/or date not set
164	Memory size of CMOS RAM not correct
201	Memory
202	Memory address line 0-15
203	Memory address line 16-32
301	Keyboard missing
302	Keyboard locked
303	Keyboard or system error
304	Keyboard or system error
401	Monochrome monitor or video adapter
501	Color monitor or video adapter
601	Floppy drive or controller defective
602	No boot sector on diskette
1780	Hard-Disk: Drive 0

Appendix B

Phoenix BIOS (continued)	
Error code	Meaning
1781	Hard-Disk: Drive 1
1782	Hard-Disk controller
1790	Hard-Disk: Drive 0
1791	Hard-Disk: Drive 1

POST Codes

POST codes listed in the following tables are specified in hexadecimal. You can read out and display these hex numbers with special diagnostic cards (POST Code cards). The codes are output to I/O port 80h during the POST.

AMI WinBIOS

Since several versions of AMI BIOS versions are available (with completely different POST codes) we cannot provide a list of all the versions. Therefore, we've included the current WIN BIOS as a substitute for the different AMI BIOS versions.

Beep Codes & POST Codes & Diagnostic Error Codes

POST code	Meaning
01	Reserved
02	Reserved
03	NMI is disabled. Test Software Reset/Power-on
04	Reserved
05	Software-Reset/Power-on detected, cache will be disabled if necessary
06	POST code being unpacked
07	POST code is unpacked, initializing CPU and CPU data range
08	CPU and CPU data range are initialized, calculating CMOS checksum
09	CMOS checksum calculated, CMOS diagnostic byte written, CMOS will be initialized if 'CMOS in every boot' Init is set
0A	CMOS initialized CMOS status register being initialized for date and time
0B	CMOS status register is initialized
0C	Keyboard controller free, output BAT commands to keyboard controller
0D	BAT commands output to keyboard controller, BAT commands being checked
0E	Keyboard controller BAT commands have been checked
0F	Initialization after keyboard controller BAT finished, writing keyboard command byte
10	Keyboard command byte written, outputs Pin 23, 24 blocking/unblocking command
11	Pin 23, 24 from the keyboard is blocked/unblocked, test whether INS key is pressed during Power on
12	Test INS key is finished, disabling DMA and interrupt controllers
13	DMA controllers #1 #2 and interrupt controllers #1 #2 are disabled, video output is disabled and Port-B is initialized, initializing chip set
14	Reserved
15	Chip set initialized, 8254 timer test begins
16	Reserved
17	Reserved
18	Reserved

AMI WIN BIOS (continued)

410

AMI WIN BIOS (continued)	
POST code	Meaning
19	8254 timer test okay, testing memory refresh
1A	Memory refresh line is switched, testing 15 microseconds ON/OFF time
20	Memory refresh period of 30 microseconds concluded, initializing 64K base memory
21	Reserved
22	Reserved
23	64K base memory is initialized, setting BIOS stack
24	Required setup prior to interrupt vector initialization finished, beginning interrupt vector initialization
25	Interrupt vector initialization finished, reading input port 8042 for turbo switch (if necessary) and deleting password (if necessary)
26	Input port 8042 has been read, initializing general data for the turbo switch
27	General data for turbo switch initialized, performing other initializations prior to setting video mode
28	Other initializations prior to setting video mode have been performed, preparing video mode setting
2A	Initializing different buses
2B	Control passed to other setups prior to a possible video ROM check
2C	Processes prior to video ROM check completed, determining whether video ROM is present
2D	Video ROM check finished
2F	EGA/VGA not found, video memory Read/Write test begins
30	Video memory Read/Write test finished, 'Retrace check' begins
31	'Retrace check' failed alternate video memory test begins
32	Alternate video memory test finished, alternate 'Retrace check' begins
34	Video test finished, setting graphics mode
35	Reserved
36	Reserved

AMI WIN BIOS (continued)	
POST code	Meaning
37	Graphics mode set, Power-on message is displayed
38	Different buses are initialized (input, IPL general devices) if they exist
39	Errors during initialization of different buses are shown
3A	New cursor position is read and stored, 'Hit-DEL message' being displayed
3B	'Hit-DEL message' has been displayed, preparing memory test in virtual mode
40	Preparing descriptor table
41	Reserved
42	Descriptor table prepared, enabling virtual mode for memory test
43	Virtual mode enabled, enabling interrupts for diagnostic mode
44	Interrupts enabled, initializing data for memory test
45	Data initialized, test begins with determination of memory size
46	Memory size calculated, writing patterns memory test
47	Patterns written to extended memory for test, writing patterns to base memory
48	Patterns written to base memory, searching for memory below 1 Meg
49	Memory below 1 Meg located, searching for memory above 1 Meg
4A	Reserved
4B	Memory above 1 Meg located, test for software reset, then clear memory below 1 Meg
4C	Memory below 1 Meg cleared, clearing memory above 1 Meg (software reset)
4D	Memory above 1 Meg cleared, backing up/securing memory size (software reset)
4E	Memory test started (hardware reset), displaying 64K blocks
4F	Memory displayed, preparing sequential and random test
50	Memory test/initialization below 1 Meg finished, setting video memory

AMI WIN BIOS (continued)	
POST code	Meaning
51	Video memory set, testing memory above 1 Meg
52	Memory above 1 Meg tested, backing up/securing memory size
53	Memory size secured/backed up, CPU register secured/backed up, setting real mode
54	Shutdown concluded, CPU in real mode, disabling Gate A20 and parity/NMI
57	Gate A20 and parity/NMI disabled, setting memory size (relocation and shadowing)
58	Memory size determined, deleting 'Hit-DEL message'
59	'Hit-DEL message' deleted, displaying 'WAIT message', DMA and interrupt controller test begins
60	DMA page register test finished
62	DMA 1st base register tested
65	DMA 2nd base register tested
66	DMA programming finished, initializing 8259 interrupt controller
67	8259 interrupt controller initialized
7F	Enable extended NMI sources
80	Keyboard test started, clearing output buffer, check whether unexpected key has been pressed
81	Keyboard reset/pressed key found, testing keyboard controller
82	Keyboard controller tested, writing command byte
83	Command byte written, general data initialized
84	Check whether memory size corresponds with CMOS
85	Memory size test complete, check whether password is set
86	Password tested, preparing Setup
87	Setup prepared, unpack Setup and run CMOS Setup
88	Back from CMOS Setup, clearing screen

AMI WIN BIOS (continued)	
POST code	Meaning
89	Display Power-on message
8B	Power-on message displayed, copying video BIOS to RAM
8C	Video BIOS copied to RAM, setting optional Setup after CMOS Setup
8D	Optional Setup after CMOS Setup set, test and initialize mouse
8E	Mouse tested and initialized, reset hard disk controller
8F	Hard disk controller reset, initializing floppy
90	Reserved
91	Floppy setup finished, executing hard disk setup
92	Reserved
93	Reserved
94	Hard disk setup executed, set base and extended memory
95	Memory set, set optional buses to address C8000h
96	Reserved
97	Initializations of C8000h finished, perform optional ROM test
98	Optional ROM test performed
99	All required initializations after ROM test finished, set setup timer
9A	Finished setting timer and printer base address, set serial base address
9B	Serial base address set, perform other initializations prior to coprocessor
9C	Other initializations prior to coprocessor performed, initializing coprocessor
9D	Coprocessor initialized
9E	Test extended keyboard and numeric keypad
9F	Extended keyboard and numeric keypad tested, output keyboard ID
A0	Keyboard output, clear keyboard ID flag
A1	Keyboard ID flag cleared, test cache memory
A2	Cache tested, output software errors

AMI WIN BIOS (continued)	
POST code	Meaning
A3	Set keyboard rate
A4	Keyboard rate set, set wait states
A5	Wait states are set, clear screen and enable Parity/NMI
A6	Reserved
A7	Parity/NMI enabled
A8	Give control to E000h
A9	Get control back
AA	Display configuration
AB	Reserved
AC	Reserved
AD	Reserved
AE	Reserved
AF	Reserved
B0	Configuration displayed
B1	Copy necessary code to special area
00	Pass control to INT #19 for booting

AWARD-BIOS	
POST code	Meaning
01	Processor test
02	Keyboard test
03	Clear 8042 interface
04	Reset 8042
05	8042 initialization
06	Initialization of chips (DMA, Interr. CMOS)
07	Processor test
08	Initialization of CMOS RAM
09	BIOS-EPROM determine checksum
0A	Initialization of video adapter
0B	Test timer channel 0
0C	Test timer channel 1
0D	Test timer channel 2
0E	Test CMOS datum
0F	Test CMOS shutdown byte
10	Test DMA channel 1
11	Test DMA channel 2
12	Test DMA page register
13	Test keyboard controller (8751)
14	Memory refresh
15	Test 64K base memory
16	Initialize interrupt vectors
17	Initialize video adapter
18	Test video memory

AWARD-BIOS (continued)	
POST code	Meaning
19	Test interrupt controller 1
1A	Test interrupt controller 2
1B	Test CMOS battery
1C	Determine CMOS checksum
1D	CMOS setup
1E	Determine memory size
1F	Test memory
20	Test interrupt controller bits
21	Test parity bits
22	Test interrupt controller
23	Test protected mode and A20 line
24	Determine memory size above 1 Meg
25	Test memory above 1 Meg
26	Test protected mode
27	Test cache controller and Shadow RAM
28	Test keyboard controller
29	Reserved
2A	Initialize keyboard controller
2B	Initialize floppy and hard drive controllers
2C	Determine and initialize RS232 interfaces
2D	Determine and initialize parallel ports
2E	Initialize hard drive
2F	Test coprocessor
30	Reserved

AWARD-BIOS (continued)	
POST code	Meaning
30	Reserved
31	Determine and initialize optional ROMs
3B	Initialize second cache (Opti chip set)
CA	Initialize cache
EE	Processor error
FF	Pass control to interrupt 19h (boot loader)

AWARD-BIOS Version 4.50	
POST code	Meaning
01	Test processor Flag
02	Test processor register
03	Initialization of timer DMA and interrupt controller
04	Read port 61h bit 4
05	Initialization of keyboard controller
06	Reserved
07	Test CMOS interface
08	Test first 64K of memory
09	First cache initialization
0A	Load interrupt vector table
0B	Check whether CMOS checksum okay or INS key pressed
0C	Initialization of keyboard
0D	Initialization of video card, detection of CPU cycle
0E	Test video memory preparation of screen for POST messages output
0F	Test DMA controller 0
10	Test DMA controller 1
11	Test DMA page register

AWARD-BIOS Version 4.50 (continued)	
POST code	Meaning
12	Reserved
13	Reserved
14	Timer test
15	Test interrupt controller 1
16	Test interrupt controller 2
17	Test for defective interrupt bit
18	Test for interrupt controller and timer functionality
19	Test NMI bits in port 61h, clear NMI, if okay
1A	Display CPU cycle
1B	Reserved
1C	Reserved
1D	Reserved
1E	Reserved
1F	Set EISA mode
20	Set EISA slot 0
21	Set EISA slot 1
22	Set EISA slot 2
23	Set EISA slot 3
24	Set EISA slot 4
25	Set EISA slot 5
26	Set EISA slot 6
27	Set EISA slot 7
28	Set EISA slot 8
29	Set EISA slot 9

AWARD-BIOS Version 4.50 (continued)	
POST code	Meaning
2A	Set EISA slot 10
2B	Set EISA slot 11
2C	Set EISA slot 12
2D	Set EISA slot 13
2E	Set EISA slot 14
2F	Set EISA slot 15
30	Determine the size of base and extended memory
31	Test memory
32	Test memory (EISA)
33-3B	Reserved
3C	Installation of setup
3D	Initialization of mouse
3E	Set cache, if enabled in setup
3F	Reserved
BF	Initialization of chip set with setup values
40	Virus warning
41	Initialization of floppy controller
42	Initialization of hard drive controller
43	Initialization of peripheral ports
44	Reserved
45	Initialization of coprocessor
46-4D	Reserved
4E	Display errors, restart if necessary
4F	Security check, password query if installed in setup

Appendix B

AWARD-BIOS Version 4.50 (continued)	
POST code	Meaning
50	Restore CMOS from RAM, clear screen
51	Enable Parity and NMI, enable cache
52	Search for optional ROM from C8000h to EFFFFh
53	Initialization of time values
54-5F	Reserved
60	Virus protection
61	Set boot cycle
62	Keyboard setup (numeric keypad and keyboard rate)
63	Selection of boot device
FF	BOOT
B0	Wrong interrupts in protected mode
B1	NMI detected
E1-EF	Setup side active (Side #1: E1, #2: E2...)

AWARD ISA/EISA BIOS	
POST code	Meaning
01	Processor test 1 (Flags,Iflags)
02	Processor test 2 (Registers)
03	Initialize chips (FPU, DMA-Page, Timer, DMA, INT-Contr. EISA-Regs)
04	Test memory refresh toggle
05	Blank video, initialize keyboard
06	EPROM checksum (=0)
07	Test CMOS interface and battery status
08	Setup low memory (first 256K, OEM chip set)

Beep Codes & POST Codes & Diagnostic Error Codes

POST code	Meaning
AWARD ISA/EISA BIOS (continued)	
09	Early cache initialization
0A	Setup INT table
0B	Test CMOS RAM checksum
0C	Initialize keyboard
0D	Initialize video interface
0E	Test video memory
0F	Test DMA controller 0
10	Test DMA controller 1
11	Test DMA page registers
12-13	Reserved
14	Test timer counter 2
15	Test 8259-1 mask bits
16	Test 8259-2 mask bits
17	Test stuck 8259's interrupt functionality
18	Test 8259 interrupt functionality
19	Test stuck NMI bits (Parity/IO Check)
1A-1E	Reserved
1F	Set EISA Mode
20-2F	Enable EISA slot 0..15
30	Size base (256K 640K) and ext. memory > 1 MEG
31	Test base 1256K 640K) and ext. memory > 1 MEG
32	Test EISA extended memory
33-3B	Reserved
3C	Setup enabled

AWARD ISA/EISA BIOS (continued)	
POST code	Meaning
3D	Initialize floppy drive & controller
3E	Setup cache controller
3F	Setup shadow RAM
40	Reserved
41	Initialize floppy drive & controller
42	Initialize hard drive & controller
43	Detect & initialize serial/parallel ports
44	Reserved
45	Detect & initialize math coprocessor
46	Reserved
47	Set speed for boot
48-4D	Reserved
4E	Manufacturing POST loop or display messages
4F	Security check
50	Write CMOS
51	Pre-boot enable (parity, nmi, cache on)
52	Initialize option ROMS (SCAN C8000h. .EFFFh)
53	Initialize timer value
63	Boot attempt
B0	Spurious (INT occurs in protected mode)
B1	Unclaimed NMI ('Press F1 disable NMI, F2 reboot')
BF	Program chip set
C0	Turn on/off cache (OEM specific)
C1	Memory presence test (OEM specific)

AWARD ISA/EISA BIOS (continued)	
POST code	Meaning
C2	Early memory initialization (OEM specific)
C3	Extended memory initialization (OEM specific)
C4	Special display switch handling (OEM specific)
C5	Early shadow (OEM specific)
C6	Cache programming (OEM specific)
C7	Reserved
C8	Special speed switching (OEM specific)
C9	Special shadow handling (OEM specific)
CA	Very early initialization (OEM specific)
D0-DF	Debug
E0	Reserved
E1-EF	Setup Pages (E1=Page 1, E2=Page)
FF Boot	

Chips & Technologies	
POST code	Description
01	Test CPU flag
02	Test CPU register
03	Determine BIOS-ROM checksum
04	Test DMA controller
05	Test timer
06	Test addressing of 64K base memory
07	Test 64K base memory
08	Test interrupt controller
09	Interrupt occurred
0A	Reserved

Chips & Technologies	
POST code	Meaning
0B	CPU is in protected mode
0C	Test DMA page register
0D	Memory refresh
0E	Test keyboard controller
0F	Test protected mode
10-15	Test CPU register
16	Test keyboard controller
17	Shutdown
18	Shutdown during memory test
19	Copyright checksum error
1A	BMS checksum error
50	Initialization of hardware
51	Initialize timer
52	Initialize DMA controller
53	Initialize interrupt controller
54	Initialization of chip set
55	Reserved
56	Switch to protected mode
57	Determine memory size
58	Reserved
59	Switch to real mode
5A	Determine memory size
5B	Relocate shadow RAM
5C	Configure EMS

Chips & Technologies (continued)	
POST code	Meaning
5D	Reserved
5E	Test 64K base memory
5F	Test shadow RAM
60	Test CMOS RAM
61	Test video adapter
63	Test interrupts in protected mode
64	Test address line A20
65	Test memory address lines
66	Test memory
67	Test extended memory
68	Test timer interrupt
69	Test clock (CMOS RAM)
6A	Test keyboard
6B	Test coprocessor
6C	Test RS232 interface
6D	Test parallel port
6E	Reserved
6F	Test floppy
70	Test hard drive
71	Check key lock switch
72	Test mouse
73-8F	Reserved
90	RAM setup
91	Determine CPU clock frequency

Chips & Technologies (continued)	
POST code	Meaning
92	Check system configuration
93	Initialize BIOS
94	Pass control to interrupt 19h (boot loader)
95	Reset hardware
96	Initialize cache controller

Hewlett Packard	
POST code	Meaning
1	LED Test
2	Processor Test
3	System (BIOS) ROM Test
4	RAM Refresh Timer Test
5	Interrupt RAM Test
6	Shadow the System ROM BIOS
7	CMOS RAM Test
8	Internal Cache Memory Test
9	Initialize the Video Card
10	Test External Cache
11	Shadow Option ROMs
12	Memory Subsystem Test
13	Initialize EISA/ISA Hardware
14	8042 Self test
15	Timer 0/Timer 2 Test
16	DMA Subsystem Test
17	Interrupt Controller Test
18	RAM Address Line Independence Test

Beep Codes & POST Codes & Diagnostic Error Codes

Hewlett Packard (continued)	
POST code	Meaning
19	Size Extended Memory
20	Real-Mode Memory Test (First 640 K)
21	Shadow RAM Test
22	Protected Mode RAM Test (Extended RAM)
23	Real-Time Clock Test
24	Keyboard Test
25	Mouse Test
26	Hard Disk Test
27	LAN test
28	Flexible Disk Controller Subsystem Test
29	Internal Numeric Coprocessor Test
30	Weitek Coprocessor Test
31	Clock Speed Switching Test
32	Serial Port Test
33	Parallel Port Test

IBM-AT-BIOS	
POST code	Meaning
01	80286 processor test (real mode),Verify flags, registers conditional jumps
02	ROM checksum test of 32K ROM modules: POST, ROM BASIC, BiOS
03	CMOS Shutdown byte test, rolling bit pattern at shutdown address
04	8254 Timer 1 all bits on, set timer count, check all bits on
05	8254 Timer 1 all bits off, set timer count, check all bits off
06	8237 DMA 0 initialization, channel register test, disable 8237, read/write all channels
07	8237 DMA 1 initialization, channel register test, disable 8237, read/write all channels

428

Beep Codes & POST Codes & Diagnostic Error Codes

Appendix B

IBM-AT-BIOS (continued)	
POST code	Meaning
08	DMA page register test, write/read all page register
09	storage refresh test, verify refresh is occurring
0A	Soft reset
0B	Reset 8042
0C	Test OK
0D	Write byte 0 of 8042 memory, base 64K read/write test, write/read data patterns AA, 55, FF, 01, 00
0E	Fill memory with data
0F	Get I/P buffer switch settings
10	Issue self test
11	Initialize display row count verify 80286 LGDT/SGDT and LIDT/SIDT instructions
12	Test protected mode registers initialize 8259 interrupt 1 controller
13	Initialize 8259 interrupt 2 controller
14	Setup interrupt vectors
15	Establish BIOS interrupt call vectors, verify CMOS checksum, verify battery OK
16	Set data segment
17	Set bad battery flag
18	Verify CMOS dividers ready
19	Set return address byte in CMOS
1A	Set temporary stack protected mode, test determine memory size, verify parity through software checks
1B	Segment address (second 64K)
1C	Set base memory size flag (512 K 640 K)
1D	Segment address (> 640K)
1E	Set expanded memory size as determined by CMOS
1F	Test address fines 19-23

IBM-AT-BIOS (continued)	
POST code	Meaning
20	Shutdown
21	Return 1 from shutdown, initialize video controller, test video write/read, reset video enable, select alpha mode, write/read patterns
22	Enable video signal and set mode CRT interface test, verify video enable and horizontal sync
23	Look for advanced video card
24	8259 interrupt controller test, read/write interrupt mask register, enable interrupts, mask device interrupts off
25	Test interrupt mask registers
26	Check for unexpected interrupts
27	Check converting logic
28	Check unexpected non maskable interrupts
29	Test data bus with timer 2
2D	Check 8042 for last accepted command read/write storage test in protected mode
30	Set shutdown return 2
31	Enable protected mode
32	Test address lines 0-15
33	Check next block of 64K
34	Enable real mode, perform additional protected mode tests (or after FA: address ok in low Megabyte)
35	Keyboard error test (or after FA: address error in low Megabyte)
36	Verify AA scan code
38	Check for stuck key
39	Check 8042 error
3A	Initialize 8042
3B	Check for 2K ROM blocks in C800-E000

IBM-AT-BIOS (continued)	
POST code	Meaning
3C	Disk attachment test
3D	Initialize floppy drive with drive type
3E	Initialize hard disk
3F	Initialize printer
40	Enable hardware interrupt if 80287 is present
41	Check for system code at E0000:0000
42	ROM found: Initialize
43	Boot via INT 19h
44	Attempt to boot from fixed disk
45	Unable to find fixed disk, jump to ROM BASIC
81	Build descriptor table
82	Enable virtual mode system initialization
90-AE	Exceptions 00 to 1 Fh occurred (here error in IBM-BIOS, Code A2 for EXC 12h and 13h)
AF-B5	Interrupt 20h to 26h occurred
DD	Transmit error code to MFG_PORT
F0	Protected Mode Test
F1	software interrupt test INT 20h
F2	Exception interrupt test INT 13h
F3	Check 80286 LDT/SDT and LTR/STR
F4	Check 80286 bound instruction
F5	Check PUSH ALL and POP ALL instructions
F6	Check access rights function
F7	Check APPL functions
F8	Check LAR instructions
F9	Check LSL instructions

Appendix B

IBM-AT-BIOS (continued)	
POST code	Meaning
FA	Low megabyte chip select function test (write to 1B000, check B000:0, B800:0, ok: => 34h, error =>35h)

MR-BIOS Version 2.0	
POST code	Meaning
00	Cold start begins (doesn't appear with software reset)
01	HOOK 00, OEM specific, normally the chip set is set to the default values
02	Critical I/Os are disabled
03	Test BIOS checksum
04	Page register test (port 81-8F)
05	8042 keyboard controller self test
06	Initialization of chips 8237,8254,8259
07	HOOK 01, OEM specific, normally the cache is disabled
08	Test refresh toggle
09	Test 8237
0A	64K base memory test
0B	Test 8259
0C	8259/IRQ test
0D	8254/channel 0 test and initialization
0E	8254/channel 2 toggle test, test speaker channel
0F	Reserved
13	HOOK 02, OEM specific, setup 8 MHz bus
10	Video initialization
11	CMOS checksum test
12	Permit memory BAT
14	Determination of size and memory test (lower 64K already finished)

MR-BIOS Version 2.0 (continued)	
POST code	Meaning
15	Access memory
16	HOOK 03, OEM specific, determination of size and cache memory test
17	Test A20 gate
18	Determination of size and extended memory test
19	HOOK 04, determination of size and system memory test ('special' OEM memory)
1A	Check timer
1B	Detection of serial port
1C	Detection of parallel port
1D	Detection and test of coprocessor
1E	Detection and test of floppy controller
1F	Detection and test of hard disk controller
20	Check and set fixed CMOS values, display the others
21	Check whether computer is locked
22	Enable NUM Lock, check whether password is set
23	HOOK 05, OEM specific
24	Set keyboard rate
28	HOOK 06, OEM specific, normally enabling of shadow, cache and turbo
25	Floppy turned on
26	Hard disk turned on
27	Video mode set on the first adapter
29	A20 gate disabled, attempt to activate C8000h-E000h ROM BIOS
2A	DOS time is set
2B	Parity check and NMI allowed
2C	E000h ROM BIOS enabled
2E	HOOK 07, OEM specific, install EMS, if available
2F	Pass control to INT19 for booting

Phoenix BIOS	
POST code	Meaning
01	CPU Register test in progress
02	CMOS write/read failure
03	ROM BIOS checksum failure
04	Programmable interval timer failure
05	DMA initialization Failure
06	DMA page register write/read failure
08	RAM refresh verification error
09	First 64K RAM test in progress
0A	First 64K RAM chip or data line failure, multi-bit
0B	First 64K RAM odd/even logic failure
0C	Address line failure first 64K RAM
0D	Parity failure first 64K RAM
10	Bit 0 first 64K RAM failure
11	Bit 1 first 64K RAM failure
12	Bit 2 first 64K RAM failure
13	Bit 3 first 64K RAM failure
14	Bit 4 first 64K RAM failure
15	Bit 5 first 64K RAM failure
16	Bit 6 first 64K RAM failure
17	Bit 7 first 64K RAM failure
18	Bit 8 first 64K RAM failure
19	Bit 9 first 64K RAM failure
1A	Bit 10 first 64K RAM failure
1B	Bit 11 first 64K RAM failure
1C	Bit 12 first 64K RAM failure
1D	Bit 13 first 64K RAM failure

Phoenix BIOS (continued)	
POST code	Meaning
1E	Bit 14 first 64K RAM failure
1F	Bit 15 first 64K RAM failure
20	Slave DMA register failure
21	Master DMA register failure
22	Master interrupt mask register failure
23	Slave interrupt mask register failure
25	Interrupt vector loading in progress
27	Keyboard Controller test failure
28	CMOS power failure and checksum calculation in progress
29	CMOS configuration validation in progress
2B	Screen initialization failure
2C	Screen retrace test failure
2D	Search for video ROM in progress
2E	Screen running with video ROM
30	Screen operable
31	Monochrome monitor operable
32	Color monitor (40 column) operable
33	Color monitor (80 column) operable
34	Timer tick interrupt in progress or failure
35	Shutdown test in progress or failure
36	Gate A20 failure
37	Unexpected interrupt in protected mode
38	RAM test in progress or address failure > FFFFh
3A	Interval timer channel 2 test or failure
3B	Time-of-Day clock test or failure
3C	Serial port test or bad

Phoenix BIOS (continued)	
POST code	Meaning
3D	Parallel port test or bad
3E	Math processor test or bad
41	System board select bad (MCA)
42	Extended CMOS RAM bad (MCA)

Quadtel	
POST code	Description
02	CPU flag test
03	CPU register test
06	Initialization of hardware
08	Initialization of chip set register
0A	Determination of BIOS ROM checksum
0C	Test DMA page register
0E	Test timer
10	Initialize timer
12	Test DMA controller
14	Initialize DMA controller
16	Initialize interrupt controller, reset coprocessor
18	Test interrupt controller
1A	Memory refresh
1C	Test addressing of 64K base memory
1E	Test 64K base memory
20	Test 64K base memory (upper 16 bits)
22	Test keyboard controller
24	Test CMOS RAM

POST code	Meaning
	Quadtel (continued)
26	Test protected mode
28	Determine memory size
2A	Test memory
2C	Interleave test
2E	Protected mode test finished
30	Unexpected shutdown
32	Output memory size
34	Relocate shadow RAM
36	Configure EMS
38	Define wait state
3A	Clear 64K base memory
3A	Get CPU clock frequency
3E	Get jumper settings (8042)
40	Set CPU clock frequency
44	Get video adapter
46	Initialize video adapter
48	Test interrupts
4A	Start second test of protected mode
4C-56	Test protected mode
58	Test address line A20
5A	Test keyboard
5C	Determine whether XT or AT keyboard
5E	Start third test of protected mode
60	Check base memory
62	Test addressing of base memory
64	Test shadow RAM

Quadtel (continued)	
POST code	Meaning
66	Test extended memory
68	Test addressing of extended memory
6A	Determine memory size
6C	Display possible errors
6E	Copy BIOS to shadow RAM
70	Test timer
72	Test clock (CMOS RAM)
74	Test keyboard
76	Initialize interrupt vectors
78	Test coprocessor
7A	Determine RS232 interfaces
7C	Determine parallel ports
7E	Initialize BIOS data range
80	Determine floppy and hard drive controllers
82	Test floppies
84	Test hard drive
86	Look for an optional ROM
88	Check key-lock switch setting
8A	Wait for <Press F1 Key...>
8C	Remaining system initialization (Cache..)
8E	Pass control to interrupt 19h (Boot Loader)
B0	Unexpected interrupt has occurred

Appendix

Pinouts And Port Assignments

Power supply plug motherboard

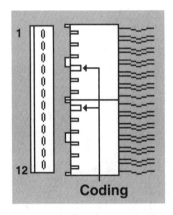

Power supply for the motherboard

Pin #	Color	Function	Pin #	Color	Function
1	Orange	Power Good	2	Red	+5V DC
3	Yellow	+12V DC	4	Blue	-12V DC
5	Black	Ground	6	Black	Ground
7	Black	Ground	8	Black	Ground
9	White	-5V DC	10	Red	+5V DC
11	Red	+5V DC	12	Red	+5V DC

Power supply plug 5.25-inch inch

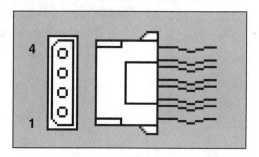

Power supply for 5.25-inch disk drives

Pin #	Color	Function	Pin #	Color	Function
1	Yellow	+12V DC	2	Black	Ground
3	Black	Ground	4	Red	+5V DC

Power supply plug 3.5-inch disk drive

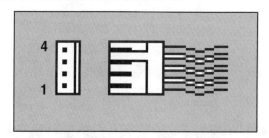

Power supply for 3.5-inch disk drives

Pin #	Color	Function	Pin #	Color	Function
1	Yellow	+12V DC	2	Black	Ground
3	Black	Ground	4	Red	+5V DC

Pinouts And Port Assignments

Serial port

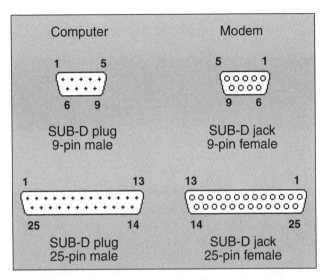

9 and 25 pin serial port

Pin # 9-pin	Pin # 25-pin	Signal	Description	Function
1	8	DCD	Data Carrier Detect	Carrier signal detected
2	3	RXD	Receive Data	Receive line
3	2	TXD	Transmit Data	Send line
4	20	DTR	Data Terminal Ready	Data terminal ready
5	7	GND	Ground	Ground
6	6	DSR	Data Set Ready	Data communications equipment ready
7	4	RTS	Request to Send	Request to send
8	5	CTS	Clear to Send	Ready to send
9	22	RI	Ring Indicator	Incoming call signal

441

Parallel port

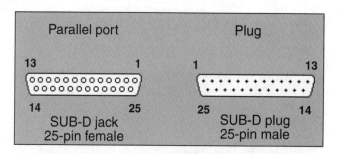

Parallel port

Pin #	Signal	Description	Function
1	STR	Strobe	Sends data to the printer
2	D0	Data bit 0	Receive line
3	D1	Data bit 1	Send line
4	D2	Data bit 2	Data terminal ready
5	D3	Data bit 3	Ground
6	D4	Data bit 4	Data communications equipment ready
7	D5	Data bit 5	Request to send
8	D6	Data bit 6	
9	D7	Data bit 7	
10	ACK	Acknowledge	Acknowledge of receive from other party
11	BSY	Busy	Other party is busy
12	PAP	PAPER OUT	No paper in printer
13	SELECT		Printer is ON-Line
14	ALF	Auto Line Feed	Printer automatically executes line feed
15	ERROR		Error at other end
16	INIT		Initializing printer
17	SLCT IN	Select In	Connected device is switched ON-LINE

Pin #	Signal	Description	Function
18	GND	Ground	Ground
19	GND	Ground	Ground
20	GND	Ground	Ground
21	GND	Ground	Ground
22	GND	Ground	Ground
23	GND	Ground	Ground
24	GND	Ground	Ground
25	GND	Gound	Ground

Parallel interface

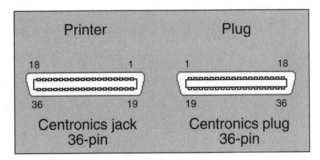

36-pin Centronics connector

Pin #	Signal	Description	Function
1	STR	Strobe	Sending data to the printer
2	D0	Data bit 0	
3	D1	Data bit 1	
4	D2	Data bit 2	
5	D3	Data bit 3	
6	D4	Data bit 4	
7	D5	Data bit 5	

443

Pin #	Signal	Description	Function
8	D6	Data bit 6	
9	D7	Data bit 7	
10	ACK	Acknowledge	Acknowledges receipt from other party
11	BSY	Busy	Other end is busy
12	PAP	PAPER OUT	No paper in printer
13	SELECT		Printer is ON-Line
14	ALF	Auto Line Feed	Printer executes automatic line feed
15	GND/N.C.	Ground	Ground or not used
16	GND/N.C.	Ground	Ground or not used
17	Chassis-GND		Ground chassis
18	External +5V		+5V for additional devices
19	GND	Ground	Ground
20	GND	Ground	Ground
21	GND	Ground	Ground
22	GND	Ground	Ground
23	GND	Ground	Ground
24	GND	Ground	Ground
25	GND	Ground	Ground
26	GND	Ground	Ground
27	GND	Ground	Ground
28	GND	Ground	Ground
29	GND	Ground	Ground
30	GND	Ground	Ground
31	INIT		Initializing printer
32	ERROR		Error at the other end
33	External GND		Ground for additional devices, usually identical to GND lines
34	N.C.		not connected
35	+5V/N.C.		+5V or not connected
36	SLCT IN	Select In	Connected device switched ON-LINE

GamePort

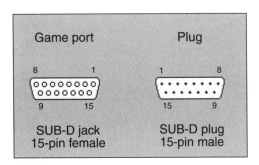

Gameport

Pin #	Signal	Function	Pin #	Signal	Function
1	Vcc	Power supply +5V	2	TA1	1st button Joystick A
3	AX	X Potentiometer Joystick A	4	GND	Ground
5	N.C.	not connected	6	AY	Y Potentiometer Joystick A
7	TA2	2nd button Joystick A	8	Vcc	Power supply +5V
9	Vcc	Power supply +5V	10	TB1	1st button Joystick B
11	BX	X Potentiometer Joystick B	12	GND	Ground
13	BY	Y Potentiometer Joystick B	14	TB2	2nd button Joystick B
15	Vcc	Power supply +5V			

The MIDI port also runs through the gameport with sound cards. Therefore, the following contacts are different than those listed above.

Pin #	Signal	Function	Pin #	Signal	Function
12	MIDI TXD	MIDI output of sound card	15	MIDI RXD	MIDI input of sound card

Keyboard connector (DIN 5-pin)

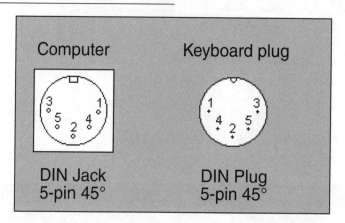

DIN keyboard connector

Pin #	Label	Function	Pin #	Label	Function
1	CLOCK	Clock line	2	DATA	Data line
3	RESET	Keyboard reset	4	GND	Ground
5	+5V	Power supply			*Not all keyboards support pin #3*

Hercules/MDA adapter

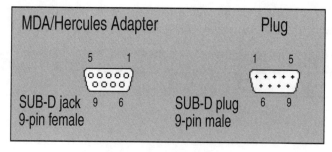

Pinout for Hercules/MDA Adapter

Pin #	Label	Function	Pin #	Label	Function
1	GND	Ground	2	GND	Ground
3	N.C.	Not connected	4	N.C.	Not connected
5	N.C.	Not connected	6	INTENSITY	Intensity
7	VIDEO	TTL video signal	8	H-SYNC	Horizontal synchronization (18.432KHz)
9	V-SYNC	Vertical Synchronization (50Hz)			

CGA adapter

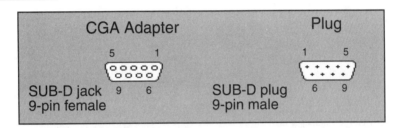

Pinout for CGA Adapter

Pin #	Label	Function	Pin #	Label	Function
1	GND	Ground	2	GND	Ground
3	RED	Red	4	GREEN	Green
5	BLUE	Blue	6	INTENSITY	Intensity
7	N.C.	Not connected	8	H-SYNC	Horizontal synchronization (15.75KHz)
9	V-SYNC	Vertical synchronization (60Hz)			

447

Pinouts And Port Assignments

EGA adapter

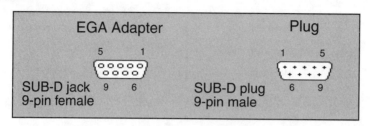

Pinout EGA Adapter

Pin #	Label	Function	Pin #	Label	Function
1	GND	Ground	2	SECONDARY RED	Red low byte
3	PRIMARY RED	Red high byte	4	PRIMARY GREEN	Green high byte
5	PRIMARY BLUE	Blue high byte	6	SECONDARY GREEN	Green low byte
7	SECONDARY BLUE	Blue low byte	8	H-SYNC	Horizontal synchronization (22KHz)
9	V-SYNC	Vertical synchronization (60Hz)			

VGA adapter

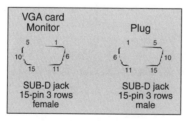

Pinout for VGA adapter

Pinouts And Port Assignments

Pin #	Signal	Description	Pin #	Signal	Description
1	RED	Red color signal	2	GREEN	Green color signal
3	BLUE	Blue color signal	4	ID2	Monitor identification bit 2
5	NC		6	GND-RED	Ground Red Signal
7	GND-GREEN	Ground Green Signal	8	GND-BLUE	Ground Blue Signal
9	N.C.	Not connected	10	GND-SYNC	Ground Sync Signal
11	ID1	Monitor Identification bit 1	12	ID0	Monitor Identification bit 0
13	H-SYNC	Horizontal synchronization	14	V-SYNC	Vertical synchronization
15	N.C.	Not connected			

floppy drive connector

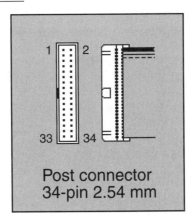

Post connector
34-pin 2.54 mm

Pinout Floppy Connector

Pin #	Signal	Description	Function
1	GND	Ground	Ground
2	HL		Write stream or rotation number change
3	GND	Ground	Ground
4	Reserved		
5	GND	Ground	Ground
6	DS3/RES	Drive Select	3rd floppy drive (normally not supported) or reserved

Pinouts And Port Assignments

Pin #	Signal	Description	Function
7	GND	Ground	Ground
8	IDX	INDEX	Displays the starting point of a track
9	GND	Ground	Ground
10	DS0	Drive Select 0	1st floppy drive
11	GND	Ground	Ground
12	DS1	Drive Select 1	2nd floppy drive
13	GND	Ground	Ground
14	DS2/RES	Drive Select 2	3rd floppy drive (normally not supported) or reserved
15	GND	Ground	Ground
16	MOTOR ON		Motor of floppy drive switched on
17	GND	Ground	Ground
18	DIR	Direction Select	Controls the direction in which the read/write head moves
19	GND	Ground	Ground
20	STEP		Step impulse for the read/write head
21	GND	Ground	Ground
22	WRITE DATA		Data written to diskette
23	GND	Ground	Ground
24	WRITE GATE	Delete written data	
25	GND	Ground	Ground
26	TRACK 00		Read/write head at track 0
27	GND	Ground	Ground
28	WRITE PROTECT		Diskette is write/protected
29	GND	Ground	Ground
30	Read DATA		Data read from diskette
31	GND	Ground	Ground
32	HEAD SELECT		Selection whether upper or lower head is active
33	GND	Ground	Ground
34	DISK CHANGE		No diskette in drive

450

IDE interface

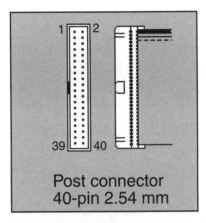

Post connector
40-pin 2.54 mm

Pinout IDE Interface

Pin #	Signal	Description	Function
1	RESET		Reset
2	GND	Ground	Ground
3	DD7	Data line 7	
4	DD8	Data line 8	
5	DD6	Data line 6	
6	DD9	Data line 9	
7	DD5	Data line 5	
8	DD10	Data line 10	
9	DD4	Data line 4	
10	DD11	Data line 11	
11	DD3	Data line 3	
12	DD12	Data line 12	
13	DD2	Data line 2	
14	DD13	Data line 13	
15	DD1	Data line 1	

Pin #	Signal	Description	Function
16	DD14	Data line 14	
17	DD0	Data line 0	
18	DD15	Data line 15	
19	GND	Ground	Ground
20	Selection for PIN 20		
21	DMARQ	DMA Request	DMA request (optional)
22	GND	Ground	Ground
23	DIOW		Write data via port address
24	GND	Ground	Ground
25	DIOR		Read data via port address
26	GND	Ground	Ground
27	IORDY		IDE device still busy (optional)
28	Reserved		Used for Cable Select with Quantum, for example
29	DMACK	DMA Acknowledge	DMA acknowledge (optional)
30	GND	Ground	Ground
31	INTRQ	Interrupt Request	Hardware interrupt request Channel 14
32	IOCS16		16 bit data transfer (8 bit with High Signal)
33	DA1		Bit 1 Address bus, for addressing the internal data register of the hard drive
34P	PDIAG	PASSED DIAGNOSTIC	Hard drive self test concluded
35	DA0		Bit 0 address bus, for addressing the internal data register of the hard drive
36	DA2		Bit 2 Address bus, for addressing the internal data register of the hard drive
37	CS0		Selection Command Block Register
38	CS1		Selection Control Block Register
39	DA/SP	DRIVE ACTIVE-SLAVE PRESENT	Hard drive is active / after reset a slave drive communicates its presence
40	GND		

50 pin SCSI Interface, Posts (A-cable, Single-Ended)

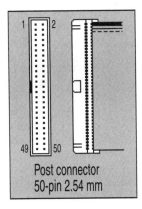

Post connector
50-pin 2.54 mm

Pinout for flat ribbon cable of SCSI interface

This interface is located on the normal SCSI bus cable as well as internal SCSI components.

Pin #	Signal	Description	Function
1	GND	Ground	Ground
2	DB0	Data Bus	Data line 0
3	GND	Ground	Ground
4	DB1	Data Bus	Data line 1
5	GND	Ground	Ground
6	DB2	Data Bus	Data line 2
7	GND	Ground	Ground
8	DB3	Data Bus	Data line 3
9	GND	Ground	Ground
10	DB4	Data Bus	Data line 4
11	GND	Ground	Ground
12	DB5	Data Bus	Data line 5
13	GND	Ground	Ground
14	DB6	Data Bus	Data line 6

Pinouts And Port Assignments

Pin #	Signal	Description	Function
15	GND	Ground	Ground
16	DB7	Data Bus	Data line 7
17	GND	Ground	Ground
18	DBP	Data Bus Parity	Parity bit for data bus
19	GND	Ground	Ground
20	GND	Ground	Ground
21	GND	Ground	Ground
22	GND	Ground	Ground
23	Reserved		
24	Reserved		
25	N.C.	Not connected	
26	TRMPWR	Terminator Power	Power supply for the terminators
27	Reserved		
28	Reserved		
29	GND	Ground	Ground
30	GND	Ground	Ground
31	GND	Ground	Ground
32	ATN	ATTENTION	Initiator reports to target that a message is ready
33	GND	Ground	Ground
34	GND	Ground	Ground
35	GND	Ground	Ground
36	BSY	Busy	SCSI bus is busy with data
37	GND	Ground	Ground
38	ACK	Acknowledge	Initiator responds to an inquiry
39	GND	Ground	Ground
40	RST	Reset	Reinitialization of the SCSI bus
41	GND	Ground	Ground
42	MSG	Message	A message is sent on the data bus

Pin #	Signal	Description	Function
43	GND	Ground	Ground
44	SEL	Select	Current initiator selects its target
45	GND	Ground	Ground
46	C/D	Control/Data	Outputs the kind of information on the data bus
47	GND	Ground	Ground
48	REQ	Request	Target indicates that it requires service
49	GND	Ground	Ground
50	I/O	Input/Output	Shows the direction of the information flow

50 pin SCSI Centronics interface (A-cable, Single-Ended)

also valid for SCSI-2 High Density

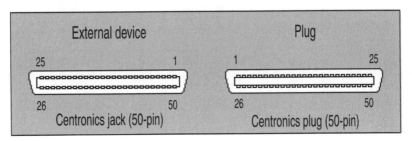

Pinout Centronics interface for external SCSI devices

Found on external SCSI components

Pin #	Signal	Description	Function
1	GND	Ground	Ground
2	GND	Ground	Ground
3	GND	Ground	Ground
4	GND	Ground	Ground
5	GND	Ground	Ground
6	GND	Ground	Ground
7	GND	Ground	Ground
8	GND	Ground	Ground
9	GND	Ground	Ground
10	GND	Ground	Ground
11	GND	Ground	Ground
12	Res		
13	N.C.		
14	Res		
15	GND	Ground	Ground
16	GND	Ground	Ground
17	GND	Ground	Ground
18	GND	Ground	Ground
19	GND	Ground	Ground
20	GND	Ground	Ground
21	GND	Ground	Ground
22	GND	Ground	Ground
23	GND	Ground	Ground
24	GND	Ground	Ground
25	GND	Ground	Ground
26	DB0	Data Bus	Data line 0
27	DB1	Data Bus	Data line 1
28	DB2	Data Bus	Data line 2
29	DB3	Data Bus	Data line 3

Pin #	Signal	Description	Function
30	DB4	Data Bus	Data line 4
31	DB5	Data Bus	Data line 5
32	DB6	Data Bus	Data line 6
33	DB7	Data Bus	Data line 7
34	DBP	Data Bus Parity	Parity bit for the data bus
35	GND	Ground	Ground
36	GND	Ground	Ground
37	Res		
38	TRMPWR	Termination Power	Power supply for the terminators
39	Res		
40	GND	Ground	Ground
41	ATN	ATTENTION	Initiator reports to target that a message is ready
42	GND	Ground	Ground
43	BSY	Busy	SCSI Bus is busy with data
44	ACK	Acknowledge	Initiator responds to an inquiry
45	RST	Reset	Reinitialization of SCSI bus
46	MSG	Message	A message is sent on the data bus
47	SEL	Select	Current initiator selects its target
48	C/D	Control/Data	Outputs the kind of information on the data bus
49	REQ	Request	Target indicates that it requires service
50	I/O	Input/Output	Shows the direction of the information flow

50-pin SCSI interface, Post (A-cable, Differential-SCSI)

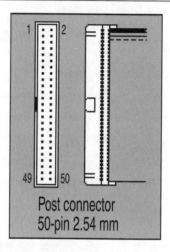

Post connector
50-pin 2.54 mm

Pinout diagram for a 50 pin post connector

Pin #	Signal	Description	Function
1	GND	Ground	Ground
2	GND	Ground	Ground
3	+DB0	Data Bus	+ Data line 0
4	-DB0	Data Bus	- Data line 0
5	+DB1	Data Bus	+ Data line 1
6	-DB1	Data Bus	- Data line 1
7	+DB2	Data Bus	+ Data line 2
8	-DB2	Data Bus	- Data line 2
9	+DB3	Data Bus	+ Data line 3
10	-DB3	Data Bus	- Data line 3
11	+DB4	Data Bus	+ Data line 4
12	-DB4	Data Bus	- Data line 4
13	+DB5	Data Bus	+ Data line 5
14	-DB5	Data Bus	- Data line 5

Appendix C

Pin #	Signal	Description	Function
15	+DB6	Data Bus	+ Data line 6
16	-DB6	Data Bus	- Data line 6
17	+DB7	Data Bus	+ Data line 7
18	-DB7	Data Bus	- Data line 7
19	+DBP	Data Bus Parity	+ Parity bit for the data bus
20	-DBP	Data Bus Parity	- Parity bit for the data bus
21	DIFFSENS		
22	GND	Ground	Ground
23	Res		
24	Res		
25	TRMPWR	Termination Power	Power supply for the terminators
26	TRMPWR	Termination Power	Power supply for the terminators
27	Res		
28	Res		
29	+ATN	ATTENTION	Initiator reports to target that a message is ready
30	-ATN	ATTENTION	Initiator reports to target that a message is ready
31	GND	Ground	Ground
32	GND	Ground	Ground
33	+BSY	Busy	SCSI Bus is busy with data
34	-BSY	Busy	SCSI Bus is busy with data
35	+ACK	Acknowledge	Initiator responds to an inquiry
36	-ACK	Acknowledge	Initiator responds to an inquiry
37	+RST	Reset	Reinitialization of SCSI bus
38	-RST	Reset	Reinitialization of SCSI bus
39	+MSG	Message	A message is sent on the data bus
40	-MSG	Message	A message is sent on the data bus
41	+SEL	Select	Current initiator selects its target
42	-SEL	Select	Current initiator selects its target
43	+C/D	Control/Data	Outputs the kind of inofrmation on the data bus

459

Pin #	Signal	Description	Function
44	-C/D	Control/Data	Outputs the kind of inofrmation on the data bus
45	+REQ	Control/Data	Outputs the kind of inofrmation on the data bus
46	-REQ	Control/Data	Outputs the kind of inofrmation on the data bus
47	+I/O	Input/Output	Shows the direction of the information flow
48	-I/O	Input/Output	Shows the direction of the information flow
49	GND	Ground	Ground
50	GND	Ground	Ground

50 pin SCSI Centronics interface (A-cable, Differential-SCSI)

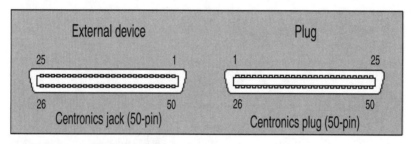

Also valid for SCSI-2 High Density

Pin #	Signal	Description	Function
1	GND	Ground	Ground
2	+DB0	Data Bus	+ Data line 0
3	+DB1	Data Bus	+ Data line 1
4	+DB2	Data Bus	+ Data line 2
5	+DB3	Data Bus	+ Data line 3
6	+DB4	Data Bus	+ Data line 4
7	+DB5	Data Bus	+ Data line 5
8	+DB6	Data Bus	+ Data line 6
9	+DB7	Data Bus	+ Data line 7

Pin #	Signal	Description	Function
10	+DBP	Data Bus Parity	+ Parity bit for the data bus
11	DIFFENS		
12	Reserved		
13	TRMPWR	Termination Power	Power supply for the terminators
14	Reserved		
15	+ATN	ATTENTION	Initiator reports to target that a message is ready
16	GND	Ground	Ground
17	+BSY	Busy	SCSI bus is busy with data
18	+ACK	Acknowledge	Initiator responds to an inquiry
19	+RST	Reset	Reinitialization of the SCSI bus
20	+MSG	Message	A message is sent on the data bus
21	+SEL	Select	Current initiator selects its target
22	+C/D	Control/Data	Outputs the kind of information
23	+REQ	Control/Data	Outputs the kind of information on the data bus
24	+I/O	Input/Output	Shows the direction of the information flow
25	GND	Ground	Ground
26	GND	Ground	Ground
27	-DB0	Data Bus	- Data line 0
28	-DB1	Data Bus	- Data line 1
29	-DB2	Data Bus	- Data line 2
30	-DB3	Data Bus	- Data line 3
31	-DB4	Data Bus	- Data line 4
32	-DB5	Data Bus	- Data line 5
33	-DB6	Data Bus	- Data line 6
34	-DB7	Data Bus	- Data line 7
35	-DBP	Data Bus Parity	- Parity bit for the data bus
36	GND	Ground	Ground
37	Reserved		

Appendix C

Pin #	Signal	Description	Function
38	TRMPWR	Termination Power	Power supply for the terminators
39	Reserved		
40	-ATN	ATTENTION	Initiator reports to target that a message is ready
41	GND	Ground	Ground
42	-BSY	Busy	SCSI bus is busy with data
43	-ACK	Acknowledge	Initiator responds to an inquiry
44	-RST	Reset	Reinitialization of SCSI bus
45	-MSG	Message	A message is sent on the data bus
46	-SEL	Select	Current initiator selects its target
47	-C/D	Control/Data	Outputs the kind of information
48	-REQ	Control/Data	Outputs the kind of information on the data bus
49	-I/O	Input/Output	Shows the direction of the information flow
50	GND	Ground	Ground

VESA Feature connector

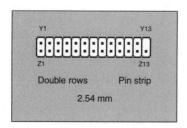

Pinout for VESA Feature Connector

Pin #	Signal	Function	Pin #	Signal	Function
Y1	Pixel Data 0		Y2	Pixel Data 1	
Y3	Pixel Data 2		Y4	Pixel Data 3	
Y5	Pixel Data 4		Y6	Pixel Data 5	
Y7	Pixel Data 6		Y8	Pixel Data 7	
Y9	Pixel Clock		Y10	Blanking	
Y11	Horizontal Sync		Y12	Vertical Sync	
Y13	Ground				

Pin #	Signal	Function	Pin #	Signal	Function
Z1	Ground		Z2	Ground	
Z3	Ground		Z4	Ext. Pixel Data Input	
Z5	Ext. Sync/Blanking Input		Z6	Ext. Pixel Clock Input	
Z7	Not Used		Z8	Ground	
Z9	Ground		Z10	Ground	
Z11	Ground		Z12	Not Used	
Z13	No Pin				

PCMCIA 2.0 Slot

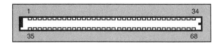

Pinout for PCMCIA interface Version 2.0

The following table gives the signals for pure memory connectors.

Pinouts And Port Assignments

Pin #	Signal	Description	Function
1	GND	Ground	Ground
2	D3	Data line 3	
3	D4	Data line 4	
4	D5	Data line 5	
5	D6	Data line 6	
6	D7	Data line 7	
7	CE1	Card Enable 1	Enables lower 8 bits of data bus
8	A10	Address line 10	
9	OE	Output Enable	Dat to be read from a PCMCIA memory card
10	A11	Address line 11	
11	A9	Address line 9	
12	A8	Address line 8	
13	A13	Address line 13	
14	A14	Address line 14	
15	WE/PGM	Write Enable / Program	Transfer write data to inserted/plugged in card
16	RDY/BSY	Ready / Busy	RDY / /BSY=0, Card still busy
17	Vcc	Power supply	
18	Vpp1	Programming power 1	
19	A16	Address line 16	
20	A15	Address line 15	
21	A12	Address line 12	
22	A7	Address line 7	
23	A6	Address line 6	
24	A5	Address line 5	
25	A4	Address line 4	
26	A3	Address line 3	
27	A2	Address line 2	
28	A1	Address line 1	
29	A0	Address line 0	

Appendix C

Pin #	Signal	Description	Function
30	D0	Data line 0	
31	D1	Data line 1	
32	D2	Data line 2	
33	WP	Write Protect	Card is write/protected
34	GND	Ground	Ground
35	GND	Ground	Ground
36	CD1	Card Detect 1	Determines whether a PCMCIA card is plugged in
37	D11	Data line 11	
38	D12	Data line 12	
39	D13	Data line 13	
40	D14	Data line 14	
41	D15	Data line 15	
42	CE2	Card Enable 1	Enables upper 8 bits of data bus
43	RFSH	Refresh	Refresh card memory
44	Reserved		
45	Reserved		
46	A17	Address line 17	
47	A18	Address line 18	
48	A19	Address line 19	
49	A20	Address line 20	
50	A21	Address line 21	
51	Vcc	Power supply	
52	Vpp2	Programming power 2	
53	A22	Address line 22	
54	A23	Address line 23	
55	A24	Address line 24	
56	A25	Address line 25	
57	Reserved		
58	RESET		Resets plugged in card

Pin #	Signal	Description	Function
59	WAIT		Card inserts wait state
60	Reserved		
61	REG	Register	Address attribute memory of card
62	BVD2	Battery Voltage Detect	Gives voltage of battery on PCMCIA card
63	BVD1	Battery Voltage Detect	Gives voltage of battery on PCMCIA card
64	D8	Data line 8	
65	D9	Data line 9	
66	D10	Data line 10	
67	CD2	Card Detect 2	Determines whether a PCMCIA card is plugged in
68	GND	Ground	Ground

Some of the contacts have a different assignment with I/O cards. So it's easier to understand, we're only listing those contacts with different assignments.

Pin #	Signal	Description	Function
16	IREQ	Interrupt-Request	Interrupt request of I/O card
33	IOIS16		Current I/O access addresses a 16 bit port
44	IORD	I/O-Read	Card passes I/O data to connector
45	IOWR	I/O-Write	Card receives I/O data from connector
60	INPACK	Input Acknowledge	Acknowledge of received data
62	SPKR	Speaker	Audio data of the card
63	STSCHG	Status Changed	PCMCIA card status has changed

Appendix C

Expansion Slot Pinout On The Motherboard

8 bit ISA Slot

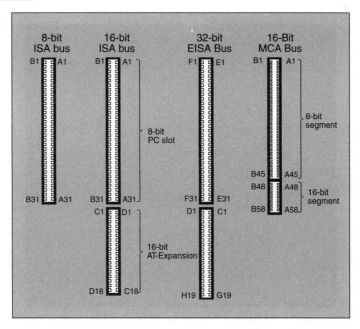

Structure of ISA, EISA and MCA slots

Pinouts And Port Assignments

Pin #	Signal	Description	Function
A1	IO CH CK	I/O Channel Check	Error channel for adapter cards
A2	D7	Data line 7 (MSB)	
A3	D6	Data line 6	
A4	D5	Data line 5	
A5	D4	Data line 4	
A6	D3	Data line 3	
A7	D2	Data line 2	
A8	D1	Data line 1	
A9	D0	Data line 0 (LSB)	
A10	IO CH RDY	I/O Check Ready	
A11	AEN	Address Enable Signal	Specifies whether CPU or DMA controller has control of the system bus
A12	A19	Address line 19 (MSB)	
A13	A18	Address line 18	
A14	A17	Address line 17	
A15	A16	Address line 16	
A16	A15	Address line 15	
A17	A14	Address line 14	
A18	A13	Address line 13	
A19	A12	Address line 12	
A20	A11	Address line 11	
A21	A10	Address line 10	
A22	A9	Address line 9	
A23	A8	Address line 8	
A24	A7	Address line 7	
A25	A6	Address line 6	
A26	A5	Address line 5	
A27	A4	Address line 4	
A28	A3	Address line 3	

Pinouts And Port Assignments

Pin #	Signal	Description	Function
A29	A2	Address line 2	
A30	A1	Address line 1	
A31	A0	Address line 0 (LSB)	
B1	GND	Ground	
B2	RES DRV	Reset Drive	Reset drive
B3	+5V	Power supply	
B4	IRQ2	Interrupt 2	
B5	-5V	Power supply	
B6	DRQ2	DMA request	Request for DMA transfer Channel 2
B7	-12V	Power supply	
B8	Reserved	Usually not not connected	
B9	+12V	Power supply	
B10	GND	Ground	
B11	MEMW	Memory Write	Write to memory
B12	MEMR	Memory Read	Read from memory
B13	IOW	Input/Output Write	Write to port address
B14	IOR	Input/Output Read	Read from port address
B15	DACK3	DMA Acknowledge	Acknowledge DMA request Channel 3
B16	DRQ3	DMA request	Request for DMA transfer Channel 3
B17	DACK1	DMA Acknowledge	Acknowledge DMA request Channel 1
B18	DRQ 1	DMA request	Request for DMA transfer Channel 1
B19	DACK0/REFRESH	DMA Acknowledge	Acknowledge DMA request Channel 0 for memory refresh
B20	CLK	System clock of computer	
B21	IRQ7	Interrupt Request	Hardware interrupt request Channel 7
B22	IRQ6	Interrupt Request	Hardware interrupt request Channel 6
B23	IRQ5	Interrupt Request	Hardware interrupt request Channel 5
B24	IRQ4	Interrupt Request	Hardware interrupt request Channel 4
B25	IRQ3	Interrupt Request	Hardware interrupt request Channel 3

Pinouts And Port Assignments

Appendix C

Pin #	Signal	Description	Function
B26	DACK2	DMA Acknowledge	Acknowledge DMA request Channel 2
B27	T/C	Terminal Count	End status counter DMA transfer, transfer complete
B28	ALE	Address Latch Enable	Valid address signlas on I/O channel
B29	+5V	Power supply	
B30	OSC	Oscillator clock 14.31818 MHz	
B31	GND		

16 bit ISA slot

Pin #	Signal	Description	Function
A1	IO CH CK	I/O Channel Check	Error channel for adapter cards
A2	D7	Data line 7 (MSB)	
A3	D6	Data line 6	
A4	D5	Data line 5	
A5	D4	Data line 4	
A6	D3	Data line 3	
A7	D2	Data line 2	
A8	D1	Data line 1	
A9	D0	Data line 0 (LSB)	
A10	IO CH RDY	I/O Check Ready	
A11	AEN	Address Enable Signal	Specifies whether CPU or DMA controller has control over the system bus

Appendix C

Pin #	Signal	Description	Function
A12	A19	Address line 19 (MSB)	
A13	A18	Address line 18	
A14	A17	Address line 17	
A15	A16	Address line 16	
A16	A15	Address line 15	
A17	A14	Address line 14	
A18	A13	Address line 13	
A19	A12	Address line 12	
A20	A11	Address line 11	
A21	A10	Address line 10	
A22	A9	Address line 9	
A23	A8	Address line 8	
A24	A7	Address line 7	
A25	A6	Address line 6	
A26	A5	Address line 5	
A27	A4	Address line 4	
A28	A3	Address line 3	
A29	A2	Address line 2	
A30	A1	Address line 1	
A31	A0	Address line 0 (LSB)	
B1	GND	Ground	
B2	RES DRV	Reset Drive	Reset drive
B3	+5V	Power supply	
B4	IRQ2	Interrupt 2	
B5	-5V	Power supply	
B6	DRQ2	DMA request	Request for DMA transfer Channel 2
B7	-12V	Power supply	
B8	0WS	0 Waitstates	Signal indicates that the peripheral device can be addressed without wait states

Pin #	Signal	Description	Function
B9	+12V	Power supply	
B10	GND	Ground	
B11	SMEMW	Small Memory Write	Write to memory (0 - 1 Meg)
B12	SMEMR	Small Memory Read	Read from memory (0 - 1 Meg)
B13	IOW	Input/Output Write	Write to port address
B14	IOR	Input/Output Read	Read from port address
B15	DACK3	DMA Acknowledge	Acknowledge DMA request Channel 3
B16	DRQ3	DMA request	Request for DMA transfer Channel 3
B17	DACK1	DMA Acknowledge	Acknowledge DMA request Channel 1
B18	DRQ 1	DMA request	Request for DMA transfer Channel 1
B19	REF	Refresh	Refreshes dynamic memory chips
B20	CLK	System clock of computer	
B21	IRQ7	Interrupt Request	Hardware interrupt request Channel 7
B22	IRQ6	Interrupt Request	Hardware interrupt request Channel 6
B23	IRQ5	Interrupt Request	Hardware interrupt request Channel 5
B24	IRQ4	Interrupt Request	Hardware interrupt request Channel 4
B25	IRQ3	Interrupt Request	Hardware interrupt request Channel 3
B26	DACK2	DMA Acknowledge	Acknowledge DMA request Channel 2
B27	T/C	Terminal Count	End status counter DMA transfer, transfer complete
B28	ALE	Address Latch Enable	Valid address signals on I/O channel
B29	+5V	Power supply	
B30	OSC	Oscillator clock 14.31818 MHz	
B31	GND		

Appendix C

Pin #	Signal	Description	Function
C1	SBHE	System Bus High Enable	Specifies that data is transferred via higher order data byte
C2	LA23	Large Address	Address line 23
C3	LA22	Large Address	Address line 22
C4	LA21	Large Address	Address line 21
C5	LA20	Large Address	Address line 20
C6	LA19	Large Address	Address line 19
C7	LA18	Large Address	Address line 18
C8	LA17	Large Address	Address line 17
C9	MEMR	Memory Read	Read from memory (0 - 16 Meg)
C10	MEMW	Memory Write	Write to memory (0 - 16 Meg)
C11	SD08		Data line 8
C12	SD09	Data line 9	
C13	SD10	Data line 10	
C14	SD11	Data line 11	
C15	SD12	Data line 12	
C16	SD13	Data line 13	
C17	SD14	Data line 14	
C18	SD15	Data line 15	
D1	MEM CS16	Memory Chip Select 16	16 bit data transfer
D2	IO CS16	I/O Chip Select	- I/O data in 16 bit ???
D3	IRQ 10	Interrupt Request	Hardware interrupt request Channel 10
D4	IRQ 11	Interrupt Request	Hardware interrupt request Channel 11
D5	IRQ 12	Interrupt Request	Hardware interrupt request Channel 12
D6	IRQ 15	Interrupt Request	Hardware interrupt request Channel 15
D7	IRQ 14	Interrupt Request	Hardware interrupt request Channel 14
D8	DACK0	DMA Acknowledge	Acknowledge DMA request Channel 0
D9	DRQ0	DMA request	Request for DMA transfer Channel 0
D10	DACK5	DMA Acknowledge	Acknowledge DMA request Channel 5

Pin #	Signal	Description	Function
D11	DRQ5	DMA request	Request for DMA transfer Channel 5
D12	DACK6	DMA Acknowledge	Acknowledge DMA request Channel 6
D13	DRQ6	DMA request	Request for DMA transfer Channel 6
D14	DACK7	DMA Acknowledge	Acknowledge DMA request Channel 7
D15	DRQ7	DMA request	Request for DMA transfer Channel 7
D16	+5V	Power supply	
D17	MASTER	Bus master on card can control system bus	
D18	GND	Ground	

32-bit EISA slot

An EISA slot is enhanced from the 16 bit ISA slots. These are the new signals:

Pin #	Signal	Meaning	Function
E1	CMD	COMMAND	Synchronization of an EISA bus cycle
E2	START	Start of an EISA bus cycle	
E3	EXRDY	EISA-Ready	Bus cycle can end without wait state
E4	EX32	EISA 32 bit signal	
E5	GND	Ground	
E6	Coding	Coding	
E7	EX16	EISA 16 bit signal	
E8	SLBURST	Slave Burst	Slave can process bursts
E9	MSBURST	Master Burst	Master can execute bursts
E10	W/R	Write/Read	Distinction EISA write/read access
E11	GND	Ground	
E12	Reserved	Reserved	
E13	Reserved	Reserved	
E14	Reserved	Reserved	
E15	GND	Ground	
E16	Coding	Coding	

Pin #	Signal	Meaning	Function
E17	BE1	Byte Enables	Data transferred on 2nd byte of 32 bit data bus
E18	LA31	Large Address	Address line 31
E19	GND		
E20	LA30	Large Address	Address line 30
E21	LA28	Large Address	Address line 28
E22	LA27	Large Address	Address line 27
E23	LA25	Large Address	Address line 25
E24	GND	Ground	
E25	Coding	Coding	
E26	LA15	Large Address	Address line 15
E27	LA13	Large Address	Address line 13
E28	LA12	Large Address	Address line 12
E29	LA11	Large Address	Address line 11
E30	GND	Ground	
E31	LA9	Large Address	Address line 9
F1	GND	Ground	
F2	+5V	Power supply	
F3	+5V	Power supply	
F4		MANUFACTURER	Can be used by board manufacturer for own purposes
F5		MANUFACTURER	Can be used by board manufacturer for own purposes
F6	CODING	Coding	
F7		MANUFACTURER	Can be used by board manufacturer for own purposes
F8		MANUFACTURER	Can be used by board manufacturer for own purposes
F9	+12V	Power supply	
F10	MI/O	Memory, Input/Output	Distinction between EISA memory and EISA bus cycle
F11	LOCK	Locked	Only bus master on motherboard has memory access
F12	RESERVED	Reserved	
F13	GND	Ground	

475

Pin #	Signal	Meaning	Function
F14	RESERVED	Reserved	
F15	BE3	Byte Enables	Data transferred on 2nd byte of 32 bit data bus
F16	CODING	Coding	
F17	BE2	Byte Enables	Data transferred on 3rd byte of 32 bit data bus
F18	BE0	Byte Enables	Data transferred on 1st byte of 32 bit data bus
F19	GND	Ground	
F20	+5V	Power supply	
F21	LA29	Large Address	Address line 29
F22	GND	Ground	
F23	LA26	Large Address	Address line 26
F24	LA24	Large Address	Address line 24
F25	CODING	Coding	
F26	LA16	Large Address	Address line 16
F27	LA14	Large Address	Address line 14
F28	+5V	Power supply	
F29	+5V	Power supply	
F30	GND	Ground	
F31	LA 10	Large Address	Address line 10
G1	LA7	Large Address	Address line 7
G2	GND	Ground	
G3	LA4	Large Address	Address line 4
G4	LA3	Large Address	Address line 3
G5	GND	Ground	
G6	Coding		
G7	D17	Data line 17	
G8	D19	Data line 19	
G9	D20	Data line 20	
G10	D22	Data line 22	
G11	GND	Ground	

Pinouts And Port Assignments

Pin #	Signal	Meaning	Function
G12	D25	Data line 25	
G13	D26	Data line 26	
G14	D28	Data line 28	
G15	Coding		
G16	GND	Ground	
G17	D30	Data line 30	
G18	D31	Data line 31	
G19	MERQ	Master Request	Master request from ext. device
H1	LA8	Large Address	Address line 8
H2	LA6	Large Address	Address line 6
H3	LA5	Large Address	Address line 5
H4	+5V	Power supply	
H5	LA2	Large Address	Address line 2
H6	Coding		
H7	D16	Data line 16	
H8	D18	Data line 18	
H9	GND	Ground	
H10	D21	Data line 21	
H11	D23	Data line 23	
H12	D24	Data line 24	
H13	GND	Ground	
H14	D27	Data line 27	
H15	Coding		
H16	D29	Data line 29	
H17	+5V	Power supply	
H18	+5V	Power supply	
H19	MACK	Master Acknowledge	Acknowledge master request for ext. device

16 bit Microchannel (MCA)

Pin #	Signal	Meaning	Function
A1	CDSETUP	Card Setup	Initialization of adapter card
A2	MADE 24	Memory Enable	Enables address line 24
A3	GND	Ground	
A4	A11	Address line 11	
A5	A10	Address line 10	
A6	A9	Address line 9	
A7	+5V	Power supply	
A8	A8	Address line 8	
A9	A7	Address line 7	
A10	A6	Address line 6	
A11	+5V	Power supply	
A12	A5	Address line 5	
A13	A4	Address line 4	
A14	A3	Address line 3	
A15	+5V	Power supply	
A16	A2	Address line 2	
A17	A1	Address line 1	
A18	A0	Address line 0	
A19	+12V	Power supply	
A20	ADL	Address Decode Latch	Valid address exists
A21	PREEMT		Device wants to become bus master
A22	BURST		Transfer takes place in burst mode
A23	-12V	Power supply	
A24	ARB0	Arbitrate	Arbitration addressbit 0
A25	ARB1	Arbitrate	Arbitration addressbit 1
A26	ARB2	Arbitrate	Arbitration addressbit 2
A27	-12V	Power supply	

Pinouts And Port Assignments

Pin #	Signal	Meaning	Function
A28	ARB3	Arbitrate	Arbitration addressbit 3
A29	ARB/GNT	Arbitrate/Grant	Master can take the bus
A30	TC	Terminal Count	End status counter DMA transfer, Transfer complete
A31	+5V	Power supply	
A32	S0	Status Bit	Status bit 0 Microchannel
A33	S1	Status Bit	Status bit 1 Microchannel
A34	M/IO	Memory I/O	Specifies whether access to RAM or I/O port takes place
A35	+12V	Power supply	
A36	CD CH RDY	Card Channel Ready	Bus cycle extension
A37	D0	Data line 0	
A38	D2	Data line 2	
A39	+5V	Power supply	
A40	D5	Data line 5	
A41	D6	Data line 6	
A42	D7	Data line 7	
A43	GND	Ground	
A44	DS16RTN	Data size 16 Return	Device works with 16 bit data capacity
A45	REF	Refresh	Refresh signal for dyn. memory
A48	+5V	Power supply	
A49	D10	Data line 10	
A50	D11	Data line 11	
A51	D13	Data line 13	
A52	+12V	Power supply	
A53	Reserved		
A54	SBHE	System Byte High Enable	higher order data bus byte contains valid data
A55	CDDS16	Card Data Size 16	16 bit wide data transfer performed
A56	+5V	Power supply	

Pinouts And Port Assignments

Pin #	Signal	Meaning	Function
A57	IRQ 14	Interrupt Request	Hardware interrupt request Channel 14
A58	IRQ 15	Interrupt Request	Hardware interrupt request Channel 15
B1	AUDIO GND		Ground of audio signal
B2	AUDIO		Signal line audio signal
B3	GND	Ground	
B4	OSC	Oscillator	Clock frequency
B5	GND	Ground	
B6	A23	Address line 23	
B7	A22	Address line 22	
B8	A21	Address line 21	
B9	GND	Ground	
B10	A20	Address line 20	
B11	A19	Address line 19	
B12	A18	Address line 18	
B13	GND	Ground	
B14	A17	Address line 17	
B15	A16	Address line 16	
B16	A15	Address line 15	
B17	GND	Ground	
B18	A14	Address line 14	
B19	A13	Address line 13	
B20	A12	Address line 12	
B21	GND	Ground	
B22	IRQ 9	Interrupt Request	Hardware interrupt request Channel 9
B23	IRQ 3	Interrupt Request	Hardware interrupt request Channel 3
B24	IRQ 4	Interrupt Request	Hardware interrupt request Channel 4
B25	GND	Ground	
B26	IRQ 5	Interrupt Request	Hardware interrupt request Channel 5
B27	IRQ 6	Interrupt Request	Hardware interrupt request Channel 6

Pin #	Signal	Meaning	Function
B28	IRQ 7	Interrupt Request	Hardware interrupt request Channel 7
B29	GND	Ground	
B30	Reserved		
B31	Reserved		
B32	Channel Check	Error channel for adapter cards	
B33	GND	Ground	
B34	Command	Data on the bus valid	
B35	CHRDYRTN	Channel Ready Return	I/O channel is ready
B36	Card Select Feedback	Addressed card is ready	
B37	GND	Ground	
B38	D1	Data line 1	
B39	D3	Data line 3	
B40	D4	Data line 4	
B41	GND	Ground	
B42	CHRESET	Channel Reset	Reset line adapter
B43	Reserved		
B44	Reserved		
B45	GND	Ground	
B48	D8	Data line 8	
B49	D9	Data line 9	
B50	GND	Ground	
B51	D12	Data line 12	
B52	D14	Data line 14	
B53	D15	Data line 15	
B54	GND	Ground	
B55	IRQ 10	Interrupt Request	Hardware interrupt request Channel 10
B56	IRQ 11	Interrupt Request	Hardware interrupt request Channel 11

481

Appendix C

Pin #	Signal	Meaning	Function
B57	IRQ 12	Interrupt Request	Hardware interrupt request Channel 12
B58	GND	Ground	

VESA local bus slot

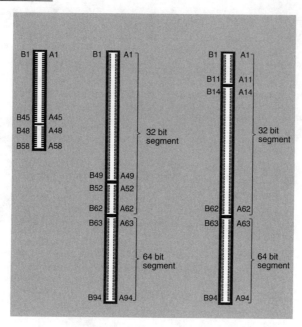

Structure of VESA local bus slot and PCI slots

Appendix C

Pin #	Signal	Meaning	Function
A1	D1	Data line 1	
A2	D3	Data line 3	
A3	GND	GND	
A4	D5	Data line 5	
A5	D7	Data line 7	
A6	D9	Data line 9	
A7	D11	Data line 11	
A8	D13	Data line 13	
A9	D15	Data line 15	
A10	GND	Ground	
A11	D17	Data line 17	
A12	Vcc	Power supply	
A13	D19	Data line 19	
A14	D21	Data line 21	
A15	D23	Data line 23	
A16	D25	Data line 25	
A17	GND	Ground	
A18	D27	Data line 27	
A19	D29	Data line 29	
A20	D31	Data line 31	
A21	A30	Address line 30	
A22	A28	Address line 28	
A23	A26	Address line 26	
A24	GND	Ground	
A25	A24	Address line 24	
A26	A22	Address line 22	
A27	Vcc	Power supply	
A28	A20	Address line 20	
A29	A18	Address line 18	

Pin #	Signal	Meaning	Function
A30	A16	Address line 16	
A31	A14	Address line 14	
A32	A12	Address line 12	
A33	A10	Address line 10	
A34	A8	Address line 8	
A35	GND	Ground	
A36	A6	Address line 6	
A37	A4	Address line 4	
A38	WBACK	Write Back	???
A39	BE0	Byte Enable	1st data byte has valid data
A40	Vcc	Power supply	
A41	BE1	Byte Enable	2nd data byte has valid data
A42	BE2	Byte Enable	3rd data byte has valid data
A43	GND	Ground	
A44	BE3	Byte Enable	4th data byte has valid data
A45	ADS	Address Strobe	Start of a bus cycle
A48	LRDY	Local Ready	Destination of a bus cycle concluded request
A49	LDEV	Local Device	Addressing detected ???
A50	LREQ	Local Request	VL bus master requests control of VL bus
A51	GND	Ground	
A52	LGNT	Local Grant	VL bus master requests control of VL bus
A53	Vcc	Power supply	
A54	ID2	Identify Bit 2	Passes VLB parameter to card
A55	ID3	Identify Bit 3	Passes VLB parameter to card
A56	ID4	Identify Bit 4	Passes VLB parameter to card
A57	LKEN	???	
A58	LEADS	Local External Address Strobe	VL bus master executes memory access

Appendix C

Pin #	Signal	Meaning	Function
B1	D0	Data line 0	
B2	D2	Data line 2	
B3	D4	Data line 4	
B4	D6	Data line 6	
B5	D8	Data line 8	
B6	GND	Ground	
B7	D10	Data line 10	
B8	D12	Data line 12	
B9	Vcc	Power supply	
B10	D14	Data line 14	
B11	D16	Data line 16	
B12	D18	Data line 18	
B13	D20	Data line 20	
B14	GND	Ground	
B15	D22	Data line 22	
B16	D24	Data line 24	
B17	D26	Data line 26	
B18	D28	Data line 28	
B19	D30	Data line 30	
B20	Vcc	Power supply	
B21	A31	Address line 31	
B22	GND	GND	
B23	A29	Address line 29	
B24	A27	Address line 27	
B25	A25	Address line 25	
B26	A23	Address line 23	
B27	A21	Address line 21	
B28	A19	Address line 19	
B29	GND	Ground	

Pin #	Signal	Meaning	Function
B30	A17	Address line 17	
B31	A15	Address line 15	
B32	Vcc	Power supply	
B32	A13	Address line 13	
B34	A11	Address line 11	
B35	A9	Address line 9	
B36	A7	Address line 7	
B37	A5	Address line 5	
B38	GND	Ground	
B39	A3	Address line 3	
B40	A2	Address line 2	
B41	N.C.	Not connected	
B42	RESET	Reset	
B43	D/C	Data/Command	Specifies the bus cycle type
B44	MI/O	Memory I/O	Specifies the bus cycle type
B45	W/R	Write / Read	Specifies the bus cycle type
B48	RDYRTN	Ready Return	VLB cycle is concluded
B49	GND	Ground	
B50	IRQ9	Interrupt Request - Hardware interrupt request Channel 9	
B51	BRDY	Burst Ready	Ends current burst transfer
B52	BLAST	Burst Last	Current burst cycle ends with next /BRDY
B53	ID0	Identify Bit 0	Passes VLB parameter to card
B54	ID1	Identify Bit 1	Passes VLB parameter to card
B55	GND	Ground	
B56	LCLK	Local Clock	Clock signal of VLB
B57	Vcc	Power supply	
B58	LBS16	Local Bus Size 16	VLB card only works with 16 bit bus

PCI bus slot 5V

Pin #	Signal	Meaning	Function
A1	TRST	Test Reset	Reset TAP control
A2	+12V	Power supply	
A3	TMS	Test Mode Select	Enables TAP control
A4	TDI	Test Data Input	Test data for JTAG-Boudary Scan Test
A5	+5V	Power supply	
A6	INTA		PCI hardware interrupt A
A7	INTC		PCI hardware interrupt C
A8	+5V	Power supply	
A9	Reserved		
A10	+5V I/O	Power supply	for universal adapter
A11	Reserved		
A12	GND	Ground	Ground
A13	GND	Ground	Ground
A14	Reserved		
A15	RST	Reset	Resets all PCI devices
A16	+5V I/O	Power supply	for universal adapter
A17	GNT	Grant	PCI device is master
A18	GND	Ground	Ground
A19	Reserved		
A20	AD30	Address/Data line 30	time division multiplexing <! Please check for technical accuracy !>
A21	+3,3V	Power supply	
A22	AD28	Address/Data line 28	time division multiplexing
A23	AD26	Address/Data line 26	time division multiplexing
A24	GND	Ground	Ground
A25	AD24	Address/Data line 24	time division multiplexing
A26	IDSEL	Initialization Device Select	specifies device to be configured
A27	+3,3V	Power supply	

Appendix C

Pin #	Signal	Meaning	Function
A28	AD22	Address/Data line 22	time division multiplexing
A29	AD20	Address/Data line 20	time division multiplexing
A30	GND	Ground	Ground
A31	AD18	Address/Data line 18	time division multiplexing
A32	AD16	Address/Data line 16	time division multiplexing
A33	+3,3V	Power supply	
A34	FRAME		launches addressing phase
A35	GND	Ground	Ground
A36	TRDY	Target Ready	Addressed PCI device is ready
A37	GND	Ground	Ground
A38	STOP		Target indicates to master process must stop
A39	+3,3V	Power supply	
A40	SDONE	Snoop Done	Query cycle completed
A41	SBO	Snoop Backoff	Shows query hit on a modified cache line
A42	GND	Ground	Ground
A43	PAR	Parity	Parity bit for address/data lines 0-31
A44	AD15	Address/Data line 15	time division multiplexing
A45	+3,3V	Power supply	
A46	AD13	Address/Data line 13	time division multiplexing
A47	AD11	Address/Data line 11	time division multiplexing
A48	GND	Ground	Ground
A49	AD9	Address/Data line 9	time division multiplexing
A50	Coding		
A51	Coding		
A52	C/BE0	Bus Command/Byte Enable	Bit 0 bus cycle type
A53	+3,3V	Power supply	
A54	AD6	Address/Data line 6	time division multiplexing
A55	AD4	Address/Data line 4	time division multiplexing
A56	GND	Ground	Ground

Pinouts And Port Assignments

Appendix C

Pin #	Signal	Meaning	Function
A57	AD2	Address/Data line 2	time division multiplexing
A58	AD0	Address/Data line 0	time division multiplexing
A59	+5V I/O	Power supply	for universal adapter
A60	REQ64	Request 64 bit Transfer	Bus master wants to perform 64 bit transfer
A61	+5V	Power supply	
A62	+5V	Power supply	
A63	GND	Ground	Ground
A64	C/BE7	Bus Command/Byte Enable	Bit 7 bus cycle type (64 bit)
A65	C/BE5	Bus Command/Byte Enable	Bit 5 bus cycle type (64 bit)
A66	+5V I/O	Power supply	for universal adapter
A67	PAR64	Parity 64 bit	Parity bit for address/data lines 32-63
A68	AD 62	Address/Data line 62	time division multiplexing
A69	GND	Ground	Ground
A70	AD60	Address/Data line 60	time division multiplexing
A71	AD58	Address/Data line 58	time division multiplexing
A72	GND	Ground	Ground
A73	AD56	Address/Data line 56	time division multiplexing
A74	AD54	Address/Data line 54	time division multiplexing
A75	+5V I/O	Power supply	for Universal adapter
A76	AD52	Address/Data line 52	time division multiplexing
A77	AD50	Address/Data line 50	time division multiplexing
A78	GND	Ground	Ground
A79	AD48	Address/Data line 48	time division multiplexing
A80	AD46	Address/Data line 46	time division multiplexing
A81	GND	Ground	Ground
A82	AD44	Address/Data line 44	time division multiplexing
A83	AD42	Address/Data line 42	time division multiplexing
A84	+5V I/O	Power supply	for universal adapter
A85	AD40	Address/Data line 40	time division multiplexing

Appendix C

Pin #	Signal	Meaning	Function
A86	AD38	Address/Data line 38	time division multiplexing
A87	GND	Ground	Ground
A88	AD36	Address/Data line 36	time division multiplexing
A89	AD34	Address/Data line 34	time division multiplexing
A90	GND	Ground	Ground
A91	AD32	Address/Data line 32	time division multiplexing
A92	Reserved		
A93	GND	Ground	Ground
A94	Reserved		

Pin #	Signal	Meaning	Function
B1	-12V	Power supply	
B2	TCK	Test Clock	Clock for test data or -commands from JTAG-Boudary Scan Test
B3	GND	Ground	Ground
B4	TDO	Test Data Output	Test data for JTAG-Boudary Scan Test
B5	+5V	Power supply	
B6	+5V	Power supply	
B7	INTB		PCI hardware interrupt B
B8	INTD		PCI hardware interrupt D
B9	PRSNT1	Present 1	Bit 1 card present
B10	Reserved		
B11	PRSNT2	Present 2	Bit 2 card present
B12	GND	Ground	Ground
B13	GND	Ground	Ground
B14	Reserved		
B15	GND	Ground	Ground
B16	CLK	Clock	PCI clock signal
B17	GND	Ground	Ground

Pin #	Signal	Meaning	Function
B18	REQ	Request	Device wants to use bus as master
B19	+5V I/O	Power supply	for universal adapter
B20	AD31	Address/Data line 31	time division multiplexing
B21	AD29	Address/Data line 29	time division multiplexing
B22	GND	Ground	Ground
B23	AD27	Address/Data line 27	time division multiplexing
B24	AD25	Address/Data line 25	time division multiplexing
B25	+3,3V	Power supply	
B26	C/BE3	Bus Command/Byte Enable	Bit 3 bus cycle type
B27	AD23	Address/Data line 23	time division multiplexing
B28	GND	Ground	Ground
B29	AD21	Address/Data line 21	time division multiplexing
B30	AD19	Address/Data line 19	time division multiplexing
B31	+3,3V	Power supply	
B32	AD17	Address/Data line 17	time division multiplexing
B323	C/BE2	Bus Command/Byte Enable	Bit 2 bus cycle type
B34	GND	Ground	Ground
B35	IRDY	Initiator Ready	Bus master is ready to conclude current data phase
B36	+3,3V	Power supply	
B37	DEVSEL	Device Select	Device is target of bus process
B38	GND	Ground	Ground
B39	/	PCI device is locked	
B40	PERR	Parity Error	Displays data parity errors in PCI processes
B41	+3,3V	Power supply	
B42	SERR	System Error	Displays address parity or other serious errors
B43	+3,3V	Power supply	
B44	C/BE1	Bus Command/Byte Enable	Bit 1 bus cycle type
B45	AD14	Address/Data line 14	time division multiplexing

Pinouts And Port Assignments

Appendix C

Pin #	Signal	Meaning	Function
B46	GND	Ground	Ground
B47	AD12	Address/Data line 12	time division multiplexing
B48	AD10	Address/Data line 10	time division multiplexing
B49	GND	Ground	Ground
B50	Coding		
B51	Coding		
B52	AD8	Address/Data line 8	time division multiplexing
B53	AD7	Address/Data line 7	time division multiplexing
B54	+3,3V	Power supply	
B55	AD5	Address/Data line 5	time division multiplexing
B56	AD3	Address/Data line 3	time division multiplexing
B57	GND	Ground	Ground
B58	AD1	Address/Data line 1	time division multiplexing
B59	+5V I/O	Power supply	for Universal adapter
B60	ACK64	Acknowledge 64	Device can perform requested 64 bit transfer
B61	+5V	Power supply	
B62	+5V	Power supply	
B63	Reserved		
B64	GND	Ground	Ground
B65	C/BE6	Bus Command/Byte Enable	Bit 6 bus cycle type (64 bit)
B66	C/BE4	Bus Command/Byte Enable	Bit 4 bus cycle type (64 bit)
B67	GND	Ground	Ground
B68	AD63	Address/Data line 63	time division multiplexing
B69	AD61	Address/Data line 61	time division multiplexing
B70	+5V I/O	Power supply	for universal adapter
B71	AD59	Address/Data line 59	time division multiplexing
B72	AD57	Address/Data line 57	time division multiplexing
B73	GND	Ground	Ground

Pin #	Signal	Meaning	Function
B74	AD55	Address/Data line 55	time division multiplexing
B75	AD53	Address/Data line 53	time division multiplexing
B76	GND	Ground	Ground
B77	AD51	Address/Data line 51	time division multiplexing
B78	AD49	Address/Data line 49	time division multiplexing
B79	+5V I/O	Power supply	for universal adapter
B80	AD47	Address/Data line 47	time division multiplexing
B81	AD45	Address/Data line 45	time division multiplexing
B82	GND	Ground	Ground
B83	AD43	Address/Data line 43	time division multiplexing
B84	AD41	Address/Data line 41	time division multiplexing
B85	GND	Ground	Ground
B86	AD39	Address/Data line 39	time division multiplexing
B87	AD37	Address/Data line 37	time division multiplexing
B88	+5V I/O	Power supply	for universal adapter
B89	AD35	Address/Data line 35	time division multiplexing
B90	AD33	Address/Data line 33	time division multiplexing
B91	GND	Ground	Ground
B92	Reserved		
B93	Reserved		
B94	GND	Ground	Ground

PCI bus slot 3.3V

The structure of a 5V adapter and a 3.3V PCI adapter differ only slightly in th earea of codings, therefore we only list the contacts with different assignments here.

Pin #	Signal	Meaning	Function
A12	Coding		
A13	Coding		
A50	GND	Ground	Ground
A51	GND	Ground	Ground
B12	Coding		
B13	Coding		
B50	GND	Ground	Ground
B51	GND	Ground	Ground

Appendix

Interface And Connection Cables

Serial connection cable for modem hookup (5 pin)

This cable is usually sufficient for connecting a modem. If some signals are still missing, upgrade to the 9 pin cable.

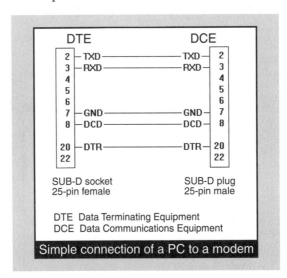

Simple connection of a PC to a modem

Serial connection cable for modem hookup (9 pin)

This cable transmits all the existing signals of the serial port (1:1 cable).

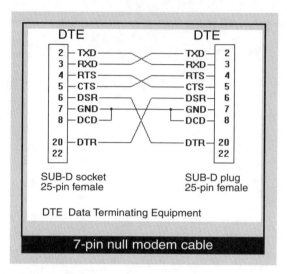

7-pin null modem cable

Null modem cable for connecting two PCs (3 pin)

This cable is sufficient for simple coupling of two PCs (e.g., for games).

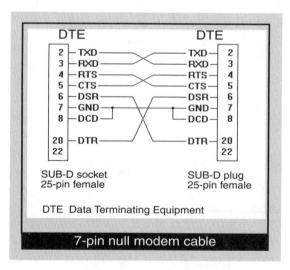

7-pin null modem cable

Null Modem Cable for connecting 2 PCs (7 pin)

General purpose null modem cable for complete connection of signals. Required for data transfer programs such as LapLink or MS-Interlink.

Appendix D

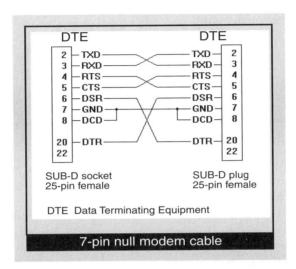

```
        DTE                      DTE
   ┌─────────────┐         ┌─────────────┐
   │ 2 ─ TXD ──┐ ┌── TXD ─ 2 │
   │ 3 ─ RXD ──┘ └── RXD ─ 3 │
   │ 4 ─ RTS ──┐ ┌── RTS ─ 4 │
   │ 5 ─ CTS ──┘ └── CTS ─ 5 │
   │ 6 ─ DSR ─┐      DSR ─ 6 │
   │ 7 ─ GND ─┤      GND ─ 7 │
   │ 8 ─ DCD ─┘      DCD ─ 8 │
   │                          │
   │ 20 ─ DTR ─      DTR ─ 20 │
   │ 22                    22 │
   └─────────────┘         └─────────────┘
```

SUB-D socket   SUB-D plug
25-pin female   25-pin female

DTE Data Terminating Equipment

7-pin null modem cable

Serial printer cable

Use this cable to connect a computer to the PC through the serial port

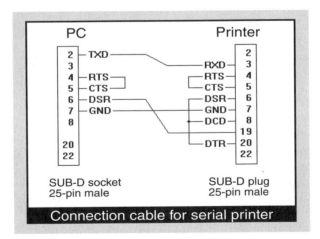

```
        PC                    Printer
   ┌─────────────┐       ┌─────────────┐
   │ 2 ─ TXD ──┐           2 │
   │ 3        └── RXD ─ 3 │
   │ 4 ─ RTS ─┐    RTS ─ 4 │
   │ 5 ─ CTS ─┘    CTS ─ 5 │
   │ 6 ─ DSR ─┐    DSR ─ 6 │
   │ 7 ─ GND ─┤    GND ─ 7 │
   │ 8        └    DCD ─ 8 │
   │                  19 │
   │ 20           DTR ─ 20 │
   │ 22               22 │
   └─────────────┘       └─────────────┘
```

SUB-D socket   SUB-D plug
25-pin male   25-pin male

Connection cable for serial printer

497

Parallel cable (Centronics cable)

A parallel cable (also called a Centronics cable) connects a printer to the parallel port on a PC. When you are calculating the length of the cable, keep in mind that some printers have trouble with printer cables that are too long (printer won't print).

```
  PC                                      Printer
  ┌──┐                                       ┌──┐
  │ 1│─STROBE───────────────────STROBE─│ 1│
  │ 2│─D0──────────────────────────D0──│ 2│
  │ 3│─D1──────────────────────────D1──│ 3│
  │ 4│─D2──────────────────────────D2──│ 4│
  │ 5│─D3──────────────────────────D3──│ 5│
  │ 6│─D4──────────────────────────D4──│ 6│
  │ 7│─D5──────────────────────────D5──│ 7│
  │ 8│─D6──────────────────────────D6──│ 8│
  │ 9│─D7──────────────────────────D7──│ 9│
  │10│─ACK─────────────────────────ACK─│10│
  │11│─BSY─────────────────────────BSY─│11│
  │12│─PAP─────────────────────────PAP─│12│
  │13│─SELECT─────────────────SELECT──│13│
  │14│─ALF─────────────────────────ALF─│14│
  │15│─ERROR──────────────────ERROR──│32│
  │16│─INIT─────────────────────────INIT─│31│
  │17│─SLCT IN──────────────SLCT IN──│36│
  │18│─GND─────────────────────────GND─│33│
  └──┘                                       └──┘
  SUB-D socket                     Centronics socket
  25-pin male                      36-pin

             Parallel cable (Centronics cable)
```

Serial adapter cable from 25 pin to 9 pin plug

Adapter cable for connecting a 25 pin port cable to a 9 pin serial port. If you require an adapter cable for converting from 9 to 25 pins, you can assemble the cable in the same manner, only the 25 pin male connector becomes a female connector and the 9 pin female connector becomes a male connector.

Interface And Connection Cables

Appendix D

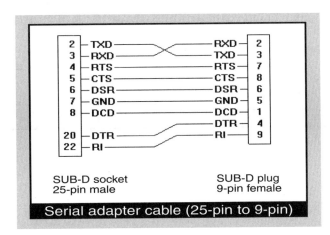

Serial adapter cable (25-pin to 9-pin)

Parallel InterLink cable

This cable enables you to exchange data between two computers over the parallel port. This cable is suitable for InterLink or LapLink.

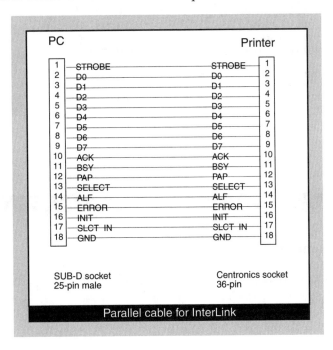

Parallel cable for InterLink

Game port Y-adapter

With sound or Multi-IO cards, both joystick ports are on the joystick jack. With the
Y adapter cable you can split up the signals for both joystick ports so that 2 joysticks
can be used.

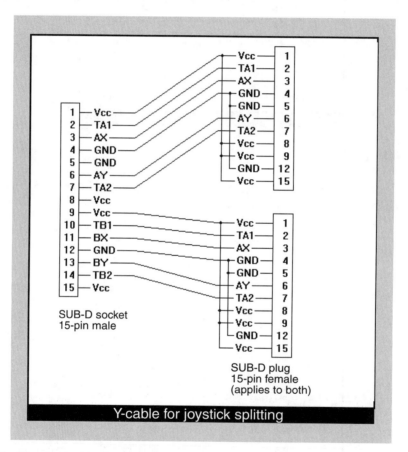

Y-cable for joystick splitting

VGA adapter from 15 pin to 9 pin

Used to connect Multiscan or Multisync monitors to a VGA card.

Interface And Connection Cables

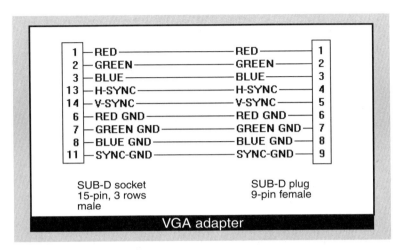

1	RED	RED	1
2	GREEN	GREEN	2
3	BLUE	BLUE	3
13	H-SYNC	H-SYNC	4
14	V-SYNC	V-SYNC	5
6	RED GND	RED GND	6
7	GREEN GND	GREEN GND	7
8	BLUE GND	BLUE GND	8
11	SYNC-GND	SYNC-GND	9

SUB-D socket
15-pin, 3 rows
male

SUB-D plug
9-pin female

VGA adapter

Game port

Structure of the GamePort with a diagram of the connected joystick.

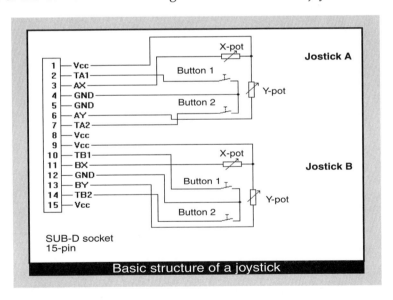

1	Vcc
2	TA1
3	AX
4	GND
5	GND
6	AY
7	TA2
8	Vcc
9	Vcc
10	TB1
11	BX
12	GND
13	BY
14	TB2
15	Vcc

Jostick A — X-pot, Button 1, Y-pot, Button 2

Jostick B — X-pot, Button 1, Y-pot, Button 2

SUB-D socket
15-pin

Basic structure of a joystick

501

Contents Of The Companion CD-ROM

We hope this book will be an indispensable reference guide to using Windows 98 on your PC. The companion CD-ROM contains many practical utilities for PC testing and maintenance. The companion CD-ROM includes dozens of megabytes of the following programs and applications:

The MENU

The most convenient method of using the companion CD-ROM is by using the MENU program. The MENU.EXE program is in the root directory of the CD and is a Windows application that lets you access the contents of the companion CD-ROM.

The CD-ROM for WIN 98 RX

The following files are on the root directory of the companion CD-ROM:

ACROREAD EXE
The fantastic portable document reader from Adobe. Use it to see book.pdf or CATALOG.PDF in the ABACUS directory.

MENU.EXE
The MAIN program for Windows users.

README .TXT
This text file.

MSVBVM50.DLL
A required file.

The following directories (with their contents) are on the root directory of the companion CD-ROM:

ABACUS (dir)

Contains the exciting and informative Abacus Catalog 1996.

ACROREAD (dir)

Adobe's Acrobat Reader directory.

DLL (dir)

This directory contains various DLLs and VBX files you may need.

PC_INFO (dir)

Our very own outstanding utility. See the section at the end of this chapter for more info.

BCM DIAGNOSTICS

Program which helps you diagnose problems of your PC running Microsoft Windows 95 operation system. It includes System Info, Processor Test, Memory Test, Audio Test, Video Test, Modem Test, Graphics Test, Harddisk Test, Floppy Test, CD-ROM Test, and Stress Test. It also has a Resource Monitor and shortcuts to Microsoft Mouse, Joystick, and ScanDisk. A System Hardware Health Monitor is also included for system containing a LM78 chip.

DT_SCAN

Scans files for times that are not plausible as well as century entries that exceed the year specified by the user. DT_SCAN helps you detect viruses that manipulate these figures.

PC_INFO

System information program with test functions. Provides detailed information about the hardware, software and programming interfaces. IMPORTANT NOTE - We have chosen to load text files rather than the DOS utilities from the DOS UTILITIES menu. This is because of the variety of user's DOS windows. You should create a directory (DOSTOOLS) and copy the files in BOOK and DOSTOOLS and run them from your DOS prompt. Editors.

F-PROT

One of the best virus scanners for DOS with an outstanding virus database. F-PROT anti-virus package contains a virus scanner combined with a disinfection program, as well as a resident monitoring program for intercepting known viruses.

504

MODEMDOC

Extensive test program for modems. The Modem Doctor checks every serial port chip (uart) register, checks cables and modems for proper handshaking signals, and will inform you if it runs across something that isn't set properly. Modems are also rigorously tested, including handshaking tests and modem self-connect tests which simulate an on-line connection. IRQ assignment errors, base port addressing errors, and a host of other settings are checked. The Modem Doctor will inform you of the type of uart and modem you have installed, and will print a copy of the test results to a printer or a file. ShareWare.

SYSCHK24

System information program with information about hardware and software and benchmark tests for the CPU, video card and hard drive.

SYSINFO

System Information. SYSINFO is a fully functional shareware DEMO from Scott Hoopes. Checks all available drives (A-Z) for free space; Extensive ROM information; more extensive ENVIRONMENT reporting; total memory and free memory; number of directories on all available drives; start-up files information; game adapter detection and more.

PC_CARE

Diagnostic program for Windows 98.

REGSRCH

Program that makes Search/Replace of the values in the Registry easier.

SAF_TNET

Saftey Net is a utility for backing up key files. It has 1 default setting - to backup key "windows" -system files - 3 user configurable options. Safety Net could easily backup all of your DOC and/or database files, for example. An added function - the files can be ZIPped to disk. It can also print your directory tree, and make a boot disk. Shareware from Ron Parker (CT Software).

VBSYS

VBSys (Windows System Monitor includes VBSys and VBSysBar). Monitors many system resources at all times and combines many utilities. It will: Monitor DiskSpace (even Networks), resources, memory, tasks, built in timer, display and set date and time, give system info, compact memory, run programs from within VBSys all in one small display. ShareWare.

PLEASE NOTE: Because of the time-lag between publishing the book and companion CD-ROM, we have included several other utilities which are not listed above. Please be sure to check the MENU program for additions.

Shareware, Freeware and Public Domain Software

Many of the programs included on the CD-ROM are fully functioning 'shareware evaluation versions' of the best programs available today. Because shareware is copyrighted, the authors ask for payment if you use their program(s). You may try out the program for a limited time, typically 10 to 30 days, and then decide whether you want to keep it. If you continue to use it, you're requested to send the author a nominal fee. Shareware benefits both the user and the author as it allows prices to remain low by avoiding distribution, packaging, and advertising costs.

The shareware concept allows small software companies and program authors to introduce the application programs they have developed to a wider audience. The programs can be freely distributed and tested for a specific time period before you have to register them. Registration involves paying registration fees, which make you a licensed user of the program. Check the documentation or the program itself for the amount of registration fee and the address where you send the registration form.

After registration you will frequently get the current full version of the program without restrictions and shareware notes as well as the option of purchasing upgraded versions later for a reduced price. As a rule, larger applications include a users manual. Shareware programs usually feature the complete performance range of the full versions. Some programs use special messages to indicate they're shareware versions. The message usually appears immediately after program startup or can be called from the Help menu.

The WIN 98 RX CD will illustrate the variety of shareware. To ensure that the program authors continue writing programs and offering them as shareware, we urge you to support the shareware concept by registering the programs that you plan to use on a permanent basis. Perhaps you have even developed your own programs that you would like to make available to other users on a later edition of this shareware CD?

You will find program instructions as well as notes on registration for the shareware propgrams in special text files located in the program directory of each program. These programs are usually called READ.ME, README.TXT or README.DOC. As a rule, the TXT, WRI or DOC extensions are used for text files, which you can view and print with Windows 98 editors.

Thanks again from the Abacus Editorial and Technical Staffs

Index

PC catalog

Order Toll Free 1-800-451-4319
Books and Software

PC INTERN
SYSTEM PROGRAMMING 6th Edition

PC memory organization
Extended & expanded memory
COM & EXE programs
DOS structures and functions
BIOS interrupts
Programming video cards
TSR programs

Michael Tischer

INCLUDES COMPACT DISK WITH SAMPLE PROGRAMS

Abacus

www.abacuspub.com

To order direct call Toll Free 1-800-451-4319

In US and Canada add $5.00 shipping and handling. Foreign orders add $13.00 per item.
Michigan residents add 6% sales tax.

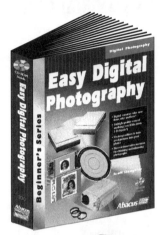

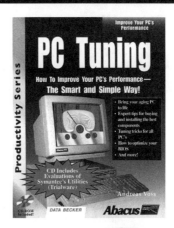